MODERNISM
AND
VIRGINIA WOOLF

MODERNISM
AND
VIRGINIA WOOLF

by

N TAKEI da SILVA

WINDSOR PUBLICATIONS

British Library Cataloguing in Publication Data
Da Silva, N Takei
    Modernism and Virginia Woolf
    I. Title
    823.912

    ISBN 1 870417 03 8
    (also in Hardback ISBN 1 870417 06 2)

Published by Windsor Publications, Windsor, England
Distributed by SPA Books Ltd, PO Box 47, Stevenage
Printed by Antony Rowe Ltd, Chippenham, England

ACKNOWLEDGEMENTS

I wish to express my gratitude to the following persons and institutions, whose assistance has been invaluable for the completion of this study. Dr. T. P. Matheson as my supervisor, provided much encouragement and criticism, while it was being prepared as a doctoral dissertation. The staff of the Shakespeare Institute at the University of Birmingham, in particular Dr. Susan Brock, the Librarian, have always been most helpful. Professor Quentin Bell, the copyright holder of Virginia Woolf's writings, kindly allowed me access to the unpublished material from the Monks House Papers. I also benefited greatly from research grants awarded by INIC, the National Institute of Scientific Research of Portugal.

I should further like to thank Ms K von Burg of Windsor Publications for her painstaking editorial and indexing work.

Last but not least, my thanks are due to my husband for his constant moral support and to my children for their patience and stoicism.

N Takei da Silva

CONTENTS

To José, Ana and Miguel

INTRODUCTION

"The 1910-1930 period was one of the great epochs of English literature," wrote John Holloway,[1] "It stands with 1590-1612, or 1710-1735 or 1798-1822. What has been written since then does not bear comparison with it for a moment."

Whether or not we agree with Holloway's final verdict, there is no doubt that to most literary scholars and critics the first 25 or so years of this century stand out for their dazzling assembly of talents and a bursting-out of artistic energies rare in the history of art and literature.

It is significant that in the above passage this period is referred to only by dates and not by any specific name and, as if to avoid the rather awkward stylistic disunity, even the other periods are indicated by dates instead of the usual epithets which are more commonly used, ie, "Elizabethan and Jacobean", "Augustan" (or "Neo-Classical") and "Romantic". In actual fact, the period did not then have a name. Only in recent years has one emerged out of several different names and established itself to identify the period and the particular nature of, if not all, the outstanding part of the art and literature of those years, namely, Modernism.

Indeed, "Modernism", along with its variant "Modernist", both often spelled with small "m", is one of the critical terms which have recently made conspicuous headway in the field of English literature. The process of its development, however, has been far from simple, and the examination of its tortuous course reveals not only interesting vicissitudes of the critical fashion but the gradual growth of awareness in the critical world of the nature and significance of the phenomenon now identified by that name. It seems worth its while at this moment, when the material about it is still fairly widely available, and especially when the memories of the backgrounds of the various different nomenclatures attached or related to it are yet relatively fresh and have not faded into oblivion, to record and analyse this process through which the new literary term and concept established themselves in the domain of English literature.

One of the primary objectives of this book is to trace the development of this term "Modernism", dividing it into three successive periods or stages: the first period, when there was not yet a clear recognition of, not to say a particular name for, what was happening in art and literature in the earlier part of this century, each individual writer, artist or movement being considered a separate and isolated entity, and when some common characteristics *were* perceived, they were called by various different names, which made their identification all the more difficult and confusing; the second period, when there was a growing awareness among critics that something special took place in the cultural arena during those years, and that there were common features and objectives that linked together all those highly individualistic writers and artists, who were then given the collective name "the moderns", in contrast to "the contemporaries", partly as a result of the influence of Stephen Spender's *The Struggle of the Modern*, one of the pioneering works in the study of Modernist literature; and the third period, when there gradually emerged a general agreement in the critical world as to the nature and the name of this particular phenomenon, "Modernism" replacing the formerly dominant "the Modern", and setting itself up as one of the generally accepted critical terms.

Consideration of what constituted the essential spirit, or nature, of Modernism leads us on the one hand back to the earlier manifestations of the similar traits in the Romantic movement, and on the other to the almost contemporary phenomenon of a different kind, the spread of the new psychological concepts, primarily of Freud, which brought about a profound change in the attitude of educated people towards themselves and their fellow human beings. In view of their respective roles as bequeather and instigator of the Modernist principles in art and literature, both Romanticism and Freudian psychology may be considered the two spiritual roots of the Modernist movement. As a result, while it is possible to concentrate upon Modernism in English literature alone, any consideration of its derivation involves the study of European Romantic literature as well as the related study of psychology.

An attempt will accordingly be made to substantiate this view that Modernism was a fruit borne of a tree with two main roots, first through the examination of the psychological theories of Freud and Jung, and then through a study of Romantic writers, English as well as German and French; this will be supplemented by consideration of such writers as Baudelaire, Dostoevsky and Nietzsche for the part they played as mediators between Romanticists and Modernists. While chronologically it may appear rather arbitrary, this arrangement has two advantages: firstly, to describe in the beginning the central concepts of modern psychology, which is by its very nature more systematic and more clearly expository, helps make explicit the common grounds or concerns that link Modernism to both modern psychology and the Romantic movement and secondly, placing the chapter on the "Romantic Ancestry" after the purely theoretical chapter on psychology will make the transition to the remaining literary study smoother than if we were to follow a strictly chronological order. The main purpose of this part, at all events, is to make sufficiently clear the outline of the lineage of Modernism.

The assumptions which are at the basis of these chapters find ample endorsement in the ideas of Surrealists and their sympathizers, a survey of which will be made in this study through the writings of André Breton, the initiator and advocate of Surrealism, that conspicuous branch of the Modernist movement, as well as its English members such as Herbert Read, David Gascoyne, etc, and through various kinds of documents which appeared in the characteristically international magazine *Transition*, including a number of articles written by its American editor, Eugene Jolas, an ardent promoter of Modernist art and literature during the heyday of the movement. All those writers show, in their artistic principles and practice, a clear awareness of the double heritage in Modernism mentioned above.

One aspect of literary Modernism that demands special attention is its impact on the English novel. The genre, which in England, unlike the Continent, had for the most part remained untouched by the successive waves of *isms* such as Romanticism, Naturalism and Symbolism, came for the first time under the influence of a prevailing movement, and perhaps for this very reason underwent a most spectacular change, a transformation unprecedented in its history. Here again, it was not very long ago that the literary men came to a realisation that this was not simply an isolated event in the field of the English novel but an integral part of the wider cultural phenomenon. In this connection Virginia Woolf, especially as a critic, emerges as a figure of considerable significance, far more significant in fact than she is usually given credit for by critics.

Thus, to clarify the nature of Virginia Woolf's unique contribution to the Modernist movement is another purpose of this book. For, besides being one of the representative Modernists in the field of fiction alongside Joyce and, with certain reservations, Lawrence, she may be considered a pioneer in establishing the concept of Modernism itself. She was, in fact, virtually the first to identify the essential nature of Modernism, and was the most articulate critic to discuss and advocate the principles of Modernist fiction consistently throughout her career.

Arnold Bennett, Woolf's worthy opponent, once wrote, "The real champion of the younger school is Mrs. Virginia Woolf. She is almost a senior; but she was the inventor, years ago, of a half-new technique, and she alone, so far as I know, came forward and attacked the old."[2] It was Virginia Woolf more than any other major modern writer, including Joyce and Lawrence, who carried on this rather brave campaign through her articles and critical essays as much as, and certainly more explicitly than, in her novels, and thus these writings give a valuable insight into the genesis of the Modernist novel in England and help make intelligible its spirit first hand. Yet, while there is a growing number of critics who recognize her as a major modern novelist without the condescension of some of the earlier critics, this side of Woolf's achievement has not so far received the amount of attention it deserves.[3] This book will concentrate its attention mainly on her critical writings, though it may refer to, or discuss, her fictional works wherever necessary.

These essays reveal that Woolf was clearly conscious of the two basic strains, or roots, of her kind of art, and her lucid, if not systematic, expositions of the essential qualities of Modernist art, to my mind, contributed greatly, especially via such a writer as Stephen Spender, to the formation of a new literary concept. This, in fact, is the reason for the choice of, and emphasis on, Virginia Woolf in the study of Modernism and its relation to the English novel. In the course of this study, I shall examine her appreciation of Freud's contribution to literature, her own interest in his ideas as well as the extent of her knowledge and intimacy with them. By doing so, I hope to throw light on the interrelation between her art and the new psychological ideas which again, it seems to me, has not hitherto been paid due attention. This, together with her recognition of the Romantic heritage and her attempt to revive its essential spirit, makes her a most fitting representative, or the embodiment, of the spirit of Modernism, which in my view was firmly based on these two elements.

I might also have examined in detail the manifestations of these elements in the novels of Woolf as well as Joyce and Lawrence, but as the works of these three writers have by now reached the status of modern classics, there is an abundance of studies which often deal, without recognizing them as such, with those particular qualities which we now understand as Modernist, whereas the kind of survey and analyses attempted in this study has not yet been fully undertaken. Thus there is a case for establishing the identity of the particular literary and artistic trend that affected these novelists as well as many other literary men and artists, and examining the part played by Virginia Woolf in this context, rather than adding another detailed study of the fictional works themselves. Nevertheless, in the concluding chapter there is a brief survey of the relation between Woolf's critical essays and her novels, which reflect to a remarkable degree her ideals and aspirations about the art of fiction expressed in the former, followed by a cursory examination of similar expressions of the Modernist spirit in the writings of Joyce and Lawrence, recognizing in this aspect of the three novelists' works the principal part of their contribution to English literature.

By going through the Modernist phase and particularly through the works of these writers, the English novel has acquired the added depth and universality, and what they achieved in their novels and other writings is bound to occupy a significant place in any assessment of the Modernist movement in the English-speaking world or even beyond. In fact, the basic concerns of these novelists, which centred on the mysteries of life and the irrational depths of the human mind and were, as we now know, characteristically Modernist, are not very far from those of Shakespeare, and it was no accident that my attention was first drawn to this aspect of the modern novel through a study of Shakespeare's plays, which in the course of time developed into an interest in its relation to the whole Modernist movement. In this sense, acknowledgement of my debt should perhaps be extended to the spirit of Shakespeare who, through his plays, has led me to the present study.

Due to the very nature of the "Movement", I have been obliged, often extensively, to discuss or refer to foreign material, including French, German and Russian literature as well as material from the field of psychology. As a general rule, when good translations are available, these have been used and acknowledged in the Notes. When no reliable translations have been found, quotations are made in the original languages, to which are added my own translations or paraphrases in English either in the text or in the Notes.

CHAPTER ONE

WHAT WAS MODERNISM?

THE QUESTION OF TERMINOLOGY

"We have grown accustomed to speak offhandedly of 'modern literature', of the 'modern temper' and even of 'the modern', but until recently we have not made much effort to analyse the meaning of the term that we find so useful."[1] In these words, the editors of a massive collection of documents on, as its subtitle puts it, *The Backgrounds of Modern Literature*, published in 1965, complain about the lack of clear definition of the term "modern" as well as the absence of an awareness even of its necessity among literary scholars. For "the modern" for them signifies "a distinct kind of imagination - themes and forms, conditions and modes of creation, that are interrelated and comprise an imaginative whole" which cannot be identified with the more chronological notion, "contemporary", and thus requires and still awaits a specific definition.

In an essay entitled "The Modern", written at about the same time (1965-1966), in which the above volume is reviewed, Frank Kermode also points out the "unexamined way" in which the word "modern" was commonly used and the meaninglessness of such practice.[2] As it is, Kermode informs us, even the then "new" *Encyclopedia of Poetry and Poetics* (1965), "the work of very learned contributors and editors", does not contain an entry on "modernism" in its widely used sense. Touch as it may on modern poetry under the heading Modern Poetics, it does not, in his view, "help us much with the modern Modern, the new New" (p.46). However, he calls our attention at the same time to a growing interest in the subject at the time, commenting "There is at present much interest in this question of the modern" (p.41), and cites Ellmann and Feidelson's *The Modern Tradition*, and Cyril Connolly's *The Modern Movement* also published in 1965, as examples of its manifestation.

In retrospect, it seems that during the 'sixties, especially towards the middle of the decade, a greater interest in and clearer notion of what we now call Modernism, or Modernist art and literature, began to emerge, and the ensuing few years saw a sudden upsurge in publication of books and articles devoted to the subject, as if in response to the clarion call of the editors of *The Modern Tradition*.

In fact, we may be able to divide the development of the concept of "the modern", or rather "Modernism" as we shall shortly explain, roughly into three stages: the first from the beginning of the movement up to the 1950s; the second, the 'sixties and a few years beyond; the third, from the middle of the 'seventies up to the present. Admittedly, even before 1960, there was clearly an awareness among literary critics and scholars that a radical change, often referred to as "a revolution", had taken place in art and literature between the end of the last century and the first quarter of this, but there seems to have been little attempt to synthesize its various elements as "an imaginative whole" and examine it as a distinctive artistic entity, nor was there any general consensus or agreement as to its name. In spite of the pioneering work done by Virginia Woolf in her critical writings as regards the particular significance of the terms "the modern" or "modernist", which we shall discuss later, critical effort of the first half of this century seems to have been devoted mainly to individual cases, be it a writer, a genre or a movement, rather than the Modernist phenomenon as a whole. Likewise, it was variously called by such names as "the modern", "the *avant garde*", "modernism", "imagism", "the Vortex" or simply "the new". The distinction between "the modern" and "the contemporary", which was to become crucial in the 'sixties, was not yet very clear either, and they were often used interchangeably. Frederick J. Karl and Marvin Magalaner, who together compiled *A Reader's Guide* to 20th century English novels, published in 1959, employ both "modern" and "contemporary" without consciously distinguishing them as most literary critics of the following decade would have done.[3]

It must be added that they were keenly aware of the singular nature of the sensibility that created those "great" novels, as well as of the particular social background which had bred that sort of sensibility, so much so that we shall find it useful to resort to their observations sometimes in the course of our discussion which follows on the present subject.

Harold Rosenberg provides another example when he discusses the special significance of Paris in relation to Modernism in an essay written in 1940 and reprinted in his book (1959). Warning against identifying the city with the "larger" artistic current - larger both in the historical and geographical sense - he observes :

> it is a mistake to see this city also as central to the modern in the larger sense, the sense in which we think of the contemporary as beginning in 1789. This larger and more fundamental span has not belonged to Paris alone. It has embraced equally the United States, South America, industrial and revolutionary China, Japan, Russia, the whole of Europe, every spot in the world touched by contemporary civilization.[4]

Clearly in the above passage, "the modern" and "the contemporary" are synonymous. Graham Hough too, like Karl and Magalaner, is aware, with more specific dating, that "the years between 1910 and the Second World

War saw a revolution in the literature of the English language as momentous as the Romantic one of a century before."[5] The statement comes from a chapter in his *Image and Experience*, entitled "Reflections on a Literary Revolution", which was first delivered, the author tells us, in a series of lectures "in the spring of 1959" (p.vii). He also confides that at that stage "we have not yet asked what the nature of the twentieth century revolution is ... " and finds it "notable that whatever was happening in those years has not yet acquired a name" (p.8). Rejecting R.P. Blackmur's term "Expressionism" which refers to "the whole European movement", including the English one, he is inclined to call it "Imagism", using the word in a wider sense than that of the particular movement associated with Ezra Pound, on the ground that "Imagist ideas are at the centre of the characteristic procedures of our time, and there is a case for giving the word a wider extension" (p.9). Elsewhere, however, he also uses quite often such words as "modern" or its derivative, "modernity", in his discussion of the same subject, as when, referring to "a feeling of the discontinuity between the literature of our century and that of any previous one" or the "singularity of modern poetry", he argues that "This consciousness of modernity is a distinctly modern thing" and "is largely the work of the revolutionary generation itself" (p.5), ie, the generation of Pound, Eliot, Joyce, Wyndham Lewis, etc. He remarks at one point on the same "modern poetry": "The new poetry was new in the '20s and it is still new in the sense that we have nothing newer" (p.6).

Thus in one volume, one and the same author refers to the same literary phenomenon by three different terms: "modern", "new" and "Imagism", perhaps a natural outcome when it "has not yet acquired a name". Peter Faulkner, in his monograph on Modernism, where he traces the history of the usage of this term as critical idiom, informs us that Hugh Kenner at about the same time (in his foreword to *Gnomen* in 1958) was also aware of this lack of a name for "the movement", and that he proposed to call it "the Vortex", a term borrowed from Wyndham Lewis, which never developed into general use.[6]

When, also in 1959, Harold Rosenberg published the book from which we have already quoted, and which dealt in most part with what we might now call Postmodernist American art scenes, such as "action painting" or "pop culture", he gave it a title, *The Tradition of the New*, indicating that his subjects are the offspring, rather than a part, of the cultural phenomenon he alternately calls "the new", "the Modern" and "Modernism", which he traces back to Baudelaire. As is implied by the title itself, he is conscious that "the new" or "the Modern" has been in existence for quite a long time – "There are people", he even remarks, "who are made nostalgic, if at all, by the sight of the Modern" - and that it in its turn has become a tradition:

> The famous "modern break with tradition" has lasted long enough to have produced its own tradition. Exactly one hundred years have passed since Baudelaire invited fugitives from the too-small world of memory to come aboard for his voyage in search of the new. (p.11)

The critics, writing towards the close of the 'fifties, show an unmistakable awareness that they are witnessing the end of an era that has produced a remarkable outburst of artistic energy and cultural excitement. The time was ripe for the closer and overall examination and analysis of the extraordinary phenomenon as a whole, and the 'sixties saw a series of initial attempts in this direction.

The growing interest in the question of "the Modern" in the 1960s must surely be due to the sense shared by many at the time that at least the peak or the height, if not the spirit, of the Modernist movement was over and already belonged to the past, as Stephen Spender in 1963 observed in his *The Struggle of the Modern:* "The modern movement, in literature at any rate, looks today like past history." [7]

In a lecture delivered in 1960 and reproduced in essay form during subsequent years in several journals and books, Harry Levin talked about "What Was Modernism?" The past tense is significant. Borrowing Arnold Toynbee's terms "Post-Modern Period", Levin called his generation "we Post-Moderns". [8] Thus when Ellmann and Feidelson describe in their Preface the general awareness of the passing of the Modernist era, they do so with particular reference to his essay: "Harry Levin's recent essay, 'What Was Modernism?' makes explicit what everyone has begun to realize, that the great age of the century's literature, the age of Yeats, Joyce, Eliot and Lawrence, of Proust, Valery and Gide, of Mann, Rilke and Kafka, has already passed into history." [9] (Note that "the great age" even here "has not yet acquired a name.") This realization enabled them to put the whole phenomenon into historical perspective - "see it in historical depth" - and made them aware of what they call a "modern tradition" which, they consider, "reaches well back into the romantic era and even beyond." At all events, looking back from a certain distance, it was possible now to see that the various movements and ideas, which had formerly appeared separate, opposed or even antagonistic to each other, actually formed an organic whole, manifesting each in its different and characteristic manner the spirit of Modernism.

Spender's *The Struggle of the Modern* occupies a significant place in the study of the Modernist movement, since it was virtually the first full-length work that attempted in-depth analyses of the Modernist spirit and of its significance and as such may be regarded as an important breakthrough in its history. It was also important in the sense that it exerted a considerable influence on the subsequent studies and discussions on the subject, especially by introducing the distinction between "the modern" and "the contemporary", which henceforward, when placed together, were rarely to be used synonymously as had often been done before, and thus establishing the identity of "the modern" as an entity clearly opposed to the rival tradition, which he called "the contemporary".[10] When Ellmann and Feidelson profess in the same Preface, "We no longer completely identify the modern with the contemporary" (p.vi), their debt to Spender's book, to which they also refer alongside Levin's essay, is apparent. Irving Howe shows an equally unmistakable sign of Spender's influence when he states in his Introduction to a collection of critical essays on Modernism and Modernist writers, published in 1967:

> In the past hundred years we have had a special kind of literature. We call it modern and distinguish it from the merely contemporary; for where the contemporary refers to time, the modern refers to sensibility and style, and where the contemporary is a term of neutral reference, the modern is a term of critical placement and judgement. [11]

Obviously it was a useful distinction, and consequently the two terms have come to enjoy wide currency as critical terminology in the 'sixties. In the Introduction to his book, Spender explains how he distinguishes the "modern", whom he also calls the "recognizers", from the "contemporaries", or "non-recognizers":

> I see the 'modern' and the 'recognisers' as deliberately setting out to invent a new literature as the result of their feeling that our age is in many respects unprecedented, and outside all the conventions of past literature and art. I see the 'contemporaries' and the 'non-recognizers' as being at least partly aware of the claim that there is a modern situation. Yet they refuse to regard it as a problem special to art. The 'contemporaries' – of whom H. G. Wells was an early example and C. P. Snow a recent one – see the changes that have taken place in civilization as the result of the developments of scientific technology, and think that, on the whole, the duty of writers is to enlist their art to support the cause of progress. The 'moderns' on the whole, distrust or even detest, the idea of progress, and view the results of science as a catastrophe to the values of past civilization ... (p.x)

We may accept these definitions as more or less appropriate, if we interpret the "cause of progress" as that of material and technological progress without implicating the development of science, or rather scientific theories, *in toto*, since the relation between "the moderns" and science was more complex and not just of simple opposition as the above quotation seems to suggest, as we shall see shortly. Later, in a chapter entitled "Moderns and Contemporaries", he elaborates on the above distinction and writes:

> Modern art is that in which the artist reflects awareness of an unprecedented modern situation in its form and idiom. The quality which is called modern shows in the realised sensibility of style and form more than in the subject matter. Thus early in the scientific and industrial era, the Age of Progress, I would not call Tennyson, Ruskin, Carlyle moderns because, although they were aware of the effects of science and most contemporary in their interest, they remained within the tradition of rationalism, unshaken in the powers of what Lawrence called the 'conscious ego'. (p.71)

For Spender those were the possessors of "the Voltairean 'I', the confidence that they stood outside a world of injustices and irrationalities", "believers in progress" who "judged the world in which they lived by the most up-to-date developments of materialist thinking" (p.72). Applying this idea to the later generation, he compares the "Voltairean I" of the "contemporaries" with the "I" of the "moderns":

> The 'Voltairean I' of Shaw, Wells and the others, acts upon events. The 'modern' 'I' of Rimbaud, Joyce, Proust, Eliot's *Prufrock* is acted upon by them. The Voltairean 'I' has the characteristics – rationalism, progressive politics, etc. – of the world the writer attempts to influence, whereas the 'modern' 'I' through receptiveness, suffering, passivity, transforms the world to which it is exposed. (p.72)

It is an opposition that originates in the writer's basic views of man and society as well as relation of these to art and literature: so far, it seems to be that of the writers as social reformers versus those dedicated to innovations, or even revolution, in art and literature. Further on in the Introduction, however, when he explains the reason for exclusion from his book of such writers as Graham Greene, Evelyn Waugh and Angus Wilson, "who did not choose either to be realist or poetic-image novelists, 'contemporaries' or 'moderns'", and names Arnold Bennett as an example of "the first category" and Virginia Woolf of "the second", he gives a wider connotation to the term "contemporary" by including in it, or identifying with it, along with the "believers in progress", such an apolitical figure as

Bennett, solely as the representative of the realist tradition. Here the opposition, or the distinction, comes to mean not only that of ideologies but that between conventional realism and the new kind of fiction advocated by Modernists, and most emphatically by Woolf, which may explain her being given as an example.

In fact, the opposition of the "moderns" and the "contemporaries" in this wider connotation was first made by Virginia Woolf as that between the "materialists" represented by Bennett, Wells and Galsworthy, and "the spiritual" young writers like Joyce and by implication herself in her essay "Modern Fiction", or as that between "the Edwardians" and "the Georgians", which is essentially the same as the former, in "Mr. Bennett and Mrs. Brown". According to Woolf, the "materialists", or "the Edwardians", are those who are concerned excessively with the material aspects of life, either for political or sociological reasons as in the case of Wells and Galsworthy or chiefly for literary purposes as in the case of Bennett, whereas the "spiritual" or "the Georgians", whom she calls "the moderns" in "Modern Fiction" and elsewhere, are those who, out of their awareness of new reality, or we may likewise say their new awareness of reality, of life, reject traditional realism as "old tools" and explore the possibility of new forms and styles more appropriate for its expression. Seen in this way, a striking affinity between Woolf's concept and that of Spender becomes more apparent. Although he does not acknowledge it explicitly, nor even mention the above distinctions made by Woolf, it is almost impossible to avoid the impression that he was, to a considerable degree, indebted to, or at least inspired by, either or both of those essays of Woolf, especially in view of the fact that he does quote from "Mr. Bennett and Mrs. Brown" towards the end of his introduction. While discussing the "reason for the difference between the traditional novels of E. M. Forster and the poetic-imagist ones of Virginia Woolf", he quotes from the essay Woolf's bold statement, "On or about December 1910 human character changed", together with her subsequent exposition on it, and argues that, while Forster assumes that human nature has not basically changed, if "manners, behaviour and ideas" have, Woolf finds a fundamental shift in "the quality of sensibility itself", and relates it to the Modernist stance as a whole:

> The moderns are therefore those who start off by thinking that human nature has changed: or if not human nature, then the relationship of the individual to the environment, forever being metamorphosised (*sic*) by science, which has altered so completely that there is an effective illusion of change which in fact causes human beings to behave as though they were different. This change,

recorded by the seismographic senses of the artist, has also to change all the relations within arrangements of words or marks on canvas which make a poem or a novel, or a painting. (p.xiii)

This last passage from Spender's Introduction shows clearly that the essay by Woolf was really the starting point of his book, and that hers was not merely, as Bernard Bergonzi puts it, "an early example of the opposition between Contemporaries and Moderns"[12] but rather its *original* version. Written in the midst of the turmoil by one of the main participants of the movement, those essays bear the character more of manifestos than careful and comprehensive studies, and naturally has less fullness and body than the book by Spender, who could take, as it were, a good view of the whole scene from a distance. The essential characteristics of "the modern" or Modernism, as well as its basic points of difference from traditional art, however, were already clearly discerned and expounded by Woolf in those two, as well as other, essays,[13] which will be discussed in a later chapter. In this sense, we may regard her as an important forerunner of Modernist critics.

It may be said that Spender took up where Woolf left off after the space of nearly forty years, and in this we may recognize part of his contribution since there had been during those years little effort, or even awareness of the need, to examine and define the Modernist movement precisely against its social and literary backgrounds. Spender's distinction, though almost identical with Woolf's in concept, must have acquired its wider currency not only because of the general awareness of the phenomenon in the critical circle but also because of the greater flexibility and usefulness of the terms employed. While Woolf was rather vague about the names of the opposition in "Modern Fiction", and that of "the Edwardians" and "the Georgians" was rather limiting in its application, Spender's "contemporaries" and "moderns" were applicable to a wider period within the twentieth century and to some extent even beyond. After the publication of *The Struggle of the Modern*, especially during the decade which followed it, these two terms came to be used quite extensively in the discussion of Modernism. Although at one point in the Introduction Spender introduces another pair of terms, "modernism" and "anti-modernism", for the same distinction, these were not taken up by critics, at least during the following decade, probably because Spender himself almost immediately drops them and consistently uses the other pair.

If the first period up to the 'fifties could not see the wood of Modernism and confused it with all the other trees that did not belong to it, even if there existed an awareness, vague or otherwise, of the phenomenon, especially towards the end of the decade, it was a classical, all too common, case of being too close to it or submerged in it.

Our second period, which corresponds more or less to the decade of the 1960s, seems to have emerged with a clearer, if not the definitive, view of the subject, and we might regard Spender as the initiator of this new phase. His book was a timely reminder for some and a revelation for others, that there existed in the recent past a special kind of art and literature of which he made the most extensive and closest study so far. It was a period when the identity of the modern or Modernism was established, and literary critics and scholars began seriously to examine its true nature. It was most often called "the modern", although "modernism" was also used simultaneously and the term "contemporary", to which "the modern" was often contrasted, was rarely to be used synonymously with it during this period. As the notion became more clarified, general interest in the subject, as was noticed by Kermode, increased, and a number of books and articles devoted specifically to it began appearing on both sides of the Atlantic, especially towards the latter half of the decade. Yet it was still too early for a clear definition or a truly comprehensive survey of the whole movement, the kind of book which Spender confesses, at the beginning of his book, to having an expectation: "In writing these loosely connected chapters, I have been haunted all the time by another book, an authoritative, extensive survey which could be written", adding that his own "contains some of the thoughts one might have when reading such a survey" (p.ix).

It was as yet a period of examination and exploration of the nature of a recently identified phenomenon. Thus, when the scene was set by Spender, and partly by Levin in his "What Was Modernism", which gave a succinct account of some of the essential characteristics of Modernism, what immediately followed was Ellmann and Feidelson's *The Modern Tradition* and *The Modern Movement* by Connolly, neither of which was "an authoritative, extensive survey" in Spender's sense. They were rather source books which provide materials for such a survey, ie, preparations for future studies. *The Modern Tradition* was comprehensive enough in time, space and subject matter, ranging from Vico to Paul Tillich, from Britain, France and Germany to Denmark and Russia, from literature and art to philosophy (Kant, Hegel, Schopenhauer, Kierkegaard, Nietzsche, etc.), as well as both natural and social sciences (Darwin, Heisenberg, Freud, Jung, Marx, etc.), but its aim was not to give a general exposition or definition of "the modern" as a whole, the need of which the editors themselves felt strongly and emphasized. As they put it,"The purpose of the book is exploratory. It is not designed to argue a general theory of modernism but to represent the various factors that any theory will be obliged to take into account. The representation is by direct quotation ... the editors have avoided extensive paraphrase and interpretation" (p.vii). Cyril Connolly's book too, as its subtitle, *One Hundred Key Books from England, France and America: 1880-1950*, suggests, is more in the nature of a critical bibliography, divided into four parts, each corresponding, except the initial one that covers the years 1880-1920, to the decades of the 1920s, 1930s and 1940s. Although, at the beginning of the book as well as of each part, he does provide commentaries by way of introduction, they are rather descriptions of historical events, both literary and social,[14] which do not amount to a clear account of what Modernism, or what he calls the "Modern Movement" is, or was. Moreover, the list of the "key" books itself is rather confusing, when writers such as Somerset Maugham, George Orwell and Graham Greene, who are now more likely to be classified as "antimodernists" are joined together with Proust, Joyce, Woolf, etc, as forming part of the "Modern Movement".[15]

The book was also limited in the sense that the list was confined to the books published in "England, France and America", and those for the most part only of poetry and fiction. No doubt it was, as the editors of *The Modern Tradition* characterized their book, an "exploratory" period, as well as one of confusion, especially at the beginning, and time was not ready for an overall survey even of literary Modernism alone. This may have been due partly to the fact, or at least to the sense, which apparently existed in many, that even if Modernism now belonged to the past, this past was a fairly recent one and the repercussions of the event were still being felt in the cultural life of the day. It was probably for this reason that when in 1967 he compiled *The Idea of the Modern*, which he described as an "anthology about literary modernism", Irving Howe, denying any intention to "provide a neatly shaped synthesis of what modernism may be", remarked:

> Since modernism is a matter close to us in time, perhaps still alive in our time, the important thing is not to be "definitive", which by the very nature of things is unlikely, but to keep ideas in motion, the subject alive. (Howe, p.12)

This sense of the continuity of Modernism, even if in a changed form, seems to have been particularly strong around the middle of the 'sixties, which may be attested by some of the writings of the period. Howe himself is not quite sure if Modernism is really dead and gone, and in a passage following the above, writes:

> Modernist literature seems now to be coming to an end, though we

can by no means be certain and there are critics who would argue
that, given the nature of our society, the modern period cannot come
to an end. (p.13)

His sympathy for those critics who claim the permanence of Modernism is apparent in a later passage, where he states that "Modernism need
never come to an end, or at least we do not really know, as yet, how it can
or will reach its end." One of the critics he had in mind may have been
Richard Chase whose article, "The Fate of the *Avant-Garde*", originally
written in 1957, Howe found relevant enough to reprint a decade later in
his anthology already mentioned. Although later in the article Chase
concedes that "'modernism' and experimentalism in the arts", which he
interprets as the "recent phase" of the *avant-garde*, "is, after forty years
of struggle, finally exhausted", his article nevertheless begins with a sort
of declaration of its permanence: "It is the custom nowadays to pronounce
the *avant-garde* dead. But the fact seems to be that under modern
conditions the *avant-garde* is a permanent movement." [16] That Chase's
avant-garde was very much the same as what others called "the modern"
or "Modernism" may be seen from the characteristics he ascribed to it:
"recurring impulse to experimentation, its search for radical values, its
historical awareness, its flexibility and receptivity to experience, it polemical intransigence". Furthermore, he traced it back, as other critics did
with Modernism, partly to the French Encyclopedists but most of all to
the "German and English, and later French romantic movements" – thus
the "Wordsworth-Coleridge group was *avant-garde* in the modern sense"
(pp.146-147) – and considered that "the vanguard of writers and artists
has been, for more than a hundred and fifty years, a necessary part of the
cultural economy", and that "the health of culture" depended upon it.
Similar sympathy for and optimism in the "avant-garde", or in this case,
"modernism", are shared by Louis Kampf. In the initial chapter of his *On
Modernism*, also published in 1967, Kampf, refusing "to discuss the
nature of modernism" itself, takes up the task of explaining the reason for
the "diversity of its offspring", ie, "What elements in the past made
possible the present diversity of artistic styles and the corresponding
diversity of roles played by artists and intellectuals?" [17]

Taking for illustration an experimental play by Jack Gelber, *The
Connection*, which was apparently performed in America around 1965,
and bore some characteristics of a "happening", such as hiring real-life
drug addicts instead of actors, while the producer himself did not know,
with only a rough framework in hand, what these "junkies" were going to
do or to say, Kampf analyses the audience's reaction to it and argues:

We now expect the work of art – and here lies both its modernity
and that modernity's permanence – to create a situation in which
we create our own values, make our own connections and shape our
own forms, whereas traditionally the work of art – since it is an
ordered object rather than a situation – was valued precisely because
of its capacity to do these things for us. (p.29)

Considering that "each of the works of modernism ... attempts to
challenge not our values but the very foundations of those values" and
that similar "Doubts about the foundations of our knowledge" are pervasive in all sectors of modern society, he thinks that this situation engenders
a "speculative freedom", with its self-perpetuating and self-enlarging
permanence", that can lead to "intellectual despair", to "a systematized
disorderliness" but possibly to "a freedom which creates order spontaneously ... ' as well, and concluded his argument by saying: "Of one thing
we can be sure, the doubts, and the freedom, have created something
which will not readily allow itself to be stopped" (pp.29-30). The chapter
has a subtitle, "The Permanence of Modernism".

Frank Kermode too had a sense, if not of the permanence of Modernism, of "a genuine continuity" in "all modernist art and literature between
the 'nineties and now [1965-1966]" *(Modern Essays,* p.40). He rejected
the idea that the Modernist movement was "all over", regarding what
others considered radically "new art" of the 'sixties, represented by such
figures as Cage, Burroughs and Warhol whom they called "post-Modern-
ists", merely as "marginal developments of older modernism" (p.61). For
him, "there has been only one Modernist Revolution", which "happened
a long time ago".(p.61) Though he distingished the older, or earlier
phase of modernism as "paleo-modernism" and its later phase as "neo-
modernism", he saw "little radical change" between the two, maintaining
"There is ... a family resemblance between the modernisms" (p.51).

Perhaps it is necessary to remind ourselves here that most critics who
claimed the permanence or continuity of Modernism were Americans -
Howe, Chase, Kampf, etc, and even Kermode, if he was not an American,
referred mainly to American writers and artists, when he discussed "neo-
modernism". It may also be expedient to remember that the first promoter
in this century of Modernist literature in England, and the English-speaking world for that matter, was an American, Ezra Pound. It may be argued
that there was something in the American temperament which, due to the
nature or the history of its society, was more congenial to experimentalism
and cosmopolitanism of the Modernist movement than the more tradition-
orientated British one.

Whatever the reasons were, the fact was that Modernism maintained its vigorous and active life much longer in the United States than in Britain where, by the 'fifties there had already emerged signs of strong reaction to it. (The reaction of the 'thirties seems to my mind a different case, since many poets and writers of the decade shared, apart from politics, the same concerns as those of the earlier generation of Modernists, as we shall see later. Nevertheless, there was undoubtedly an almost universal "sense of an ending", in both the old and the new worlds, of a phase, a period, an age or a movement, depending upon interpretation; many seem to have felt an urge to reflect upon the past phenomenon and have a clearer view of it, so that even Kermode, towards the end of his essay, "The Modern", concedes, "The fact that defining the modern is a task that now imposes itself on many distinguished scholars may be a sign that the modern period is over" (p.66).

In spite of this sense of the necessity of definition, however, many scholars, as we have seen, "postponed the task of defining" the term, "the modern" or "modernism", describing them as "intimate and elusive" (Ellmann & Feidelson, p.v) or "elusive and protean ... its definition hopelessly complicated" (Howe, p12), in preference to the examination or exploration of some particular aspects or writers of the Modernist movement, as well as of its general characteristics. A good example of this is Howe's *The Idea of the Modern* in which, while the compiler discusses the general characteristics of "Modernism" in the titular, introductory chapter, other critics examine either its particular aspects or particular writers, not only of English language but of other languages, such as Gide, Mann and Proust. It also includes "two manifestos", one of Italian Futurism, the other of Russian Modernism. Thus it may be said to have fairly international perspective, which seems to be a prerequisite for any general discussion of Modernism, although it still remains an "anthology" of independent essays and documents, collected together without a unifying principle, and falls short of giving an overall picture of Modernism. Nor was this, as we have already seen, the professed aim of the book. Besides those books and articles already discussed, we may mention Anthony Cronin's *A Question of Modernity* (1966), which is a collection of essays mainly on Modernism and Modernist writers, especially Joyce and his fiction. In the initial essay, which gave the book its title, Cronin maintains that the nature of the "revolution" which "was sometimes referred to as 'the modern movement'", was misunderstood both in its day and at the time of his writing the essay: "One might say that the nihilism of the revolution was exaggerated by entrenched academicism then, just as its radicalism is minimalized by entrenched academism now".[18] He makes out his case for greater recognition of the "radical and revolutionary" role of the movement, despite the "talk about 'tradition'" among some of its progenitors themselves (p13), especially in relation to poetic language, which was given new life and almost transformed by Modernism and in particular under Pound's tutelage – "make it new" was his message to his fellow poets.

The 1960s, especially the years between 'sixty five and 'sixty seven when there was a virtual outburst of the writings on the subject of Modernism, was a period which, to use Irving Howe's expression, kept "ideas in motion, the subject alive", even if it was not yet ready to be "definitive". As a result, by the time our second period approached its end, there was more or less a common understanding of "the idea of the Modern", or Modernism. Thus, when Bernard Bergonzi edited the volume on the 20th century of *Sphere History*, he wrote at the outset of the opening chapter, "The Advent of Modernism 1900-1920" :

> Until a few years ago, 'modern' literature might have been equally well described as 'contemporary' or 'recent' or 'twentieth-century' literature, and all of these terms would have been understood in much the same way. But as our century has moved into its final decades, a refinement of critical language has taken place: the word 'modern' is increasingly used to refer to a particular period - that is to say, the years between 1900 and 1930 - the kind of writing that flourished at the time. It has become another descriptive term, like Augustan or Romantic, to be freely used or misused by literary historians. (p.17)

Although the book itself was published in 1970, his essay was apparently written during the last years of the 'sixties and, comparing the above comment with the complaints of the editors of *The Modern Tradition* or Kermode in the mid-'sixties, we can detect quite a rapid change in critical climate that took place during the intervening years. Looking back on the British literary scene and "the Modern Movement" from the vantage point of "the [late] 1960s", Bergonzi, however, characterizes the movement as "a creative explosion" rather than "the decisive revolution", drawing our attention to the persistent survival of the "anti-modern 'native' English ... tradition" and sums up the current situation thus: "Modernist and traditionalist (or Contemporary) attitudes continue to co-exist in a state of fluctuating stasis". (After denying the status of "revolution" to Modernism in Britain, he makes a parenthetical qualification: "the American situation is quite different"(pp.19-20).

The concluding years 1970-1971 of this second period saw again publication of quite a few writings on our present subject. In an essay, entitled "The Birth of the Modern: 1885-1914", in the sixth volume of

French Literature and Its Background, Gabriel Josipovici discusses "the modern movement", as a reaction against, but at the same time the continuation of, Romanticism.[19] When the essay was reprinted the following year in his *The World and the Book*, the title was changed to *Modernism* and *Romanticism*. H.T. Moore's *Age of the Modern*, written also in the late 'sixties but published in a book with the same title in 1971, makes a fairly synthetic, if in part rather cursory, survey of what is "modern" or "20th-centuryish" in art and literature, which includes the examination of the background of "Today's Thought"with emphasis on the influence of, among others, Rousseau, Darwin, Marx, Einstein and above all, Freud, as well as the discussion of "kinships of modernity"[20] that exist among literature (Mann, Joyce, Woolf, etc), visual arts (Picasso, Marcel Duchamp, etc.) and music (Schoenberg, Stravinsky, etc.). In the same year (1971), Irving Howe, in the Preface to his significantly titled book *The Decline of the New*, while confessing that the "problem of literary modernism" has been a recurrent interest and the centre of his critical work in recent years, admits to "the possibility [even in America] that we are now living through the unsettling moral and intellectual consequences of the breakup of modernist culture, or the decline of the new."[21] In "Beliefs of the Masters", one of the essays included which seems to have been written a few years earlier, he records the changing attitude of the reading public towards such Modernist "masters" as "Eliot, Yeats and Lawrence", comparing it with that in the 'fifties and early 'sixties when they "were accredited culture-heroes of the literary young", observing: "By now, all this has changed. Young people interested in literature have, so far as I can tell, no special concern for Eliot, Yeats and Pound, though a few still celebrate Lawrence. They tend to look upon the literary "modernism" of the last seventy-five or hundred years as a period tucked away in a dim past"(pp.34-35). Here there is little uncertainty about the end of Modernism which characterized his *The Idea of the Modern:* it is presented almost certainly as passé, although curiously enough Howe's own titular essay from the earlier book is reprinted under an altered title, *The Culture of Modernism*, but with little alteration in the text, thus retaining the notion of the permanence of Modernism, which seems rather incongruous with the new tenet of the book.

We may conclude perhaps that by the end of the second period "the Modern" or Modernism had become clearly identifiable as a cultural movement or phenomenon, and at the same time the sense of its passing into history had grown even more definite than at the beginning. One uncertainty, however, still remained, ie, that of the term to be used for it. The word most favoured, perhaps due to Spender's influence, was the "modern", but "modernism" was used quite often, sometimes simultaneously in the same essay (both written at times with a capital M), and critics seem to have been unable to decide upon a single term. Malcolm Bradbury calls our attention to this fact in his *The Social Context of Modern English Literature* (1971) in which he gives an extensive discussion of the nature and origin of the particular cultural phenomenon, as the chapter headings such as "Modernity in England", "The Coming of the Modern in English Writing" or "The Making of the 'Modern' Tradition " may indicate. Referring to the "vast stylistic upheaval" that took place "from about 1880 to 1914", and which he earlier compared to "Neo-Classicism" and "Romanticism" for its impact, he finds it necessary to state, and re-state that, unlike those older movements, "There is ... no one clear word that suggests the nature of this movement",[22] which indeed seems to reflect the current situation of criticism. Yet Bradbury does suggest "one word", which he thinks "convenient" but "must be used with caution", that is, "modernism" (p.xxiv), while expressing a reservation that "it is not entirely comprehensive" (p.70). In fact, it is probable that there was at the time a general tendency to employ this term in preference to the formerly more popular "the modern". Alteration of the title of Josipovici's essay, "The Birth of the Modern", to "Modernism and Romanticism", or that of Howe's 1967 essay, "The Idea of the Modern", to "The Culture of Modernism" may be considered some indication of this changing attitude. In any case, in the essay, "The Novel", in *The Twentieth Century Mind*, published the following year (1972), Bradbury himself shows no hesitation in adopting the term "modernism" exclusively. At the same time, both "modern" and "contemporary", shedding their recently acquired literary connotations, regain their original chronological meanings, although in the case of "modern", further socio-historical significance is attached, as seen by his definition: "the modern as a world environment of change in a recognizable, post-industrial direction."[23] As we shall see presently, Bradbury's usage of these terms foreshadows the general tendency of the ensuing period.

After a lull of a few years, the third period makes a rather impressive start with a thick, closely printed volume with the title *Modernism: 1890-1930*, published in 1976. Edited by Malcolm Bradbury and James McFarlane, the book seems to have come closest, to date, to that which is said to have "haunted" Stephen Spender when he was writing *The Struggle of the Modern*, "an authoritative, extensive survey", as far as literary Modernism is concerned. Limited for the most part to the major European countries and to literature only, although it covers poetry, drama and the novel respectively, it may be, as the editors admit, far from "a comprehensive survey" of Modernism, nor can it be "a tidily finished account" when, in their words, "the critical arguments about it are still not yet out of the formative stage".[24]

Yet within these limitations, it may be considered the most extensive survey - the editors themselves prefer to use the term "anthology" - of the movement so far, consisting of two parts, Part One ranging from the examinations of more general character, as may be suggested by the headings, "The Name and Nature of Modernism", and "The Cultural and Intellectual Climate of Modernism", to the geographical survey of the different centres of Modernism in Europe, eg, Berlin, Vienna, Prague, etc, besides the usual Paris and London, as well as the critical analyses and assessment of the various literary movements, such as Imagism, Futurism, Dadaism and Surrealism, which are considered to be the component parts of Modernism, while Part Two is devoted entirely to the discussion of the different aspects of the three above mentioned genres. With contributions from 23 writers specializing in various fields and different languages the book succeeds, to a considerable degree, in providing the international as well as the multiple perspectives of this complex subject.

As to the name itself, although there is some discussion of the general use of the word "modern" and its variants, including "Modernism", the editors seem to have settled on the latter, and throughout the book "Modernism" is used, along with its adjective form, "Modernist".

Although it is difficult to know to what extent the book influenced the general critical practice - the book's choice of the term itself may be a reflection of the general tendency - it is significant that the subsequent publications on the subject that have come under our notice all adopt the term "Modernism", as well as "Modernist", both sometimes written with a small "m". The following year 1977 saw the publication of Peter Faulkner's book under the title *Modernism* which, declining to be "ency-clopedic", declares to deal specifically with "English literary Modern-ism", ie, "the writings above all of T. S. Eliot, Ezra Pound, James Joyce and Virginia Woolf" (p.ix). The fact that it was published as part of "The Critical Idiom" series, which includes volumes on Romanticism, Natural-ism, Classicism, etc, may indicate the general critical climate of the time, in which "Modernism", and not "the modern", was more or less estab-lished as a critical term, and had achieved the status, to use the General Editor's expression, of one of "the key terms in our critical vocabulary" (p.vi). It is quite possible that in this, Penguin *Modernism* had played a considerable role.

In the same year appeared David Lodge's *The Modes of Modern Writing*, in which the word "Modern", as was presaged by Bradbury, no longer signified the particular kind of literature associated with Eliot, Joyce or Virginia Woolf, which in the '60s it would surely have meant. As may be seen from the author's rephrasing of the word "modern" into "the modern era" or "in the modern period", here again, it bears primarily chronological connotations, and thus "Modern Writing" embraces "the variety of literary forms". In the section "Two Kinds of Modern Fiction", "Modern Fiction" obviously is not used in the exclusive sense given by Virginia Woolf, but includes both the "Modernist" fiction of Woolf and Joyce and its rival, the novels of traditional realism of Wells and Bennett, which Woolf did not consider "modern". The "modern" in her sense, and in Spender's sense, is consistently referred to in this book as "modernism" or "modernist".

Thus we have the third part, headed "Modernists, Antimodernists and Postmodernists", where he discusses the representative writers of the Modernist movement, those who reacted against it as well as those who inherited its legacy but developed their own characteristics. The same practice is carried on in his next book *Working with Structuralism* (1981). Here, particularly in the essays, "Modernism, Antimodernism and Post-modernism" and "Historicism and Literary History: Mapping the Modern Period", the author traces the rise and fall of, or "the oscillating pattern of dominance"[25] by, "modernism" and "antimodernism" (that is, "traditional realism"), and the transformation of the former into "postmodernism" of the more recent period. (It is interesting that Lodge should have reverted to the "Modernism-Antimodernism" contrast, tentatively adopted but eventually abandoned by Spender.) Clearly he found the word "modern-ism" (or "modernist"), together with its derivatives with their respective prefixes, useful as a framework for "mapping" literature of the modern period. Significantly, in the Preface to *The Modes of Modern Writing*, he explains that the book originates in his work as a contributor to the *Penguin book of Modernism.*[26] Gabriel Josipovici, the writer of the 1970 essay "The Birth of the Modern", also published a book in 1977 under the title *The Lessons of Modernism*, where he discussed among others such European Modernists as Kafka and Fernando Pessoa,[27] and the signific-ance of Modernism for modern English literature.

It is perhaps symptomatic of this situation that, while the 1965 *Ency-clopedia of Poetry and Poetics*, as Kermode complained, did not contain any entry on Modernism, the 1977 *Fontana Dictionary of Modern Thought* has quite an extensive one on the subject, which gives a compact and sympathetic account of the whole Modernist movement, making full use of the recent development in criticism in this particular area. It is also

aware of the shift in terminology, which we have been tracing, and thus
its entry under the heading "modernism" begins:

> Although the adjective 'modern' has (cf. *avant-garde* and *contem-
> porary*) been applied to many different phenomena at different
> times, 'modernism' (or the 'modern movement') has by now ac-
> quired stability as the comprehensive term for an international
> tendency, arising in poetry, fiction, drama, music, painting, archi-
> tecture and other arts of the West in the last years of the 19th century
> and subsequently affecting the character of most 20th century art.[28]

A most recent publication which supports our analysis is an essay by
Jeremy Hawthorn, "Individuality and Characterization in the Modernist
Novel" (1982), in which the author attempts a defence of Modernist
fiction against the criticisms made by Marxist critics (above all, Georg
Lukács), although his defence itself is based largely on sociological
concern. In the initial part of the essay Hawthorn, quoting Peter Faulkner's *Modernism*, makes a particular mention of the fact that "The term
'modernism' is ... one which has assumed wide currency only in the last
decade or so," and after giving a brief definition of the term, states
expressly: " 'The modernist novel' in this essay should be taken to refer
to writers such as Virginia Woolf, James Joyce, Franz Kafka and Albert
Camus".[29] That the author felt the need for such explanation and definition indicates the still recent arrival on the scene of these terms, ie,
"modernism" and "modernist", yet at the same time this essay, which uses
them consistently throughout in accordance with the critical principle
expressed in the above statement serves as a good example to illustrate
present critical practice in which such terms as "the moderns" and "the
'modern' novel" that had formerly characterised Woolf, Joyce, Kafka, etc,
and their works have become completely obsolete.

A large part of this change in critical terminology may be explained by
sheer passage of time. As the century moved further towards its end, the
writers and cultural phenomena, dubbed either "modern" or "contemporary", that belonged to its earlier part may no longer appear so "contemporary" or "modern". In the 'sixties some of the "moderns" and
"contemporaries", eg, Eliot, Pound and Snow, were still alive and the
death of the others like Joyce and Woolf was as yet relatively fresh in the
memory - at least fresh enough to regard them as belonging roughly to the
same period. In the late 'seventies and 'eighties, however, these figures
began to assume the remoteness, and sometimes the stature, of classical
writers (their works are now often called "modern classics"). In such a
situation, those terms which suggest immediacy and closeness may no
longer appear adequate. Furthermore, there is an obvious inconvenience

in attributing the specific cultural meanings to the two words and depriving them of their original chronological ones, since each age and period require these terms in their original roles for their own use. After all, the earliest date given by the *Oxford English Dictionary* for the word "modern" in the current chronological sense is 1585, and those for "contemporary" are 1631 in the form of "cotemporary", and 1655 in the present form. Surely the connotations of these words in earlier times were different from those of today, and those of the next century will be different from today's.

It is therefore not surprising that, as time went on and as the need for these words in new chronological contexts came to be felt, the more distinctly "qualitative" and specific term "Modernism", which had always coexisted, if not so popular, with "modern",[30] began to replace it, which, together with "cotemporary", now seems to be restored to its primary function, as it clearly is for example in David Lodge's recent books. In the study that follows, when referring to the particular cultural movement of the early part of this century, following what seems to be the critical consensus of today, we shall use the term "Modernism" as well as its adjective form "Modernist," which seems to have established itself as a critical term alongside Classicism, Romanticism, etc.

CHAPTER TWO

THE NATURE AND ROOTS OF MODERNISM

AS it is impossible to mark precisely and objectively the beginnings and the terminations of most cultural phenomena, the date given to the Modernist movement also varies according to the views of individual critics, some examples of which we have already seen during our discussion of the terminology. Like Irving Howe, who claims "In the past hundred years [presumably 1867-1967] we have had a special kind of literature called 'modern' or 'modernist' literature", or Graham Hough who thinks "a revolution in English literature" took place in the "years between 1910 and the Second World War", some critics give a greater time span for the phenomenon. In most cases, however, they concentrate their attention on a narrower period, usually the first quarter or so of this century, with or without adding the last years of the preceding century as its preliminary stage. Cyril Connolly, who sets the point of departure of "the Modern Movement" in 1880, sees its "peak period ... from about 1910 to 1925" (*The Modern Movement*, p.4). Even Frank Kermode, who considers Modernism to continue to exist from the end of the last century to the 1960s, regards "the period between 1907 and, say, 1925" as the most important for "anybody who thinks what modernism now means" ("The Modern", p.40).

Often the titles of the books or the essays themselves clearly indicate the authors' points of view. Bernard Bergonzi's introductory chapter in the *Sphere History* has, as we have seen, "The Advent of Modernism 1900-1920" for its title, although in the text he mentions "the years between 1900 and 1930" as the period increasingly being referred to as "modern". Gabriel Josipovici's essay was entitled, we recall, "The Birth of the Modern: 1885-1914". Although Malcolm Bradbury in *The Social Context of Modern English Literature* is not quite specific about the date of what he describes as "The positive assertion of the idea of a distinctively modern tradition in the arts", stating that it belongs to "a fairly narrow period of time – the last years of the nineteenth century and the first years of this" (p.85), this idea takes a clearer shape in one of the Pelican Guides as *Modernism:1890-1930*, while his remark that Modernism had its "flowering in the first third of this century" (p.74) indicates that these are no watertight datelines.

Seen in this way, it becomes apparent that, apart from the few that extend to longer periods, all those dates that do have differences in details in fact converge on roughly the same period, that is, the final decade or two of the last century and the first three decades of this. In this respect too, we may assume that there is now a broad agreement among critics, and regard Bradbury and McFarlane's title, *Modernism:1890-1930* as a sort of synthesis of those varying views.

Here it may be expedient to ask again the oft repeated question: what was Modernism? What were its main characteristics? One of the most prominent facts about it is that, unlike Classicism or Romanticism, to which it has often been compared, the spirit of Modernism did not have a single dominant mode of expression or style, manifesting itself in manifold, sometimes even contradictory ways. *The Fontana Dictionary of Modern Thought* states:

> As a stylistic term modernism contains and conceals a wide variety of different, smaller movements usually reckoned to be those post-dating Naturalism and characterized by the anti-positivistic ... and anti-representational leanings of many late-19th century artists and thinkers. It would thus include the tendencies of SYMBOLISM, IMPRESSIONISM and DECADENCE around the turn of the century; FAUVISM, CUBISM, POST-IMPRESSIONISM, FUTURISM, CONSTRUCTIVISM, IMAGISM and VORTICISM in the period up to and over World War I; and Expressionism, Dada and Surrealism during and after that war.[1]

The editors of Penguin *Modernism*, after giving a similar list of "a wide variety of movements" comment: "even these are not ... all movements of one kind, and some are radical reactions against others".[2] Bradbury elsewhere writes about "pluralism" as a marked feature of Modernism:

> If anything marks the new mood in the arts it is the very pluralism of art itself – the very heterodoxy of the forms of the new, the very breadth of expression involved in the conviction that the modern was here. Hence the difficulty of identifying the 'modern' in literature with any one particular style, any one mode of the new. If the changed mood is marked by anything, it is not by a single new style or manner or movement, but by the way the developing situation seemed to throw any single tendency into question.[3]

Thus Gabriel Josipovici, when considering the case for the emergence of "the modern movement in arts" and its "specific features", self-consciously reminds us of the "absurdity" of such enquiry itself, saying:

> There is no specific thing called 'modernity' which we can extract from the variety of individual works of art and hold up for inspection. Every modern artist of any worth has achieved what he has precisely because he has found his own voice and because this voice is distinct from those around him.[4]

Anthony Fothergill puts it laconically: "Modern*ism* ... embodies a logical contradiction."[5]

This variety, which may be considered one of the essential characteristics of Modernism, is closely related to, or indeed we might say derives from, another of its features, individualism or its emphasis on the self, either of the artist, the creator or the characters created by him, rather than society and its norms, as is explicit in the above statement of Josipovici. Walter Allen found, in all the varied artistic trends and talents of the early years of this century (for which, significantly, he had not yet had a unifying name), "one thing in common": that is, "they emphasize the individual reaction".[6] James McFarlane, in his essay "The Mind of Modernism", analyses and emphasizes the central place individualism occupies in the new cultural and artistic climate at the turn of the century:

> Perceptibly in the 'nineties and even more markedly in the early years of the new century, the custody of life's integrities began to pass from society to the individual who necessarily commanded some unique perception of the things of life, who embodies some secret essence which alone gave the world its legitimation.[7]

"The wanderer, the loner", whose origin, as we shall see later, we may trace back to Romanticism, as well as the newer breed, "the exile, the restless and homeless individual" were, according to McFarlane, "no longer the rejects of a self-confident society but rather those who, because they stood outside, were uniquely placed in an age when subjectivity was truth to speak with vision and authority" (p.82). As a result, in Howe's words, "Subjectivity becomes the typical condition of the modernist outlook".[8] It is no coincidence, then, that Virginia Woolf, who called herself and her like "the moderns" or "modernist[s]", set so much store by individual visions and "solitude", a subject which will also be dealt with later.

All the same, in spite of this difficulty of finding a clear identity of Modernism and the bewildering variety of the movements and talents related to it, there is now a general agreement, as was evidenced by the foregoing examination and sanctioned, so to speak, by an entry in the *Fontana Dictionary*, that there was a distinct break with the past traditions in the arts towards the end of the nineteenth century, which reached its climax in the 1920s; that, in the words of Josipovici, "something *did* happen to art, to all the arts, around the turn of the century, and that Proust, Joyce, Picasso, Klee, Schoenberg and Stravinsky, for all their manifest differences, do have something in common" (p.1). The list of names may vary – Josipovici himself gives a slightly longer list in *The Lessons of*

Modernism (p.109) – but what is common to all such lists drawn up by critics and scholars is that they include writers and artists of various nationalities as well as various genres. This fact is noteworthy, as it indicates the two other features of Modernism, namely, its international or cosmopolitan nature and the merging of, or interaction between, different genres and arts.

The already quoted definition, or description, of "modernism" by the *Fontana Dictionary* as "the comprehensive term for an international tendency, arising in the poetry, fiction, drama, music, painting, architecture and other arts" itself consists of these two factors. This "cross-fertilisation between countries and also among the different arts" (p.396) is so ingrained in the nature of the movement that it becomes almost prerequisite for the critics who undertake the discussion or examination of Modernism to focus their attention on this aspect, as is evident in the books and articles discussed so far.

We may recall, for example, H.T. Moore's examination of "kinships of modernity" among literature, visual arts and music in his "Age of the Modern" (each art being represented by artists of various national origins), or how the editors of *Modern Tradition* were compelled to embrace a wide range of genres and fields as well as countries when they compiled the source book for the study of Modernism. Merging of poetry and prose, characteristic of modern fiction – and especially predominant in Virginia Woolf's novels – may be considered a manifestation of this aspect of the movement. Surrealism, which affected poetry, fiction, painting, sculpture, film and to a certain extent even architecture, and exerted an almost worldwide influence too, may be given as a typical example to represent the abovementioned characteristics. In fact, in respect of internationalism, Modernism goes further than the older movement that also crossed national boundaries and in many ways may claim its ancestry, Romanticism. For while the latter was above all a European movement the former, as Harold Rosenberg pointed out, extended itself to the countries of North and South America as well as to the Far East, that is, most parts of the world which were affected by modern, post-industrial civilization.

Another trait which lies, as it were, at the heart of Modernism and which may be considered its focal point, as many other features including the aforementioned individualism or subjectivity, anti-realism (or -naturalism), experimentalism and so forth may be said to derive from it, was its anti-positivism, or its concern with the inner realities of the mind. The *Fontana Dictionary* confirmed its major significance when it recognized "the anti-positivistic ... and anti-representational [ie, anti-realist] leanings" as the common characteristics that bind together all the multifarious and idiosyncratic movements within the Modernist fold. The editors of *Modernism: 1890-1930* seem to regard it as the central driving force of the movement when they state: "it is precisely in the breaking up of the naturalistic surface and its spirit of positivism that one senses the growth of Modernism" (p.44).

Quoting H. Stuart Hughes' statement that "Nearly all the students of the last years of the nineteenth century have sensed in some form or other a profound pyschological change",[9] they interpret this "change" as "a reaction against positivism, toward a fascination with irrational or unconscious forces". This echoes Hughes' own view which emphasizes this aspect in the intellectual current of the period: "Unquestionably the major intellectual innovators of the 1890s were profoundly interested in the problem of irrational motivation in human conduct. They were obsessed, almost intoxicated, with a rediscovery of the non-logical, the uncivilized, the inexplicable" (p.35). In the chapter entitled "The Decade of the 1890s: The Revolt against Positivism", from which the above quotations are taken, Hughes argues that the writers like Freud, Weber, Croce, Bergson, Jung and others thought of their innovatory work "as a revolt against positivism", 'positivism' which they used "almost interchangeably with ... 'materialism', 'mechanism' and 'naturalism' " (pp.37-38).

The fact that both books cover exactly the same dates, and that Bradbury and McFarlane found it expedient to quote Hughes when explaining the initial phase of Modernism makes it abundantly clear that this was not simply a movement engendered within the realm of art and literature alone. In fact, it becomes almost compulsory to cast even a cursory glance over the other areas of human activities when we discuss the phenomenon of Modernism. For this reason we shall examine briefly the general intellectual climate which has so much bearing on the birth of Modernism.

The concluding years of the last century were indeed a critical period not only in art and literature but also in other spheres, especially science, both natural and social, as well as philosophy, in which new and completely altered images of man and the world were emerging. While society outwardly seemed to be marching confidently forward with its claim for technological advance and material progress, almost simultaneous and sometimes correlated questionings and reassessment of the established and generally accepted ideas that formed the very basis of such a claim began to take shape both in art and science towards the end of the nineteenth century. As the artists began to doubt the validity of the conventional realism in their attempt to recreate in their work the realities as they saw them, the scientists and philosophers, finding the traditional theories limiting and insufficient to explain the real nature of man and the world around him, began to produce a host of new theories which, sometimes confirming what artists had been instinctively and vaguely perceiving (as did to a great extent Freud's theories), profoundly affected man's view of himself and his world. As Frederick Karl and Marvin Magalaner put it :

> Several of the scientific discoveries of the last century have worked together to remake man's vision of himself, to turn heroes into fallible men. From Darwin's evolutionary theories through Freud and Max Planck and Einstein, the nature of the universe has undergone a number of different interpretations. (p.32)

Frank Kermode picks out 1900 as one of the critical years of the change and, listing the works by Freud, Husserl, Russell and Planck published in that year, comments to a similar effect:

> Thus within a few months, were published works which transformed or transvalued spirituality, the relation of language to knowing, and the very locus of human uncertainty, henceforth to be thought of not as an imperfection of the human apparatus but part of things, a condition of what we may know.[10]

We might also add the name of Nietzsche, who died in that year and who questioned the very premise of Cartesian logic and rationalism and whose writings had exerted an enormous influence during the preceding decade or so on social thinkers as well as literary men all over Europe. It was five years later – in 1905 to be precise – that Einstein published his Theory of Relativity which rejected the idea of the absolute, stationary frame of reference in the external world, which may be compared to Nietzsche's rejection of Descartes' final and fixed frame of reference in the inner world, the conscious "I" of "Cogito". This comparison is not altogether whimsical since, as science started to explore the regions beyond man's visible, empirical world, it too began to shed its, so far characteristic, positivistic quality and present sometimes an appearance even of fantasy or science fiction, as McFarlane points out:

> New concepts in science more and more took on the nature of poetic conceits; the crucial advances in science (not merely in the relatively new field of psychology but also in the more traditional physical sciences) followed the exploitation of the same kind of imaginative, intuitive insight that went towards the making of a poem. The physicist found himself having to acknowledge the existence of new and disturbingly different laws, in which conventional logic and common sense played a greatly diminished role ...

imaginative and even fantastic speculation invaded scientific thought on a scale as never before.[11]

This fact did not ecape a writer's notice either; in her last novel, *Between the Acts*, Virginia Woolf writes as a fragment of the conversation among the spectators at a village pageant: " ... It's odd that science, so they tell me, is making things (so to speak) more spiritual ... The very latest notion, so I'm told, is, nothing's solid ... "[12] Although this is presented as a layman's knowledge through hearsay - note the repetition of "so they tell me" and "so I'm told" - of the general trend in science in the year 1939, in which the novel is set, the process had started almost half a century before. Levin recognizes in this a link with Modernism and states: "Science no longer underprops our world view with rationalistic or positivistic reassurances. It has undergone a modernist phase of its own, and seen its solid premises subverted by such concepts as relativity and indeterminacy."[13] The result of all this was that the classical, or traditional, sense of the solid, hierarchical and rational order of the world and man was drastically shaken, and was taken over by a greatly altered vision which inevitably affected the atmosphere of the whole of society and especially its most sensitive sector, art and literature.

Of all the theories that thus affected man's consciousness at the turn of the century it was perhaps Freud's, most writers concur, that made the greatest impact, especially in the field of art and literature. Alan Bullock epitomizes the opinion of the many when, discussing the significance of the new scientific thoughts and discoveries in the 1900s, he comments: "No single man, probably, has exercised a greater influence on the ideas, literature and art of the twentieth century than Freud".[14] H. Stuart Hughes, while viewing "the major intellectual innovators of the 1890s", declares: "Obviously the towering figure of the era is Sigmund Freud", who surpasses in importance all the others such as Weber, Durkheim, Bergson, etc. (p.19). H.T. Moore, who thinks: "Perhaps no influence on modern literature has been so direct as that of Freud",[15] sets aside a section (under the title, "The Power of Freud") in his discussion of Modernism, for the explication, however cursory, of Freud's theories, maintaining that "a partial understanding" of his works "is requisite for a thorough knowledge of twentieth century literature" (p.101). Graham Hough goes so far as to compare him to "Plato in the Renaissance" as the "thinker who above all others loomed behind the contemporary artistic imagination",[16] and writes:

If one were asked to name the most profoundly revolutionary

influence on the imaginative writing of this century, one would be compelled to cite the name of a scientist – Freud. (p.133)

What Freud revolutionized was, of course, the way man looked at and understood himself: the convention of the predominantly two-dimensional way of understanding man gave way to that with three or four dimensional, in short, multiple, outlooks. As one commentator aptly stated: "it was like the discovery of perspective by the early Italian painters".[17] As such terms as "Freudian slip", "Oedipus complex", "repression" or "wish fulfilment" became incorporated into everyday language, it was no longer possible for most people not to be aware of the deeper layers of the mind, or hidden or unconscious motives for human behaviour. As Kathleen Cannell puts it: "Nowadays no one is innocent of Freud ... "[18] It does not mean that the recognition of this aspect of human reality had not existed before: men of genius, like Shakespeare in literature and Bosch in painting, intuitively explored and revealed in their work the more obscure regions of man's mind, and more lately, as we shall examine in detail, the poets and writers of the Romantic movement were particularly concerned with it.

These had been, however, either isolated cases or minority concern. Now it has become the concern of the whole society, or at least of the educated sector of it. Freud brought to the mind of common people the understanding, or recognition, of the complexity of the human mind which had hitherto been the privilege of a few great artists and thinkers who had achieved it through their insight and intuitive faculty. Ernest Jones, in his biography of Freud, reflecting on various examples of Freud's influence on social life, concludes:

> Most important, however, is the increasing sense people have of being moved by obscure forces within themselves which they are unable to define. Few thinking people nowadays would claim a complete knowledge of themselves or that what they are consciously aware of comprises the whole of their mentality. And this recognition ... we owe above all to Freud.[19]

Karl and Magalaner elaborate on this point specifically in relation to the novel:

> Freudian psychology precluded the nineteenth-century conception of the soul as an entity in which a character was either "good" or "bad", a view that often resulted in melodrama and/or sentimentality. After Freud, the soul – or man's personality – was seen as having a multiplicity of aspects, which the novelist uses to demonstrate the controlled disorder of the human mind. (p.29)

Although this transformation was spectacular above all in the field of the novel, recognition and exploitation of the newly revealed, or confirmed, complexity of man's inner world became the dominant preoccupation of modern art and literature, and especially of the Modernists. This brings us back to our earlier discussion of the main features of Modernism, in which the awareness of this complexity and richness of the inner life of man occupied the central place. Eugene Jolas, the editor of *Transition*, the characteristically international magazine for Modernist art and literature, based in Paris, may be considered to be speaking for the whole movement, when he said: "We felt the importance of the problem of reality – the new reality of our twentieth century in relation to our inner world ..." [20] Stephen Spender illustrates how this particular concern linked various writers and movements together:

> There is in much modern literature an evocation of compensatory depths in individual human life. Everyone carries around an infinity, if not in his head, then in his sex. If his thoughts are cupboard-size, nevertheless, his dreams open to prairies, constellations. Art invokes the subconscious world to counterbalance the conscious result of materialism. [21]

After discussing its manifestation in the works of Joyce and Lawrence, he concludes:

> It is this appeal to forces stronger than those in conscious individuality but which yet *are* the individual, and of which he can be made conscious, that writers as opposed as Lawrence and Joyce, movements as divergent as futurism, dadaism, surrealism and existentialism, yet have in common.

Even in the above passages alone the influence of Freud, together with that of his one-time disciple and later dissenter, Jung, is apparent in the terminology as well as in the concepts on which Spender bases his argument. Seen in this way, the kind of pyschological knowledge Freud introduced to the public in the early years of this century may be regarded as an important source of inspiration for the Modernist movement, and indeed as one of the main roots from which Modernism grew and flowered. Alfred Kazin expresses essentially the same view when he remarks:

> It is impossible to think of the great names in modern literature and art - Thomas Mann, James Joyce, Franz Kafka, Ernest Hemingway, William Faulkner, Pablo Picasso, Paul Klee – without realizing our debt to Freud's exploration of dreams, myths symbols and the imaginative profundity of man's inner life. [22]

If we turn our eyes, however, from this more or less contemporary source of influence to another direction, to the field of literature itself, and further back in time, we encounter a movement which foreshadowed many of the characteristics of Modernism, and in this sense may be called its precursor, or even its forebear. As our references, during the discussion of the main features of Modernism, to their earlier manifestations in Romanticism have already indicated, the legacies of this older movement are clearly discernible in the later movement. In the earlier days, however, this kinship between the two, again, was not easily recognizable or tended to be ignored, since Modernism did react to certain aspects of Romanticism (eg, Eliot's reaction against Shelley) and initially differences stood out more than similarities. Thus Randall Jarrell noted: "What has impressed everyone about modernist poetry is its differentness",[23] and that "Modernist poetry – the poetry of Pound, Eliot, Crane, Stevens, Cummings, Macleish, etcetera – appears to be and is generally considered to be a violent break with romanticism ..." (p.159). Yet his own proposition was counter to this general assumption: "it is actually, I believe, an extension of romanticism, an end product in which most of the tendencies of romanticism have been carried to their limits ...", which explains the title of his article, "The End of the Line". After commenting that "all Pound's early advice to poets could be summed up in a sentence, half of which is pure Wordsworth: Write like prose, like speech – and *read French poetry!*" (p.161), he lists some of the characteristics of Modernist poetry to show its resemblance to Romanticism. The fact that at the end of his article he felt obliged to make the following, rather elaborate, apology indicates how inconceivable and unpopular such a suggestion was around 1942 when it was first published:

> I am afraid that my hypothesis about romanticism and modernism, without the mass of evidence that can make a theory plausible, or the tangle of extensions and incidental insights that can make it charming, may seem improbable or unpleasant to some of my readers. It is intended to be partial ... (p.166)

However, as the nature and the identity not only of Modernist poetry but of the Modernist movement as a whole came to be more generally recognized, this situation also seems to have changed and we find critics writing towards and during our second period showing increasing awareness of its kinship with Romanticism. Here again Spender, in his *Struggle of the Modern*, may be said to have set the tone:

> We are confronted with a paradox that although there has been a reaction against the Romantics and back towards the poets who

preceded them, nevertheless, the same poet-critics who made his revolt have taken over the subjective view of the imagination which was Romantic. Joyce, Yeats (in his later works), Eliot and Pound combine critical awareness in the *act* of writing, with the instinctive subjective consciousness in their use of material from dreams, as well as in their fragmentariness, obscurity, mysteriousness and the like. (p.48)

Another apology, this time at the end of Josipovici's "The Birth of the Modern: 1885-1914" (later "Modernism and Romanticism"), reflects a situation in 1970 which was almost the complete reverse of Jarrell's:

It has ... been necessary as a matter of strategy, to make the division between the Romantics and the Moderns sharper than it really is. For however much the modernist movement is a reaction to a decadent Romanticism, its basic assumptions are still the Romantic ones: a refusal to rely on any external system of values, moral or epistemological, the attempt to discover and communicate the uniqueness of the individual and of each object. (p.18)

Bradbury too, while describing Modernism as "a change away from romanticism" (*The Social Context*, p.69) and the "most visible mark of literature and art's passing beyond the environment of Romanticism and Victorianism" (p.74), nevertheless regards it as "very much an internal development within the history of the romantic art themselves" and sees many of its basic premises deriving from Romanticism: "Romanticism ... was an international movement of revolutionary sensibility; and it certainly marks the beginning of the aesthetic transition into the modern age. It set out the basis of an essentially modern view of art ... and basically modern view of the artist ... " (p.75). These examples, though each stressing different points of similarities, seems to testify that by the '60s there was a common understanding of recognition among critics that Modernism, in spite of its apparent novelty or differences, was in fact a spiritual offspring of Romanticism. Thus towards the end of the following decade, in 1977, Peter Faulkner summed up the general critical climate: "Modernism has come to seem a broadly homogeneous movement, with roots in Romanticism and a flowering in the first third of this century." (*Modernism*, p.74)

Cyril Connolly had earlier defined the "modern spirit" as "a combination of certain intellectual qualities inherited from the Enlightenment: lucidity, irony, scepticism, intellectual curiosity, combined with the passionate intensity and enhanced sensibility of the Romantics" (*The Modern Movement*, p.1), and certainly the highly developed critical intelligence characteristic of many Modernist writers may, to some extent, be regarded as a legacy of the Enlightenment.

Yet, in the final analysis, the "Voltairean I" and the "modern I", as was discussed by Spender, hold virtually opposite views of man and the world, and any resemblance between them does not seem to go beyond the surface. Besides, some of the qualities Connolly lists in relation to the Enlightenment such as "irony" or "scepticism", especially towards the established norms of society of their time, are not unknown to the Romantics, and as to critical intelligence Romantic poets and writers, such as Wordsworth, Coleridge and Hazlitt, are now often regarded as the initiators of modern literary criticism. As far as the focal point of Modernism, ie, its concern with, or interest in, the inner reality was concerned, there is no doubt that, as some of the Modernists themselves (eg, Surrealists, those related to the magazine *Transition,* Virginia Woolf, etc.) were acutely aware of, Romanticism was its immediate and direct ancestry. Stuart Hughes, who was impressed above all by "the profound psychological change" setting into the mainstream of European thought towards the end of the last century, was at one point even "tempted to characterize" the new attitude as "neo-romanticism or neo-mysticism" and observed:

> Unquestionably the turn towards the subjective that we find in so much of the imaginative and speculative writing of the quarter century between 1890 and the First World War recalls the aspirations of the Original Romanticists. It is not difficult to think of writers who in the 1890s or early 1900s felt that they were reaching back over a half-century gap to restore to honor those values of the imagination that their immediate predecessors had scorned and neglected.[24]

Clearly this was the case with those Modernists mentioned above who, as we shall see, express this belief in their manifestos and critical writings.

Thus it might be said that when it comes to its major feature, the concern with the inner life or non-logical side of man, Modernism had two roots, one contemporary, the other in the past, namely, Freudianism and Romanticism. These two roots, though aparently belonging to different fields, were in fact not altogether unrelated in their turn, and we may even discern a sort of family relationship between them. Freud himself, who called creative writers "valuable allies", was the first to recognize and emphasize in his writings the kinship between literature and psychology as well as the latters's debt to the former which often anticipated it. Thus he wrote in a paper: "The description of the human mind is indeed most his [the writer's] own; he has from time immemorial been the precursor of science, and so too of scientific psychology".[25] More particularly, the Romantic poets and writers, whom we shall later examine in detail, foreshadowed the major concerns and theories of Freudian psychology to such an extent that there even seems in some respects a direct link between them. It was no doubt with this in mind that Lionel Trilling commented: "psychoanalysis is one of the culminations of the Romanticist literature of the nineteenth century";[26] or that Frank Kermode succinctly described the age of Romanticism as "the period when literary men were doing the preparatory work of psychoanalysis".[27]

CHAPTER THREE

MODERNISM AND THE ENGLISH NOVEL

ONE of the most notable facts about Modernism in England is that its impact, as well as its manifestations, was especially dramatic, or spectacular, in the field of the novel. This was, to my mind, largely due to the particular nature of the traditional English novel which, having little to do with inner visions or realities, concerned itself mainly with the external world, with the description of manners and criticism of society, the two summits of which we may see in Jane Austen and Charles Dickens, though the two traits often, perhaps inevitably, intermingled. As Robert Kiely points out, "at its very foundations, the English novel was a social genre, not taking its earliest inspirations from fear of God or love of nature, but from a preoccupation with the structure of society."[1] Virginia Woolf called it "the sociological novel" (see p.192). Unlike its counterparts in France or Germany, the English novel, at least its mainstream, had been little affected by, or formed part of, the Romantic movement, which in England was concerned almost exclusively with poetry.

It is significant that, whereas on the Continent the same writer was often simultaneously an important poet and novelist, as in the case of Novalis or Nerval (see Chapter 6), poetry and the novel in England, since the establishment of the latter as a genre, seem mostly to have maintained a separate existence. If anything, Romanticism in the English novel appeared in that peculiar form, the Gothic romance, which rather anticipated, or initiated, Romanticism than was influenced by it, and which has often been treated by the literary establishment as an inferior type of fiction, a second class citizen in the Republic of Letters. In many books on the history of English literature, it is not mentioned at all, and when it is, it is referred to merely in passing in relation to the main current of the English novel, only to be dismissed most of the time in such terms as "that ... extreme form of 'sentimental' expressionism, Gothic horror",[2] or the "subliterary depths of romanticism".[3] Robert D. Hume in fact points out that "There is a persistent suspicion that Gothicism is a poor and probably illegitimate relation of Romanticism, and a consequent tendency to treat it that way", and that there are even those who deny the relation altogether. In his effort to revalue the Gothic novel, Hume emphasizes its close kinship with Romanticism, while admitting to the essential difference that exists between them (see p.239, note 27) by describing the basic concerns common to both:

Gothic and romantic writing are closely related chronologically and share some themes and characteristics, such as the hero who is a guilt-haunted wanderer. Both have a strong psychological concern with interior mental processes. The realistic novel, the novel of manners and neo-classical poetry generally lead the reader to contemplate the exterior actions of life around him. In sharp contradiction, Gothic and Romantic writing usually lead the reader to consider internal mental processes and reactions. The one sort of writing is basically social in its concern, the other essentially individual. It is this absorbtion with the individual that Gothic and romantic writing gain their preoccupation with the mind. (pp.288-289)

It is significant that the description here of the contrast between Romanticism and Neo-classicism, between the Gothic novel and the novel of manners, may be used almost verbatim for that between Modernist fiction and the nineteenth century realistic novel against which the former reacted. It is no accident that this should be so, since, if we believe the initiator of the genre, Horace Walpole, the Gothic novel was started for very much the same reason as was Modernist fiction .

In his Preface to the Second Edition of *The Castle of Otranto* (1764), Walpole reveals that in writing this first work of the genre – "an attempt", in his words, "to blend the two kinds of romance, the ancient and the modern" – he was largely motivated by his dissatisfaction with the latter, ie, the contemporary novel, whose main aim, he points out, was always to copy nature successfully [ie, realism] and in which, consequently, "the great resources of fancy have been dammed up, by a strict adherence to common life" and "nature has cramped imagination ..."[4] The same complaints will be repeated later by Modernists and especially by Virginia Woolf in her essays. Thus it is again no accident that André Breton, that "Magus of Surrealism", should have found kindred spirits in the Gothic writers, and discussed them in several of his writings including his *First Manifesto* (1924), acclaiming them enthusiastically. We may say that he was one of the first, or even the first, to recognize the real significance of the Gothic novel, and may detect his influence behind the recent trend to revalue it.

Gillian Beer, who defends the genre against the usual ridicule: "Despite its incidental absurdities the Gothic romance is a serious form which freed the primal material of dreams and terrors back into fiction",[5] expressly sympathizes with the Surrealists' appreciation of it. David Punter, who sees "Gothic fiction [as] a process of cultural self-analysis, and the image which it throws up [as] the dream-figures of a troubled social group",[6] bases his revaluation on partly the Marxist but largely the Freudian approach, which recapitulates that of Breton and his fellow Surrealists.

How the Gothic novel could grasp the fundamental problem of life, which is even more relevant today, may be illustrated by Mary Shelley's minor masterpiece, *Frankenstein*, which portrays man's dreams of creative power turning into a nightmare – a problem, a threat, which we are witnessing almost daily in various forms in today's world. Be that as it may, Gothicism, or Romanticism in fiction, never occupied a legitimate place in the history of the English novel, nor did it really affect its main body in depth, merely showing itself, if at all, in such an isolated case as *Wuthering Heights*, which is indeed a great Romantic novel, or in some elements in such works as *Jane Eyre* and some of Dickens' novels.

While attempting to reassess the Gothic romance as the forerunner of the "romantic novel" in England, Kiely confesses at the outset to the problem of such classification itself: "The English romantic novel is, in some ways, an embarrassing subject. There is, first of all, the question of its existence."[7] In fact, Gothicism in its heyday, as Punter emphasizes in his study, was affiliated more with poetry than with fiction, and it was the Romantic poets, such as Blake, Byron, Coleridge, Keats and Shelley, who were most deeply influenced by it and who in their turn contributed to its tradition.[8] In the field of fiction, however, where it seems never to have risen above its subordinate status, if not in popularity at least in its public estimate, the elements it represented had rarely received due recognition nor been explored to the full and, as time went on, deteriorated further into such "subliterary" genres as ghost or detective stories and horror films.

The "great tradition" of the English novel had remained largely that of realism, which dealt mainly with the realities of the external rather than the internal world. Even when it concerned itself with the interior of its characters, this was usually restricted to the psychology of daytime, of the conscious level, rarely going beyond to reach the concealed depths of the mind. It virtually excluded from its confines what Jung called the "nightside of life", the irrational depths of man's existence which, however temporarily, had found expression, an outlet, in the Gothic novel. The real message of Gothicism may thus be said to have been transmitted to posterity, especially to the Modernists, not through its own genre, the novel, but through Romantic poetry which, though belonging to a different genre, was nevertheless its closest spiritual kin.

To all this too, however, "something did happen" and the change is all the more dramatic due to its contrast with the realistic tradition of the English novel. Bernard Bergonzi talks of "the sense of development and spectacular advance [in the novel] that was apparent between 1890 and 1930",[9] and thinks that fiction, which had been steadily opening up a new territory, occupied "the last piece of territory ... in the decades between 1910 and 1930, in the work of Proust and Joyce, to whom Moravia has referred as 'the gravediggers of the nineteenth century novel'" (p.23). Alan Friedman, in *The Turn of the Novel*, points out "the unmistakable shift, and a period of transition"[10] in the novel, which "was gradual, but ...took place ... with great velocity at about the turn of the century" (p.14). Malcolm Bradbury, elaborating on this " 'turn' of the novel", writes:

> It is a turn which distinguishes, say, the later work of Henry James from that of George Eliot, or separates the work of Lawrence from the work of Hardy. This change is not one kind and is not total or inclusive, for some novelists seem not to be touched by it; nonetheless it brought about an enormous alteration in the novel's nature, structure and mode of activity, so that a new period or phase of style seems to emerge.[11]

Analysing it further, he continues:

> The change has something to do with the fortunes of realism and liberalism in the novel ... An essential feature of the twentieth century novel is the presence of a new kind of self-awareness, an introversion of the novel to a degree unprecedented in its fortunes.

And this coincides with the "essential feature" of the whole Modernist movement. The degree of the "introversion of the novel" may indeed have been "unprecedented", but not unanticipated if we take into account the existence of the Gothic novel. In a sense, we might say that modernist fiction attempted to realise the full potentiality of the Gothic heritage, handed down by the Romantic movement. Virginia Woolf was one, along with Breton, who was aware of the true significance of the Gothic novel, hidden behind its often absurd or fantastic façade, and almost intuitively of its link with Modernist fiction. In "Phases of Fiction" (1929), while discussing Mrs. Radcliffe's *The Mysteries of Udolpho* which, she admits, "have been so much laughed at as the type of Gothic absurdity that it is difficult to come at the book with a fresh eye", Woolf nevertheless finds in it, alongside the artificiality and "absurdity of romance", "the force which the romantic acquires by obliterating facts":

> With the sinking of the lights, the solidity of the foreground disappears, other shapes become apparent and other senses are roused. We become aware of the danger and darkness of our existence; comfortable reality has proved itself a phantom too. Outside our little shelter we hear the wind raging and the waves breaking.[12]

This evocative passage reminds us very much of the middle section, "Time Passes", which dwells on death, decay and chaos, of her own *To the Lighthouse*, written two years before. Besides, to be liberated from "facts" alone and to "become aware of the danger and darkness of our existence" formed an important part of Woolf's art. Yet, in an earlier essay, "Gothic Romance" (1921), originally a *Times Literary Supplement* review of Edith Birkhead's study of the genre, Woolf herself is rather dismissive of the subject, describing it as "a parasite, an artificial commodity", condescendingly smiling at "the absurdity of the visions" conjured up by the same Mrs. Radcliffe, Monk Lewis, *et al*, and mentioning Scott, Jane Austen and Peacock as those mainstream authors who "stooped from their heights to laugh at the absurdity of the convention and drove it" into its subsequent subterranean existence.[13]

Obviously a considerable change took place in her views during the eight years that separate the two essays which, significantly, include the publication of Breton's *Manifestos*. It must be noted, however, that even in the earlier essay Woolf, almost in spite of herself, seems to sense the underlying link between the generally depreciated genre and the kind of fiction with which she is affiliated, when she expounds on what, with self-congratulation, she termed "our improvement" on the former:

> In our days we flatter ourselves the effect is produced by subtler means. It is at the ghosts within us that we shudder, and not at the decaying bodies of barons or the subterranean activities of ghouls. (p.133)

Surely, "our improvement" unwittingly assumes a common basis, suggests a certain sense of continuity? When she acknowledges by implication that modern fiction aims at the same effect as the Gothic romance, though it be "by subtler means", it is only one step from seeing "the decaying bodies of barons, etc." as projections of "the ghosts within us". It is also notable that following the above passage, Woolf speculates on possible modifications of "the Gothic romance of the future" due to the influence of scientific development ("with the aeroplane and the telephone") and observes: "Already the bolder of our novelists have made use of psychoanalysis to startle and dismay" (p.133).

It is significant that Woolf relates psychoanalysis to what she seems to regard as an extension, or modern version, of the Gothic novel. For modern, and above all Modernist, fiction which made use of or, more often, was inspired by, psychoanalysis may indeed be considered the spiritual descendant of Gothicism in that it was motivated by the same concern with man's inner life as the latter, which was the very reason for using, or being affected by, psychoanalysis, and that both reacted against the prevailing mode of external realism, which they considered to be stifling and ignoring this side of human reality. This awareness, or concern, thus may be said to be the essential factor that interrelates Modernism, the Gothic novel (which may be considered the earliest manifestation of Romanticism), and Freudian psychology.

Clearly, there were obvious differences between the eighteenth century Gothic romance and the twentieth century Modernist fiction, and the greatest and most manifest of them all was perhaps the place each occupied, ie, their status, in the literary hierarchy of their time. In contrast to the obscure and inferior role assigned to the former, the latter came to occupy, though not without some initial struggle, the forefront of the early twentieth century literary scene, becoming its vanguard in every sense of the word. Its impact, the weight of its presence, was such that it almost completely overshadowed the other type of fiction, the traditional realist novel, for some time, so much so that such critics as Bernard Bergonzi and David Lodge found it necessary to draw attention to its survival or coexistence during the Modernist phase of the English novel. This no doubt had much to do with the already discussed general climate, social as well as cultural, that had undergone considerable transformation under the influence of the new scientific theories and the ideas of the anti-positivist thinkers of the period, of which the most significant for the English novel was, as for modern art in general, those of Freud, and later Jung. As Freud recognized and appreciated the significance of literature for psychology, literary men, especially novelists, on their part, came to realise the essential kinship between their own work and those psychological theories, that they were based on common ground: the human mind and behaviour. Some even regarded the psychologists as, in Freud's own words for writers, "valuable allies", and the customary distinction, or boundary, between literature and science was all but obliterated. Explaining why "Freud, surely more than Planck and Einstein appealed to the novelists", the editors of *The Reader's Guide* write:

> Several of his theories on sex and psychopathology had always been the commonplaces of literature and were now interpreted by many as literary, not scientific, doctrines.[14]

As pointed out by W. H. Auden who, though a generation younger than the representative Modernists, shared many of their concerns, there were "certain obvious technical influences" Freud had on literature in such aspects as "its treatment of space and time" [orderly arrangement of space and chronological time came to play an increasingly minor role] and "the use of words in associational rather than logical sequence",[15] which we may think derived from Freud's method of free association, the "stream of consciousness" technique being one of its manifestations in literature. But more important were his theories about the significance of dreams and the role of the unconscious in man's daily life which preceded, or rather gave rise to these technical innovations, and which had been guessed at and explored by some writers of genius and the Romantics but by no means "the commonplaces of literature". Acknowledging this debt which literature owes to Freud, Auden continues: "He has directed the attention of the writer to material such as dreams and nervous tics hitherto disregarded; to relations as hitherto unconsidered as the relations between people playing tennis; he has revised hero-worship." (Note the repetition of "hitherto disregarded" and "hitherto unconsidered".)

The new techniques were part and parcel of those new subject matters. Karl and Magalaner expressed this in these words: "the new psychology of Freud and his followers gave the modern novelist new themes almost ready made for artistic dramatisation and new means to conceive these schemes" (p.29). This, then, was what has often been described as "the revolutionary influence of Freud" on literature. It did not, however, mean that the modern novelist constructed his work entirely and faithfully on the basis of Freud's or Jung's pyschological theories, nor that all the novelists were affected by them; hence Virginia Woolf's condemnation of the "materialists" and Stephen Spender's distinction between "the modern" and the "contemporary". It meant that for those writers who increasingly felt dissatisfied with the conventional mode of writing a novel – its characterisation, subject matter and style – these theories opened up a new perspective, new possibility. It meant more than anything else that they created a general atmosphere, "provided the inescapable environment of ideas",[16] in which a new kind of fiction with its altered visions of man and the world, conceived and presented by some of the most perceptive and creative of the novelists of the period could be, unlike its spiritual forebear, the Gothic romance, incorporated into "official" literature, to such an extent that it was even regarded for some time, while Modernism was at its height, as the mainstream of the English novel, resulting in an almost total eclipse of convenional realism. This must be what Bradbury meant when he said, "The change has something to do with the fortunes of realism ... in the novel", and the influence of Freudian psychology, as we have seen, contributed greatly to this "unprecedented" "introversion of the novel", which became the hallmark of Modernist fiction.

The exploration of the inner world gained momentum with the trauma of the War, and the Modernist movement which had been gathering strength since the last years of the nineteenth century reached its culminating point during the postwar period, namely in the 1920s. World War I was in many ways a veritable turning point, a crucial landmark, for the whole of European culture and society. It was "a truly apocalyptic moment for Western civilization ... a very recognizable point of transition in ideaology, mores and social change, and possibly the mark of the collapse of an entire civilized order,"[17] and so it was for the novel.

The "civilized" attitude, which had prevented the full exploration of deeper truths about man and life in the name of propriety and discretion was, as it were, blown up by the blast of the bombs, which brought in its place the recognition that beneath the "civilized" surface, there lay the primaeval force that had persistently maintained its existence throughout the centuries of apparent progress and development. Walter Allen, seeing a clear break between the prewar and the postwar English novels, refers to the arrival after the war of "a new generation" of novelists who were very different from their predecessors. Borrowing the label Wyndham Lewis put to Pound, Joyce, Eliot and himself, and including further in the group, as a "reasonable" extension Lawrence, Woolf and Dorothy Richardson, he calls them the "Men of 1914" and comments:

> All break up the accepted realistic surface of things and emphasize, at the expense of the rational and mechanical, of the scientific in its simpler manifestations, the irrational, the unconscious, the mythical. Reality lies in a hitherto unsuspected labyrinthine complexity beneath the surface of things; and to be content with the surface of things is, these events [ie, publication of Freud's and Jung's psychological theories, the War, etc.] seem severally to argue, to be content with unreality. Indeed, this is precisely the burden of Virginia Woolf's attack on the Edwardian novelists ... [18]

John Gross expresses a similar view when he remarks:

> In the 1920s the dominant characteristic of modern literature was felt to be a bringing to light of hidden areas of the personality, an enlarging and refining of consciousness. Joyce's interior monologues, Lawrence's insistence that "you mustn't look in my novel for the old stable ego of the character", Virginia Woolf's flow of tremulous imagery, whatever the difference between them, could all be taken as pointing in broadly the same direction – towards a picture of individual experience as more fluid, denser, more disorderly, less subject to rational control than earlier generations had dared to admit.[19]

It was a picture, he adds, which was made "easier to accept after the upheavals of war", and confirmed by "the rapid if confusing spread of what used to be known in those days as Depth Psychology".

Although neither of the two comments, written respectively in 1964 and 1969, mentions Modernism, it is precisely its "dominant characteristic", discussed earlier in this chapter, that they describe in relation to those novelists whom Allen called the "Men of 1914", and the fact that Gross apparently regards the characteristic as that of "modern literature" in general indicates the degree of predominance of Modernist fiction at the time. It is also noteworthy that both critics emphasise the role of the war as well as Freudian, or "depth" psychology either in relation to the emergence (Allen), or the public's reception (Gross) of this kind of fiction.

Following the above comment, Gross writes further about this "spread" of the new psychology in England: "The Freudian ideas which were an unheard-of novelty when they were discussed in *The New Age* in 1912 had become common knowledge among most educated people a dozen years later." This, however, is slightly misleading, for, while it is perfectly true that it was in the 1920s both in England and America that Freud's theories made dramatic headway, though not without opposition or confusion Gross mentions, they were by no means "an unheard of novelty" in 1912 as he claims. As we shall discuss this point later, it may suffice to point out here that, in the wake of the American tour of Freud and Jung in 1909 and publication of their lectures and some of Freud's theories in English the following year, some writers and intellectuals were quick to realise their implication in the field of art and culture in general. As to the American situation, F. J. Hoffman, while admitting that its "popularisation" did not reach the stage of "tidal wave of interest and controversy [that] swept the United States in the 'twenties", writes, "Intellectuals and artists early saw the possibilities of the new psychology", and quotes a remark by A. A. Brill, pioneer and loyal advocate of Freudian psychology in America, that writers "came to me from everywhere wanting to know about it" after the publication of his paper on dreams "sometime in 1910", which "had received a two-page notice in the New York Sunday Times".[20]

England does not seem to have lagged far behind, since in his autobiography Leonard Woolf, reminiscing of his youth, names Freud, alongside Rutherford and Einstein, as a contributing factor to the exciting atmosphere "in London in 1911" (see p.179). During the ensuing years his ideas seem to have spread steadily through newspaper and magazine articles, conversation among friends as we shall see in a sketch "According to Freud" (1914?) by Lytton Strachey, or through "parlour game" dream analysis and drawing room conversation, these two latter apparently particularly popular in America.[21]

This inevitably meant that they were, in the hands of these popular media and channels, often misrepresented, misinterpreted or even distorted, while heated controversy between supporters and detractors added to the confusion. But, as Hoffman puts it, "One thing was sure to happen – a doctrine so avidly condemned was bound to interest the thoughtful people of the time (p.56). He considers it "hardly likely", on both sides of the Atlantic during the following decade, "that any thinking, literate person who in any way associated himself with the world of letters failed to encounter the new psychology. It is more than likely that he was unable to escape getting too much of it". Only "if he did not read or speak to people," was he safe from it" (pp.70-71).

Obviously there were many who, having learned his theories only through hearsay or popularized versions in magazines, tended to misunderstand or abuse them, but at the same time there were those, especially among writers and intellectuals, who took serious interest in them and possessed an accurate understanding of the subject. Among the latter we may count the Woolfs who, as publishers of most of Freud's works in England, had direct access to them and were well read, we have ample evidence to believe, in his theories.

Although D. H. Lawrence reacted rather strongly against Freud and Jung, he shared with the psychologists the same serious concern for the aspect of human reality first resurrected by Freud, as is testified by his *Fantasia of the Unconscious* and *Psychoanalysis and the Unconscious*, both published in 1923 as his own version of the new psychology, as well as by his fictional works. James Joyce characteristically never discussed the subject in the form of criticism or essay like Virginia Woolf or Lawrence and showed apparent dislike or antipathy towards the psychologists,[22] yet in his actual works made good use of the knowledge of man's inner life brought in by them, and his huge dream book *Finnegans Wake* appropriately abounds in references to psychoanalysis as well as to Freud and Jung.[23] In any case, conception of such work as *Finnegans Wake* and some parts of *Ulysses,* especially the Nighttown sequence in the "Circe" episode seems, if not impossible, highly improbable without the kind of environment created by the advent and popularisation of the new psychology in which they were written. It is no accident that the commentators either on Joyce or on those works often find it useful, or are obliged, to refer to the theories or the names of Freud and Jung.[24]

In the following chapters we shall see how the modern psychological theories and the Romantic movement performed, to adapt Kermode's expression, "the preparatory work" for Modernism.

CHAPTER FOUR

THE ROLE OF THE PSYCHOLOGISTS (1)

SIGMUND FREUD

to us he is no more a person
now but a whole climate of opinion
under whom we conduct our different lives

AS is evidenced by such terms in current use as "pre-Freudian" and
"post-Freudian", the name of Freud often stands for the landmark indicating the radical change which occurred in man's consciousness as well as
in the field of psychology at the beginning of this century. There is no
doubt that Freud played an epoch-making role in the history of psychology. Through his theories of the unconscious he showed that age-old
subject, the human mind, in a new light and opened up ways for unprecedented development in that field. His influence was not, however,
confined to the domain of pychology alone, but by its very nature extended
to the whole cultural milieu of his time. The above lines from W. H.
Auden's "In Memory of Sigmund Freud",[1] written after Freud's death in
September 1939 as a tribute to the psychologist, succinctly describe the
situation.

Freud himself often admitted that he was not the first to "discover" the
unconscious. One of the earliest examples is Plato's indication of some
awareness of the unsconscious activities of the mind, though he does not
call them by any specific name. In Book IX of his *Republic*, he speaks of
"some lawless pleasures and appetites" which "are probably to be found
in us all". Although in some they are controlled and elimated by the power
of reason, they remain "stronger and more numerous in others".[2] These
are the desires

> that awakened in sleep when the rest of the soul, the rational, gentle
> and dominant part, slumbers, but the beastly and savage part, replete
> with food and wine gambols and, repelling sleep, endeavours to
> sally forth and satisfy its own instincts. You are aware that in such
> case there is nothing it will not venture to undertake as being
> released from all sense of shame and all reason. (p.337)

And he concludes: "in fact there exists in every one of us, even in some
reputed most respectable, a terrible, fierce and lawless brood of desires,
which it seems are revealed in our sleep ..." (p.339)

There is a remarkable similarity, immediately recognizable, between
Plato's observations here and Freud's theory of dreams. In the field of
psychology itself names such as Herbart, whose theory of the unconscious

Freud is said to have studied at school, and Edward von Hartmann, who had published *The Philosophy of the Unconscious* (1869), to which Freud himself makes several references in his *Interpretation of Dreams* (1900),[3] are often cited as Freud's immediate predecessors.

Yet Freud, to quote Alfred Kazin, "had the ability, such as is given to very few individuals, to introduce a wholly new factor into human knowledge ... He revealed a part of reality that many before him had guessed at, but which no one before him was able to describe so systematically and convincingly. In the same way as one associates the discovery of certain fundamentals with Copernicus, Newton, Darwin and Einstein, one identifies one's deepest motivations with Freud."[4] It is to Freud's credit that he called wide public attention to the unconscious activities of the mind and their significance, and made people realize that there was a vast unknown territory within themselves awaiting exploration. Whether or not they accepted all of his theories, or even read him directly (his theories and ideas spread in various popularized versions, which was often the cause of misunderstanding) their way of looking at themselves and their concept of man and his behaviour nevertheless underwent a profound and almost irreversible change.

Freud's theories were first received with such hostility by his colleagues and medical society in general that later, in his *Introductory Lectures* (1916-1917), he compared his predicament with that formerly suffered by Copernicus and Darwin. He explained this hostile reception as the expression of man's reluctance to accept the unpleasant and undesirable fact that he does not have the real control even of his own mind, that "the ego ... is not even master in its own house." This was, he claims, the "third and most wounding blow" to "human megalomania" which had already twice suffered humiliation on the discoveries that the earth is not the centre of the Universe and that mankind is of no more noble and privileged origin than any other animal.[5]

Opposition was particularly strong to his theories on sexuality, such as repressed sexual wishes in the unconscious and infantile sexuality. In fact, his detractors may be said to have been the very same adversaries of the Romantic and the Symbolist, as well as the Modernist, poets and writers, namely the nineteenth-century middle class, or bourgeoisie, with its rigid sense of respectability, which often accompanied moral attitudes that might be termed philistine, and essentially materialistic ideals which dismissed anything that might disturb the established norms of society. In short, it was the age of "Victorian morality", which is now regarded as virtually synonymous with "hypocrisy".

Assessing Freud's significance, Jung stated:

> The historical conditions which preceded Freud were such that they made a phenomenon like himself necessary, and it is precisely the fundamental tenet of his teaching – namely, the repression of sexuality – that is most clearly conditioned in this historical sense.[6]

concluding:

> Like Nietzsche, like the Great War and like James Joyce, his literary counterpart, Freud is an answer to the sickness of the nineteenth century. That is indeed his chief significance.[6] (p.37)

Above all, the Great War shattered the self-complacency and assurance of nineteenth century men, and demanded a drastic revision in the view of man and civilization which now appeared to be a mere façade. They were obliged to look inwards and re-examine themselves, and Freud's theories provided them with useful clues and directions in their search for self-knowledge. Thus his ideas were absorbed by a wider public in Europe and America[7] and even beyond. In *An Autobiographical Study* (1925), Freud himself recalls:

> Both in Germany and in the countries of Western Europe the war had actually stimulated interest in psycho-analysis. The observation of war neuroses had at last opened the eyes of the medical profession to the importance of psychogenesis in neurotic disturbances ...[8]

In order to clarify the interrelationship between the new trend in psychology initiated by Freud and the two artistic movements, Romanticism and Modernism, it would be useful first to take a cursory glance at Freud's theories themselves. Of all the works of the psychologist, *The Interpretation of Dreams,* published in 1900, is generally considered to be the most important. Freud himself supports this view in his Preface to the Third English Edition (1932) when he writes:

> This book, with the new contribution to psychology which surprised the world when it was published (1900), remains essentially unchanged. It contains, even according to my present-day judgement, the most valuable of all the discoveries it has been my good fortune to make. Insight such as this falls to one's lot but once in a lifetime.[9]

It was also the book which exerted the greatest influence on modern literature and art, and for this reason our survey will be centred mainly on this work, with references and digressions to other works whenever necessary.

Through the collaboratory work with his senior colleague Breuer, published in 1895 under the title *Studies in Hysteria*, Freud had discovered that patients with hysteria "suffer mainly from reminiscences" - long forgotten, or banished into the unconscious, because of their forbidden or disturbing nature, which was often sexual, yet still operating forcefully at a level unknown to the patients themselves. It had also been observed that these repressed thoughts or wishes often found their way into the patients' dreams. By analyzing these dreams with the help of patients' free associations, Freud often succeeded in discovering the real, yet unconscious, causes of their mental disorder. Thus he came to realize the significant role played by dreams and unconscious mental activities in human life. Discovery of the significance of dreams was important, because not only the mentally sick but also perfectly normal and sane people dream. Reflecting thirty-two years later on his theory of dreams, Freud recognized it as "a turning point in the history of psychoanalysis".[10] He also expressed his belief in the signifance of dreams in that famous axiom of his:

> The interpretation of dreams is in fact the royal road to a knowledge of the unconscious.[11]

This was almost a revolutionary change in the attitude towards dreams for, apart from their religious significance in primitive society and occasional remnants of superstitious beliefs in civilized societies, men had more often than not treated them with ridicule and scorn, and looked down on them with what Freud called "the arrogance of consciousness" (p.39). We may find its classic expression in Mercutio's comment on them:

> True I talk of dreams
> Which are the children of an idle brain,
> Begot of nothing but vain fantasy;
> Which is as thin of substance as the air,
> And more inconstant than the wind ...
> (Romeo and Juliet, I, iv, 96-100).[12]

Jung, in his "In Memory of Sigmund Freud", writes about the reactions of his contemporaries to Freud's book:

> For us young psychiatrists it was a fount of illumination, but for older colleagues it was an object of mockery ... At the turn of the century ... it was an act of the greatest scientific courage to make anything as unpopular as dreams an object of serious discussion. What impressed us young psychiatrists most was neither the technique nor the theory, both of which seemed to us highly controversial, but the fact that anyone should have dared to investigate dreams at all.[13]

This attitude of mockery and scorn towards dreams had persisted for centuries, although there had existed simultaneously superstitious or religious beliefs, and artists' intuitive interest in them.[14] By making dreams an object of serious study and investigation, Freud might be said to have saved them from both mockery and superstition. He claimed that dreams had a sense and a specific function in our mental lives, his basic contention being that "a dream is the fulfilment of a wish,"[15] – of a wish which was repressed or frustrated in the sleeper's waking life. We must not, he warns us, take the "façade" of the dream as it is, but must get to the real meaning hidden behind it. Throughout his works, he repeatedly maintains that we must distinguish the "manifest content of the dream", as we remember it in the morning, from the "latent-dream thoughts" which he considered to be present in the unconscious, between which there is little logical relation. Distinguishing between the two in *The Interpretation of Dreams*, he explains:

> The dream-thoughts and the dream-content are presented to us like two versions of the same subject-matter in two different languages. Or, more properly, the dream content seems like a transcript of the dream thoughts into another mode of expression, whose characters and syntactic laws it is our business to discover by comparing the original and the comprehensible, as soon as we have learnt them. The dream-content, on the other hand, is expressed as it were in a pictographic script, the characters of which have to be transposed individually into the language of the dream-thoughts. If we attempted to read these characters according to their pictorial value instead of according to their symbolic relation, we should clearly be led into error. (p.277)

The dream reveals thoughts which were banished into the unconscious because they were incompatible with, and unacceptable to, the ego, the conscious self, by means of the disguises provided by the preconscious, which enable them to pass the ego's censorship. [The pre-conscious is one of the two kinds of the unconscious which Freud postulates to exist in the mind and terms respectively the Ucs. (Unconscious) and the Pcs. (Preconscious). "Both are unconscious in the sense used by psychology," yet, while the Ucs. is "inadmissible to consciousness", the Pcs. is "able to reach consciousness", which "stands like a screen between the system Ucs. and consciousness" (pp.614-615). The "motive force for producing dreams is supplied by the Ucs." but it can obtain access to consciousness only via the preconscious (pp.541-542).]

Freud calls this process the "dream-work", the main features of which are "condensation", "displacement", "transformation of thoughts into images", "symbolism" and, though arguably, "secondary revision." By condensation he means that the manifest content is only an abbreviated expression of the latent-thoughts – "dreams are brief, meagre and laconic in comparison with the range and wealth of the dream-thoughts."[16] For example, a person who appears in a dream can be an amalgamation of several people in real life, with different characteristics from each combined into one. Dream-displacement, says Freud, is one of the chief methods by which dream-distortion is achieved (p.308), a mechanism through which some highly charged emotions are transformed or displaced from their true objects to comparatively insignificant ones so that they can escape the censorship imposed by resistance. Thus "the apparently innocent dreams turn out to be quite the reverse when we take the trouble to analyse them. They are, according to Freud, "wolves in sheep's clothing" (pp.182-183). For example, a woman dreamed one night that she was strangling a little white dog. Later, through analysis, the dog transpired to be a substitute for her sister-in-law, against whom she had a grudge and with whom she had had a violent quarrel some days before. The sister, moreover, was short and of very pale complexion, which seemed to confirm the interpretation (This example, in fact, is not given by Freud, but by Ferenczi, one of his pupils).[17]

The third, which Freud thinks to be "psychologically the most interesting,[18] is plasticity of most dreams or transformation of thoughts into visual images, although "some of them retain their form and appear as thoughts or knowledge in the manifest dream as well". Nor are the visual images the only form into which latent thoughts are transformed, but they nevertheless, according to Freud, "comprise the essence of the formation of dreams." A dream, for example, may represent such an abstract idea as "adultery" (in the original German *"Ehebruch"*, literally meaning "breach of marriage") by another breach – a broken leg (*"Beinbruch"*).[19]

Dreams also make use of symbolism "for the disguised representation of their latent thoughts." Freud conjectures that "Things which are symbolically connected today were probably united in prehistoric times by conceptual and linguistic identity,"[20] and that the dream symbolism is of the same primitive origin. How may we come to know then, Freud asks, "the meaning of these dream symbols, upon which the dreamer himself gives us insufficient information or none at all?" To this he replies:

> we learn from very different sources – from fairy tales and myths, from buffoonery and jokes, from folklore (that is, from knowledge about popular manners and customs, sayings and songs) and from poetic and colloquial linguistic usage. In all these directions we

come upon the same symbolism, and in some of them we can understand it without further instruction. If we go into these sources in detail, we shall find so many parallels to dream symbolism that we cannot fail to be convinced of our interpretations.[21]

Dream-symbols, Freud maintains, are "almost exclusively for the expression of sexual objects and relations," while those in the other fields mentioned above are not necessarily so (p.166). Both in *The Interpretation of Dreams* and *Introductory Lectures*, he gives the by now famous list of these symbols, while admitting the incompleteness of our knowledge of them and the ambiguity of dream-symbols themselves. To give some typical examples: "The Emperor and Empress (or the King and Queen) as a rule really represent the dreamer's parents; and a Prince or Princess represents the dreamer himself or herself ... All elongated objects, such as sticks, tree trunks and umbrellas ... may stand for the male organ ... as well as all long, sharp weapons such as knives, daggers and pikes ... boxes, cases, chests, cupboards and ovens represent the uterus, and also hollow objects, ships and vessels of all kinds ... Rooms in dreams are usually women ... There is no need to name explicitly the key that unlocks the room ...," etc. Although the idea of symbolism in dreams seems to have been widely accepted, Freud's method of interpreting them has been the subject of great controversy, and many recent psychologists are still critical of it. As is well known, it was one of the causes for schism between Freud and Jung, who thought Freud's interpretation was too narrow, attaching only personal and sexual significances to the symbols. C. S. Hall, an American psychologist, on the other hand, claims that the use of symbols in dreams is not a means of disguise, as Freud postulates, but a device for expressing complex conceptions in a compact form, as is used in waking life.

He includes as the last part of the "dream-work" both in *The Interpretation of Dreams* and in earlier works what he termed "secondary revision", namely, the effort of the mind to make sense of the seemingly chaotic and absurd contents of dreams by means of interpolations and additions[22] by filling "the gaps in the dream-structure with shreds and patches" and making a more or less coherent and intelligible whole. Since this process, in his theory, is carried out by the psychical function essentially identical with "waking (preconscious) thinking", Freud increasingly came to doubt its validity as part of the dream-work, whose primary significance lies precisely in its unconscious nature, and in his later works excluded "secondary revision" from the dream-work altogether.

In the field of literary criticism, however, the idea of "secondary revision," often in the more popularly-known form, "secondary elaboration," retains its place as a stage in the process of artistic creation, along with "condensation" and "symbolism". In this sense, these terms may be said to have been integrated into the vocabulary of modern literary criticism. In fact, the whole concept of Freud's dream-work is often applied to the analysis of the creative process as its near equivalent or a convenient approximation, thus showing the degree of penetration of Freud's ideas into the field of literature.

To come back to Freud's theory of dreams, the task of the psychoanalyst, Freud tells us, is to disentangle these complicated dream-works and relate the manifest content to the dream-thoughts lying beneath it, with the help of the dreamer's free association. He maintains that it is impossible to interpret dreams without the dreamer's association, and thus even in the case of dream symbols, emphasizes the "decisive significance" of "the comments made by the dreamer", while describing "the translation of symbols," as illustrated above, as "an auxiliary method."[23] There is a well-known episode concerning this point: Breton and other Surrealist poets once sent their dreams to Freud, asking him to interpret them, whereupon Freud flatly denied them their request on the ground that he could not interpret the dreams on their own, *en vacuum*, without the dreamers' associations.

What is the function, then, of dreams which disguise themselves so elaborately to escape the censorship and creep into our sleep? In short, Freud believes that the purpose of all dreams is fundamentally the fulfilment of wishes, and that if they are not recognizable as wishes, or appear absurd, it is because of the influence of the psychic censorship.[24]

He also observes the dreamer's tendency to regress to his childhood and his earliest experiences. In *The Interpretation of Dreams* he writes: "To our surprise, we find the child and the child's impulses still living on in the dream" (p.191). He maintains that all the characteristics of childhood mentality, such as egoism, its "incestuous" wishes, dominance of instinctual impulses, even the method of expression available to a child, are revived in them (pp.189-219; pp.533-549). Dreams "carry us back every night to this infantile level."[25] Freud conjectures that behind this we are able to detect a picture of the development of the human race, which the individual's development recapitulates. Supporting Nietzsche's assertion that in dreams "some primaeval relic of humanity is at work which we can now scarcely reach any longer by a direct path,"[26] he writes: "we may expect that the analysis of dreams will lead us to a knowledge of man's archaic heritage, of what is psychically innate in him."

Totem and Taboo (1912-1913) may be said to be his first and in a sense only attempt at an enquiry into such "archaic heritage" in man, though it was carried out not through analyses of actual dreams as he proposes here but through studies of Darwin's theory of the primitive state of human society as well as the writings and reports on contemporary primitive societies by such anthropologists and psychologists as J.G. Frazer, Wundt, Durkheim and Lang.[27] This resulted in a hypothesis that the Oedipus complex, which Freud recognized as a central cause for neuroses in his patients, had originated in the primal patriarchal family system in which the father dominated the whole "horde" to such an extent that he kept all the females for himself and drove away his sons as they grew up. One day, Freud conjectures, the exiled sons united themselves and "killed and devoured their father and so made an end of the patriarchal horde."[28] According to Freud, devouring of the father signified the sons' identification with him and their acquisition of a part of his envied strength and position, which was later to be repeated and commemorated by totem meals. When the misdeed was accomplished, however, love for him returned and with it a sense of guilt, for the sons, Freud tells us, had the same ambivalent feeling, ie, love as well as hate, towards the father as that of neurotic patients and children of today.

Out of this feeling of remorse, maintains Freud, were born totem and taboo, ie, the substitution of the totem animal for their father and prohibition against incest, in other words, renunciation of their claim to the women of the same family or tribe for whose acquisition the strife had originally begun (pp.142-143). It is no coincidence – Freud regards it as predetermined – that the two repressed wishes of the Oedipus complex correspond exactly to those two fundamental taboos of primitive society. In brief, he postulates that the Oedipus complex has an origin in the remote, primaeval past of mankind, and that it has genetically been passed on until today.

Freud regards the Oedipus complex of these primaeval tribesmen not only as the origin of totemism but as the beginning "of social organisation, of moral restrictions and religion" (p.142). He later makes the still broader claim "that its outcome shows that the beginning of religion, morals, society and art converge in the Oedipus complex" (p.156). He argues that the suffering of the Hero in Greek tragedies is the re-enactment of "the great primaeval tragedy" in a form distorted by "refined hypocrisy," where the Hero's "tragic guilt" – often that of rebellion against some authority, divine or human – really belongs to the Chorus, "the company of brothers," but is transferred or projected to the Hero, whose suffering relieves them of their collective guilt (pp.155-156). Although Freud does not claim to have found an overall explanation for those complex cultural phenomena, he nevertheless maintains that the Oedipus complex by its very nature "could not but play any other than a central part" in any attempt to synthesize the explanations" (p.157).

His enquiry into and, for that matter, his interest in, the ancestry of pyschic phenomena, however, seem to have been limited to this particular phase, as we do not find further attempts in the same line, except the repetition of the same thesis on the Oedipus complex in his later philosophical writings such as *The Future of an Illusion* (1927), *Civilization and its Discontents* (1920) and *Moses and Monotheism* (1939).[29] Nor did he, in actual practice, make much use of such anthropological theories and information as he used in *Totem and Taboo*. In contrast to Jung who, in his dream interpretations and psychoanalytical practice resorted extensively to studies in mythology, comparative religion, fairy tales and anthropology; references to these fields formed an essential part of his psychological system. Freud's interest, on the other hand, was concentrated mainly on the significance of childhood in an individual's development, with emphasis on his personal background and on the different psycho-sexual phases in the course of his growth.

A male child, through his early total dependence on his mother, develops a strong unconscious sexual attraction to her; because of his wish to have her exclusively to himself he begins to feel jealous hostility towards his father whom he regards as his rival. The resultant feelings of guilt and emotional conflict within him are repressed, banished into the unconscious, emerging only occasionally in "typical dreams" concerning the death of his father or lying with his mother.[30]

Freud argues that these wishes within us respond profoundly to the ancient tragedy of *Oedipus Rex* – "His destiny moves us only because it might have been ours – because the oracle laid the same curse upon us before our birth as upon him."[31] He believes that the play derives from some old "dream-material":

> There is an unmistakable indication in the text of Sophocles' tragedy itself that the legend of Oedipus sprang from some primaeval dream-material which had as its content the distressing disturbance of a child's relation to his parents owing to the first stirring of sexuality. (p.263-264)

and quotes as evidence Jocasta's speech which she addresses to Oedipus, who is troubled by the recollection of the oracle:

> Many a man ere now in dreams hath lain
> With her who bare him. He hath least annoy
> Who with such omens troubleth not his mind.[32]

Finding a typical situation to support his theory in Sophocles' tragedy, he gave it the name of the Oedipus complex, and regarded the play as the fulfilment, through imagination, of the universal childhood wishes of man.

Another example from classical literature which he quotes to illustrate his point is Shakespeare's *Hamlet*. Though it is rooted, Freud claims, in the same soil as *Oedipus Rex,* it shows greater repression in its treatment of the material, thus revealing the difference in the mentality of the two widely separated periods of civilization. "In *Oedipus* the child's wishful fantasy that underlies it is brought into the open and realized as it would be in a dream. In *Hamlet* it remains repressed; and – just as in the case of a neurosis – we only learn of its existence from its inhibiting consequences" (p.264). These inhibiting consequences Freud recognizes in Hamlet's hesitation and delay in fulfilling the task of revenge assigned to him by the Ghost, which had long been the enigma of the play and roused a variety of interpretations as to their cause. Rejecting the previous views which found it in his "irresolute character" or his "excessive" intellectualism that blunted the power of direct action, Freud maintains:

> The answer, once again, is that it is the peculiar nature of the task. Hamlet is able to do anything – except take vengeance on the man who did away with his mother and took that father's place with his mother, the man who shows him the repressed wishes of his own childhood realized. Thus the loathing which should drive him on to revenge is replaced in him by self-reproaches, by scruples of conscience, which remind him that he himself is literally no better than the sinner whom he is to punish.[33]

Hamlet's aversion to sexuality itself, he argues, has the same origin. He further traces it back to the playwright himself – "For it can of course only be the poet's own mind which confronts us in *Hamlet*- and claims that Shakespeare's own feelings about his father who had died not long before (and the memory of his own dead son Hamnet) are at the heart of the creation. He is, however, prudent enough to add that he is merely trying to interpret the "deepest layer of impulses of the mind of the creative writer," admitting that "all genuinely creative writings are the product of more than a single motive and more than a single impulse in the poet's mind" and thus "are open to more than a single interpretation."[34]

Whatever the reasons for the denunciation and criticisms at the first publication of the theory of the Oedipus complex,[35] it appears that psychologists today generally accept it with reservations. According to recent development in the study of other cultures and other societies, it has become known that the Oedipus complex is not biologically innate to all mankind as Freud claimed, but that there are some societies where it does not exist. In other words, Freud's theory was based on the observation of a particular society, and cannot be assumed to be a universal, or absolute, law of Nature, applicable to all humanity.[36]

The personality division observed by Freud in the dream censorship was later developed into a theory of the total personality, or pyschical structure, through such works as *Beyond the Pleasure Principle* (1920)and *The Ego and the Id* (1923), and synthesized in one of his last works, *An Outline of Psychoanalysis* (1940). According to his assumption, the human psyche can be divided into three layers, or regions (though these words Freud warns, should not be understood to indicate locality),[37] formed in the course of the individual's development, namely, id, ego and superego. Of the three, the "id" is the oldest part, and "contains everything that is inherited, that is present at birth," ie, all the inherited instinctual drives or forces which constitute the unconscious. As the child grows up, one part of the id, under the influence of the external environment, undergoes a special development, forming a separate entity, which "acts as an intermediary between the id and the external world."[38] This part is called the "ego", which is conscious and has voluntary movement at its command. It deals with external events and stimuli, and controls the demands of the instincts, in such a way as befits its task, self-preservation. The influence of the parents left on the mind of the individual comes to form the part named "super-ego", which is only partly conscious. Even when the individual is no longer dependent on his parents, their influence is retained by the super-ego and supervises the ego's action and thoughts – this function of the super-ego is usually called "conscience".[39] This parental influence includes "not only the personalities of the actual parents but also the family, racial and national traditions handed on through them, as well as the demands of the immediate social *milieu* which they represent."[40]

The later influences of teachers and of those public figures whom the individual regards as ideals also contribute to the constitution of the super-ego. In brief, it may be said to be of largely social and cultural nature, in contrast to the id's instinctual and primitive nature. Despite their fundamental differences, however, the id and the super-ego "have one thing in common: they both represent the influence of the past – the id the influence of heredity, the super-ego the influence, essentially, of what is taken over from other people ..." (p.147). What determines the ego, on the other hand, is largely the individual's own experience of accidental and contemporary events, ie, the influence of the present. The ego in Freud's system is the unifying agent of the three psychical parts, or forces. It strives to reconcile, and satisfy, the demands of the id, of the super-ego and of the external reality which, being not always harmonious, could present psychological conflicts and problems.

Towards the end of his career, Freud wrote several books which were more in the nature of cultural criticism or philosophical speculation than scientific treatises. *The Future of an Illusion* (1927) was an attempt to explain the origin and nature of religion, which he regarded essentially as an illusion, a phase of neurosis in the course of human evolution, comparable to "the obsessional neurosis of children,"[41] that was eventually to be replaced by science and its rational, realistic way of thinking. *Civilization and its Discontents* (1930) traces civilization back to its beginning and analyses the process of cultural development, with a particular concern for the individual's often hostile, and at best ambivalent, relationship to society and civilization. His last complete work, *Moses and Monotheism* (1939) aims at a genealogical exposition of Judaism and Christianity, as well as an analysis of anti-Semitism, which was highly relevant to the period immediately preceding the Second World War and Nazi persecution of the Jews. The common theme that links all three is his earlier hypothesis that morality, religion, art and society – in other words, all aspects of civilization – originated in the Oedipus complex, in the sense of guilt that the sons of the "primal horde" acquired at the killing of their father.[42]

The Oedipus complex, Freud further explains, consists of two contradictory instincts, namely Eros, love in its widest sense and the civilizing element in man, and the Death instinct which manifests itself as aggressiveness or destructiveness and directly opposes Eros. The evolution of civilization is thus described as "the struggle between Eros and Death, between the instinct of life and the instinct of destruction"[43]. Civilization, which is based on the renunciation, or at least sublimation, of man's primal instincts of aggression and destruction, is, according to Freud, essentially incompatible with the individual happiness which consists in the fulfilment of those very instincts – hence the potential hostility of the individual to civilization and society. He believes that "human life in common" becomes possible only when "the power of the individual is replaced by the power of the community" (p.95), and concludes his argument with these words: "The fateful question for the human species seems to me to be whether and to what extent their cultural development will succeed in mastering the disturbance of their communal life by the human instinct of agression and self-destruction. It may be that in this respect precisely the present time deserves a special interest."[44]

Ironically, Freud, whose main purpose was to put man's instinctual impulses under the control of reason and science, has often been taken for an advocate of licentiousness. Psychoanalysis, as F. J. Hoffman tells us, was often condemned or used as "a rationalisation of sex-looseness,"[45] and Freud, in his psychological studies, was considered to be presenting, in the words of an article in *The Times* (December 4th, 1920), "a justification of immorality by science."[46] It is a good example of how misconception or distortion can occur as a result of popularization of a theory.

For Freud, to bring through psychoanalysis the unconscious and repressed wishes into the open was the first step towards controlling and mastering them. For the mental and somatic power of a wishful impulse, he believes, is far stronger when it is unconscious. Moreover, an "unconscious wish cannot be influenced," whereas those which have become conscious could be "destroyed by the rational mental activity of the better impulses that are opposed to them."[47] This is possible, says Freud, because repressed wishes usually have infantile origins which, when exposed, often prove to be easily manageable by the maturer and stronger personality of adults. Renunciation thus becomes feasible.

Even when the renunciation has not been achieved, however, a path is left for the wishful impulses to find fulfilment, instead of developing into neuroses, that is, by being channeled into socially more acceptable or desirable courses. This he calls "sublimation", which he regards as the most important of all the transformations an instinct can undergo:

> here both object and aim are changed, so that what was originally a sexual instinct finds satisfaction in some achievement which is no longer sexual but has a higher social or ethical valuation.[48]

All creative and mental activities in the fields of science, art and ideaology, according to Freud's theory, belong to this "higher and finer" class of psychical activities. They are, in his view, essentially substitute satisfactions for instinctual wishes, whose merit is highly valued by him. "It is probable," he writes, "that we owe our highest cultural successes to the contributions of energy made in this way to our mental functions."[49] Sublimation of instinct, Freud considers, is "an especially conspicuous feature of cultural development,"[50] and a valuable alternative, apart from renunciation, to neurosis or a more primitive state of mankind.

His views on art and literature are naturally closely linked with his ideas of sublimation and the substitute satisfaction of wishful impulses. These two points may be said to form the basis of his arguments about the subject – "wish fulfilment" as the motive or the aim of works of art and "sublimation" as the psychological process involved in the act of creation. In fact, he does not go very far beyond them. Here we may as well remember that Freud himself admits the limitation of psychoanalysis in this field. It is beyond the scope of psychoanalysis, he concedes, to explain the nature of artistic talent, or "the beauty of human forms and gestures, of natural objects and landscapes and of artistic and even scientific creations" (p.82), or why such things strike us as beautiful and give us pleasure. As to artistic talent, he writes :

> Instincts and their transformations are at the limit of what is discernible by psychoanalysis. From that point it gives place to biological research. We are obliged to look for sublimation in the organic functions of character on which the mental structure is only afterwards erected. Since artistic talent and capacity are intimately connected with sublimation we must admit that the nature of the artistic function is also inaccessible to us along psychoanalytic lines.[51]

On the subject of beauty, after attacking aesthetics for its incapacity to give any explanation of the nature, origin and enjoyment of beauty which "has a peculiar, mildly intoxicating quality of feeling," Freud confides: "Psychoanalysis, unfortunately, has scarcely anything to say about beauty either. All that seems certain is its derivation from the field of sexual feeling. The love of beauty seems a perfect example of an impulse inhibited in its aim."[52]

Setting aside such fundamental questions, Freud's attention mainly focuses on the kinds or aspects of art which best serve to illuminate his own psychoanalytical theories. He uses them to explain works of art and conversely uses works of art to explain his theories. The kinds of art cited by Freud are for the most part literature and plastic art, above all literature in its various forms. He recognizes the particularly close relationship between literature and psychology, and acknowledges the contribution of creative writers to the understanding of the human mind, praising their insight sometimes above scientific knowledge. In an essay devoted entirely to a study of a piece of fiction, perhaps the only one of its kind among his works, Freud writes:

> ...creative writers are valuable allies and their evidence is to be prized highly, for they are apt to know a whole host of things between heaven and earth of which our philosophy has not yet let us dream. In their knowledge of the mind they are far in advance of us everyday people, for they draw upon sources which we have not yet opened up for science.[53]

The overlapping of the boundaries of literature and the kind of psycho-

logical study in which he was involved was already noted at the beginning
of his career. In his first published book, *Studies on Hysteria*, he observes:

> it still strikes me as strange that the case histories I write should read
> like short stories and that, as one might say, they lack the serious
> stamp of science. I must console myself with the reflection that the
> nature of the subject is evidently responsible for this, rather than
> any preference of my own. The fact is that local diagnosis and
> electrical reactions lead nowhere in the study of hysteria, whereas
> a detailed description of mental processes such as we are accus-
> tomed to find in the works of imaginative writers enables me, with
> the use of a few psychological formulas, to obtain at least some kind
> of insight into the course of that affection.[54]

This statement reminds us of the essential kinship betwen the two
fields, and perhaps explains the mutual interest often found between them.
He further confirms this when he says:

> ...the creative writer cannot evade the psychiatrist nor the psychia-
> trist the creative writer, and the poetic treatment of a psychiatric
> theme can turn out to be correct without any sacrifice of its beauty.[55]

From the point of view of a literary man, Lionel Trilling expresses
much the same view on the mutual indebtedness between psychology and
literature:

> the human nature of the Freudian psychology is exactly the stuff
> upon which the poet has always exercised his art. It is therefore not
> surprising that the psychoanalytical theory has had a great effect
> upon literature. Yet the relationship is reciprocal, and the effect of
> Freud upon literature has been no greater than the effect of literature
> upon Freud.[56]

Freud, in fact, was widely read in both classical and modern literature
and made extensive use of material from it as well as from the other arts,
Shakespeare being one of his favourites and the most often quoted.

In order to understand this correlation between literature and Freudian
psychology, it may be expedient to examine those of his works in which
literature and writers, and more generally art and artists play the principal
role. While he wrote neither systematically nor extensively on artistic
subjects, he did write several short papers exclusively on literary and
artistic themes. His views on art and artists are also to be found scattered
in many of his writings. According to the angle from which he discusses
his subjects, we may roughly classify his writings in this field into three
groups: those in which works of art are meant to illustrate and support his
psychoanalytical theories, those in which he employs his theories to

explain particular artists or works of art, and those which are of more independent character and may be considered as general theories of art and literature, although these are comparatively few and are again based essentially on his major pyschoanalytical concepts.

We are already acquainted with an instance of the first in the examination of *Oedipus Rex* and *Hamlet* in relation to the theory of the Oedipus complex. We may further add such essays as "Delusions and Dreams in Jensen's *Gradiva* " (1907) and "Some Character-Types Met with in Psycho-Analytic Work" (1916). In spite of its detailed analysis of the story, which partly resembles literary criticism, the former is, as Freud himself makes clear at the outset, primarily an attempt to prove, with the help of fiction, the theses of his *Interpretation of Dreams*, namely, that dreams have meanings and that they are fulfilled wishes, which at the time were "far from being generally believed".[57]

Gradiva (1903), a novella by a German author, Wilhelm Jensen, tells the story of a young archaeologist who falls in love with a classical marble relief of a girl. He calls her Gradiva and his preoccupation with her grows until it reaches a state of delusion. After having a dream in which he, transported back in time, meets her in person in ancient Pompeii, he feels compelled to make a trip to the ruined city himself. There, to his amazement, he finds an exact replica of Gradiva as he saw her in his dream, who turns out to be his childhood friend, Zoë Bertgang. By her, he is eventually brought back to reality, finding there the fulfilment of the love he cherished in fantasy. Freud argues that it was the memory of his childhood, of his playmate, that the relief, because of its close resemblance to the object of his childhood love, stirred up in him, though without his being aware of it. He "had in fact transferred his interest from the living girl to the sculpture." As for the dream, Freud recognizes in it obvious, though slightly disguised, erotic wishes and interprets, "The latent dream-thoughts, which were bound to remain unconscious, sought to change the sculpture back into the living girl" (p.60). He commends the author upon his use of a dream to bring about the further development of his character's delusion as an ingenious notion and true to reality. In fact, as the details of the story so well agree with his psychoanalytical findings, Freud even observes that "the author has presented us with a perfectly correct psychiatric study, on which we may measure our understanding of the workings of the mind – a case history of a cure which might have been designed to emphasise certain fundamental theories of medical psychology" (p.43). It does not mean that the author knew anything about these psychological rules and principles: he may, says Freud, disavow them in good faith. Nevertheless, he thinks that

We probably draw from the same source and work upon the same
subject, each of us by another method. And the agreement of our
results seems to guarantee that we have both worked correctly.
(p.92)

and reaches the conclusion that "either both of us, the writer and the
doctor, have misunderstood the unconscious the same way, or we have
both understood it correctly." He found in the story by Jensen an assurance for his theories of the importance of the childhood experience and
of the nature and the function of dreams. The Editor's Note informs us
that the author himself, in the ensuing short correspondence with Freud,
"appears ... to have accepted the main line of interpretation" (p.3).

"Some Character-Types Met With in Psycho-Analytic Work" is a
collection of three essays, each dealing with a particular character trait
that Freud observed in his patients which, though usually dormant and
often unrecognized by the individual himself and people around him, give
rise to, as well as reveal themselves in, neuroses. To illustrate his point,
instead of disclosing the case histories of his patients, he makes use of the
"figures which great writers have created from the wealth of their knowledge of the mind,"[58] owing to the considerations for the intimate and
delicate nature of the former. For instance, Shakespeare's *Richard III*
exemplifies a type called the "Exceptions," who, through some experience
or suffering in their childhood or resentment against hereditary disorders
– in Richard's case, his inborn deformity – which they consider disadvantages unjustly imposed upon them, develop the idea that, as they have
suffered and sacrificed enough, they are entitled to refuse any more
demands from life, that they are "exceptions", a privilege they claim as a
compensation for the injustice done to them. This sense of injustice, Freud
argues, is more or less present in all of us – "Richard is an enormous
magnification of something we find in ourselves as well" (p.315) – and it
is to this that Shakespeare appeals, to arouse in the audience sympathy
and fellow-feeling for the villain-hero of the play. "We all think," Freud
continues, "we have reason to reproach Nature and our destiny for
congenital and infantile disadvantages; we all demand reparation for early
wounds to our narcissism, our self-love. Why did not Nature give us the
golden curls of Baldur or the strength of Siegfried or the lofty brow of
genius or the noble profile of aristocracy? Why were we born in a middle
class home instead of in a royal palace?" (This last point, the theme of
"family romance", is also touched upon by Jung as a component of
archetypal thinking – see p.130)

Freud also quotes Lady Macbeth, again from Shakespeare's play, and
Rebecca Gamvik of Ibsen's *Rosmersholm,* in explanation of another type,

"Those Wrecked by Success," as examples of those who "fall ill precisely when a deeply rooted and long-cherished wish has come to fulfilment" (pp.317-318). It is, according to him, the "forces of conscience", or the conflict between the libidinal wish and the censuring ego, that causes this failure to enjoy the achieved goal. In the case of Lady Macbeth, however, after trying some hypotheses on the themes of parricide (the murder of Duncan) and of childlessness (taken as the punishment for the crime), which may be considered to cause the sense of guilt and despair in the protagonists, Freud in the end concludes that it is impossible to give any definite explanation, due to "the bad preservation of the text, the unknown intention of the dramatist and the hidden purport of the legend." (p.323)

As for Rebecca, he is more confident and ascribes the "forces of conscience," or the sense of guilt, to her Oedipus complex, apparent in her admiration of and attachment to her foster (though suspectedly actual) father; her feelings are later transferred to Rosmer, master of the house where she has been working and for whose love she contrives to bring his wife to suicide. In Rebecca Gamvick Freud recognizes a representation of the common fantasy among young girls newly employed in a house-hold, who dream of the mistress of the house disappearing and herself taking over as the wife of the master. It is, according to Freud, a day-dream well known to practising pyschoanalysts, and Ibsen's play, he considers, is "the greatest work of art" that deals with the subject. In conclusion, he reaffirms "the complete agreement" between literature and clinical experience, and repeats his thesis that the forces of conscience, or the sense of guilt in general, "are closely connnected with the Oedipus complex, the relation to father and mother" (p.331).

Although these essays were written primarily as expositions of his psychological theories, they read quite well as literary criticism because Freud, in his efforts to be objective, sticks closely to the literary works themselves without, like much of the later psychoanalytical criticisms, arbitrarily applying the fixed patterns or preconceived ideas,[59] though it does not necessarily mean that one accepts either his conclusions or his theories.

Great artists and their works seem to have had an infinite fascination for Freud, and as a psychologist his interest in them led to enquiries into the motive forces behind their creative activities that had given particular shapes to their creations. "Leonardo da Vinci and a Memory of His Childhood" (1910) and "Dostoevsky and Parricide" (1928) are such attempts. In both cases, he gives up the idea of explaining the secret of artistic genius itself as being unassailable by psychoanalysis.[60] In both, the starting point - and, in fact, his basic concern throughout – is the artist's childhood experiences which he believes to have had a decisive influence on his later development as a man and an artist.

The main source of his study, which he calls "pathography", is thus the biographical data of the artist's life: "on the one hand the chance circumstances of events and background influences and, on the other hand, the subject's reported reactions," as he puts it in "Leonardo" (p.135). As to Leonardo, Freud attached the greatest importance to his childhood family situation – to the fact of his illegitimate birth and the consequent excessive love of his mother who sought in him a substitute for her husband and the fact that he was later taken to his father's house, where he was to be brought up by his stepmother. He also emphasizes the significance of Leonardo's childhood fantasy, or dream, of a vulture, which he relates to his deprived mother's almost violent passion towards her son. His consequent fixation upon her, Freud conjectures, caused his sexual repression, which for the most part was to be sublimated later into artistic activities and scientific researches, but which also produced a latent homosexual trait. [Freud, incidentally, was apparently in error in describing the bird of prey as a "vulture" (in German: *"Geier"*): the editor of the *Standard Edition* points out that in Leonardo's original notebooks this bird is called *"nibio"* which is the Italian word for "kite". The origin of Freud's mistake, according to the editor, seems to lie in the German translations which Freud used, all of which adopted the word *"Geier"* (ie, "vulture") instead of *"Milan"*, the German word for "kite". While admitting that this fact invalidates some of the arguments in this paper, he considers that it does not affect the main body of Freud's study, and acknowledges its significance for the light which it throws upon various aspects involved in the creative process (pp.61-62).]

In Leonardo's paintings Freud recognizes the reflection of the influences of his childhood – the mysterious smile of Mona Lisa reveals the memory of his mother; the painting of St. Anne with her daughter Mary and the child Christ "contains the synthesis of the history of his childhood."[61]

In conclusion he writes that it seems "as if only a man who had Leonardo's childhood experiences could have painted the Mona Lisa and the St. Anne." While admitting that psychoanalysis may not help our understanding of a great artist's achievements nor throw light on the fact of his artistic gift, "it at least," Freud claims, "renders its manifestations and its limitations intelligible to us" (p.136).

"Dostoevsky and Parricide", initially written as an introduction to the German translation of *The Original Version of The Brothers Karamazov* (1928), is very much in the same vein, though with Dostoevsky Freud is definitely inclined to think of him as a neurotic whereas with Leonardo he expressly denies that he has ever considered him "a neurotic or a 'nerve case'" (p.131). He conjectures that Dostoevsky's reputed epilepsy was actually a symptom of hysteria, a form of neurosis, and not an organic disease, as had usually been believed. He traces its origin to the Oedipus complex in Dostoevsky which was germinated in his childhood and which first manifested itself as a series of "death-like attacks," consisting of "lethargic, somnolent states" preceded by a fear of death. These earlier "hysterical" attacks, according to Freud, were a form of self-punishment, brought about by the sense of guilt for the hatred and death-wish which Dostoevsky harboured against his hard and violent father. The traumatic event in his eighteenth year, the murder of his father, became, for its very realization of his own wish, the turning point of his neurosis,[62] which now came to assume the more severe form, epilepsy. Dostoevsky's epileptic attacks, writes Freud, signified, as did those milder attacks in his childhood an identification with his father as a punishment. To support his argument on the significance of these attacks, Freud quotes Dostoevsky's own comments to his friend that "his irritability and depression after an epileptic attack were due to the fact that he saw himself as a criminal and could not rid himself of the feeling that he had a burden of unknown guilt upon him, that he had committed some great misdeed which oppressed him" (p.187) ; only they became now more terrible, befitting his father's violent death. As to the writer's well known mania for gambling, he explains that gambling too was a self-inflicted punishment to satisfy his sense of guilt – "He never rested until he had lost everything. For him gambling was a method of self-punishment as well" (p.191). [In the ensuing part, Freud further analyses the meaning of addiction to gambling, quoting Stefan Zweig's short story, *Four and Twenty Hours in a Woman's Life*, and giving a psychoanalytical interpretation to the story of a brief affair between an elderly woman and a young man obsessed by gambling.]

In fact, Dostoevsky, Freud maintains, "never became free of the feelings of guilt arising from his intention of murdering his father" (p.187), and these feelings, he continues, also determined his attitudes towards the authority of the State and belief in God, his submission to and veneration for both the Little Father, the Tzar and God the Father. It was because of this "filial guilt," says Freud, that Dostoevsky instead of becoming "a teacher and liberator of humanity," ended up as "a reactionary." He also detects in the novelist's sympathy for the criminal, which he considers is boundless and goes far beyond what pity they deserve, his identification with them "on the basis of similar murderous impulses – in fact, a slightly displaced narcissism" (p.190). This, he believes, played a decisive role in determining Dostoevsky's choice of material. Most of his major characters, in fact, may be termed criminals: according to Freud, the novelist, after dealing first with the common criminal and then with the political and religious criminal, came back, at the end of his life, to "the primal criminal, the parricide" to "use him, in a work of art, for making his confession."

It is a matter for debate how far we can go with Freud's argument, especially in its details. Joseph Frank, for example, contests Freud's basic contention that Dostoevsky's epilepsy was not an organic disease but "a case of hysteria", originating from his Oedipus complex. He claims that quite a few instances of Freud's dating of the significant events in the writers life are wrong, and that the psychologist ignored some of the biographical evidences and arbitrarily interpreted others in such a way as to suit his theory.[63] The essay is nevertheless interesting as an interpretation of the biographical facts of a writer that may have influenced his choice of subject-matter and his treatment of it. Freud's "Dostoevsky", together with his "Leonardo", set a model for later literary criticism and biography in the psychoanalytical line, whose influence we can clearly see, for example, in Jean-Paul Sartre's *Baudelaire* and *St. Genet.*[64]

"Psychopathic Characters on the Stage", written probably between 1905 and 1906, and posthumously published in 1942, is an example of the third kind, which analyses the nature of drama and the audience's reaction to it, with some reference to lyric and epic poetry. It is of more general nature than those we have so far treated, in the sense that it does not concentrate on a particular author or work, and that it has less direct relationship to his psychological theories. Freud's argument is essentially based on the Aristotelian theory of "catharsis," which he, we may say, paraphrases in psychoanalytical terms. The main factor of dramatic experience, as Freud describes it, is "to get rid of one's own emotions by 'blowing off steam'," the enjoyment derived from which corresponds to "the relief produced by a thorough discharge."[65]

The spectator is a person, he writes, who feels that he is a "poor wretch to whom nothing of importance can happen." By identifying himself with the hero of the play, he is enabled to experience all the adventures and climactic moments, the excitements and deeper emotions that are prohibited to him in his daily life. Through the hero's experiences on the stage, he gets vicarious or substitute satisfaction for his suppressed desires for action, and is able to give vent to his pent-up, ie, repressed, emotions. The enjoyment is all the greater, says Freud, as the spectator is aware at the same time that he himself, unlike the hero, is at a safe distance from these experiences which might jeopardize his life, that it is after all a "game". His "enjoyment is based on an illusion" (p.306). The audience at a performance of a play or a spectacle is compared by Freud to children at play, and he develops this idea further in his later paper, "The Relation of the Poet to Day-Dreaming" (1908), where he applies it more widely to poetic creation and imaginative writing in general.[66]

In fact,"The Relation of the Poet to Day-Dreaming", with its more detailed discussion of the origin of creative activities, may be said to form the basis of Freud's Poetics, or theory of art, and is one of the most important papers as far as his views on art and artists are concerned. Freud finds man's first imaginative activity in children's play, recognizing an affinity between a creative writer and a child at play in the fact that each creates his own world of fantasy – "he arranges the things of his world and orders it in a new way that pleases him better"[67] – which, though distinguishing perfectly from reality, they both take very seriously. This essential kinship between the two, observes Freud, is retained in the use of such terms as "plays" and "players" to indicate a certain field of artistic activity. As the child grows up, he ceases to play and appears to give it up, which in fact he never does. Freud maintains that human beings never "give up a pleasure they once tasted" – "We only exchange one thing for something else" (p.175). A grown-up who appears to have given up play, according to him, actually finds its substitute in building "castles in the air," in creating fantasies or "what are called day-dreams". Thus, says Freud, "Day-dreaming is a continuation of play."

Behind a child's play, there is his *"one* wish, which is to be grown up." The driving forces behind adult fantasies too are wishes that are unsatisfied. Freud even maintains that "happy people never make phantasies, only unsatisfied ones." "[E]very separate phantasy," he continues, "contains the fulfilment of a wish, and improves on unsatisfactory reality."[68] This statement at once brings us back to his theory of dreams and, in fact, by calling our attention to the linguistic link between the two subjects, dreams and daydreams, alias fantasies, he emphasizes the fundamental tie between them. Thus he claims that "our nocturnal dreams are nothing but such phantasies," and that "Nocturnal dreams are fulfilments of desires in exactly the same way as daydreams are" (p.179).

After the comparison of a child at play to a creative writer, and of daydreams to children's play, the argument comes full circle when Freud compares an imaginative writer to a daydreamer and his poetic creation to a daydream. It must be added, however, that he excludes from his discussion ancient writers of epics and tragedies who did not create their material but borrowed from existing versions, along with those great writers "who are most highly esteemed by critics." He will choose for his subject, he tells us, "the less pretentious writers of romances, novels and stories, who are read all the same by the widest circles of men and women"(p.179), which seems to imply writers of popular fiction as distinct from serious writers. We must assume, therefore, that here he does not intend a general theory of literature and that his argument is to be applied only to the particular kind of literature designated, though rather vaguely, by Freud. If we understand it as a theory of popular fiction, or romances, it seems to clarify some essential qualities of this genre of literature. One distinct characteristic of this type of fiction, says Freud, is that "they all have a hero who is the centre of interest, for whom the author tries to win our sympathy by every possible means, and whom he places under the protection of a special providence" (p.179). The invulnerability given to such a hero makes Freud perceive the existence of "His Majesty the Ego, the hero of all daydreams and all novels" (p.180). The "egocentric" nature of these stories also affects their mode of characterization, which divides people sharply into good and bad – those who help the ego and those who are its enemies. Freud claims that many imaginative works, which appear far removed from such crude original patterns, could still be related to the type. For example, he points out that in "many so-called psychological novels," only one person, the hero, is described from within – "the author dwells in his soul and looks upon the other people from outside." Perhaps with the more complex works in mind, he adds:

> The psychological novel in general probably owes its peculiarities to the tendency of modern writers to split up their ego by self-observation into many component egos, and in this way to personify the conflicting trends in their own mental life in many heroes.

This certainly seems to pinpoint one of the characteristics which we recognize in modern, not to say psychological, novels.

Freud assumes that in a fantasy, or daydream, three periods of time are involved: the present – the current event which arouses a wish; the past – the memory of childhood when it was fulfilled; and the future – imaginary fulfilment of the wish. A similar idea is applied to the process of creative writing itself which he, as we know, identifies with daydreaming. He writes :

> Some actual experience which made a strong impression on the writer had stirred up a memory of an earlier experience, generally belonging to childhood, which then arouses a wish that finds a fulfilment in the work in question, and in which elements of the recent event and the old memory should be discernible. (p.182)

A work of fiction, in Freud's view, is a construction in verbal form of the future part of a fantasy, the imaginary fulfilment of a wish.

Now if they spring from the same source, what is it that distinguishes poetic creation from the daydreams of ordinary people or of the neurotic? The major difference, Freud thinks, lies in the effect which they create in the mind of the audience. Private daydreams disclosed, he maintains, only repel us, whereas imaginative writing based on such daydreams gives us pleasure. "The essential *ars poetica*", therefore, "lies in the technique by which our feeling of repulsion is overcome." According to Freud's analysis,

> The writer softens the egotistical character of the daydream by changes and disguises, and he bribes us by the offer of a purely formal, that is, aesthetic, pleasure in the presentation of his phantasies. (p.183)

There are two points here: one is the elimination from the daydream of "the egotistical character," ie, the personal element, which Freud seems to think causes repulsion, and the other the addition of "aesthetic pleasure", or pleasure derived from formal beauty, which he considers to be the writer's "bribe" to win us over. These, we may assume, are the essentials of literary art, or rather technique, as Freud sees it. Through these means, he conjectures, creative writers are able to put us "into a position in which we can enjoy our own daydreams without reproach or shame" (p.183). The release of tension – "catharsis" in Aristotle's word – thus derived is, in his opinion, the true enjoyment of literature.

Apart from the question of all daydreams being repulsive to others as he claims, Freud's argument here seems to be quite valid, so long as we emphasize his own reservation, for later in the essay he half-retracts it when, commenting on those who used the ready-made material, he says that such material itself "is derived from the racial treasure house of myths, legends and fairy tales", which are, in all probability, the "distorted vestiges of the wish-phantasies of whole nations – the age-long dreams of young humanity". We may also remember that he described *Oedipus Rex* as "the fulfilment of our own childhood wishes" by imagination. We must therefore restrict application of Freud's argument to a certain kind, or aspect, of literature, which we may call "literature of wish-fulfilment", such as popular novels and romances and even some classical, or serious, works of literature. The least disputable example may be the romantic fiction found in traditional women's magazines, which was so superbly parodied by Joyce in the Gerty MacDowell episode in *Ulysses*. Though far more subtle and complex, Shakespeare's last plays, which are also called "Romances" may, in the final analysis, be said to belong to this category. The relevance of Freud's theory on romances especially will be confirmed by quoting a critic's exposition of the genre, which is almost identical to the foregoing argument:

> Romance was the non-realistic, aristocratic literature of feudal-ism. It was non-realistic in the sense that its underlying purpose was not to help people cope in a positive way with the business of living but to transport them to a world different, idealised, *nicer* than their own. ... ...
>
> It is not, of course, that only the leisured read or listen to romantic literature; on the contrary its quality of 'substitute-living' (the evocation of a kinder, more glamorous world) especially recom-mends it to the unleisured, those who most need the consolations of an escape from a cruel or humdrum reality.[69]

In the course of time, however, Freud discards these qualifications, and in many of his later writings he presents the view as an all-embracing theory of literature and art in general.[70] He also comes to associate writers or artists more distinctly with the neurotic,[71] a standpoint which was not very apparent in the earlier essay. According to this view, an artist is a person "oppressed by excessively powerful instinctual needs," an intro-vert "not far removed from neurosis."[72] As his wishes, be they for fame, power, wealth or love, meet in reality resistance and frustration – the familiar clash between the pleasure principle and the reality principle – he withdraws, like the neurotic or any other unsatisfied man, from unsatisfying reality into the world of imagination, where he creates for himself substitute satisfactions in fantasy. This is a course which may lead to actual neurosis but, thanks to his artistic gift – the psychological mystery – "he can transform his phantasies into artistic creations instead of into symptoms."[73] By so doing, Freud maintains, the artist, unlike the neurotic, finds his way back to reality instead of losing himself totally in the fantasy world and thus regressing to infancy. The constitution of the artist, he thinks, "includes a strong capacity for sublimation and a certain degree of laxity in the repressions which are decisive for a conflict."[74] This latter quality also explains his richer resources of fantasy than ordinary people's.

In *An Autobiographical Study*, reminiscing his past "attempt at an analysis of poetic and artistic creation in general," Freud epitomizes his theory of art:

> His [the artist's] creations, works of art, are the imaginary satisfac-tions of unconscious wishes, just as dreams are ... But they differ from the asocial, narcissistic products of dreaming in that they are

calculated to arouse sympathetic interest in other people and are able to evoke and satisfy the same unconscious wishful impulses in them too. Besides this, they make use of the perceptual pleasure of formal beauty as what I have called an 'incentive bonus'.[75]

This is almost a summary account of his views in "The Relation of the Poet to Daydreaming," and it is evident that he later came to think that the theory which he had developed in the earlier paper was universally applicable to all forms of art and creative activity. His idea of formal beauty as something auxiliary and separate from the content, an embellishment for the purpose, so to speak, of seduction, also remains the same: only it is now called an "incentive bonus", while formerly it was described as a means through which the writer "bribes" the reader. His confession that psychoanalysis is powerless before the problem of artistic talent or genius, too, is restated here: "It [Psychoanalysis] can do nothing towards elucidating the nature of artistic gift, nor can it explain the means by which the artist works – artistic technique" (p.65).

It is not surprising that Freud's theory of art has met serious objections from artists, especially from literary men. For while, as discussed, there does exist a field or genre, or even an aspect, in literature, of which the main concern is wish-fulfilment or an escape from reality, his thesis that works of art in general are essentially the fulfilment of instinctual wishes, transformed through sublimation and trimmed by artistic technique, into universally acceptable and enjoyable forms seems to most literary minds far from sufficient to explain the whole variety of creative writings and the range of experience and enjoyment to be derived from them. Lionel Trilling, though a great admirer of Freud, complains, for example, of the psychologist's "too limited an application", when judging literature, of the pleasure and reality principles, while conceding that representation of the opposition between the two principles is essential in both literature and psychology. Paradoxically, in the final analysis it was not so much Freud's theories of art and literature proper as his purely psychological theories of dreams and the unconscious activities of the mind that had such an impact on writers and artists as well as on the general public. Besides *The Interpretation of Dreams*, which Freud himself regarded as the most important, such works as *The Pyschopathology of Everyday Life* (1901), and *Jokes and their Relation to the Unconscious* (1905), which are in the same line as the earlier work and may be considered its extension, played a considerable role in bringing to the layman deeper understanding of man and his behaviour, since as in the case of dreams they both deal with such perfectly normal and "everyday" phenomena as the sudden forgetting of proper names or words, slips of the tongue and pen, misreadings, errors of memory, etc, as well as jokes and wit, and revealed their possible unconscious origins or motives that were hidden or disguised. In a later chapter we shall see, through fictional form, an instance which shows how *The Pscyhopathology of Everyday Life* popularized Freud's psychological theories among the intellectuals around the time of its first appearance in English translation in 1914 (see pp.181-185). With Freud, psychology ceased to be the science merely of the sick mind, which formerly it had predominantly been. Trilling sums up literature's debt to Freud thus:

> it is certainly true that, whatever natural affinity we see between Freud and literature, however great a contribution to the understanding of literature we judge him to have made, it must seem to a literary man that Freud sees literature not from within but without. The great contribution he has made to our understanding of literature does not arise from what he says about literature, but from what he says about the nature of the human mind; he showed us that poetry is indigenous to the very constitution of the mind; he saw the mind as being in the greater part of its tendency, exactly a poetry making faculty.[76]

An Address, presented personally by Thomas Mann to Freud on the latter's 80th birthday (May 6th, 1936), conveys vividly the sense of indebtedness and respect the writers and artists of the time felt towards the psychologist, and for this reason, though rather lengthy, we shall quote it in full:

> 'The 80th birthday of Sigmund Freud gives us a welcome opportunity to convey to the pioneer of a new and deeper knowledge of man our congratulation and veneration. In every important sphere of his activity, as physician and psychologist, as philosopher and artist, this courageous seer and healer has for two generations been a guide to hitherto undreamt-of regions of the human soul. An independent spirit, "a man and knight, grim and stern of visage" as Nietzsche said of Schopenhauer, a thinker and investigator who knew how to stand alone and then drew many to him and with him, he went his way and penetrated to truths which seemed dangerous because they revealed what had been anxiously hidden, and illumined dark places. Far and wide he disclosed new problems and changed old standards; in his seeking and perceiving he extended many times the field of mental research, and made even his opponents indebted to him through the creative stimulus they derived from him. Even should the future remould and modify one result or another of his researches, never again will the questions be stilled which Sigmund Freud put to mankind; his gains for knowledge cannot permanently be denied or obscured. The conceptions he

built, the words he chose for them, have already entered the living language and are taken for granted. In all spheres of humane science, in the study of literature and art, in the evolution of religion and prehistory, mythology, folklore and pedagogics, and last not least in poetry itself his achievement has left a deep mark; and, we feel sure, if any deed of our race remains unforgotten it will be his deed of penetrating into the depths of the human mind.

'We the undersigned, who cannot imagine our mental world without Freud's bold life-work, are happy to know that this great man with his unflagging energy is still among us and still working with undiminished strength. May our grateful feelings long accompany the man we venerate.'[77]

Ernest Jones, who recorded in his biography of Freud this remarkable expression of appreciation of Freud's achievement and contribution, informs us that "the undersigned" included Thomas Mann himself, Romain Rolland, Jules Romain, H. G. Wells, Virginia Woolf, Stefan Zweig and 191 other writers and artists. It is interesting to see as one of the signatories H. G. Wells, whom Virginia Woolf classified as a "materialist" and condemned for not showing interest in the inner world of his characters, along with herself. The occasion must have been the first of its kind in the history of either psychology or art and literature.

The foregoing short survey is by no means comprehensive, but is merely intended to cover the major issues in Freud's psychological system relevant to our present subject. For, though his contribution to psychology was great, his influence – as the above quotations amply demonstrate – has been far-reaching, and there have been few writers and artists, especially of the Modernist era, who could remain totally indifferent to him. In this sense, we must regard him as a cultural phenomenon as well as a scientific one. H. T. Moore observes in his essay "Age of the Modern": "The art of our time, whether by Salvador Dali or James Joyce or a hundred or a thousand others, abounds in Freudian ideas and forms",[78] while Auden's description of Freud, quoted at the beginning of this chapter, as "no more a person now but a whole climate of opinion" would seem a most apt rendering of this phenomenon.

CHAPTER FIVE

The Role of the Psychologists (2) – C. G. JUNG

WHEN Jung equated Freud in terms of revolutionary impact with Nietzsche, the Great War and James Joyce, "his literary counterpart", he was fully aware of Freud's cultural and historical significance. Yet, by singling out this aspect of his contribution, he was also trying to show Freud's limitations from the "scientific" point of view. Critical of Freud's theories which he considers to reduce "all complex psychic phenomena like art, philosophy and religion" to "'nothing but' repressions of the sexual instinct",[1] he believes that "This essentially reductive and negative attitude of Freud's towards accepted cultural values" is the product of the historical conditions in which Freud had been working.[2] Regarding "Freud's revolutionary passion for negative explanations" as a "reaction against the Victorian tendency to see everything in a rosy light and yet to describe everything *sub rosa*," Jung claims:

> If Freud is viewed in this retrospective way as an exponent of the resentment of the new century against the old, with its illusions, its hypocrisy, its half-truths, its faked, overwrought emotions, its sticky morality, its bogus, sapless religiosity and its lamentable taste, he can be seen, in my opinion, much more correctly than when one makes him out as the herald of new ways and new truths. He is a great destroyer who breaks the fetters of the past. He liberates us from the unwholesome pressure of a world of rotten habits.[3]

Freud had an "historical task" – the task of a "destroyer", which Jung agrees Freud had fulfilled, but we cannot expect more since, "For those with a forward-looking view he offers no constructive plan."[4] Moreover, Freud's theory, based on "the malformations of the nineteenth century", Jung implies, cannot claim itself to be scientific, and be applied as a "general pyschological theory" to the problems of different sorts of societies. "Freud had not penetrated into that deeper layer which is common to all man," for this, according to Jung, was imcompatible with his "historical task" (p.40). He also accuses Freud, who does not recognize this fact, of "absolutism", conditioned by the "nineteenth century scientific materialism" (pp.33 and 47).

Though Jung was clearly confusing the issues when he criticized Freud for his "negative attitude" and lack of "constructive plan" some of his criticisms are shared by others, even by the psychologists of the Freudian school today.[5] However, our main concern here is not to analyse the scientific validity of Jung's criticisms but to examine his own theories, which have had perhaps no less, if not more, influence on modern writers than those of Freud.

What distinguishes Jung from Freud and other psychologists is mainly his concept of the unconscious. As we have already observed, Jung was not altogether satisfied with the way Freud treated the subject. One of his complaints was that with Freud the unconscious is "nothing but the gathering place of forgotten and repressed contents" and consequently "of an exclusively personal nature", although he did admit that Freud is not unaware of its archaic and mythological thought-forms.[6] For Jung, the unconscious contents do not only consist of those which were once conscious and have later turned into unconscious complexes by being repressed:

> Quite otherwise, the unconscious has contents peculiar to itself which, slowly growing upward from the depths, at last come into consciousness. We should therefore in no wise picture the unconscious pysche to ourselves as a mere receptacle for contents discarded by the conscious mind.[7]

Thus, in the Jungian system of psychology there are two kinds of unconscious: at a more or less superficial level the one which owes its existence to personal experience, and accordingly is called the "personal unconscious", and the other which he believes is not a personal acquisition but inborn, which forms the deeper layer of the psyche. This Jung calls the "collective unconscious", the term "collective" denoting that this phase of the unconscious is "not individual but universal." Jung considers the latter, in contrast to the personal psyche, to be identical in all men, thus constituting a common psychic substrata of a suprapersonal nature which is present in every one of us.[8] Again, unlike the personal unconscious, "the contents of the collective unconscious have never been in consciousness, and therefore have never been individually acquired, but owe their existence exclusively to heredity."[9] As to what constitutes these contents, Jung states that, while the personal unconscious consists chiefly of "the feeling-toned complexes", the collective unconscious is made up essentially of "archetypes".[10]

What are these archetypes, then, the concept of which forms perhaps the most important ingredient of Jung's psychological system? He traces the idea itself as far back as to Plato's *eidos* (ideal forms or archetypes) and to Philo Judaeus, the first century Jewish philosopher, who used the term "archetype" with reference to the "God-image" in man. More recently, he relates his archetypes to the anthropologist Lévi-Bruhl's *"représentation collective"* which signifies the "symbolic figures in the primitive view of the world".[11] [It is one of Jung's characteristics to correlate his theory with other fields of study, such as religion, mythology, anthropology and literature.] Jung's own definition of his archetypes is accordingly not very far from this: they are "archaic or ... primordial types" or "universal images that have existed since the remotest times" (p.5). He postulates that the human psyche retains the traces of a prehistoric ancestry, of the instinctual experiences of primitive man – his fears and desires, joys and sorrows – in spite of the later evolution that has taken place, just as the body keeps the traces of its evolutionary past. Originally he based his idea on Freud's theory that childhood psychology is a recapitulation of the early stage of mankind and that this infantile thinking is banished to and survives in our dream life (see p.52). In his earlier work, *Psychology of the Unconscious*, which first established his standpoint, he argues that, although marriage by capture, the cult of the phallus worship and other primitive and ancient customs and beliefs may have disappeared from civilized society and be regarded as superstitious,

> all of this does not affect the fact that we, in childhood, go through a period in which the impulses toward these archaic inclinations appear again and again, and that through all our life we possess, side by side with the newly recruited, directed and adapted thought, a phantastic thought which corresponds to the thought of antiquity and barbarism. Just as our bodies still keep the reminders of old functions and conditions in many old-fashioned organs, so our minds, too, which apparently have outgrown those archaic tendencies, nevertheless bear the marks of the evolution passed through, and the very ancient re-echoes, at least dreamily, in phantasies.[12]

Whereas this thesis does not assume a major role in Freud's psychology, it forms almost the core of all Jung's theories. If dreams are the manifestation of the unconscious, the archetypes of the collective unconscious become indispensable factors in dream interpretation. They are also important in psychotherapy, as Jung recognizes in abnormal states of mind such as the delusions of paranoiacs not only the personal complexes but the archetypal material which could never come from patients' personal experiences. His interpretations of literature and works of art are also founded on this basic concept. To illustrate his approach in contrast to Freud's, we may quote Jung's own comparison between his interpretation and that of Freud concerning the painting by Leonardo da Vinci of the infant Christ and the Virgin Mary and St. Anne.[13]

Jung explains this as the motif of the dual mother, well known in such fields as mythology and comparative religion, an archetype which can be found in these fields in varied forms. One such form is the motif of the dual descent, which signifies the descent from both the human and divine parents. Hercules, for example, was born of a human mother, Alcimena, but was later given immortality by Juno who fed him, unknowingly, with her divine milk. Jung traces the motif back to the ritual in ancient Egypt, where Pharoah, who was "twice-born", once as a human, then as a god, was supposed both human and divine by nature. Christ himself, reborn through the baptism given in the Jordan, says Jung, is another example. It is retained in the present-day custom of giving children a "godfather" and a "godmother". Jung finds this idea of second birth "at all times and in all places"; it is the central mystical experience in many religions and can also be recognized in the infantile fantasy of many children who wistfully think that they are not the children of their ordinary parents and that their real, more glamorous parents, exist somewhere else.[14]

The archetypes are, according to Jung, "the inherited powers of human imagination", the most ancient and the most universal 'thoughtforms' of humanity".[15] They are at the heart of all psychic activities, including the creation of art, in which motifs from myths and legends repeat themselves in identical forms, and also of the delusions of mental patients who "can reproduce exactly the same images and associations" as those in the old texts that are completely unknown to them. It is not, argues Jung, that ideas as such are inherited, but that the possibility or the potentiality of those ideas are. Those "primordial" images, as Jung quotes Jakob Burkhardt's term, lie dormant in the deeper layer of the unsconscious, well up as is dictated by occasions and reach consciousness in various forms.[16]

Although Jung expressly states that the best source of study of the archetypes is dreams – because the "evolutionary stages through which the human psyche has passed are more clearly discernible in the dream than in consciousness" and that dreams with their language of images can give expression to "instincts that are derived from the most primitive levels of nature"[17] – he believes that they are also manifest in primitive tribal lore, myths and fairy tales and considers the comparative study of all these essential to the understanding of archetypes and dreams. For they are, says Jung, all expressions of the archetypes, though in these they have already been submitted to and modified by conscious elaboration, and so cannot be regarded as immediate data of psychic experience.[18]

Myths, for example, may appear to be the attempts of primitive man to explain the natural phenomena in his world and universe. In fact, according to Jung, it is the contrary: primitive man makes use of natural phenomena to express his psychic experience. He does not draw a clear distinction between psychic and physical events: the psychic and the objective merge in the external world. "Primitive man is unpsychological", maintains Jung, "Psychic happenings take place outside him in an objective way."[19] In this state of mind, he has an irresistible urge to identify his inner, psychic life with the events of the outer world. The rising and setting of the sun, the changes of the seasons, become assimilated to the rise and fall of a god or a hero who dwells in his soul, or to the fate of man:

> All the mythological processes of nature, such as summer and winter, the phases of the moon, the rainy seasons, and so forth, are in no sense allegories of these objective occurrences; rather they are symbolic expressions of the inner, unconscious drama of the psyche which becomes accessible to man's consciousness by way of projection - that is, mirrored in the events of nature.[20]

Jung claims that "the psyche contains all the images that have ever given rise to myths", and that primitive man only "rediscovers" the inner drama, "by means of analogy", in the process of nature.[21]

Primitive tribal-lore consists also of the archetypes transformed into conscious formulae of "esoteric teaching" handed down generation after generation. All such teachings, according to Jung, are man's attempts to "apprehend the unseen happenings in the psyche", and the same may be said of the great religions of the world,[22] although this may be further removed from the original experience because of the critical and evaluating influence of conscious elaboration which has refined and sophisticated them.

Indispensable as they are for the study of archetypes, myths, folklore, religions and fairy tales have all undergone elaboration by consciousness and thus are more or less "indirect" expressions of the archetypes which Jung calls, using Lévi-Bruhl's term, *représentations collectives*" – "symbolic figures in the primitive view of the world". In order to look for the immediate manifestation of them he turns to other sources: besides dreams in general, those listed by Jung are what he calls "active imagination,"[23] "the delusions of paranoiacs, the fantasies observed in trance-states, and the dreams of the childhood, from the third to fifth year" (p.50). Even these materials, however, would be valueless, warns Jung, unless through comparative studies with parallel symbols in mythology they are found to bear similar contexts and the same functional meanings in those contexts.

Dreams above all are important, as they "have the advantage of being involuntary, spontaneous products of the unconscious psyche (p.48) that are not falsified by any intervention from arbitrary will. For this reason, Jung regards them as "a highly objective, natural product of the psyche, from which we might expect indications, or at least hints, about certain basic trends in the psychic process."[24] They, in other words, "give information about the secrets of inner life and reveal to the dreamer hidden factors of his personality".[25]

Although Jung partly agrees with Freud's theory of the wish-fulfilling and sleep-preserving function of dreams - for there are, he admits, dreams which do fulfil the "repressed wishes" - and thinks that the basic idea of a compensatory biological function is correct, he strongly disputes Freud's thesis that all dreams are wish fulfilments, regarding it as "too narrow".[26] (For there is no ground, says Jung, for the assumption that the unconscious processes underlying the dream are more limited and one-sided in form and content than conscious processes. He would expect the contrary.[27]) After studying many dreams, Jung himself came to the conclusion that "all dreams are compensatory to the content of consciousness" (p.250). Our psyche, according to Jung, is "a self-regulating system" which maintains its equilibrium in the same way as our body does:

> Every process that goes too far immediately and inevitably calls forth a compensatory activity. Without such adjustments a normal metabolism would not exist, nor would the normal psyche. We can take the idea of compensation so understood, as a law of psychic happening.[28]

In short, the "relation between conscious and unconscious is compensatory." So is the relation between consciousness and the dreams which are the expressions of the unconscious.

In interpreting dreams, therefore, Jung's first concern is "to establish the context with minute care" (p.14), and the best way for this, he claims, is to ask the dreamer, before starting to interpret: What conscious attitudes does it compensate? He even maintains that "it is impossible to interpret a dream with any degree of certainty unless we know what the conscious situation is" (pp.21-22). Although this is basically not very far from the standpoint of Freud who insisted that no interpretation could be undertaken without the dreamers' associations, Jung rejects Freud's method of free association as too loose and arbitrary, and condemns it on the ground that it allows the dreamer to move away from the dream itself. Free association, he considers, will be useful to uncover all the hidden complexes of the dreamer but won't be of any help in getting to the real meaning of the dream – "If we associate freely to a dream, our complexes will turn up right enough, but we shall hardly ever discover the meaning of the dream" (p.15). For Jung, a dream is "something like a text that is unintelligible". And it is unintelligible not because, as Freud claimed, it is disguised and has a façade, but because we simply don't know how to read it. The first thing for us to do, therefore, is to try to read it, keeping as close as possible to the particular dream-images themselves:

> When a person has dreamed of a deal table, little is accomplished by his associating it with his writing desk which is not made of deal. The dream refers expressly to a deal table ... I say to my patients: "Suppose I had no idea what the words 'deal table' mean. Describe this object and give me its history in such a way that I cannot fail to understand what sort of thing it is." We succeed in this way in establishing a good part of the context of that particular dream image. When we have done this for all the images in the dream, we are ready for the venture of interpretation. (pp.15-16)

Jung also believes that it is difficult to interpret on its own a single obscure dream with any certainty, but that with a series of dreams we can recognize better the basic themes and important contents, which repeat themselves. It is also possible to correct the mistakes in earlier interpretation by later dreams, which makes the interpretation more reliable. Thus Jung recognizes the significance of the "unconscious process spontaneously expressing itself in the symbolism of a long dream series – and calls it "individuation process."[29]

He likewise disputes the Freudian treatment of dream-symbols. Jung does not accept his "hard and fast sexual 'symbols' " as symbols: in his opinion they are rather signs, "for they are made to stand for sexuality, and this is supposed to be something definitive". True symbols are "expressions of something not yet consciously recognized or conceptually formulated". Dreams must be treated, maintains Jung, as symbols in this sense, not as "signs or symptoms of a fixed character". He does admit that there exist relatively fixed symbols, but it does not necessarily follow that they have fixed meanings or content. In order to understand all their implications, we must take into consideration the dreamer's philosophical, religious and moral convictions, just as, when interpreting a dream, we take into account full details of his conscious situation.[30]

To give an example of Jung's interpretation of dreams: a young girl who was suspected of an organic disease as well as hysteria, told him a series of dreams. In one of them she dreamed that, on coming back home at night, she found her mother hanging from the chandelier and swinging to and fro in a cold wind blowing in through the open window. In another, she heard a terrible noise in the house at night and saw a frightened horse tearing through rooms before finally jumping through the window from the fourth floor down into the street. She was terrified to see its mangled body lying below. Whereas Freud might interpret the first dream as a disguised death wish of the dreamer against her mother and the second one perhaps as an elaboration or the further disguise of the same dream, Jung calls our attention to the two distinct symbols, "mother" and "horse", and points out their affinity – they both commit suicide. Both the mother and the horse symbol, according to Jung, are archetypal. The mother "refers to a place of origin, to nature, that which passively creates, hence to substance and matter, to material nature, the lower body (womb) and the vegetative functions". It connotes also "the unconscious, natural and instinctive life, the psychological realm, the body in which we dwell or are contained ... it thus stands for the foundations of consciousness". Being contained in something also suggests darkness, a state of anxiety. All this, explains Jung, is not derived from the girl's personal knowledge but is the idea of the mother that has undergone mythological and etymological transformations. It is "a bequest from the past", the archetypal dream-content.

Jung's interpretation, based on these concepts, of the meaning of the first dream is that the unconscious life destroys itself. "Horse" is another archetype which is found widely in mythology and folklore and represents the sub-human, animal side, ie, the unconscious side of man. It is closely related to the mother-archetype as a beast of burden – eg, the Trojan horse which contained the Greek warriors.[31] It too symbolizes the lower part of the body and the animal drives arising hence – it is, in short, a symbol of instinctive drives. It is connected with magic spells and omens as well, eg, the black night horse, the herald of death. It is evident, Jung concludes, that "horse" is the equivalent of "mother" with a slight shift of meaning – "The mother stands for life at its origin and the horse for the merely animal life of the body". Accordingly, the meaning of the dream is: the animal life destroys itself. The two dreams give virtually the same message, though the second, says Jung, is more specific, as is usually the case. His final interpretation of those dreams is that they both "point to a serious, even fatal, organic disease". He tells us that his prognosis was shortly afterwards proved by fact.[32]

To those critics who accuse him of undermining culture and exalting primitivism "at the cost of our highest values", Jung answers that "the unconscious is not a demonic monster, but a thing of nature that is perfectly neutral as far as moral sense, aesthetic taste and intellectual judgement go". Danger arises only when our conscious attitude is falsified by repression or depreciation of that side of our pysche (pp.19-20). If our life becomes thus one-sided, the psyche, in order to redress the balance, goes autonomously to the other extreme, which may completely overcome the conscious life of the person concerned – examples of which we often observe in real life and literature. Usually, however, as soon as the person begins to assimilate the previously unconscious contents into his life, such dangers diminish, and the wholeness of his personality is restored.

The process of assimilation of the conscious and the unconscious contents, including the already mentioned dream series, is called by Jung "individuation", which means to become "a single homogeneous being". It is also explained as "coming to selfhood" or "self-realization",[33] which we could paraphrase in Jung's own words as the "spontaneous realization of the whole man".[34] The "self" in Jungian terminology means the total personality, the "whole man", the synthesis of the conscious and the unconscious. It is an entity, composed of multifarious psychic factors. One of them, the centre of the field of consciousness, is the ego, to which all conscious contents are related: Jung calls the outermost aspect of the conscious personality "persona", using a term which originally meant the mask worn by an actor, signifying the role he played.[35] Society expects – and indeed must expect – says Jung, every individual to play the part assigned to him. The "persona" is thus assumed like a mask, "designed on the one hand to make a definite impression upon others,and on the other, to conceal the true nature of the individual" (p.190). Although the persona, "the ideal picture of a man as he should be", is a necessary factor in man's adaptation to society, there will be a serious danger to his personality if his ego assimilates itself entirely to this social role. For the persona, according to Jung, is only one side or the façade of his personality, and realization of the whole personality therefore cannot possibly be achieved by it alone. In such cases, the unbalance often reveals itself in the form of psychic disorder – "These identifications with a social role are a very fruitful source of neuroses" – or in more ordinary, milder cases, as "bad moods, affects, phobias, compulsive ideas, backsliding, vices, etc.". In any case, "A man cannot get rid of himself", maintains Jung, "in favour of an artificial personality without punishment."[36]

The more the individual identifies himself with the mask, the more likely he is to be at the mercy of the opposing forces from the inside, because the psyche tries to compensate what is neglected with corresponding intensity. For against the persona or mask there always exists, according to Jung, a "shadow", the negative or inferior side of the personality. "To become conscious of it", observes Jung, "involves recognising the dark aspects of the personality as present and real". It meets considerable resistance from the ego and demands a great deal of moral effort. Yet "This act", he believes, "is essential for any kind of self-knowledge".[37] A move towards wholeness, which is "not so much perfection as completeness", is possible only when this hidden and darker side of one's personality is brought into consciousness and integrated with the ego.

The difficulty will be greater, says Jung, when the subject's disorder is rooted not in the personal unconscious, but deeper in the collective unconscious, in the neglect of one's archetypal element. The archetypes which, together with the shadow, have "the most frequent and the most disturbing influence on the ego" (p.8) are, according to Jung, the "anima" and the "animus". He bases his concepts of the anima and the animus on the biological fact that the greater number of either masculine or feminine genes determines the sex of an individual. No one, therefore, can be said to be entirely feminine or masculine – "Either sex is inhabited by the opposite sex up to a point.[38] Thus a very masculine man can have a very soft emotional life, "carefully guarded and hidden."[39] The feminine or masculine character remains unconscious because of its subordinate position, yet it nevertheless plays a vital role in composing the personality of the individual. The feminine element in a man is called the anima and the corresponding masculine element in a woman is named the animus.

The anima, which compensates the masculine consciousness, is considered by Jung to be the soul of man, not the "soul" in the dogmatic or philosophical sense, but a natural archetype of "chaotic life urge". Jung sometimes calls it Maya, the "Spinning woman" – a terminology borrowed from the East - "who creates illusion by her dancing".[40] It is an "inherited collective image of woman that exists in man's unconscious, with the help of which he apprehends the nature of woman" (p.188). The image is first projected on to his mother, and then to any woman whom he comes to love – "Every mother and every beloved is forced to become the carrier and the embodiment of this omnipresent and ageless image".[41] It corresponds, says Jung, to the deepest reality in a man. While the anima affords him compensation and solace for the bitterness of life, she is at the same time, "the great illusionist, the seductress, who draws him into life with her Maya - and not only into life's reasonable and useful aspects, but into its frightful paradoxes and ambivalences where good and evil, success and ruin, hope and despair, counterbalance one another." In other words, because the anima wants life – and life itself is not only good but also bad – she wants both good and bad.[42] History, mythology and literature abound in such anima-figures, like Venus, Helen of Troy (and we may add, Cleopatra), etc.

As a man is said to be compensated by the anima, a woman is said to be compensated by the masculine element which Jung calls the animus, signifying "mind or spirit". Her unconscious has therefore a masculine trait. Whereas the anima could be related to "the maternal Eros", whose main function is that of personal relationship, the animus could be related to "the paternal Logos" with its faculty of discrimination and cognition, and in its negative way can lead a woman into an argument in which she holds her opinion with baseless, irrational conviction. It is because

The animus is rather like an assembly of fathers or dignitaries of some kind who lay down incontestable 'rational' *ex cathedra* judgements. In closer examination these exacting judgements turn out to be largely sayings and opinions scraped together more or less unconsciously from childhood on, and composed into a canon of average truth, justice and reasonableness; a compendium of presuppositions which, whenever a conscious and competent judgement is lacking (as not infrequently happens), instantly obliges with an opinion.[43]

The anima produces "moods", the animus "opinions"; so it very often happens, says Jung, that men have "irrational moods" and women have "irrational opinions" for they both come from the unconscious (p.205).

The animus, however, like the anima, is said to have a positive aspect. As the latter gives a man's consciousness "relationships and relatedness", the former gives "a capacity for reflection, deliberation and self-knowledge" to a woman's consciousness. It also gives rise to spirituality and aspiration for higher ideals."[44]

As his theory of the unconscious originated in criticism of the Freudian theory, so Jung's views on literature and art and their relationship to psychology are based on his critical attitude towards Freud's approach to them and, as we shall see presently, for much the same reason. His first paper on the subject is "On the Relation of Analytical Psychology to Poetry" (1922).[45] Jung concedes in the first place that, although the act of creation is a psychological activity and as such can be a subject of psychological investigation, the psychologist can never answer the question of what art is in itself. In his own words, "Whatever the psychologist has to say about art will be confined to the process of artistic creation and has nothing to do with its innermost essence" (p.66). In this respect, his standpoint is not very far from that of Freud who disengaged himself from such essential questions as aesthetic beauty and artistic talent, and limited the subject of his enquiry to the psychological motives behind creative activity. Jung's main concern was to form an hypothesis as to how creative activity is motivated and what psychological factors are involved in the process of creation.

His argument begins with a critique of the Freudian approach to literature and art, the main target of which is the emphasis Freud's method places on the personal background of the artist in interpreting works of art. Jung himself believes that "Personal causes have as much or as little to do with a work of art as the soil with the plant that springs from it" – "The plant is not a mere product of the soil;" on the contrary, "the special significance of a true work of art", he maintains, "resides in the fact that it has escaped from the limitations of the personal and has soared beyond the personal concerns of its creator" (pp.71-72). While Freud is interested mainly in that aspect of a work of art which he thinks manifests the artist's personal complexes, Jung rejects this as an identification of the artist's personality with his work, on the ground that the latter does not necessarily spring from a personal cause but may have a deeper source. He goes so far as to say that a work of art is

> a living being that uses man only as a nutrient medium, employing his capacities according to his own laws and shaping itself to the fulfilment of its own creative purpose. (p.72)

In this view, art is not a means to express the artist's personality; it is on the contrary the artist who is a means, a "medium", for the work to realize itself.[46]

However, not all works of art, says Jung, are produced in the way described above. He classifies them, according to their mode of creation, into two categories: the introverted art and the extraverted art. Those which belong to the former are the product of conscious creative activity. They are designed and shaped throughout by the conscious intention of the artist: "His material is entirely subordinated to his artistic purpose: he wants to express this and nothing else."[47] Here, the consciousness of the artist is completely at one with the creative process. The effect of the works of art thus created is conditioned, as a rule, by the artist's intention, and would rarely go beyond it. The latter works, on the other hand, "flow more or less complete and perfect from the author's pen", ie, without much conscious designing on the author's part. The extraverted attitude, according to Jung, is characterized by the artist's subordination to the creative impulse, with which his consciousness has little or nothing to do. "These works positively force themselves upon the author; his hand is seized, his pen writes things that his mind contemplates with amazement." Here the man and the creative process are not identical: "he is aware that he is subordinate to his work or stands outside it as though he were a second person" (pp.72-73). In other words, he becomes the "medium" for the nascent work. Works of this kind, says Jung, bear "suprapersonal" characters and defy our understanding "to the same degree that the author's consciousness was in abeyance during the process of creation". They would normally display such characteristics as "a strangeness of form and content, thoughts that can only be apprehended intuitively, a language pregnant with meanings and images that are true symbols because they are the best possible expressions for something unknown – bridges thrown out towards an unseen shore" (pp.75-76). Schiller's plays, according to Jung, are the example of the first kind and Goethe's *Faust* II that of the second. The two categories, however, are said not to be exclusive, so that it is possible for the same artist to produce both kinds of work. To illustrate his point, he gives the example of Nietzsche who was the author of both the "well-turned aphorisms and the rushing torrent of *Zarathustra*". Schiller in his philosophical writings and Goethe in his "perfectly formed poems" are also said to have written the type of works opposite to those mentioned earlier.

It is mainly the second class of works, the extraverted art, with which Jung is concerned in relation to his psychology. He calls them, because of their predominant use of symbolism, "symbolic works", and believes that the creative urge, or impulse, that moves an artist to produce this kind of work exists as "a living thing implanted in the human psyche". It is "a split-off portion of the psyche, which leads a life of its own outside the hierarchy of consciousness", which he names an *autonomous complex* (p.75). It is defined as:

> a psychic formation that remains subliminal until its energy charge is sufficient to carry it over the threshold into consciousness ... it is not subject to conscious control, and can be neither inhibited nor voluntarily reproduced. Therein lies the autonomy of the complex. ... The creative complex shares this peculiarity with every other autonomous complex. In this respect, it offers an analogy with pathological processes, since these two are characterized by the presence of autonomous complexes, particularly in the case of mental disturbances. The divine frenzy of the artist comes perilously close to a pathological state, though the two things are not identical.[48]

In an autonomous complex itself, however, Jung finds nothing morbid or pathological since its domination occurs even in normal people. The presence of the autonomous creative complex can be detected only through the analysis of symbols and images in finished works of art. If a work has no symbolic value, it is self-explanatory, and does not invite, nor require, any analysis or interpretation – "it is no more than what it *seems* to be".[49] This explains why his interest is predominantly in symbolic works. In regard to this type, he quotes Gerhard Hauptmann's words, "Poetry evokes out of words the resonance of the primordial word", and maintains that the essential question is, "What primordial image lies behind the imagery of art?" (p.80)

It may readily be recalled that in Jungian psychology the "primordial image" has another name, the "archetype". That is to say, Jung considers that imagery in art is an expression, or a revelation, of the archetypes, the psychic residues of the typical experiences of our ancestors, which supposedly reside in the collective unconscious and are often projected into mythological figures. In short, he assumes that symbolic works have their origin not in "the personal unconscious" but in "the collective unconscious". Admitting that the former may contribute to the creation of art, he believes that its predominance merely turns a work of art into a symptom (which he claims is best dealt with by the "purgative methods" of Freud), instead of a symbol. Works of art which spring from the collective unconscious, however, are of a totally different nature. "Whoever speaks in primordial images speaks with a thousand voices ... He transmutes our personal destiny into the destiny of mankind." The secret of great art and its effect upon us, explains Jung, is precisely this (pp. 80-82).

The creative process of this kind of art is thus described by him as consisting in "the unconscious activation of an archetypal image, and in elaborating and shaping this image into the finished work" (p.82). The artist, according to him, is a man "who takes to the back streets and alleys because he cannot endure the broad highway", ie, the general trend of the time followed by "the normal man". This relative lack of adaptation, Jung thinks, is in fact his advantage: "it enables him to follow his own yearnings far from the beaten path, and to discover what it is that would meet the unconscious needs of his age (p.83). While the general trend is bound to exclude many psychic elements that are incompatible with it, the artist goes back to the "deepest springs of life", seizes the image in the unconscious "best fitted to compensate the inadequacy and one-sidedness of the present" and shapes it into a concrete form of art. By so doing, he makes it accessible to his contemporaries who would otherwise remain unconscious of it, and enables them to realise "in what the age is most lacking". In this Jung recognises the social significance of art. It has for him the same corrective and compensatory function as he finds in dreams. He concludes:

just as the one-sidedness of the individual's conscious attitude is corrected by reactions from the unconscious, so art represents a process of self-regulation in the life of nations and epochs.

"Pyschology and Literature", first published in German in 1929,[50] and perhaps the most popularly known of Jung's writings in this field, is essentially the continuation, or reaffirmation of his original stand in the preceding paper. Here he lays special emphasis on the distinction between the artist and the work of art, maintaining that, in spite of their close interrelationship, we cannot fully explain one with the other. They present for him "two separate and distinct tasks" which require totally different approaches. He divides his discussion accordingly into two parts, under the respective title, "The Works of Art" and "The Poet". As to the work of art, he first calls our attention to the distinction between the "psychological" and the "visionary" modes of creation, which in many ways corresponds to that between the "introverted art" and the "extraverted art". For example, "psychological" works of art, like the introverted art, is said to belong to the realm of consciousness, drawing from the "conscious life of man, and his feeling for life in particular", such material as "the lessons of life ... emotional shocks, the experience of passion and the crises of human destiny in general.[51] The author's job in this kind of work being "an interpretation and illumination of the contents of consciousness", there is no obscurity about them: "they fully explain themselves" (p.180).

This is precisely the reason, Jung explains, why the so-called "psychological novels", which in his view belong to this class of literature do not, against popular expectation, interest the psychologist. What is of interest as well as a challenge to him is the other kind, ie, the "visionary" works of art. In these works what we encounter is no longer the expression of familiar experiences of life, but something out of the ordinary which can even be demonic or grotesque. In Jung's words, it is "a strange something that derives its existence from the hinterland of man's mind", a "disturbing vision of monstrous and meaningless happenings that in every way exceed the grasp of human feeling and comprehension" (pp.180-181). He believes that a vision of this nature represents "a deeper and more impressive experience than human passion", and describes this as "a genuine, primordial experience". According to Jung, human passion belongs to the sphere of conscious experience, whereas the subject of the vision lies beyond it. The vision is an intimation given to man, who "protects himself with the shield of science and the armour of reason", who wishes to believe that he has complete command over his own soul, that there is a level of reality beyond his conscious will (p.187). It is "true symbolic expression", says Jung, "the expression of something existing in its own right, but imperfectly known, which reminds us not "of everyday, human life, but rather of night-time fears and the dark recesses of the mind that we sometimes sense with misgiving". For this reason, Jung associates the vision with the night-world, while associating conscious experience with the day time. When he links the visionary artist with "the seers, prophets, leaders and enlighteners", as one of those who are "in touch with the night-side of life", his alliance with traditional mysticism becomes clearly recognizable. As in the case of symbolic works – and indeed in Jung's discussion "visionary" and "symbolical" are synonymous – the origin of the vision is traced to the collective unsconsicous, and it is emphasized again that each manifestation of the collective unconscious is compensatory to the conscious attitude of the age. The examples of such visionary works and artists given by Jung are Dante, *Faust* II, Nietzsche with his "Dionysian exuberance", Wagner's opera cycle *Der Ring des Nibelungen*, the poetry of William Blake, Jacob Boehme's "philosophic and poetic stammerings", etc.

His argument on the poet is to a large extent a restatement of the view expressed in his first paper as well as in the preceding section. His main thesis is that a creative artist is "a duality or a synethsis of contradictory attitudes" in that he is on the one hand "a human being with a personal life" and on the other "an impersonal creative process" (p.194). Admitting that the investigation of his psychic make-up is necessary in order to know the personality of the man, it is only through his artistic achievement, maintains Jung, that we can understand the artist. It is a sad mistake, he thinks therefore, to approach a work of art through the personal life of the artist. An artist in his view is, besides being an individual, " 'man' in a higher sense – he is collective man – one who carries and shapes the unconscious, psychic life of mankind". He is a chosen instrument for the spirit of the age to express its unconscious needs and restore its psychic equilibrium; in other words, "The artist is not a person endowed with free will who seeks his own ends, but one who allows art to realize its purposes through him" (p.195). In the realm of art, the personal aspect, considers Jung, is a limitation, even a sin. The dichotomy of the man and the artist in a creative person naturally causes in him conflicting forces: a longing for ordinary human happiness on the one hand and the passion for creation on the other. More often than not, however, the ruthlessness of the creative urge overrides all his other desires; then

> The work in process becomes the poet's fate and determines his
> psychic development. It is not Goethe who creates *Faust*, but *Faust*
> who creates Goethe. (p.197)

This is a complete reversal of the Freudian point of view, and again is a reassertion of his notion of the artist as a medium, and not a personality, expressed in the earlier paper. As already pointed out, this shows close affinity with the artist's own way of looking at the subject, and poets and writers have voiced much the same feelings about their relation to their own works. A good example may be found in a poem by the great Portuguese poet, Fernando Pessoa, where he writes :

> *Às vezes tenho ideias felizes,*
> *Ideias sùbitamente felizes, em ideias*
> *E nas palavras em que naturalmente se despegam ...*
>
> *Depois de escrever leio?*
> *Por que escrevi isto?*
> *Onde fui buscar isto?*
> *De onde me veio isto? Isto é melhor do que eu ...*
> *Seremos nós neste mundo apenas canetas com tinta*
> *Com que alguém escreve a valer o que nós aqui*
> *traçamos? ...*[52]

(Sometimes I have happy ideas,
Ideas suddenly happy, in ideas
And in the words, into which they naturally form
      themselves ...

After writing down, I read ...
Why did I write this?
Where did I find this?
From where did this come to me? This is better than I ever ...
Can it be that we in this world are nothing but pens
      filled with ink
With which someone actually writes what we here
      merely trace? ...)

Pessoa successfully conveys to us the sensation a poet experiences at the moment of inspiration, when he virtually loses his own identity in relation to his work and feels that he has become an instrument, or medium, which writes at the dictates of something beyond his conscious control. Indeed, it is not Pessoa who creates a poem, but a poem that creates Pessoa. William Faulkner too, in an interview, refuses any personal questions on the grounds that what matters about a writer is only his work, and says:

> If I had not existed, someone else would have written me, Hemingway, Dostoevski, all of us. Proof of that is there are three candidates for the authorship of Shakespeare's plays. But what is important is *Hamlet* and *Midsummer Night's Dream*[sic], not who wrote them, but that somebody did. The artist is of no importance. Only what he creates is important ...

Also on the nature of the artist:

> An artist is a creature driven by demons. He don't [sic] know why
> they choose him and he is usually too busy to wonder why...

> The writer's only responsibility is to his art. He will be completely
> ruthless if he is a good one. He has a dream. It anguishes him so
> much he must get rid of it. He has no peace until then. Everything
> goes by the board: honour, pride, decency, security, happiness, all
> to get the book written.[53]

Incidentally, Faulkner tells us he has never read Freud – neither did
Shakespeare, nor Melville, he adds – and does not even mention Jung's
name, which is all the more significant as it shows Jung's inherent affinity
with the artists.

The final passage of "Psychology and Literature" seems to give a fair
summary of Jung's basic views on the nature of art and the artist, echoing
much of what Faulkner said in the interview:

> The secret of an artistic creation and of the effectiveness of art
> is to be found in a return to the state of *participation mystique* – to
> that level of experience at which it is man who lives, and not the
> individual, and at which the weal or woe of the single human being
> does not count, but only human existence. This is why every great
> work of art is objective and impersonal, but none the less profoundly
> moves us each and all. And this is also why the personal life of the
> poet cannot be held essential to his art – but at most help or
> hindrance to his creative task. He may go the way of a Philistine,
> a good citizen, a neurotic, a fool or a criminal. His personal career
> may be inevitable and interesting, but it does not explain the poet.[54]

What we have discussed so far may be called Jung's general theory of
literature, and as such it seems to have been more favourably accepted by
literary men than that of Freud. One reason for this may very likely be
the already mentioned proximity of Jung's way of thinking to that of the
artist.

As to the specific and independent application of his psychological
theories to actual works of art or artists, there are not many examples,
perhaps even fewer than in Freud's case. More often than not, works of
art, and mostly literary works at that, form an integral part of his phsycho-
logical theories, as in the case of the figures from *Faust* or *Zarathustra*
quoted in many of his writings, or Rider Haggard's character used to
illustrate his "mana-personality".[55] However, we may mention two essays written about the same time, in which Jung deals with a particular
work of art and a particular artist, namely Joyce's *Ulysses* and Picasso.

"*Ulysses:* A Monologue", first published in a journal (1932), was later reprinted and included in a book (*Die Wirklichkeit der Seele,* 1934). In a headnote attached to the latter version, Jung writes :

> This literary essay ... is not a scientific treatise, any more than my *aperçu* on Picasso. I have included it in the present volume because *Ulysses* is an important "*document humain*" very characteristic of our time, and because my opinions may show how ideas that play a considerable role in my book can be applied to literary material. My essay lacks not only any scientific but also any didactic intention, and is of interest to the reader only as a subjective confession.[56]

In other words, he makes it clear that in writing these essays he did not intend scientific treatises but literary essays of a subjective nature in which his psychological theories may be applied. Consequently, compared with Freud's writings in this field, which are closely and consistently bound to his theories, these essays may be said to have more tenuous relationship to Jungian psychology.

Jung's initial response to *Ulysses* seems to have been far from favourable. He confides that he felt bored and vexed; he could not find anything meaningful in it:

> ...utterly hopeless emptiness is the dominant note of the whole book. It not only begins and ends in nothingness, it consists of nothing but nothingness. It is all infernally nugatory. (p.110)

He feared that the book was "the product of an author's negative mood", as he found in it "nothing pleasing, nothing refreshing, nothing hopeful" but only things "from the seamy side of life". Since there was in the book "no tendency for reconstruction", he suspected that destructiveness had become an end in itself. In its concentration on visceral thinking and sense-perception, with "severe restriction of cerebral activity", he also recognized a striking resemblance to the schizophrenic mentality, although this did not lead him to conclude that *Ulysses* was a product of schizophrenia. For one thing, he explains, the book lacks the stereotyped expression which is the characteristic mark of the composition of the insane; for another, he recognises throughout the book the presence of "a unified personal will and directed intention" (pp.115-126). "Ulysses", Jung argues, "is no more a pathological product than modern art as a whole". Using a term for the plastic art, he describes the book as "cubistic" in the sense that "it resolves the picture of reality into an immensely complex painting whose dominant note is the melancholy of the abstract objectivity" (p.117). Apparent resemblance between cubism

and schizophrenia, according to Jung, comes from the tendency common
to both to treat reality as if it were strange to one or to estrange oneself
from reality. While this in the insane is a symptom resulting from the
disintegration of personality, in the case of modern artists it is far from a
sign of any disease in the individual but the manifestation of the collective
psyche of the age.[57] The proof of this, says Jung, is that it creates identical
phenomena in widely different fields, such as literature, painting, sculpture and architecture.

"The distortion of beauty and meaning by grotesque objectivity or
equally grotesque irreality" is, in his view, not a consequence of disease,
but is based on a creative purpose. "Far from his work being an expression
of the destruction of his personality", he claims, "the modern artist finds
the unity of his artistic personality in destructiveness" (pp.117-118). He
finds a similar tendency for destructiveness in the art and spirit of other
periods in history, such as the epoch of Akhnaton, the early Christian era,
the Baroque and the Pre-Raphaelite, each of which, he thinks, represents
in its own way the rejection and destruction of past values and the
anticipation of the new era.

Thus viewed in historical perspective, and considered as part of a
collective phenomenon, *Ulysses*, with all its "destructiveness", begins to
bear new significance for Jung. He now thinks that he "can ascribe a
positive, creative value and meaning" to the book as well as to "its artistic
congeners". The abuse heaped on *Ulysses,* in his opinion, originates in
"the resentment of the unmodern man" who refuses to see the unseemly
side of life, who is "stuck in medievalism up to the ears" (pp.118-119).
Ulysses and its kindred works of art, says Jung,

> are drastic purgatives whose full effect would be dissipated if they
> did not meet with an equally strong and obstinate resistance ... They
> have this in common with Freudian theory, that they undermine with
> fanatical one-sidedness values that have already begun to crumble.
> (p.119)

Both Freud and Joyce, according to him, are the "prophets of negation"
who are needed to reveal to their contemporaries the "shadow side of
reality": thus the destruction in *Ulysses* is in fact a "creative destruction".
What first seemed to him negative elements comes to have a positive
function as the indication of and the counterbalance for the malaise in
society. The "evil and destructive elements" are the antidote for the notion
of the "good" handed down from the past, which in his view is actually
"a ruthless tyrant, an illusory system of prejudices that robs life of its
richness, emasculates it and enforces a moral compulsion which in the

end is unendurable" (p.121). It is the "objective" recognition of his world
and of his own nature, claims Jung, that frees the prisoner of a system.
The lack of feeling – "Everything is desouled, every particle of warm
blood has been chilled, events unroll in icy egoism" (p.114) – too has its
role to play: a compensation for the excess of sentiment, particularly "too
much false feeling". Jung is "deeply convinced that we are not only stuck
in the Middle Ages but are also caught in our own sentimentality". Joyce
therefore is "a prophet" who arose "to teach our culture compensatory
lack of feeling".[58] He believes that the world of *Ulysses* is, paradoxically,
"a better one than the world of those who are hopelessly bound to the
darkness of their spiritual birthplace" (p.121).

Besides these "positive virtues", Jung senses that there is a secret
purpose behind the book which makes it meaningful and of value.
Ulysses, in his view, is not symbolic in his sense of the word (see p.87):
it is not a dream, nor a revelation of the unconscious. On the contrary, it
seems to him to have a strong purposiveness and sense of direction.
According to Jung's interpretation, what the book aims at, its real secret,
is detachment of consciousness, "to be an eye of the moon, a consciousness detached from the object, in thrall neither to the gods nor to sen-
suality, and bound neither by love nor by hate, neither by conviction nor
by prejudice" (p.124). It is a spiritual state which he compares to that of
Yogi, a Buddha or a Christ, who, through overcoming of their egos, of "a
fool's world", attained the higher, "more objective state of the self".
Ulysses, considers Jung, represents this state of the higher self which is
able to absorb the opposite, can embrace "the ego and the non-ego, the
infernal regions, the viscera, the *Imagines et lares,* and the heavens"
(p.125). It is a picture of the world in its totality, and Ulysses, who never
appears in the book is, according to Jung, the creator-god who presides
over it, unseen but omnipresent. [It seems that Jung here is unaware that
Joyce conceived of the character of Bloom as the modern Ulysses.] He is
the "symbol of what makes up the totality, the oneness, of all the single
appearances in *Ulysses* as a whole ...", in short, a "microcosm of James
Joyce". He is the symbol of the "higher self", or the detached consciousness which has freed itself from entanglement in the pysical and mental
world. The "whole basis and highest artistic achivement of *Ulysses*" in
Jung's view, is this "detachment of human consciousness and its consequent approximation to the divine" (p.126). At the end of the essay, he
describes in a sentence what he considers to be the signifance of the book:
"A world has passed away, and is made new" (p.132).

His short essay on Picasso was written on the occasion of the Picasso
Exhibition in Zurich in 1932, and was published the same year, closely

following the publication of the essay on Joyce. As his recognition of the spiritual kinship between the painter and the writer – Joyce is described as Picasso's "literary brother"[59] – may indicate, the main drift of "Picasso" is not very far from that of the preceding essay.

Jung concedes at the outset that he has nothing to say on the question of Picasso's art but only on the psychology underlying his kind of artistic creativeness. He had for many years used painting for therapeutic purposes with his patients, and in the light of his experience he claims, the psychic problems expressed in Picasso's works are "strictly analogous to those of [his] patients" (p.135). He points out those elements in Picasso's painting that "do not correspond to any outer experience", and do not at all agree with general expectations. These, he assumes, cannot be derived from consciousness but must originate in the "inside", ie, the unconscious psyche of the painter. This "inside", though invisible, can have, according to Jung, profound effects on consciousness, and to those of his patients who suffer mainly from these effects, he advises that they give them expression in pictorial form so as to make them accessible to their consciousness. All such pictorial representations of the unconscious contents, says Jung, are "symbolic" and give one "the feeling of strangeness and of a confusing, incomprehensible jumble" (p.136). One does not know, he continues, what is actually meant or what is being represented. He makes it clear that by all this he is simultaneously describing what he thinks are the characteristics of modern art, when he admits that the pictures of his patients, because of their simplicity due to lack of artistic imagination, are nevertheless relatively easier to understand than those of the modern artists.

Jung divides his patients into two groups, the neurotics and the schizophrenics, although they are said to have one thing in common in that they both produce pictures with symbolic content. The main difference lies in the fact that the painting by the former has a "synthetic character" and "unified feeling-tone", while the pictures of the latter "immediately reveal their alienation from feeling", "contradictory feelings or even a complete lack of feeling" (p.137). Whereas the neurotic strives to communicate his meaning to the beholder, the schizophrenic, observes Jung, hardly shows any such inclination. [Repeating word for word what he said about Joyce, he comments: "nothing comes to meet the beholder, everything turns away from him" (p.138).] Their pictures, according to him, show the characteristic fragmentation in form, and preoccupation with "the ugly, the sick, the grotesque, the incomprehensible, the banal" in content. Picasso is said to belong to this second group,[60] just as Joyce at one point in the other essay is related to the schizophrenic. The artistic development of Picasso's painting is thus analysed in the light of the psychological development Jung observed in his patients' pictures. These are said to show a series of images, starting with "the symbol of Nekyia – the journey to Hades", ie, "the descent into the unconscious", which is followed by further images of symbolic nature that give "intimations of a hidden meaning" (p.138). Picasso, Jung thinks, follows more or less the same pattern, the pictures of his relatively early Blue Period corresponding to the Nekyia, the process of descending into the unconscious. The change of colour – does he refer to the so-called Rose Period that follows? – signifies the entry into the "underworld" where the "world of objects is death-struck" and Picasso, according to Jung, encounters a number of dead souls like his own. He recognizes in Picasso a "personality"

> which suffers the underworld fate - the man in him who does not turn towards the day-world, but is fatefully drawn into the dark; who follows not the accepted ideals of goodness and beauty, but the demonical attraction of ugliness and evil. (p.138)

In this, however, says Jung, Picasso is not alone but his contemporaries, the modern man, all share the same "anti-Christian and Luciferian forces". He is "a sign of the times", like Joyce.

In the "underworld", Picasso is said to undergo a metamorphosis and reappear in the form of the "tragic Harlequin", a motif of many of his paintings. Jung also claims that the "descent into ancient times" is always associated with the "Nekyia", and that it revives the ancient and primitive elements in man. Thus his patients, with few exceptions, are said to "go back to Neolithic art forms or revel in evocations of Dionysian orgies" (p.139). Picasso likewise, "conjures up crude earthly shapes, grotesque and primitive, and resurrects the soullessness of ancient Pompeii in a cold glittering light", which seems to allude to his cubism and classicism. In all the varied forms Picasso explores, Jung senses the presence of the Harlequin – since even wine and lutes are considered to be his manifestations – and wonders what is the significance of "his wild journey through man's millennial history". What symbol, he asks, will appear as the final cause and meaning of all this disintegration? As "the dazzling versatility of Picasso", he confesses, is too daunting for him to "hazard a guess", he draws an answer from his interpretation of his patients' pictures. The "Nekyia" in their case, he maintains, is "no aimless and purely destructive fall into the abyss" but an attempt to restore, "by awakening the memories in the blood", the whole man, the "*homo totus*", lost in one-sidedness of the modern man. After the symbols of madness of the period of disintegration comes the images representing the "coming together of the opposites" such as light/dark, male/female, etc. He recognizes the same sign in Picasso's latest (ie, ca. 1932) paintings, which show "the motif of the union of opposites ... in their direct juxtaposition" (p.140), although he refrains from further "prophecy" as to Picasso's future course.

As his comments on and interpretations of Picasso's paintings are not always convincing enough, the essay, in spite of his claim does not seem to help us to understand the psychology underlying Picasso's art, but rather reveals what Jung thinks of artists and works of art, which is essentially a confirmation of what we have already seen in the previous essays.

Though, outside his own school, Jung has often been accused of mysticism or of being unscientific[61] – and the accusation sometimes seems to be faily justified – by literary men at least his theories were often more favoured than those of Freud, perhaps because of the very lack of scientific determinism as well as their rather speculative and philosophical nature. For example, Eugene Jolas, to whom we shall return later, clearly valued Jung more highly than Freud, although he did recognize and appreciate Freud's pioneering role. Jorge Luis Borges too confessed in a conversation that he "always disliked Freud" and continued: "I read Jung in the same way as, let's say, I might read Pliny or Frazer's *Golden Bough*. I read it as a kind of museum or encyclopedia of curious lores."[62] (In both cases, the motive for preferring Jung was what Jolas termed Freud's "pan-sexualism".) According to J. A. C. Brown, "many critics have commented that the Jungian theory is more like a metaphysical system than a school of scientific psychology". Quoting another critic, he continues: "Rightly or wrongly it seems that there is something in Jung's writings which ... must ever repulse those whose training and bias has taught them to rely upon logical reason as the only legitimate method of learning and adaptation (J. E. Nicole, *Psychopathology*)."[63] This may be precisely the reason why they tend to appeal more to the literary mind.

CHAPTER SIX

THE ROMANTIC ANCESTRY

IN the history of European literature, there were those who preceded
Freud and his fellow psychologists in recognizing the significant role
played in man's life by the non-rational or the unconscious part of the
mind. This fact was, indeed, pointed out by the psychologists themselves.

Apart from a few individual artists gifted with extraordinary insight
into the most subtle and secret workings of the human mind, such as
Shakespeare, the main trend of European literature had been relatively
unconcerned with this side of man and more often than not downright
scornful of it. This culminated in the eighteenth century Neo-classicism
which placed supreme importance on man's rational faculty with almost
total subordination or suppression of his other qualiities such as emotion
or imagination. Paradoxically, it was precisely this Age of Reason which
gave rise to the first manifestation of the more or less collective awareness
of the other side of human nature, which expressed itself in the form of
the Romantic movement.

In reaction to the exaggerated, and what they considered misconceived,
emphasis on rationalism in general and the classic decorum in the field of
art, the Romantic poets and writers of the late 18th and early 19th centuries
deliberately turned their eyes to the so far neglected or rather, ignored,
and often depreciated side of man, ie, the private and inner world of his
mind, and emphasized in almost inverse proportion, the significance of
dreams and fantasies, making them virtually the mainspring of their
creative activities. Throughout Europe, literary men started showing
greater, sometimes even obsessive, interest in and concern for that part of
man's life which was often baffling, defying logical or rational explanation and comprehension. Since all those dreams, fantasies and reveries,
which seemed to reveal the secrets of this hidden side of human nature
are related to the realm of imagination, or considered to spring from it,
this faculty, imagination, in clear contrast to the previous age, came to
occupy the central place among the Romantics and this attitude towards
imagination became one of the most important legacies of Romanticism.
Those modern writers whom we call Modernists, in whom also imagination plays a crucial role as regards their creative process as well as their
artistic beliefs, may be considered to have revived, after an interval of
almost a century, and in spite of some apparent differences, the essential
spirit of Romanticism, and may thus be regarded as its direct descendants.
Their interest in, and concern with, the inner life of man was indeed an

integral part of the Romantic heritage; it was further reinforced by the spread of the new psychology of Freud and Jung which itself had had its way prepared by the Romantic movement. By examining some of the main features of Romanticism that are especially relevant to our present subject, we may have a clearer notion of the nature of the legacies it bequeathed to Modernists, as well as the interlinking ties that bind together Modernism, modern psychology and Romanticism.

Those concerns of the Romantics which seem to me to be central, namely those which particularly anticipate the major preoccupations of the modern psychologists and writers may be said to be recognition of the significance of childhood, emphasis on the individual sensibility or the Self, and the concern with the irrational, or non-rational, side of the mind. In this chapter we shall deal with some of the Romantic poets and writers who best illustrate these aspects in their writings.

Just as it was Freud who first revealed the importance of childhood in the individiual's development in the field of psychology, so in literature it was the Romantics who first brought man's attention to the significance of childhood which until then had barely been noticed. William Blake is a poet who is remembered above all for the poems which dealt specifically with the themes of childhood. For him they represented an ideal state, unspoiled and undefiled by hypocrisy and worldly considerations of the grown-ups (as seen in "The Lamb" in *Songs of Innocence*), and as such, the state all men should strive for. Contrary to the conventional view, it is the children who perceive the truths about life and the world better than the adults. For example, on the subject of the incomprensibility of his works, he wrote in his letter to Trustler (23rd August, 1799), "But I am happy to find a Great Majority of Fellow Mortals who can Elucidate My Visions, Particularly they have been Elucidated by Children..." For Blake "Neither Youth nor Childhood is Folly or Incapacity".[1] As a result, they are often regarded as the victims of the cruel and uncomprehending adults (eg, "Holy Thursday", "The Chimney Sweeper", "A Little Boy Lost" in *Songs of Experience*). In this sense, childhood for Blake presents a clear contrast to adulthood which is essentially corrupt and wicked. Although he must be the first major poet who recognized a great significance in childhood, his attitude towards it differs from that of the modern psychologists who regard it as an embryonic stage for later development and see an essential continuity between childhood and adulthood.

William Wordsworth is another poet who attached an immense importance to childhood, and devoted some of his most important works to it. The titles themselves of the works like "Poems Referring to the Period of Childhood", "Ode: Intimations of Immortality from Recollections of

Early Childhood", and the early Books of *The Prelude*, such as "Childhood and School-Time", clearly show Wordsworth's preoccupation with this period of life. For him it also meant a blessed state, a state of grace, but unlike Blake he did not regard adulthood as the antithesis to childhood, but rather its continuation though with less intensity and decreased visionary power. This continuity between childood and adulthood is well emphasized in the "rainbow" poem:

> My heart leaps up when I behold
> A rainbow in the sky;
> So was it when my life began;
> So is it now I am a man
> So be it when I shall grow old,
> Or let me die!
> The Child is father of the Man;
> And I could wish my days to be
> Bound each to each by natural piety.[2]

The central idea here that "The Child is father of the Man", anticipates that of modern psychologists, although the basic idea underlying it may be different. One variation of the same theme can be found in Freud's theory of artistic creation in which he regards the artist's creative activities as the continuation of the play of children. His theory of the Oedipus complex is also based on a similar line of thinking. The difference for Wordsworth between the two stages lies in the decrease in the later years in the ability to respond spontaneously and intensely to the appeal of Nature. For "Heaven lies about us in our infancy!" when "The earth, and every common sight" seem to be "Apparrelled in celestial light, / The glory and freshness of a dream" ("The Immortality Ode", 2-5). It was when the poet

> ... held unconscious intercourse with beauty
> Old as creation, drinking in a pure
> Organic pleasure from the silver wreaths
> Of curling mist, or from the level plain
> Of waters coloured by impending clouds.
> (*The Prelude*, I, 562-566)

Although Wordsworth's main concern was the communion with Nature throughout a man's life, which occupied the most important place in his poetry as well as in his life, he may be said to be one of the precursors of modern psychology in recognizing and expressing this essential continuity between childhood and manhood.

Coleridge expresses a similar idea about the validity of childhood experience and sensibility when, quoting from his own pamphlet *The Friend*, he says that

> To carry on the feelings of childhood into the powers of manhood; to combine the child's sense of wonder and novelty with the appearances which every day for perhaps forty years had rendered familiar ... this is the character and privilege of genius, and one of the marks which distinguish genius from talent.[5]

Although he did not write poems specifically on childhood, here we can recognize his belief in it, and in the positive combination of childhood and adulthood, in very much the same vein as Wordsworth's.

The theme of the exploration of "the Self", or the individuality, is closely related to the last of the three aspects of Romanticism under consideration, the emphasis on the irrational. For non-rational activities like dreams, fantasies and reveries are all extremely personal and private ones, and when the Romantics valued these elements in life, to be oneself alone and solitude inevitably became almost a prerequisite condition for their poetic creation. This is in strong contrast to the preceding age when poetry was often used as a public weapon to satirise the state of affairs in society or criticize some particular well-known public figure, or as a means of preaching some socially accepted moral norms. The subject matter too was naturally about the individuals or the poet himself. With the Romantics, we most often find them musing alone, or walking in solitude, like Wordsworth who "wandered lonely as a cloud" and later lay down on a couch to bring up the vision of the "golden daffodils" in a manner quite reminiscent of the free association method of the modern psychologists. In his autobiographical poem, *The Prelude*, he makes a point of saying that he speaks only about himself, the inner world of his Self:

> My theme has been
> What passed within me. Not of outward things
> Done visibly for other minds, words, signs,
> Symbols or actions, but of my own heart
> Have I been speaking, and my youthful mind.
> (III, 172-176)

And again,

> A Traveller I am
> Whose tale is only of himself ...
> (III, 195-196)

For him everybody is ultimately alone and unique:

> Points have we all of us within our souls
> Where all stand single ...
> (III, 185-186)

He also confesses his appreciation of solitude, of standing "single":

> ... I had learnt betimes to stand unpropped,
> And independent musings pleased me so
> That spells seemed on me when I was alone,
> (III, 227-229)

while conceding that his natural inclination loved society. In the Preface
to *The Excursion*, quoting from his own poem "The Recluse", he says:
"On Man, on Nature, and on Human Life, Musing in solitude ..." (1-2),
which indicates the importance of solitude and solitary musing for the
poet's creative activity.

Many of the subjects of Wordsworth's poems are also solitary individuals. In "Lucy Gray", the little girl is described as the "solitary child",
who after her death may be seen "Upon the lonesome wild", singing "a
solitary song". In *Resolution and Independence*, the poet imagines the
old leech gatherer, whom he met on "the lonely moor", to "pace about the
weary moors continually, Wandering alone and silently" (129-131). In
"The Solitary Reaper", the title itself is significant, and almost every line
of the first stanza emphasizes her state of loneliness:

> Behold her, single in the field,
> You solitary Highland Lass!
> Reaping and singing by herself;
> Stop here or gently pass!
> Alone she cuts and binds the grain,
> And sings a melancholy strain.

The settings for Coleridge's poems are very often night, sleep and
dreams which are naturally states of solitude. In "Frost at Midnight", he
is left alone to his musings:

> The owlet's cry
> Came loud – and hark again! loud as before.
> The inmates of my cottage all at rest,
> Have left me to that solitude which suits
> Abstruser musings ...[4]

As is well known, "Kubla Khan" which has a sub-title, "A Vision in a
Dream", was claimed by the poet to have been composed in a dream.
However, we may discuss this subject more in detail later. Many of Keats'
poems also deal with solitary contemplations and nocturnal musings.

"The Ode to a Grecian Urn" and "The Ode to a Nightingale" are good examples of these. The knight-at-arms in his "La Belle Dame sans Merci" too is found "alone and palely loitering" at a deserted lakeside.

Even when the Romantic poets deal with more general and philosophical themes, the ideas expressed are not the socially accepted norms or decorum, but the results of intensely personal contemplations and experiences, as in the case of Blake and his *Marriage of Heaven and Hell*, or Wordsworth who tried to convey his characteristic moral sense through his own experience of Nature. [The already quoted poem on the rainbow is a good example; "The Immortality Ode" and a great deal of *The Prelude* may also serve as illustrations.] In his essay, "Literature and Society", F.R. Leavis, contrasting Blake's individualism against the Augustan writers' conformism and identification with current social values, interprets Blake's attitude as follows:

> Blake in his successful work says implicitly: 'It is I who see and feel. I see only what I see and feel only what I feel. My experience is mine, and in its specific quality lies its significance.[5]

It is interesting to note that in *Biographia Literaria* Coleridge states a very similar view:

> Though I have seen and known enough of mankind to be well aware that I shall perhaps stand alone in my creed, and that it will be well if I subject myself to no worse charge than that of singularity ...(p.7)

At about the same time William Hazlitt described the poet as one who

> lives in the solitude of his own breast, without wife or child or friend or enemy in the whole world. His is the solitude of the soul, not of woods or trees or mountains – but the desert of society – the waste and oblivion of the heart. He is himself alone.[6]

The main concerns of the Romantics were his own experiences, his own personal response to the world and the secrets of his own inner self.

Closely related to this attitude was their interest in the irrational aspect of man. As Jung observed, on the publication of Freud's *Interpretation of Dreams*, how it became "an object of mockery" for his older colleagues and that it required "the greatest scientific courage to make anything as unpopular as dreams an object of serious discussion", it had been customary until quite recently for people to mock at dreams as shadowy, insubstantial "nothing". If there were any who did not laugh at them, who on the contrary took them very seriously, even before Freud, it was the Romantics. In contrast to and reaction against the previous century in which reason was the dominant force, the Romantics either ignored or gave the secondary place to reason, placing the highest importance on imagination and imaginative or irrational activities of the mind, such as reveries, daydreaming, visions, sleep and dreams.

Again William Blake sets the tone. In *The Marriage of Heaven and Hell*, he reverses the conventional evaluation of good and evil and along with it that of reason and passion, or life force which he calls Energy. Reason, which is related to good and Heaven is presented as a passive and negative force, while Energy related to Evil and Hell is presented as the active and positive force in life. Thus:

Energy is the only life, and is from the Body; and Reason is the bound or outward circumference of Energy.

Energy is Eternal Delight. (p.149)

It is clear that the reason here is regarded as something that controls and limits the natural impulses and activities of the life force, and this in itself is considered evil in Blake's new mythology:

Those who restrain desire, do so because theirs is weak enough to be restrained; and the restrainer or reason usurps its place and governs the unwilling. (*Ibid*)

Further he writes in condemnation of rational control and in praise of free exercise of Energy:

The Roads of excess lead to the palace of wisdom.
Prudence is a rich, ugly old maid courted by incapacity.
Bring out number, weight & Measure in a year of dearth.
The cistern contains: the fountain overflows.
Damn braces: Bless relaxes.
Exuberance is Beauty. (pp.150-152)

Blake also regarded his visionary experiences as the important source of his artistic creation, but found the general tendency of the society antagonistic to such an attitude. He wrote in relation to the rationalistic philosophers and scientists like Bacon, Newton, Locke and Burke: "They mock Inspiration & vision. Inspiration and Vision was then, & now is, & I hope will always Remain, my Element, my Eternal Dwelling place; how can I then hear it Condemned without returning Scorn for Scorn?"[7] Blake, in the words of his first biographer Frederick Tatham, "always asserted that he had the power of bringing his imagination before his mind's eye, so completely organized and so perfectly formed ...that while he copied the vision (as he called it) upon his plate or canvas, he could not err".[8] Morton D. Paley considers that Blake possessed "a highly developed capacity for what is now called eidetic imagery".[9] In any case, there is no doubt that Blake believed in the truth of his visions and drew inspiration from them for his art and poetry. In his *Note-book* (1810) he states:

> The Nature of my Work is Visionary or Imaginative; it is an Endeavour to Restore what the Ancients call'd the Golden Age. (p.605)

For him, as to many other Romantic poets, imagination was not another name for shadowy fantasy, but a real creative and revelatory power in man: "Vision or Imagination is a Representation of what Eternally Exists, Really and Unchangeably" (p.604).

Wordsworth describes the child's joyful communion with Nature "the vision splendid". It is the disappearance of this "visionary gleam" that the poet of the "Immortality Ode" laments. In his infancy Nature was adorned with "The glory and the freshness of a dream"; now he has to ask: "Where is it now, the glory and the dream?" The "vision" and the "dream" in this context have nothing to do with the conventional shadowy images of these terms, but rather an implication of the positive, moving experiences in life, something essential in man's existence. For Wordsworth nature was the source of these visions, and of the mysterious communication with the primordial world:

> I would stand,
> Beneath some rock, listening to notes that are
> The ghostly language of the ancient earth,
> Or make their dim abode in distant winds.
> Thence did I drink the visionary power;
> (*The Prelude*, I, 306-311)

He was also aware of the undercurrent of the unconscious activities of the mind which express themselves in irrational fears and dreams. In the "Ode", he is grateful for his childhood memories which maintain in him

> Blank misgivings of a Creature
> Moving about in worlds not realized
> High instincts before which our mortal Nature
> Did tremble like a guilty thing surprised;
> (148-151)

In *The Prelude,* after describing the awesome experience he had in a stolen boat when he was a boy, the poet writes:

> For many days my brain
> Worked with a dim and undermined sense
> Of unknown modes of being; o'er my thoughts
> There hung a darkness, call it solitude

> Or blank desertion. No familiar shapes
> Remained, no pleasant images of trees,
> Of sea or sky, no colours of green fields;
> But huge and mighty forms, that do not live
> Like living men, moved slowly through the mind
> By day, and were a trouble to my dream.
> (I, 391-400)

And in the already quoted Preface to *The Excursion,* he explains the nature and the subject matter of his poetry:

> ... I must tread on shadowy ground, must sink
> Deep ... (27-28)

and continues:

>   Not chaos, not
> The darkest pit of lowest Erebus,
> Nor aught of blinder vacancy, scooped out
> By help of dreams – can breed such fear and awe
> As fall upon us often when we look
> Into our minds, into the Minds of Man –
> My haunt, and the main region of my song. (35-41)

Here Wordsworth intimates his knowledge of the mysterious and sometimes awe-inspiring workings of the depth of the human mind, and declares quite categorically that it is there that he finds the material for his poetry: "My haunt, and the main region of my song".

Coleridge, discussing the obscurity or the unintelligibility of Wordsworth's poems to some readers, took the "Immortality Ode" as an example and defended him in these terms:

> But ode was intended for such readers only as had been accustomed
> to watch the flux and reflux of their inmost nature, to venture at
> times into the twilight realms of consciousness and to feel a deep
> interest in modes of inmost being to which they know that the
> attributes of time and space are inapplicable and alien, but which
> yet cannot be conveyed save in symbols of time and space.[10]

This statement shows clearly that Coleridge grasped the essential nature of Wordsworth's poetry and that he himself was well acquainted with "the twilight realms of consciousness" and the "modes of inmost being" which defied the expression in the normal use of language and could not be expressed "save in symbols".

For Coleridge himself was greatly concerned about this aspect of the human mind, and his poetry may be said to bear marks of the influence of the irrational and the unconscious more distinctly than any other English poet of the Romantic period. He kept in his notebooks minute records of his own dreams and nightmares which often tormented him during sleep [11] and which found either direct or indirect expression in his poems. Perhaps because of the strong impact and half-frightening, half-fascinating details of these dreams, he even observes in one of the entries: "I must devote some one or more Days exclusively to the Meditation on *Dreams*. Days? Say rather Weeks!"[12] "The Pains of Sleep" deals directly with the theme of the nightmare. He describes how he was awaken, troubled and tortured by a bad dream:

> Yesternight I prayed aloud
> In anguish and in agony,
> Up-starting from the fiendish crowd
> Of shapes and thoughts that tortured me:
> A lurid light, a trampling throng,
> Sense of intolerable wrong ... (14-19)

It also carries a strong sexual undertone and a sense of guilt:

> Desire with loathing strangely mixed
> On wild or hateful objects fixed.
> Fantastic passions! maddening brawl!
> And shame and terror over all!
> Deeds to be hid which were not hid,
> Which all confused I could not know
> Whether I suffered, or I did:
> For all seemed guilt, remorse or woe,
> My own or others still the same
> Life-stifling fear, soul-stifling shame. (23-32)

Here we have some clearly recognizable characteristics of dreams such as confusion of the subject and the object and the naked expression of the normally hidden desires. The poet describes this as "The unfathomable hell within" and confesses his "horror of their deeds to view, / To know and loathe, yet wish and do!" Evidently here is a typical situation of the conflict between instinctual wishes and the repression. Preceding its publication in 1816, Coleridge sent to Thomas Poole a letter, dated October 3, 1803, in which he included a portion of a draft of the poem (11.18-32) and described in most vivid terms the nature of his dream experiences it illustrated:

> ... God forbid that my worst Enemy should ever have the Nights and the Sleep that I have had, night after night – surprised by Sleep, while I struggled to remain awake, starting up to bless my own loud

Screams that had awakened me – yea, dear friend! till my repeated
Night-yells had made me a Nuisance in my own House. As I live
& am a man, this is an unexaggerated Tale – my dreams became the
Substance of my life ... [13]

This leaves little doubt as to the place dreams occupied in Coleridge's
life. "The Visionary Hope", a poem written seven years later in 1910, deals
with the same subject, using words and expressions very similar to those
in the letter and the earlier poem:

> Though obscure pangs made curses of his dreams,
> And dreaded sleep, each night repelled in vain,
> Each night was scattered by its own loud screams: (12-14)

It is indeed not difficult to imagine how familiar the poet was with those
nightly visions which are born out of the "obscure pangs", the undefinable
anxieties and desires hidden in the dark regions of the mind.

Coleridge's two most important poems, "Kubla Khan" and "The
Ancient Mariner", were both claimed to have either an unconscious or a
half-conscious origin. As is well known, since it has become the subject
of many controversies, "Kubla Khan" has a sub-title, "A Vision in a
Dream. A Fragment" and in the Preface that follows, Coleridge gives a
lengthy account of how the poem was first composed in a dream during
a sleep induced by an anodyne (opium), and how it had to remain a
fragment, due to an interruption by a visitor while, after waking, he was
copying it from memory. Norman Fruman argues convincingly against
the authenticity of the poet's claim on the evidence of the existing variants
and corrections of the poem, which are the proofs of more elaborate
process of composition than the unconscious and spontaneous creation in
a dream. He concedes, however, that it may have been composed in a
kind of reverie, as Coleridge himself in his so-called Crewe manuscript
stated: "This fragment with a good deal more, not recoverable, composed
in a sort of Reverie brought on by two grains of Opium ... at a Farm House
... in the fall of the year, 1797."[14] Assuming that what Coleridge states
in the 1816 Preface is not true, the fact remains that the poem has a certain
enigmatic and mysterious quality of a dream or a vision, and that even its
structure reminds us of fragmentariness and lack of logical sequence of a
dream. It is possible that the poem in its original conception had something to do with a certain state of mind, in which consciousness was not
completely in control or dominant. Whatever the case may be, Coleridge's statements, regarding both the dream and the reverie, prove his
serious interest in dreams and the irrational activities of the mind. "The
Ancient Mariner" is another example that supports this view. It is well

known, through the account given by Wordsworth, that the poem is founded on a dream of Coleridge's friend, Cruickshank, who saw in it "a skeleton ship with figures in it", and whatever conscious elaboration it went through afterwards, it still retains the weird and spellbinding quality of a nightmare:

> He holds him with his glittering eye –
> The Wedding-Guest stood still,
> And listens like a three years' child:
> The Mariner hath his will. (13-16)

Or

> The very deep did rot: O Christ!
> That ever this should be!
> Yea, slimy things did crawl with legs
> Upon the slimy sea. (123-126)

And the skeleton ship with Death and Life-in-Death on board:

> Are those *her* ribs through which the Sun
> Did peer, as through a grate?
> And is that Woman all her crew?
> Is that a Death? and are there two?
> Is Death that woman's mate?
>
> *Her* lips were red, *her* looks were free,
> Her locks were yellow as gold:
> Her skin was white as leprosy,
> The Night-mare Life-in-Death was she,
> Who thicks man's blood with cold. (185-194)

It is obvious that the primary thing that occupied the poet's mind was not the moral at the end of the poem, but all those dream-like images of horror and mystery which pervade the whole:

> Farewell, farewell! but this I tell
> To thee, thou Wedding-Guest!
> He prayeth well, who loveth well
> Both man and bird and beast.
>
> He prayeth best, who loveth best
> All things both great and small;
> For the dear God who loveth us,
> He made and loveth all. (610-616)

In the later editions of *Lyrical Ballads* (1800, 1802, 1805) in which it was included, Coleridge added a sub-title, "a poet's Reverie". It is

significant that these two best poems which have either dream-like or
nightmarish quality are both related by the poet to reverie. R. C. Bald, in
his article "Coleridge and 'The Ancient Mariner'", discusses the poet's
idea of reverie as follows,

> But, between the normal modes of mental *activity* and the passivity
> of dreaming there are various states in which the usual controls
> imposed by the will and the reason are relaxed in differing degrees,
> and to these Coleridge applied the inclusive term 'reverie'. It
> included not merely ordinary daydreaming but, as we have seen,
> opium reveries and 'nightmares' as well.[15]

There seems to be little doubt that these poems were initially conceived
in a state in which rational or conscious controls were more or less
diminished. In any case, in these two poems Coleridge exploited to the
full the essential characteristics of dreams and nightmares. "Christabel",
though incomplete, also abounds in the nightmarish atmosphere and
images. The daydream was also used for the title and the subject in two
of his poems, "A Daydream" and "The Daydream". These examples
demonstrate clearly Coleridge's familiarity with and awareness of the
unconcsious and the irrational in man. Indeed, his concepts of dream and
the unconscious seem to concern the basis of his idea of poetic creation.
In one of the entries in his notebook, he writes:

> Poetry a rationalized dream dealing [? about] to manifold Forms
> our own Feelings, that never perhaps were attached by us conscious-
> ly to our own personal Selves. – What is the Lear, the Othello, but
> a divine Dream / all Shakespeare, & nothing Shakespeare. – O there
> are truths below the surface in the subject of Sympathy, & how we
> *become* that which we understandly [*sic*] behold and hear, having
> how much God perhaps only knows, created part even of the
> Form.[16]

It is evident in the above passage that Coleridge recognized the
importance of the role played by the unconscious in the process of poetic
creation. Poetry has the same origin as a dream, but unlike a dream, it has
to go through conscious shaping and reshaping, and this seems to be
exactly what happened with "Kubla Khan" and "The Ancient Mariner".
They are both "rationalised" dreams.

In a more traditional way, which dates back to the Classical and
Biblical periods, dreams and visions were the favourite means that the
Romantic poets used to reveal the hidden truths to the characters in their
poems. Coleridge uses a vision in "Christabel", and Keats too uses
dreams in this way in many of his poems. In "Isabella", or "A Pot of

Basil", though through Boccaccio, he uses a dream-vision to disclose the murder of her lover to the heroine. The murderers themselves are tormented by dreams, owing to their sense of guilt. In "La Belle Dame sans Merci", the knight is warned in a dream by "pale kings and princes", as well as by "Pale warriors", of the danger he is in: "La Belle Dame sans Merci/Hath thee in thrall!" In "Endymion", the protagonist, after seeing in a dream a most beautiful maiden, becomes obsessed with the image. To his sister who tries to dismiss it, saying:

> How light
> Must dreams themselves be; seeing they're more slight
> Than the mere nothing that engenders them!
> (Book I, 754-756) [17]

Endymion answers, expressing his belief in the truth of his dream-vision:

> Look not so wilder'd; for these things are true,
> And never can be born of atomies
> That buzz about our slumbers, like brain-flies,
> Leaving us fancy-sick. No, no, I'm sure,
> My restless spirit never could endure
> To brood so long upon one luxury,
> Unless it did, though fearfully, espy
> A hope beyond the shadow of a dream.
> (Book I, 850-857)

In "The Fall of Hyperion", which has a sub-title, "A Dream", the whole poem, though unfinished, is supposed to be a dream dreamt by a poet. As is clear from its introductory part, the dream here is another name for the poetic vision of a poet, and closely related to his creative imagination. Conceding that all men dream, including fanatics and the savage, the narrator goes on:

> But bare of laurel they [fanatics and the savages] live,
> dream and die;
> For poesy alone can tell her dreams,
> With the fine spell of words alone can save
> Imagination from the sable charm
> And dumb enchantment. (7-11)

Poetry is the only means, he declares, that can express men's dreams, the products of imagination.

The division between dream and reality is sometimes not very clear either. At the end of the "Ode to a Nightingale", when the bird, after leading the poet into meditation on life and death, on the world of the past and far away, leaves him behind, he wonders:

> Was it a vision, or a waking dream?
> Fled is that music: – Do I wake or sleep?
> (VIII, 9-10)

In the "Ode to Psyche", the poet sees a vision of the Goddess and questions himself:

> Surely I dreamt today, or did I see
> The winged Psyche with awaken'd eyes? (5-11)

His preference for Psyche, the Goddess of soul, is also significant. He professes himself to become her priest and build a temple in a most secret part of his mind: "some untrodden region of my mind", where his diverse thoughts murmur like trees in the wind. Here we find the poet paying homage to the mysteries of the innermost region of the mind.

In relation to the dream-theme, the themes of night and sleep are also prominent in Romantic literature. In both "Sleep and Poetry" and the sonnet "To Sleep", Keats praises the virtues of sleep and in the latter makes invocations to sleep, expressing his desire for the unconscious state, in rejection of the shining day and the "envious conscience". Shelley too, in his "To Night", invokes the "Spirit of the Night", which with its "dreams of joy and fear" are both "terrible and dear" to the poet. The conventional praise of the day and the sun (eg, Shakespeare's "Shall I compare thee to a summer's day? ... ") is inverted, and it is night that is "long-sought" and "beloved", while day is something to be endured. The poet calls to the Night:

> When I arose and saw the dawn,
> I sighed for thee;
> When light rode high, and the dew was gone,
> And noon lay heavy on flower and ree
> And the weary Day turned to his rest,
> Lingering like an unloved guest,
> I sighed for thee. (15-21)[18]

The day is "heavy" and "an unloved guest". What distinguishes Shelley from the other Romantic poets in this poem is that he does not associate Night with Death and Sleep, both of which he rejects. Otherwise, this is very much in the tradition of the night-poem of Romantic literature. Shelley also shows an awareness of the existence of the mysterious and unexplored region of the unconscious during sleep. In a fragment he writes:

> I went into the desert of dim sleep –
> That world which, like an unknown wilderness,
> Bounds this with its recesses wide and deep. (p.633)

He also demonstrates a sort of belief in the reality – at least emotional reality – of the dream. In a poem entitled "Marianne's Dream", Dream tells a lady that he can reveal to the sleeper "the secrets of the air" and the things that "are lost in the glare of day". The poem ends with a description of the lady who woke up after seeing a series of fantastic visions:

> As she arose, while from the veil
>   of her dark eyes the dream did creep,
> And she walked about as one who knew
> That sleep has sights as clear and true
> As any waking can view. (536-539)

James Thomson, an ardent admirer of Shelley who, taking the latter's middle name as his pseudonym, together with an anagram of the German poet Novalis, called himself Bysshe Vanolis or "B.V.", followed this tradition of the night-poem when he wrote *The City of Dreadful Night.* Here night and death are closely associated together, as is clear from the beginning of the poem:

> The City is of Night; perchance of Death,
>   But certainly of Night; for never there
> Can come the lucid morning's fragrant breath.[19]

The "City of Night" is a metaphor for the desolate and hopeless state of the mind. It is a city where "The sun has never visited", since "it dissolveth in the daylight fair". The city dissolves, the poet continues, "like a dream of night", but if it is a recurrent dream which visits one every night, then it becomes as real to one as any material reality:

> But when a dream night after night is brought
> Throughout a week, and such weeks few or many
> Recur each year for several years, can any
>   Discern that dream from real life in aught? (p.3)

Here again the division between dream and reality becomes blurred and the inner reality outweighs the external one.

Novalis, with whom Thomson somewhat wrongly identified himself, is the author of the famous night-poem, *Hymns to the Night (Hymnen an die Nacht).* In a sense, the themes of night and dreams were more central to the works of German Romantics than to their English counterparts, and Novalis' *Hymns* is one of the representative works in this line. There night, love, sleep, death and dreams are all united in one praise, and as in the case of Shelley, we see the reversal of the conventional evaluation, the morning and the daylight being given only negative values:

> Must ever the morning return?
> Endeth never the thraldom of Earth?
> Unhallowed affairs swallow up
> The heavenly coming of Night?[20]

The morning is an unwelcome and "unloved guest", while the coming of night is longed for as "heavenly". Whereas the Light, or the day, is given only a limited time, infinity, timelessness and holiness are associated with night and sleep:

> Timeless the rule of the Night;
> Without end the duration of sleep.
> Holy Sleep!

For Novalis sleep is holy, because it brings the key to heaven, and is "A silent messenger / Of infinite mysteries". When the poet was in deep grief, moaning the death of his beloved, sleep, which he calls "Inspiration of the Night, Slumber of Heaven", comes over him and brings new life to his spirit: "All that lay round me softly arose, above it hovered my unbound, newly-born spirit" (p.29). And in this sleep he encounters his deceased love – "the glorified features of the Beloved", which "was the first dream" he saw of her.

The dream "passed, but its image remained – the eternal, unshakeable belief in the heaven of Night, and its sun, the Beloved." The night became for him a "New World", "new land", and the "fruitful womb of revelations". In one of his writings, Novalis expresses his faith in dreams in a more direct and explicit manner:

It seems to me that the dream is a barrier against the regularity and commonness of life, a free diversion of the enchained imagination, where it tumbles together all images of life and interrupts the constant seriousness of the adult with a happy children's game. Surely we would age more quickly without dreams, and thus we may consider the dream, if not as given us directly from above, yet as a divine inspiration, a friendly companion on the pilgrimage to the holy grail.[21]

Eugene Jolas, the translator of the above passage, states in his article, "Homage to Novalis":

In his poetry and prose he expressed the miraculous, explored the mysteries of the night and the chthonian, and gave voice to his longing for death, which he felt would be a creative act and objectivation of his desires.

It is not to be wondered at that the dream became a factor of the utmost importance in his life ... In the dream he found the very roots of poetry. He worshipped all the manifestations of the pre-logical and the mythic. In his *Heinrich von Ofterdingen*, the dream of the blue flower became the symbol of his longings, and the quintessence of an entire state of mind. (p.72)

From this attitude comes his famous equation, *"Die Welt wird Traum, der Traum wird Welt"*,[22] (The world becomes the dream, the dream becomes the world). For the same reason he regarded *"Märchen"*, or the fairy tale, as "the canon of poetry", for *"Märchen"* and the dream were virtually synonymous for Novalis. *"Märchen"* is the expression in literary form of the dream, and is in his own words "really like a dream – without inner connection – an ensemble of wonderous things and events", wherein we find "the true anarchy of nature. Abstract world, dream-world ... "[23]

Ralph Tymms, in his study of German Romantic literature, comments on what the dream and *"Märchen"* meant for Novalis:

> Because the ideal can only be achieved in the dream or *Märchen*, the magus therefore enters into his ideal kingdom by means of the dream or *Märchen*; consequently they both play an important part in the works of the aspirant magus Novalis himself. (p.154)

It is not surprising to hear the same poet express his deepest interest in the mysteries of man's mind:

> We dream of voyages through the universe; but is not the universe in us? We do not know the depths of our spirits. Into the interior leads the mysterious road. In us or nowhere is the infinite with its world, past and future. The exterior world is a shadow world ...[24]

The question he puts at the beginning of this passage is the one we still put to ourselves now when the dream of "voyages through the universe" are partially fulfilled, and when he says, "The exterior world is the shadow world", he is expressing one of the essential creeds of the Romantic movement.

Whereas in England Romanticism was predominantly a movement in the field of literature, on the Continent it extended to many other fields, such as the visual arts, music, philosophy and religion. Again, unlike England where the Romantic movement was, even in the field of literature, limited mainly to poetry, and novels remained largely unconcerned with it, in Germany and France the writers of fiction also occupied a central place in the Romantic movement.[25] Also, the same writer produced works in several different fields. Novalis, for example, was a poet, but he also wrote several novels in which he put his literary creeds into practice. Another example is E. T. A. Hoffmann, a representative writer of late German Romanticism, on whom Novalis had a great influence. He was at the same time a composer, music critic and novelist. As a composer, he composed several operas as well as chamber and orchestral music. For him music was, to use René Wellek's words, "not only an emotional release and exaltation but a secret language of the beyond, a door to the supernatural and divine."[26] He had, however, another "door to the supernatural and divine" which was "the creative imagination of the poet and the unconscious workings of our dream life" (Wellek), that is to say, the world of fiction in which the dream played, as in the case of Novalis, a very significicant role. Hoffmann is remembered above all as the author of *The Tales*, and as such, occupies an important place in the history of world literature.

In these *Tales*, he made use of the device of *Märchen*, advocated by Novalis, to the full, moving freely between the world of reality and that of fantasy and dreams. In them, the most fantastic and uncanny, the weird and even grotesque co-exist, without clear division or distinction, with the banal and prosaic everyday reality. For example, in *The Golden Flower Pot*, the main character, the student Anselmus, lives in the two worlds at the same time. The one is the world of reality, that of the burghers of nineteenth century Dresden, where he is a poor, clumsy young man prone to all sorts of blunders; the other is a dream world where the most incredible happenings can take place, and in which the student is loved by a gold-green snake, Serpentina, who represents ideal love and true happiness. After experiencing several times this second world, which is also described as "the new life" or "a higher world", the student Anselmus says to himself: "... I now see and feel clearly that all these foreign shapes of a distant wonderous world, which I never saw before except in peculiarly remarkable dreams, have now come into my waking life ... "[27] In short, his daily life is invaded by the dream life, which causes all kinds of weird events as well as humorous confusions. He finally chooses betwen the two, which presents itself as a choice between Veronica, the Conrector's daughter, with the prospect of worldly success, and Serpentina, the symbol of the world of the ideal, who consequently signifies devotion to the ideal. He chooses the latter, moves into the ideal world which is called Atlantis, and becomes a poet. Atlantis is a kind of Utopia, which exists not in the physical sense but only in the imagination of the poet. What this ideal world means we may partially understand from the statement

Anselmus makes towards the end of the story: "Serpentina! Belief in you, love of you, has unfolded to my soul the inmost spirit of nature! You have brought me the lily which sprang from gold, from the primaeval force of the world ... this lily is knowledge of the sacred harmony of all beings; and in this I live in highest blessedness for ever more. Yes I, thrice happy, have perceived what was highest ..." (p.69). The narrator of the story describes him as "happy Anselmus, who has cast away the burden of everyday life ... and now lives in rapture and joy ... in Atlantis" (p.69). Clearly, the dream world, Atlantis, is invested by the author with higher values than everyday life, as indeed it is sometimes called, "a higher world". Tymms, contrasting later German Romantics with Novalis, comments:

> Later romantics ... often kept in touch with reality, even when they soared off into their escapist world of fancy from the tedious restrictions of everyday existence. To them the *Märchen* afforded precisely the opportunities for bringing out the effective contrast between the real and the ideal which Novalis failed to show.[28]

Hoffmann is said to have made "much of this contrast, from a number of aspects".

The world of reality and that of fantasy or dream in Hoffmann, however, merge without incongruity or discordance. The reader moves from one to the other smoothly, sometimes even without noticing it. For that matter, the characters themselves are often unaware of the change. In the foreword to another story, *A New Year's Adventure*, the author himself points out this fact, saying that the main character of the story

> has apparently not separated the events of his inner life from those of the outside world; in fact we cannot determine where one ends and the other begins. But even if you cannot see this boundary very clearly, dear reader, the *Geisterseher* may beckon you to his side, and before you are even aware of it, you will be in a strange magical realm where figures of fantasy step right into your own life ...[29]

This merging of the two worlds is done very often by skilful use of some of the characteristics of dreams and nightmares. For example, an innocent visit to a house turns out to be a nightmarish experience when a door-knocker suddenly changes into the growling face of the Apple-woman whose stall the hero formerly overturned and who, moreover, proves to be a witch, or when the characters gathered in a drawing room come to a sudden realization that the messenger they just saw off was actually a parrot. Invasion of the fantasy world into ordinary everyday life is done through such abrupt but apparently smooth changes of shapes and characters as those with which we are all familiar in our dreams. In many of his stories he makes use of this technique to intermingle fantasy with reality. Besides, he uses dreams as the expression of subconscious, or unconscious fears and desires which are very often fantastic, but at the same time relevant and convincing in relation to the main theme of the story. This may be the reason why, in spite of all the fantastic settings, his stories are psychologically credible and acceptable to the reader. Tymms regards Hoffmann as "without doubt the best of the romantic story-tellers", "the one who brought to its culminating point of excellence the art of *Kunstmärchen*", and considers him to be a precursor of modern fiction "who points forward, for all the deceptive artlessness of his fairy-tale technique, to the concern of later psychological realists with the substrata of consciousness as the origin of motives for action."[30] Leonard J. Kent and Elizabeth C. Knight, the co-editors of his *Selected Writings,* also express a similar appreciation:

...the whole literary world of psychological fiction owes Hoffmann an inestimable debt. Hoffmann shifted the scene of man's incessant conflict from the external world to the mind ... There is no question but that Hoffmann anticipated much of what psychologists were later to uncover. Hoffmann seems to have been aware of organic and functional psychoses long before modern science defined them and twentieth century literature exploited them ...[31]

Although in England he was neither popular nor very highly regarded, his influence in France, Russia and the United States seems to have been considerable. Among those who felt it most strongly were Baudelaire, Saint-Beuve, Nerval, Pushkin, Turgenev, Gogol, Dostoevsky, Hawthorne, Irving and Poe.[32]

Gérard de Nerval was a French Romantic poet and novelist, on whom the influence of Hoffmann and other German Romantics (he was also a translator of many German authors) was particularly notable. For him too dreams and the life of imagination had a tremendous signifance in his work as well as in his actual life. In almost all his works, eg, *Les Filles de Feu, Les Chimères* and *Aurélia*, dreams and fantasies play important roles, and as in the case of Hoffmann's tales the boundary between reality and illusion, the real and the imaginary, sometimes becomes indistinguishable.

At the outset of his major prose work, *Aurèlia,* the author explains that, in writing this confessional novel, he is following the examples of *The Golden Ass* of Apuleius and Dante's *Divine Comedy*, which he regards as "two poetic models" of the studies of the human soul. "I am going to try", he says, "to describe the impressions of a long illness which took place entirely within the mysteries of my soul."[33] What follows is a series of detailed accounts of his dreams as well as the visions and hallucinations he experienced during the attacks of insanity, interspersed with the descriptions of his normal, waking life. The book has a subtitle, *The Dream and Life (Le Rêve et la vie)* and from this alone it is not difficult to see how important Nerval considered the dream to be in relation to life. The waking life and the dreams represent the two opposing worlds of the visible and the invisible, the latter being no less real or true than the former. The book begins:

> Our dreams are a second life. I have never been able to penetrate without a shudder those ivory or horned gates which separate us from the invisible world. (p.115)

This invisible world, the dream life, is also described by him as the "spirit world" that "opens before us" after the short transitory period during which everything is vague and hazy. The book is in a sense a record of Nerval's travel between the daily world and the spirit world, and the dreams and visions were the essential means of transportation for this trip.

In fact, at several points in the narrative, he repeatedly expresses his faith in the validity of dreams as a means of communication with the spirit world:

> With my idea that dreams opened up to man intercourse with the spirit world, I hoped ... (p.154)

Since he believed, as most Romantics did, so firmly in the power of imagination that anything which springs from imagination, including legends, myths and dreams, he believed to be true:

> I do not think that human imagination has invented anything which is not true either in this world or in others ... (p.139)

When he is at a loss how to think of a certain situation, he even tries to solve it through dreams: "Then I thought I would appeal to sleep" (p.138). Thus it is not surprising that he should find profound revelations and messages in dreams. The focal point of the book is Aurélia (or the actress Jenny Colon) whom the narrator-Nerval loved for years, both in life and after death, with almost religious intensity and devotion. As the thought of her is his main preoccupation day and night, we naturally find many of his dreams associated with her. At one time he sees a premonitory dream of her death, in which he sees a lady vanishing into the sky and hear the voices crying, "The universe is in darkness". He himself cries "Don't leave me! ... For with you Nature itself dies." He finds himself in a graveyard which in the same dream was formerly a beautiful garden, with a bust of a woman in his hand in which he recognized Aurélia's features. Only much later, he says, he discovered the meaning of his dream which perplexed him deeply: that "Aurélia was dead" (p.131). In another of his dreams, he sees "a marvellous vision" of a goddess who says to him:

> I am the same as Mary, the same as your mother, the same being also whom you have always loved under every form. At each of your ordeals I have dropped one of the masks with which I hide my features and soon you shall see me as I really am. (p.162)

Obviously it is an idealized image of Aurélia who, to use Jung's term, must have represented the Anima, or the archetypal woman for the narrator, although as the phrase "the same as your mother", indicates, it could also be interpreted in Freudian terms as some critics actually do with the whole of this work.[34] After a long period of inner torment, longing for forgiveness by God and by his deceased lover for his "life spent in foolish dissipation" and the wrongs he believes he has done to her during her life and after death, he finally sees "a very sweet dream":

> I saw the woman I loved, radiant and transfigured.
> Heaven opened in all its glory and I read the word
> *forgiveness* written in Christ's blood.
> A star shone suddenly and revealed the spirit of the
> world of worlds to me. (p.174)

He is now convinced that he is forgiven; he was given this reassurance through the dream.

His dreams also reveal to him the secret of the immortality of the soul. In a dream he finds himself in an ancestral house, where he meets his grandfather's soul typically in the shape of a bird on the clock, which talks like a human being. It later changes its shape into an old man and takes the dreamer to meet his dead relations, with whom he could communicate without words. He exclaims to his dead uncle: "Then it's true ... that we are immortal and retain here the replicas of the world we once inhabited. What happiness to think that everything we loved will always exist around us!" (p.125) Then he sees men and women of all races and nationalities – "all appeared to me distinctly at the same time, as if my faculties of observation had been multiplied – and yet not muddled – by a phenome-non of space comparable to that of time, whereby a century of action is concentrated in a minute of dream (pp.125-126). And in this conglomer-ation of people he perceived a sensation of universal harmony which he finds impossible to communicate in words. His guide then is transformed into a young man, who takes him to an unknown city, where the layers of the buildings of the successive centuries coexist, and finally leads him to the dwelling place of the pure and uncorrupted primitive race. He is so charmed by them, feels such love towards them that he is even reluctant to go back to the normal, waking life:

> I felt bitterly that I was only a wayfarer in this strange land that I loved, and I trembled at the thought that I had to return to life. (p.129)

This was a dream-vision he had during one of the attacks of his mental illness and indeed during these attacks he had such vivid and revealing visions and hallucinations and experienced such a heightened imaginative capacity that there even creeps in a note of regret when he talks of his return to normality, or restoration of reason at the beginning of the book:

> I do not know why I use the word "illness", for as far as my physical self was concerned, I never felt better. Sometimes I thought my strength and energy were doubled. I seemed to know everything, understand everything. My imagination gave me infinite delight. In recovering what men call reason, do I have to regret the loss of these joys? (p.115)

He therefore feels greatly irritated by people who attribute these dreams and visions to the deranged state of his mind, since for him they are the visions of truth, belief in which brings him immense happiness and joy:

> For thus the eternal doubt about the mortality of the soul, which troubles the greatest minds, had been solved for me. No more death, no more sadness, no more cares. My loved ones, relatives, and friends, had given convincing proof of their eternal existence, and I was only separated from them by the hours of the day. I waited for the hours of the night with a gentle melancholy. (pp.129-130)

Another dream confirms him in this belief. Later he talks about these inspirations or revelations he drew from his dreams, ie, forgiveness that was granted him and the assurance of immortal existence, in these terms:

> The consciousness that henceforth I was purified from the faults of my past life gave me infinite mental delight; the certainty of immortality and of co-existence of everyone I had loved was, as it were, a material reality for me now, and I blessed the fraternal soul who had brought me back from the depths of despair to the clear path of religion. (p.177)

There is no doubt that Nerval thought of dreams as the messages from the invisible, spiritual world – brought by "the fraternal soul" – and that what he saw in them acquired in his mind the solid existence of "material reality" itself. So firmly did be believe in the existence of the spiritual life in dreams that he even wished to control it deliberately – "Is it not possible to control this fascinating, dread chimera, to rule the spirits of the night which play with our reason? (p.176) – and unite the spiritual and the phyical, dream life and the conscious life into one:

> ... I have never felt any rest in sleep. For a few seconds I am numbed, then a new life begins, freed from the conditions of time and space, and doubtless similar to that state which awaits us after death. Who knows if there is not some link between these two existences and if it is not possible for the soul to unite them now? (*Ibid*)

Even if this was impossible, he continually thought that there was a link or bond between the two existences, though he was unable to give any rational explanation for it:

> ... in my belief terrestrial events were linked up with those of the invisible world. It is one of those strange relationships which I do not understand myself, and which is easier to hint at than to define ... (p.143)

And again:

> I seemed to understand that there was a bond between the external and internal worlds: that only inattention or spiritual confusion distorted the outward affinities between them ... (p.177)

This may be interpreted in terms of mysticism, or of modern psychology which finds reflections of the unconscious life in the words and deeds of a person's waking life. In any case, for Nerval, dreams and visions played an essential role in bridging the visible and the invisible, the material and the spiritual worlds. "The dream", René Wellek comments in relation to the German Romantics and Nerval, "as with so many poets of the time – from Novalis to Nerval – is the ivory gate through which we enter the realm of truth and beauty."[35]

It must have been due to his reverence towards and profound interest in dream life, which found ample expression in his writings, that the twentieth century Surrealists recognized in Nerval a precursor of their literary movement. Anna Balakian writes in her study of Surrealism:

> ... the Surrealists believed that the supernatural character of legendary material and illogical phenomena in dreams could be effectively utilized as the expression of surreal, of the plane of existence lying between the visible and the invisible.[36]

and continues that they found "the first definite examples of this tendency" in "many of the writings of Nerval", as well as in the tales of Achim
von Arnim, whose *Contes Bizarres* they read through the translation by
Théophile Gauthier, fils. Indeed, André Breton, in his *First Surrealist
Manifesto* (1924), discusses Nerval's use of the word "supernaturalism"
in one of his dedications and finds it almost identical to his artistic creed,
Surrealism. We shall examine this point in more detail later.

The Romantic poets and writers in England, Germany and France, all
showed serious and profound interest in dreams and the irrational, imaginative side of man, which was a marked contrast to the previous age and
to the conventional attitude towards them. They found in it the one-sidedness which was grossly lacking in the true knowledge and understanding
of the total existence and reality of man. Thus we find one of the great
German Romantic poets, Friedrich Hölderlin, making in his epistolary
novel, *Hyperion,* an unusual combination of poetry and philosophy,
claiming poetry to be the real source and spring of philosophical knowledge, in defiance of the common notion which regards them as antitheses,
philosophy being the product of the cold intellect and reason and poetry
that of imagination and feeling - one of the characters says as much: "What
has philosophy ... what has the cold sublimity of philosophical knowledge, to do with poetry?" However, for the titular hero, Hyperion, who
is very much the mouthpiece for the author, "Poetry ... is the beginning
and the end of philosophical knowledge. Like Minerva from the head of
Jupiter, philosophy springs from the poetry of an eternal, divine state of
being ... "[37], since

> "Mere intellect produces no philosophy, for philosophy is more than
> the limited perception of what is.

> "Mere reason produces no philosophy, for philosophy is more than
> the blind demand for ever greater progress in the combination and
> differentiation of some particular material. (p.95)

Hyperion, whom another character calls "Visionary!", criticizes German society for its predilection for reason and intellect and for encouraging people to be "judicious", "reasonable", "shrewd" and to "become a
conscious intelligence" before developing to the full the "capacity for
feeling", before "ingeniousness has achieved its beautiful end", indeed
even "before one is a child", "Pure intellect, pure reason" being "always
the kings of the North" (p.94). For Hyperion-Hölderlin, however, "the
oneness of the whole man" is of supreme importance, and "Reason
without beauty of spirit and heart is like an overseer whom the master of
the house has set over the servants ... " (p.95). He also believes that "pure

intellect has never produced anything intelligent, nor pure reason anything reasonable" (p.94). Childhood, upon which a nostalgic glance is repeatedly cast, is regarded by Hölderlin, as by Blake, Wordsworth and other Romantics, as an ideal state, or the state of grace in which this wholeness of existence was possible:

> When I was still a child and in quietude, knowing nothing of all that is about us, was I not then more than now I am, after all my trouble of heart and all my thinking and struggling?

> Yes, divine is the being of the child, so long as it has not been dipped in the chameleon colours of men.

> The child is wholly what it is and that is why it is so beautiful. (p.24)

It is a state in which the crippling division between thinking and feeling, between the mind and the heart has not yet taken place. For a person who has not fully experienced this state of wholeness it is difficult to achieve the totality of existence later in life: "he who was not once a perfect child is hard put to it to become a perfect man" (p.90). However, Hölderlin's German society did not allow its people full development of their childhood. He calls his compatriots who, in his view, are mainly motivated by material expediency: "these all-calculating barbarians" who pursue even what is usually held sacred "as one pursues any trade, and cannot do otherwise; for where a human being is once conditioned to look, there it serves its ends, seeks its profit, it dreams no more ... " (p.165). In his condemnation of the materialism of bourgeoisie and the sterility of their imaginative life Hölderlin was a typical Romantic, and so was he in his faith in dreams, or the power of imagination. To say, "it dreams no more" amounts to the final damnation for a poet who declares:

> Oh, a man is a god when he dreams, a beggar when he thinks; and when inspiration is gone, he stands, like a worthless son whom his father has driven out of the house, and stares at the miserable pence that pity has given him for the road. (p.23)

The French literary critic, and advocate of the Romantic movement, Albert Begin, writes on the significance that the dream had for the Romantics:

> ... for him [the Romantic poet] the dream is vaster than the waking state, the world of the Conscious is a restricted world as compared with that of the Unconscious.[38]

> ...they [the Romantics] usually agree in regarding the generative force of dreams as the creative imagination which, for many of

them, is identified with the inner or universal sense, a vestige of our primal faculties. (p.210)

The Romantics reversed many orthodox and conventional values, especially those of reason and imagination, or the rational and the irrational. Begin summarizes the basic attitude of the Romantics as follows:

> For those who set up as sane and normal a state of consciousness merely sufficient to ensure decent social conduct, the Romantic has no esteem; that which is morbid, in his eyes, is not the influence of the subconscious, but the overweening consciousness of modern times, which aspires to a monopoly of our personality at the expense of all our other faculties, all our other contacts with the Real, our metaphysical perplexities and spontaneous acts, our autonomous poetic dreams. To live only in the consciousness is to simplify oneself to the point of insanity, and to reduce existence to a series of never-comprehended acts ...True understanding brings entire being into play, and calls on interests and faculties of apprehension that are infinitely more subtle and mysterious than those of intellect. (p.213)

The attitude against which the Romantics rebelled prevailed throughout the nineteenth century, until towards its end when, as we have seen, there were growing signs of change in diverse cultural and artistic fields. However, until the mid-century it had grown, if anything, more predominant throughout Europe with the spread of industrialization and the establishment of the middle class with its faith in material and technological progress, accompanied by the proportionate progress of man as a rational, "civilized" being. In fact, Hölderlin's strictures on the Germans were applicable to most European societies where the above phenomena took place, not least to England, the birthplace of the industrial revolution.

Meanwhile, the Romantic movement declined, itself in turn reacted against by later literary movements such as Naturalism and Realism. Modernism itself, in spite of its inseparable link with Romanticism, is generally considered to have reacted to its certain aspects. The essential spirit of Romanticism, however, did not die out with the decline of the movement, and found successors in the latter half of the century in such individual thinkers and writers as Nietzsche, Dostoevsky and the poets of French Symbolism, especially its central figure, Baudelaire, all of whom, as far as their essential spirits are concerned, may be regarded as the true heirs of Romanticism, and with their immense influence on modern thought and literature were, so to speak, the intermediaries between the Romantics and the Modernists.

The Romantic faith in the supremacy of imagination was taken over by Baudelaire,[39] who describes it as this "Mysterious faculty", "this queen of all faculties – *Mysterieuse faculté que cette reine des facultés!*"[40] Like Coleridge, he distinguishes it from fancy, in his words, *"la fantasie"*, as well as mere sensibility, endowing it with almost divine quality that is able to perceive the deeper secrets, the hidden relatedness, *"les correspondances"*, between things, which is beyond philosophy: *L'imagination n'est pas la fantasie; elle n'est pas non plus la sensibilité ... L'imagination est une faculté quasi divine qui perçoit tout d'abord, en dehors des methodes philosophiques, les rapports intimes et secrets des choses, les correspondances, et les analogies"* (p.63). He shares with Coleridge, Hölderlin and others the belief that imagination can, as the Bard put it, "apprehend / More than cool reason ever comprehends." (*A Midsummer Night's Dream*, V, I, 5-6). Baudelaire's idea of "correspondances", that the external world conceals behind it deeper reality, that there is secret interrelatedness between things, and that even familiar objects are symbols for some hidden meanings or ideals – hence Nature is a sacred temple which we reach through the "forests of symbols"[41] – is important not only because of its initiating role in the French Symbolist movement but also because of its far-reaching effect, direct or indirect, on literature outside France, English literature being no exception. It is common knowledge that it greatly influenced the two representative figures of the English Modernist poetry, Yeats and T. S. Eliot, in the latter's case especially through the later Symbolist, Laforgue. Its influence on modern, or rather Modernist, English fiction was as great, especially on Joyce, who derived his inspiration for technical innovation mainly from French literature and whose idea of "epiphany" is essentially the same as Baudelaire's "correspondances". Likewise undeniable is its influence, above all through Proust, on another Modernist writer, Virginia Woolf. It also anticipates Freud's theory of dreams that behind the "manifest content" of a dream lies its "latent content", the dream being the symbolical expression of hidden meanings.

The spirit of Romanticism also visibly marks the works of Dostoevsky, who explored the mystery of human nature to the full, often delving into the darker, irrational region of the minds of his characters, and thus revealing his remarkable knowledge of and insight into the psychology of man, unusual among the novelists of his period which was dominated by external realism. The influence of the fantastic tales of Hoffmann, together with that of the Gothic romance,[42] is particularly conspicuous, as is most clearly shown in one of his earliest works, *The Double* (1846), but also in such later masterpieces as *Crime and Punishment* (1866) and

The Brothers Karamazov (1879). Charles E. Passage, who made an exhaustive study of Hoffmann's influence on Dostoevsky throughout the latter's literary career, observes that "Dostoevski's Hoffmannism was truly no slight episode. Rather it was a deep and far-pervading force."[43] Dostoevsky himself claimed that he read the "whole of Hoffmann in Russian and German"[44] and made frequent references, in his works, letters and apparently in his conversation as well, to the German Romanticist whom he regarded as a great poet. *The Double*, as the title itself suggests, deals specifically with the theme of the "double" or one's alter ego. Though a favourite theme among many German Romantic writers, it was Hoffmann who most extensively exploited and developed it in such works as *Signor Formica* and *The Devil's Elixirs*, and popularized it throughout Europe. Deriving originally from the *"Doppelgänger"* of German folktale, it was given new significance by Hoffmann, who transferred it from the realm of the supernatural to the inner world of man. It was this tradition of Hoffmann that Dostoevsky followed, the full significance of which he clearly recognized. [In fact, he was greatly censured by critics for deserting the Gogolian realism of his first work, *Poor Folk*, which had won him instant and universal acclaim, and reverting to the outmoded Hoffmannesque fantasy in his second novel (see pp.2 and 12).]

Actually, the concept of the double, or the existence of one's *alter ego*, renders itself quite readily, or perhaps it seems so after Freud and Jung, to psychological interpretation as, apart from the split personalities of schizophrenia, the co-existence of one's conscious self on the one hand and the unconscious, often repressed self on the other. In literary terms, it may be presented as two sides of one character, as in the case of Stevenson's Gothic tale, *Dr. Jekyll and Mr. Hyde* (the names themselves are significant), or as two separate characters, though the inferior or undesirable (or at least for the main character), and sometimes devilish character in such a fiction often never leaves but positively haunts and torments the other, supposedly better character, as in the case of Dostoevsky's doubles, Mr. Golyadkin and "another Mr. Golyadkin", who is "a completely different one, and yet at the same time very like the other", who has the same name, looks exactly the same but behaves completely differently.[45]

Later, Dostoevsky makes more subtle and complex use of these devices, eg, in *The Brothers Karamazov*, in which Ivan, the Hamlet-like intellectual, has two doubles, one a separate character, Smerdyakov, and the other the hidden side of himself which reveals itself in the form of the Devil in his hallucinations or nightmares, though naturally these two have a great deal in common. In more sophisticated versions, they may be

completely independent and may even never meet, as Clarissa and Septimus Warren Smith in Virginia Woolf's *Mrs. Dalloway*, who as we know
from her Preface to the Modern Library edition of the novel were originally conceived as doubles by the author. The motif of the doubles is an
important one for Dostoevsky, who repeatedly used it in his later major
works in such pairs as Myshkin-Rogozin (*The Idiot*), or the already
mentioned Ivan-Smerdyakov; Ivan-the Devil, etc. He must have found
in it a convenient means to explore the complexity of the human mind. It
may not be idle to conjecture that Virginia Woolf, a great admirer of
Russian novelists and especially of Dostoevsky – through many of her
critical writings it is clear that she regarded Proust and Dostoevsky as
models in the art of fiction – was inspired by the latter's example when
she created her doubles in *Mrs. Dalloway*,[46] though the experience of her
own mental illness, as is often pointed out, may also have played a part
in it. In any case, being obsessed herself with the mystery and complexity
of the human mind, and especially with the idea of the multiplicity of the
self, she must have found this aspect of Dostoevsky's novels most com-
pelling.

Later, in his significantly titled *Notes from the Underground* (1864),[47]
Dostoevsky presents through a narrator, who claims to have buried
himself "in a cellar for 40 years out of spite" (p.22) for himself and
mankind, an impassioned argument for the forcefulness of this shadow
side, the often unconscious, irrational drives represented by the double,
in direct contradiction to the simplistic rationalism and utilitarian belief
in scientific and social progress of his time, which tried to ignore it.[48] To
his imaginary readers, who are convinced that common sense and science
will eventually enable men, imperfect as they still are, to acquire the habit
of "acting as reason and science direct," that science will teach men that
they "are no more than a sort of piano keyboard or barrel-organ cylinder"
without "will or fancy", that with the discovery of the laws of nature all
human actions can "be worked out by those laws, mathematically, like a
table of logarithms" and finally that "a new political economy ... also
calculated with mathematical accuracy" will solve all problems "in the
twinkling of an eye, simply because all possible answers to them will have
been supplied" (pp.32-33), to the believers in those "progressive" ideas,
the "underground" man expounds what he views to be unalterable truths
about human nature: "a man, whoever he is," he maintains, "always and
everywhere likes to act as he chooses, and not at all according to the
dictates of reason and self-interest; it is indeed possible, and sometimes
positively imperative (in my view), to act directly contrary to one's own
interests."[49] "One's own free and unfettered volition" which causes this,

he continues, "is the one best and greatest good, which is never taken into consideration because it will not fit into any classification, and omission of which always sends all systems and theories to the devil." He then asks: "Where did all the sages get the idea that a man's desires must be normal and virtuous? Why did they imagine that he must inevitably will what is reasonable and profitable?" (pp.33-34) Further explaining the nature of what he calls "volition", he states:

> You see, gentlemen, reason is a good thing, that can't be disputed, but reason is only reason and satisfies only man's intellectual faculties, while volition is a manifestation of the whole of life, I mean the whole of human life including both reason and specula- tion. And although in this manifestation life frequently turns out to be rubbishy, all the same it is life and not merely the extraction of a square root. After all, I, for example, quite naturally want to live so as to fulfil my whole capacity for living, and not so as to satisfy simply and solely my intellectual capacity which is only one-twen- tieth of my whole capacity for living. What does reason know? Reason knows what it has succeeded in finding out (and perhaps there are some things it will never find out ...) but man's nature acts as one whole, with everything that is in it, conscious or unconscious, and although it is nonsensical, yet it lives. (pp.35-36)

Along with this wish to grasp human existence in its entirety, Dostoev- sky shared with the Romantics a belief in the creativity of dreams, and the perception of the deep-lying reality in our fantasy life. In *The Brothers Karamazov*, the Devil, Ivan Karamazov's *alter ego* who appears to him in his dream, maintains:

> Listen, in dreams and especially in nightmares, from indigestion or anything, a man sees sometimes such artistic visions, such complex real actuality, such events, even a whole world of events, woven into such a plot, with such unexpected details from the most exalted matters to the last button on a cuff ... The subject is a complete enigma. A statesman confessed to me, indeed, that all his best ideas came to him when he was asleep. Well, that's how it is now, though I am your hallucination, yet just as in a nightmare, I say original things which had not entered your head before. So I don't repeat your ideas, yet I am only your nightmare, nothing more.[50]

True, it is spoken by a fictional character (and the Devil at that), and obviously we cannot easily identify what he says with the author's own views, but when Dostoevsky writes: "I have my own idea about art, and it is this: What most people regard as fantastic and lacking in universality,

I hold to be the inmost essence of truth. Arid observation of everyday trivialities I have long ceased to regard as realism – it is quite the reverse,"[51] and when we note in his works the pervasive nightmarish and dreamlike atmosphere, together with the frequent use of the actual dreams themselves, out of which emerges the author's understanding of the secrets of the inner man, it does not seem to be altogether unreasonable to assume that the above passage reflects to a considerable degree Dostoevsky's own view of fantasy and dreams.

In his insight into the depth and the mystery of the human soul, he may be compared with Shakespeare, as indeed it is Shakespeare who often comes to our mind while reading works by the Russian novelist. Dostoevsky himself was quite aware of the enormous significance in this sense of Shakespeare whom he apparently considered "colossal" and "eternal",[52] of how the dramatist had succeeded in capturing the innermost secrets of human reality. Shakespeare's, he declares, echoing his own words on "realism", "is not a simple reproduction of everyday life":

> The whole of reality is not exhausted by everyday life, for a great [*sic* – crossed out by Dostoevsky] huge part of it is present in it in the form of a still latent, unexpressed, future word. From time to time there appear prophets who divine and express this integral word. Shakespeare is a prophet, sent by God, so as to reveal to us secrets about man, about the human soul. (p.375)

Would it be too much to make a similar claim for Dostoevsky himself?[53] Later, when Nietzsche made the "belated discovery" of Dostoevsky, he was to remark that here "was the only psychologist from whom he could learn anything."[54] In any case, in his awareness of and concern with the shadow side in man and the consequent rejection of the mechanical positivism and optimistic progressionism of the nineteenth century, Dostoevsky may be regarded as the true precursor of the Modernist movement.

Although Nietzsche's role in shaping the modern spirit is generally acknowledged to be great and his concept of the Apollonian and Dionysian principles in art are well known, his influence, so far as English writers are concerned, may not be immediately appreciable, except in such an obvious case as Bernard Shaw, and, to a certain extent, D. H. Lawrence. Yet even here the sense of his significance increases considerably when we think of the debt Freud and Jung owed to the philosopher and the influence exerted, directly or indirectly, by these psychologists, on modern writers.

Not only is Nietzsche the writer whom both Freud and Jung most often quoted, along with Shakespeare, Goethe or Schiller, to illustrate their theories, but it even seems that sometimes he may actually have inspired the formation, or germination of some of them. Ernest Jones wonders, for example, how far Freud was influenced by "Nietzsche's doctrine of the 'eternal recurrence of the same'," when he developed his purely psychological notion of "repetition-compulsion" based on his clinical observation, into the metapsychological theory of the Death Instinct.[55] In calling the unconscious, instinctual part of the mind "*Es*" (translated in the English edition as "Id"), Freud was actually using, as he himself admits, Nietzsche's terminology,[56] and to a certain extent his concept as well. For Freud acknowledges at the same time his debt to the German physician, Georg Groddeck, in consolidating his idea of the instinctual drives, but interestingly enough, Groddeck in his turn admits the influence of Nietzsche in forming his notion of the "unknown and uncontrollable forces" *by which we are "lived"* [my italics].[57]

In *Beyond Good and Evil*, Nietzsche, while discussing the problem of "instinct and reason", declares that Déscartes, whom he calls "the father of rationalism", was "superficial," since he "recognized only the authority of reason" when "reason is only a tool."[58] Earlier in the book, without mentioning Déscartes, he tries to demolish the basic assumption of the Cartesian system of cognition, and thus prepares the ground for the above pronouncement. For Déscartes, the "I" that questions and thinks about every phenomenon was the last foothold – "the thing in itself" that cannot be doubted – for knowing the reality of the world. Now, Nietzsche submits the French philosopher's "*Cogito* – I think" to a closer scrutiny and categorically rejects the idea that "I", as the "immediate certainty" or "the thing in itself" (S.16), can be the cause for the action "think", on the ground that "a thought comes when 'it' wishes, and not when 'I' wish (*ein Gedanke kommt, wenn 'er' will, und nicht wenn 'ich' will*")."[59] Thus "it is a perversion of the facts of the case," he maintains, "to say that the subject 'I' is the condition of the predicate 'think'. In actual fact it is 'it' that thinks (*"Es denkt"*) and not 'I', so that it is more accurate to say: 'think' the condition, and 'I' the conditioned."[60] Then Nietzsche denies an easy equation between "this 'it' (*dies "es"*)" and "that famous old 'I' (*jenes alte beruhmte "ich"*)", calling it "to put it mildly, only a supposition, an assertion,and assuredly not an 'immediate certainty'".[61] Seen in this way, the "I" ceases to be the final, "absolute knowledge" in Déscartes' sense, and becomes "only a synethesis which has been *made* by thinking itself" (S.54).

It is only one step from here to Freud's theory of the structure of the psyche, which regards the self as a "synthesis" of multiple psychological functions, which he calls Id (It=*Es*), *Ego* (I=*ich*) and Super-*Ego* (Super-I=*Über-Ich*). What Freud did was to analyse the content of Nietzsche's "synethesis" and set up an hypothesis about its components. If we compare the terminologies which Freud used for them, as well as the title of his book which dealt specifically with this subject, *Das Ich und der Es* (*The Ego and the Id*), with Nietzsche's argument about the statement, "I think," the close link between the philosopher and the psychologist becomes aparent. Nietzsche certainly saw through the falsity of the general assmption of his contemporaries when he said: "We all feign to ourselves that we are simpler than we are" (S.108).

We also remember that when Freud postulated his theory of regression in dreams he implied that it was a vindication of "Nietzsche's assertion that in dreams 'some primaeval relic of humanity is at work which we can now scarcely reach any longer by a direct path,'" claiming at the same time that "the analysis of dreams will lead us to a knowledge of man's archaic heritage, of what is pyschically innate in him."[63] However, as we have already seen, Freud increasingly put more emphasis on the individual's personal childhood than the "phylogenetic" one, except in his later, more speculative theories, and this line of study was taken up chiefly by Jung.[64] In fact, though he tells us that it originated in his own dream (p.182), it even seems that Jung's theory of the collective unconscious was developed partly under the influence of Nietzsche, of whom he seems to have been an avid, though not entirely uncritical, reader. In his *Psychology of the Unconscious* (1912), the book in which Jung first expounded his own idea of the unconscious, thus making the final, irrevocable break with Freud, he quotes extensively from Nietzsche's *Human, All-Too-Human* (Part I, S.12), even a part of which shows how close it is to Jung's idea of the collective unconscious or the racial memory:

> In our sleep and in our dreams we pass thorugh the whole thought of earlier humanity. I mean, in the same way that man reasons in his dreams, he reasoned when in the waking state many thousands of years ago. The first *causa* which occurred to his mind in reference to anything that needed explanation, satisfied him and passed for truth. In the dream this atavistic relic of humanity manifests its existence within us, for it is the foundation upon which the higher rational faculty developed, and which is still developing in every individual. The dream carries us back into earlier states of human culture, and affords us a means of understanding it better.[65]

Then one of the aphorisms in the same book bears an uncanny resemblance to Jung's theory of the archetype, Anima: "INHERITED FROM THE MOTHER – Everyone bears within him an image of woman, inherited from his mother: it determines his attitude towards women as a whole, whether to honour, despise, or remain generally indifferent to them."[66]

The question of influence, however, is a notoriously complex and elusive one,[67] and here it may be enough to point out the facts that Nietzsche in many of his writings foreshadowed the psychological theories which Freud and Jung developed later, and that both psychologists were well acquainted with his work or ideas, which they used in various forms in their writings.

As may be apparent from the quotations made by Freud and Jung in relation to their theories of dreams, Nietzsche clearly recognized the signifiance of this unconscious activity in its various aspects as few men had ever done before him. He knew that dreams can reveal the hidden thoughts of which even the dreamer himself is not aware: "Signs from Dreams - What one does not know and feel accurately in waking hours... is revealed completely and unambiguously by dreams."[68]

Reminiscent of Nerval, he attached an equal importance to both dream and waking life, and considered that dreams not only reflect our repressed wishes but can positively affect our conscious life:

> *Quidquid luce fuit, tenebris agit:* but also contrariwise. What we experience in dreams, provided we experience it often, pertains at least just as much to the general belongings of our soul as anything "actually" experienced; by virtue thereof we are richer or poorer, we have a requirement more or less, and finally, in broad daylight, and even in the brightest moments of our waking life, we are ruled to some extent by the nature of our dreams.[69]

His concept of the Apollonian and the Dionysian in art, for that matter, was based on his belief in creativity of dreams and the forcefulness of the instinctual drives in man, both of which he shared with Dostoevsky. He describes the Apollonian, which he associates with plastic art and poetry, as "dreamland" or the "beauteous appearance of the dream-worlds," and while explaining "the mysteries of poetic inspiration," quotes a stanza from *The Mastersingers:*

> My friend, just this is poet's task:
> His dreams to read and unmask.
> Trust me, illusion's truths thrice sealed
> In dream to man will be revealed.
> All verse-craft and poetisation
> Is but soothdream interpretation.[70]

He thinks it justifiable to designate "the dreaming Greeks as Homers and Homer as a dreaming Greek" (p.29). The Dionysian, on the other hand, is associated with music, and defined as "drunkenness", which originated in the Dionysian orgies of ancient Greece but was later developed into transcendental "ecstasy" that "even seeks to destroy the individual and redeem him by a mystic feeling of Oneness," to achieve "the highest gratification of the Primordial Unity" (pp.27-28). It is this that gives substance to the Apollonian form, and it is for Nietzsche an important concept, closely related to his doctrine of the "Eternal Recurrence" which occupies the central place in his philosophy. It recurs in his writings throughout his career, and he repeatedly expounds the idea. We find a clearer definition of it, for example, in *The Will to Power*:

> The word "Dionysian" expresses: a constraint to unity, a soaring above personality, the commonplace, society, reality, and above the abyss of the *ephemeral*; the passionately painful sensation of super-abundance, in darker, fuller and more fluctuating conditions; an ecstatic saying of yea to the collective character of existence, as that which remains the same, and equally mighty and blissful throughout all change; the great pantheistic sympathy with pleasure and pain, which declares even the most terrible and most questionable qualities of existence good, and sanctifies them; the eternal will to procreation, to fruitfulness, and to recurrence; the feeling of unity in regard to the necessity of creating and anhililating.[71]

The opposing principles, Nietzsche believes, found an ideal balance in "the equally Dionysian and Apollonian art-work of attic tragedy."[72]

The concept of the Apollonian and the Dionysian had a considerable influence on later writers, which we may trace in the works of Thomas Mann, Kafka and others. In those modern writers, however, the distinction between the two seems to have become blurred, or rather merged into one, and dreams, instead of presenting the "beauteous appearance of the dream-worlds", ie, the perfect world of the Apollonian forms, tend to demonstrate the Dionysian world of dark impulses and submerged fears and desires as may be seen, for example, in Aschenbach's dream in Mann's *Death in Venice,* or in practically all of Kafka's works. Perhaps we need to remind ourselves that *The Birth of Tragedy* was the earliest of Nietzsche's major works and that, as we have seen while discussing his later works, identification of dreams simply with the ideal world of beauty was a stance which the philosopher himself was to discard in his more mature years. It may be said in any case that Nietzsche was one of the first, if not the first, to deal in a most imaginative and evocative way, with this perennial problem of form and content which was to occupy the minds of the Modernists in particular. In this too he may be considered their precursor.

Maintaining that it was this "[a]lertness to human illogicality", which we have been discussing so far, and which was "rare in the nineteenth century ... that enabled Nietzsche to exert such an enormous influence on the twentieth," Ronald Hayman considers that "almost every major writer in the German language has been profoundly indebted to him,"[73] naming as examples, along with already mentioned Kafka and Mann, Rilke, Musil, Benn, Heidegger and Freud, and extends the list further by including in the Nietzschean orbit such non-German writers as Gide and Valéry as well as Shaw and Lawrence. It does not take us too long to note that most of those named represent the Modernist phase of European culture and art, and indeed Stuart Hughes points out that those writers who, in the 1890s and early 1900s reacted against "their immediate predecessors" who "had scorned and neglected" the values of imagination, ie, the initiators of the Modernist movement, "established the cult of Dostoevsky and Nietzsche as the literary heralds of the new era" (Hughes, p.34). It is not surprising that those who reminded Hughes of, as quoted earlier "the aspirations of the original Romanticists" and nearly made him characterize their attitude as "neo-romanticism", should have turned towards Nietzsche and his spiritual brother, Dostoevsky, in order to reinstate the reign of imagination and restore the wholeness of life. For, whatever they say about the old Romanticism, they were, along with Baudelaire, essentially the inheritors of the true Romantic spirit, and as such, played an important role as the link between Modernism and Romanticism.

The desire to understand man in his entirety, the quest for wholeness, which results from a sense of frustration at the fragmentation of the modern man, is at the basis of most modern literature, and particularly of such Modernist writers as Joyce, Woolf and Lawrence. T. S. Eliot's famous complaint about "dissociation of sensibility" may also be considered one of its manifestations. When Albert Begin says: "Our first duty is to keep ourselves complete, and it is by paying due attention to the night life that we are most likely to achieve this" (Begin, p.24), or "The dream is revelatory, but poetically revelatory ... the world we see there actually exists. We *are our* dreams as well as our waking state" (p.215), he is reiterating the convictions not only of the Romantics but also of the modern writers and psychologists who are essentially the spiritual descendants of the Romantic forebears whose lineage we have traced briefly in this chapter.

CHAPTER SEVEN

SURREALISM AND ITS SYMPATHIZERS

Perhaps the imagination is on the verge of regaining its rights. – André Breton[1]
We re-established the reign of the imagination. – Eugene Jolas[2]

THE heritage of Romanticism and the influence of the psychological theories of Freud and later Jung were often recognized by modern writers, and most openly and emphatically acknowledged by the Surrealists and their sympathizers.

Surrealism was one of the most important artistic movements of the twentieth century – *the most important* literary movement, according to the dustwrapper notes of the 1979 Gallimard edition of the *Manifestes du Surréalisme*: "*le mouvement littérraire le plus important de notre siècle*" – and its influence, in spite of the derision and hostility which it initially received from the general public, has penetrated into our daily life, manifest in films, television programmes, even in children's lives in the form of collages and "Surrealist" paintings they are encouraged to produce in nursery schools and kindergartens. As the dustwrapper notes put it, "*son infuence a été immense dans tous les pays du monde et a débordé le domaine littéraire. Il a marqué notre façon de penser et même notre mode de vie.*" Indeed, it has affected our way of thinking and looking at things, and altered our sense of beauty. And for the formation of this epochal movement, the influence of Freud was decisive.

Surrealism was a continuation, or rather a culmination, of a rebellion against the established values and orders, initiated by Dadaists in Zurich during World War I, which was later to spread to other capitals in Europe, above all to Paris, the centre and the melting pot of European culture at the time. The effect of the war, as has already been mentioned, was crucial to the artists. Robert Short writes in his essay, "Dada and Surrealism":

> ... it was the impact of the First World War which persuaded poets of the younger generation that western culture was mortal and had been touched in its foundations, that the victor countries had suffered a dèbacle in ideas and ethics as dramatic as that of the regimes, aristocracies and frontiers among the defeated. The war confirmed a growing conviction – hardly there in the pre-war Cubists and Futurists – that the West's obsession with technological advance and the over-estimation of reason at the expense of feeling led straight to destructive megalomania.[3]

It was significant that Surrealism was born in France, where in spite of the intermittent bouts of Romanticism and Symbolism, the tradition of authoritarian Classicism and Cartesian rationalism remained strong.[4] As the Romantics revolted against the extremes of rationalism of the Age of Enlightenment, so did Surrealists rebel against the basic assumption of pre-war Europe, the idea of material and moral progress based on the belief in reason and logic, which had proved totally inadequate. It was natural that André Breton, the chief advocate of Surrealism[5] who in his 1924 *Manifesto* defined man as the confirmed dreamer – *"L'homme ce rêveur definitif"*,[6] who preferred, in the words of a former Surrealist, "Imagination, folly, dream, surrender to the dark forces of the unconscious and recourse to the marvellous" to "all that arise from necessity, from a logical order, from the reasonable,"[7] – should have placed at the outset of the Manifesto the defence of imagination and critique of rationalism and materialism:

> *Cette imagination qui n'admettait pas de borne, on ne lui permet plus de s'exercer que selon les lois d'une utilité arbitraire; elle est incapable d'assumer longtemps ce rôle inferieur ...* [8]

(This imagination, which used to admit no boundary, is no longer allowed to exercise itself except in accordance with the laws of arbitrary utility; imagination cannot continue to assume such an inferior role for long ...)

> *Réduire l'imagination à l'esclavage ... c'est se dérober à tout ce qu'on trouve, au fond de soi, de justice suprême. Le seul imagin- ation me rend compte de ce qui peut être, et c'est assez pour lever un peu le terrible interdit; assez aussi pour que je m'abandonne à elle sans crainte de me tromper ... (p.13)*

(To reduce the imagination to slavery ... is to deprive our innermost self of the supreme justice. Imagination alone can reveal to me what is possible, and this is enough to lift even a little that terrible inhibition; enough also for me to abandon myself to it without fear of committing errors ...)

He also writes:

> *Nous vivons encore sous le règne de la logique ... Mais les procédés logiques, de nos jours, ne s'appliquent plus qu'à la résolution de problèmes d'intérêt secondaire. Le rationalisme absolu qui reste de mode ne permet de considérer que des faits relevant étroitement de notre expérience...Inutile d'ajouter que l'expérience même s'est vu assigner des limites. Elle tourne dans une cage d'ou il est de plus en plus difficile de la faire sortir. Elle s'appuie, elle aussi, sur l'utilité immédiate, et elle est gardée par le bon sens. Sous couleur de civilisation, sous prétexte de progrés, on est parvenu à bannir de l'espirit tout ce qui se peut taxer à tort ou à raison de superstition,*

de chimère; à proscrire tout mode de recherche de la vérité qui n'est pas conforme à l'usage (pp.18-19).

(We are still living under the reign of logic ... But the logical methods of our time are applicable only to the solution of problems of secondary interest. The absolute rationalism which remains to be fashionable allows us to consider only those facts that are closely related to our experience ... It goes without saying that experience itself is given limits. It moves around in a cage of which it is increasingly difficult to make it get out. Experience too relies on the immediate usefulness, and is guarded by common sense. Under the pretence of civilization, under the pretext of progress, we have come to banish from our minds all that may rightly or wrongly be accused of being superstition, of being chimaera; to ban all manners of the search for truth that do not conform to convention.)

However, in this "reign of logic" and rationalism, where everything outside the narrow confines of reason and utility is banished in the name of "civilization" or "progress", he sees an encouraging sign of re-emergence to the fore of "by far the most important" but so far ignored "part of intellectual life" and for this he gives all the credit to Freud: "*Il faut en rendre grâce aux découvertes de Freud*" (p.19). With the aid provided by Freud's "discoveries" for furthering the exploration of the secrets of the human mind, he even expects the restoration of imagination to its proper status: "*L'imagination est peut-être sur le point de reprendre ses droits*" (Perhaps the imagination is on the verge of regaining its rights) (p.19).

In Breton's mind, as in the minds of the Romantics, imagination is closely related to and almost identified with the unconscious and the subconscious activities of the mind, which have now the endorsement of Freud's theories.[9] This inevitably leads him to the discussion of the dream as his central concern, in which, acknowledging the justice done by Freud to the subject, he wonders at the "extreme disproportion in the importance and seriousness" normally given to events in the waking state and those of sleep, when these two states share almost equal amount of time in a man's life. It is really "inadmissible" for him that so little attention has been paid to "this important part of psychic activity" (p.20). With the hope for future possibility of fathoming the mysteries of the dream in its entirety, he expresses his belief in "the future resolution" of these two apparently contradictory states, ie, "dream and reality," into "a sort of absolute reality," or "surreality":

Je crois à la résolution future de ces deux états, en apparence si contradictoire, que sont le rêve et la réalité absolue, de suréalité, *si l'en peut ainsi dire* (pp.23-24).

This total vision of life, the synthesis of the inner and the outer worlds was indeed the final goal of the Surrealists.

As a method of achieving this, Breton resorted to "pure psychic automatism", or automatic writing which, he explains in the *Manifesto*, derived from Freud. One night a bizarre sentence[10] that had nothing to do with his conscious knowledge came to his mind out of nowhere, which so fascinated him that he decided to apply to himself Freud's methods of examination with which he was familiar – he was, he says, totally preoccupied with Freud at the time – and which he had occasionally practised on the sick during the war as a doctor. In other words, he tried to obtain from himself what he sought to obtain from his patients, "namely a monologue uttered as rapidly as possible", without the control of the subject's critical judgement and "unhampered by any reticence, which should be as much as possible *spoken thought*" (pp.33-34). This method, in relation to Freud, clearly refers to that of free association.[11] The first fruit of the experiments in automatic writing, undertaken in collaboration with Philippe Supault, was published as *Les Champs Magnetiques (The Magnetic Fields)* in 1921,[12] three years before the publication of the *First Manifesto*.

Breton gives the "final" definition of Surrealism in these words:

SURRÉALISME, n.m. *Automatisme psychique pur par lequel on se propose d'exprimer, soit verbalement, soit par l'écrit, soit de toute autre manière, le fonctionnement réel de la pensée. Dictée de la pensée, en l'absence de tout contrôle exercé par la raison, en dehors de toute préoccupation esthétique ou morale.*

(SURREALISM, n.m. Pure psychic automatism through which we intend to express either verbally or in writing, or in any other manner, the real function of thought. Dictation of thought itself, without any control exercised by reason, and beyond all aesthetic or moral preoccupations.)

ENCYCL. *Philos. Le surréalisme repose sur la croyance à la réalité superieure de certaines formes d'associations negligées jusqu'a lui, à toute-puissance du rêve, au jeu désinteressé de la pensée. Il tend à ruiner définitivement tous les autres mecanismes psychiques et à se substituter à eux dans la résolution des principaux problèmes de la vie* (pp.37-38).

(ENCYCL. *Philos.* Surrealism is based on the belief in the superior reality of certain forms of associations hitherto neglected, in the omnipotence of the dream and in the distinterested play of thought. It leads to the final destruction of all other psychic mechanisms and its own substitution for these in the solution of the principal problems of life.)

Surrealism, equated here with "pure psychic automatism", is a means of capturing and expressing the true workings of the mind, which rejects any dictates from reason or rational considerations, either aesthetic or moral. It reverses, as did the Romantics, the conventional standard of value, and believes in "the superior reality of certain hitherto neglected forms of association, in the omnipotence of the dream", as well as in "the distinterested play of thought." What he aimed at was a total liberation of man from the conventional, logical mode of thinking, in order to seize the wealth offered by imagination and achieve the complete realization of life.[13]

As the forerunners of Surrealism, Breton names Dante, Shakespeare "in his best days", Edward Young of *Night Thoughts*, adding a list of poets and writers whom he regards as Surrealist each in a certain specific aspect: Swift, Sade, Poe, Baudelaire, Rimbaud, Mallarmé, etc (pp.38-39). However, it seems to have been with Gérard de Nerval that he felt the closest kinship – Nerval for whom, as we have seen, dream and waking life were often united into one. While explaining the origin of the term Surrealism, which Breton and Soupault borrowed from Apollinaire, he states that they could have used, even more justifiably, "supernaturalism", the term used by Nerval in his dedication to *Filles de Feu*, since Nerval, he thinks, possessed to a remarkable degree the "spirit" of Surrealism, while Appollinaire possessed only its "letter" and even that was imperfect (p.36). This may partly explain why the origin of Surrealism is often traced back to Romanticism: "Surrealism was heir to an indigenous tradition with its roots in Romanticism."[14] Breton himself emphasizes this link when, in the *Second Manifesto*, he describes Surrealism as "the tail, but then such a prehensile tail" of Romanticism.[15] Besides the concern for the irrational and the unconscious, the Surrealists share with their precursors recognition of the significance of childhood[16] and the importance of individual experience or descent into the Self, though this latter is given in the case of the Surrealists more collective or universal implications. Romanticism, after a century of existence, is not, for Breton, a spent force, but still in its vigorous youth, perhaps reborn as Surrealism.[17]

Although Surrealism is said to "have gone beyond the purely literary domain" (*a debordé le domaine purement littéraire*), this, in fact, is nothing to be wondered at, since it was from the beginning not a purely literary movement. It was aimed at changing the whole attitude towards life, a revolution of man's whole sensibility and consciousness; as Waldberg puts it, "surrealism at its inception was intended to be a way of thinking, a way of feeling and a way of life" (p.12). Significantly, Breton and Soupault engaged themselves in the first attempt at automatic writing, "with a laudable contempt for what might result in terms of literature" (Breton, p.34). What was important for them was not to write poetry but, in Breton's words, *de pratiquer la poesie* (to practise poetry) (p.28). This was the reason why the movement, from its early stage onward, involved not only poets and men of letters but also painters, sculptors, photographers and film-makers. (It has, as has often been pointed out, been especially fruitful in the field of painting, perhaps because dream[like] visions are most appropriately, or at least most readily, rendered into visual images.) Politics too played an important part in it. Rejection of the conventional values and attitudes led to the negation of the social system that produced and supported them: "We hold the liberation of man to be the *sine qua non* condition of the *liberation of the mind*, and we can expect this liberation of man to result only from the proletarian revolution."[18] Thus they increasingly came to express their commitment to Marxism, which becomes apparent in the *Second Manifesto*, in contrast to the *First Manifesto*, which is mainly devoted to literary and psychological considerations under the strong influence of Freud. In fact, it may be said that Surrealism was a movement which was propped up theoretically by the two pillars, Freud and Marx, and as such may be regarded as a remarkable reflection of the 'twenties and 'thirties over which, in F. J. Hoffman's words, "The figures of Freud and Marx dominated."[19]

In retrospect, however, this political aspect of Surrealism seems to be of little significance, and many commentators on the movement often, and perhaps justifiably, ignore it completely. Moreover, as Breton himself reveals in the *Second Manifesto*, the relationship between the Surrealists and the official organ of Marxism, the Communist Party was, to say the least, not a happy one.[20] In spite of the Surrealists' repeated pronouncement of their "adherence to historic [or dialectical] materialism", the Communists regarded them with suspicion, considering the movement "essentially ... anticommunist and counter-revolutionary" (p.98).

Given the Marxist idea that all the spiritual and cultural outputs of a society are reflections – the superstructure – of its economical and material conditions, *vis-à-vis* the Surrealists' belief in the autonomy of imagination and the "omnipotence of the dream," two mutually exclusive and contradictory stances, the latter's distrust is understandable. The Surrealists seem to have made a typically Surrealistic synthesis of the two opposing and contradictory principles, accepted only by themselves. The strained, and sometimes stormy relationship eventually came to an end – though the Surrealists did not abandon the Marxist ideology itself – with the expulsion in 1933 of Breton, Paul Éluard and René Crevel from the Party.[21]

The incompatibility between the artists and the political activists became still clearer when in the following year the Party laid down the official line of "Socialist Realism" in matters of art, subjugating art to its political purposes. André Breton who, as early as in 1926, insisted on freedom of art, or rather, "the experiments of the inner life ... without external or even Marxist control,"[22] predictably rejected it totally as an "erroneous" conception. In an essay which he contributed to a volume devoted to Surrealism and published in England in 1936, he explains the reasons for his opposition and writes:

> Above all we expressly oppose the view that it is possible to create a work of art or even, properly considered, any useful work by expressing only the manifest content of an age. On the contrary, Surrealism proposes to express its *latent content.*[23]

The "fantastic" which is totally denied by socialist realism, Breton believes, is the best means to capture this "latent content", to explore "the secret depths of history":

> It is only at the approach of the fantastic, at a point where human reason loses its control, that the most profound emotion of the individual has the fullest opportunity to express itself: emotion unsuitable for projection in the framework of the real world and which has no other solution in its urgency than to rely on the eternal solicitation of symbols and myths.

To illustrate his point, he draws our attention to the flourishing of the Gothic novels, or the "*romans noirs*" at the end of the 18th century which, in spite of their recent fall into disrepute and insignifance enjoyed, he maintains, great popularity and exerted a considerable influence on many writers of the day. Those influenced or inspired by the works of Mrs. Radcliffe, Monk Lewis or Maturin that Breton names includes Byron, Hugo, Balzac, Baudelaire and Lautréamont. Breton explains the significance of the Gothic novels in these terms: "The attention of humanity in its most universal and spontaneous form as well as its most individual and purely intellectual form, has been attracted not by the scrupulously exact description of exterior events of which the world was the theatre, but rather by the expression of the confused feelings awakened by nostalgia and terror. The pleasure principle has never avenged itself more obviously upon the principle of reality."[24] After analysing the symbolical meanings of each setting of the Gothic novels, such as the ruins, the ghosts, the subterranean passages, etc, he sums up his argument by saying that "Such

... turbulent background" combines "in the highest degree the struggle between the instinct of death on the one hand which, as Freud has shown, is also an instinct of preservation and on the other, Eros who exacts after each hecatomb the glorious restoration of life" (p.108). What is particularly significant for Breton, moreover, is the fact that the "scenery of the romantic type" used in these novels was by no means a conscious contrivance by the authors: "Their undoubted innocence in this respect gives greater importance to their sensitive testimony" (pp.108-109). Rather than being a conscious effort, the style of the Gothic novels, Breton thinks, "may be considered as pathognomonic of the great social troubles in which Europe was enveloped at the end of the 18th century" (*Ibid*, p.109). To prove his point that these novels were the unconscious "testimony", ie, the *latent content* of the age, he quotes from a letter (9th March, 1765) written by Horace Walpole (who as a politician as well as a man of letters knew well the political situation of the time), relating how his Gothic tale, *The Castle of Otranto*, came into being:

> Shall I even confess to you, what was the origin of this romance? I waked one morning in the beginning of last June, from a dream, of which all that I could recover was, that I thought myself in an ancient castle (a very natural dream for a head filled like mine with Gothic story), and that on the uppermost banister of a great staircase I saw a gigantic hand in armour. In the evening I sat down, and began to write, without knowing in the least what I intended to say or relate. The work grew on my hands, and I grew fond of it - add that I was very glad to think of anything, rather than politics - in short, I was so engrossed with my tale, which I completed in less than two months, that one evening I wrote from the time I drank my tea, about six o'clock, till half an hour after one in the morning, when my hand and fingers were so weary, that I could not hold the pen to finish the sentence. (pp.110-111)

This Breton finds so close to Surrealism in spirit that it seems to him as though in his *Manifeste de Surréalisme* he "had only paraphrased and generalized without knowing the affirmations" the letter contains (p.110). Indeed, Walpole reveals that the message was obtained, as Breton emphasizes, through "*dreams*" and "*automatic writing*", without intervention of the conscious control or intentions.

Breton's sympathy with and estimation of the Gothic novel may be understandable when we recognize that it shares its basic spirit with Romanticism, with which Breton nearly identified himself. As Bigsby succinctly puts it, "The Gothic romance implied that the world is dominated by forces not acknowledged by the rational mind. It broke free of the novel of manners and didactic sensibility to take account of areas of

experience hitherto disregarded."[25] This is exactly what Breton wanted
to be expressed in art and that is why he exempted the Gothic novel from
the general condemnation of the novel form as *"un genre inferieur"* (an
inferior genre)[26] in the *First Manifesto*. Although Bigsby points out the
Gothic novel's propensity to capitulate in its endings "to rationalism,
denying the very force which gave it its energy and compulsive mystery"
and thus betraying "its own assertions",[27] this aspect does not seem to
have troubled Breton very much, who no doubt was concerned more with
its positive qualities. While declaring that the "self-allotted task" of
Surrealism, which is "the elaboration of the *collective myth* belonging to
our period,"[28] will continue in the face of any intimidation, he regards the
Gothic romance as his model that achieved the same task in relation to its
time:

> Human psychism in its most universal aspect found in the Gothic
> castle and its accessories a point of fixation so precise that it
> becomes essential to discover what would be the equivalent for our
> own period... However, Surrealism is still only able to point out the
> change which has taken place from the period of the *'roman noir'*
> to our time, from the most highly charged emotions of the miracu-
> lous *apparition* to the no less disconcerting, *coincidence*, and to ask
> us to allow ourselves to be guided towards the unknown by this
> newest *promise*, brighter than any other at the present time, isolat-
> ing it whenever possible from the trivial facts of life. (pp.112-113)

In this effort to create a "collective myth", it is necessary, Breton
maintains, to "gather together the scattered elements of this myth,
beginning with those which proceed from the oldest and strongest traditions (p.115). He finds this tradition "to be more enduring in England than
anywhere else" today. Far from being, as is often claimed, "an unsurpass-
able obstacle" for new ideas, it is indeed a source from which Surrealism
itself had drawn deeply. In fact, Surrealism, says Breton, "has sought to
carry with it all that is most fecund in the art and literature of the past, so
that necessarily it was obliged to pay a considerable tribute to the literature
and the art of England."

In spite of this ingratiating gesture from Breton, England did not
reciprocate the enthusiasm and Surrealism never really took root, nor
gained such momentum, in England as in its birthplace, France. There
were, however, brief and tentative activities by the English Surrealists
during the 1930s, which culminated in the International Surrealist Exhibition, held in London in 1936.[29] It was in the same year that a book entitled
Surrealism, in which Breton's preceding essay appeared, was published,
with Sir Herbert Read as editor, who also provided an introduction.

Besides Breton and Read, the contributors included Hugh Sykes Davies as well as Paul Éluard and Georges Hugnet from France. A perusal of the English contributions to the book, which was prepared, in Read's words in the Introduction, as the "definitive manifesto" - the English counterpart of Breton's *Manifestes*- "in the hope of extending its membership",[30] may give us an idea about the basic stance of the English Surrealists.

In this lengthy introduction Read, as one of the leading figures of the English Surrealist movement, expounds what he then believed to be the essential spirit of Surrealism, and of true art for that matter.[31] It is based on his belief that "superrealism in general is the romantic principle in art,"[32] manifestations of which he abundantly sees in English tradition:

> The evidences on which we base the claims of Surrealism are scattered through the centuries, the partial and incoherent revelations of permanent human characteristics; and nowhere however are these evidences so plentiful as in England.[33]

The main purpose of the Introduction, he claims, is to relate "this English evidence" to "the general theory of Surrealism."

Since Romanticism is the sole, permanent and universal creative principle for Read, Classicism does not, as it usually does, present a rival or alternative concept to it. The "classic" and "romantic" are not the thesis and the antithesis, the contradiction of which should be resolved by synthesis: "They correspond rather to the husk and the seed, the shell and the kernel" (p.26). The conflict between the two should be solved only by liquidation of Classicism, "by showing its complete irrelevance, its anaesthetic effect, its contradiction of the creative impulse," since

> Classicism, let it be stated without further preface, repesents for us now, and has always represented, the forces of oppression. Classicism is the intellectual counterpart of political tyranny. It was so in the ancient world and in the medieval empires; it was renewed to express the dictatorship of the renaissance and has ever since been the official creed of capitalism. (p.23)

Whereas the Classical spirit represents that "of order, of control and of repression," the Romantic spirit is essentially the "principle of life, of creation, of liberation" (p.26). While we may detect the influence of Marxist ideology in this argument, that of Freud becomes evident when he later identifies Romanticism with the artist and Classicism with society. According to Read, the artist is characterized by this "failure in social adaption," but he directs his whole effort "towards a reconciliation with society." What he produces and eventually "offers to society" in the process is not his personal "idiosyncracies, but rather some knowledge of the secrets to which he has had access, the secrets of the self which are buried in every man alike, but which only the sensibility of the artist can reveal to us in all their actuality" (p.27). The "self" here is clearly not a personal one: it is largely made up," Read maintains, "of elements from the unconscious," which appears more and more collective as our knowledge of it deepens (p.27). It represents "universal truths", "a body of common sentiments and thoughts," which was in fact a claim made for Classical art by Sir Herbert Grierson, whose view on Classicism and Romanticism Read had already refuted earlier in the essay. For him, "the universal truths of Classicism may be merely the temporal prejudice of an epoch," while "the universal truths of romanticism are coeval with the evolving consciousness of mankind" (pp.27-28). In concluding the argument, he reasserts his earlier contention, saying that "It is in this sense, then, that Surrealism is a reaffirmation of the romantic principle" (p.28). In this definition of Romantic literature by Read, we may clearly detect the influence of Freud's theory that defines the artist as a neurotic, or near neurotic, who finds his way back to society through their creative activities, tinged with Jung's theory that true artists find expressions for the collective unconscious of a society, or of mankind.[34]

Thus in the literary and artistic beliefs of Herbert Read, the psychological theories and the spirit of Romanticism are inseparably linked together. On this basis, he proposes revaluations of the various aspects of English literature of the past, such as "ballads and anonymous literature", the significance of the irrational quality of Shakespeare's genius, the personality and the works of Blake, Shelley, Byron, Swinburne, the nonsense literature of Edward Lear and Lewis Carroll which is "actually charged with ... unconscious significance" – Carroll is even said to have "affinities with Shakespeare" (pp.55-56) – as well as the Pre-Raphaelite movement, which in its essential spirit was not unlike Surrealism but, lacking the latter's dialectic and scientific method and energy was, in Read's view, "incapable of really comprehensive reaction – a revolution" and degenerated into sentimentalism: "They should have developed romanticism from the stage Coleridge left it; instead, they developed nostalgia" (pp.59-60). (He measures the failure of the Pre-Raphaelites and their followers by contrasting Morris with Marx.) In the field of fiction, too, he maintains that "the whole field of English fiction must be reviewed," and thinks that the Gothic novelists in that event may "occupy a much higher rank" than Scott, Dickens and Hardy (p.56), a notion clearly inspired by Breton's appreciation of the Gothic romance.

His Surrealist belief in dreams and the unconscious workings of the mind becomes apparent when he discusses the use of the images found in dreams, which he compares to the "found objects" – *objéts trouvés* – valued by Surrealist painters. After explaining how the conscious mind has in the past inhibited the direct use of dream imagery, he states boldly:

> But now we turn to the dream with the same confidence that formerly men placed in the objective world of sensation, and we weave its reality into the synthesis of our art. (p.65)

He considers, moreover, that in some dreams "the work of synthesis is already done" and the dream itself becomes an artistic entity. Thus, while conceding that most dreams contain "elements that are merely the casual residues of the day's anxieties," he observes:

> We find also the day-world transformed, and occasionally this new reality presents itself to us as a poetic unity. (p.65)

Recognizing close similarity between the creation of a poem and the formation of a dream – "poetic inspiration has an exact parallel in dream formation" (p.66), – he tries to explain the mechanism of the creative process of a poem by Freud's theory of the dream work, applying such concepts as regression, displacement, condensation and secondary elaboration, and illustrates his point with his own poem, which was actually inspired by a "vivid dream", though finally completed with conscious elaboration by the poet. He concludes that "every authentic image is conceived in the unconscious" (p.77). For Read,

> Poetry, to adapt a saying of Picasso's, is found, not sought. It emerges, perhaps not easily but at any rate directly, from the well of the unconscious. (p.78)

Naturally, he considers "the faculty of a Pope or a Dryden" to be "an inventive wit," but "not essentially a poetic gift." As the examples in which the "surreality, the something-more-than-conscious naturalism" is achieved, or nearly achieved, he quotes from Blake's *Jerusalem* and Shelley's *Speculations on Metaphysics*, and maintains that in such works as *The Marriage of Heaven and Hell* and *Jerusalem*, "there is a realisation of the fundamental contradictions of reality, and a movement towards a synthesis ..." and that Shelley, in spite of the general assumption that he ended up as a neo-platonic idealist, actually "arrived at a dialectical synthesis of the real and the unreal, actuality and hallucination ..." (pp.78-82), which, as we have seen, is the final goal of the Surrealists. He ends his Introduction by defending Surrealism from J. B. Priestley's charges and restating its professed aims.

We may say that in *his* manifesto of Surrealism, Herbert Read went further than Breton in emphasizing its link with Romanticism, to the extent of almost identifying it with the latter, evidence for which he abundantly saw in the English tradition and which he tried to support, as Breton did in his, with the modern psychological theories provided by Freud.

In "Surrealism at this Time and Place", Hugh Sykes Davies deals more specifically with this link with English tradition, especially the nineteenth century English Romanticism. Davies' basic contention is that for English writers to become Surrealists was not a "violent act of conversion" but "the inevitable outcome of the historical situation in England, as elsewhere" (p.167). The "Surrealists in England," he argues, "have not heard a message from France in a cloud of fire. Surrealism is the natural and inevitable product of historical forces; it is not inspired, it is caused; it did not arise from sudden divine illuminations but, like every other valuable movement, from a profound clarification of problems historically handed down to us by the culture into which we were born" (pp.120-121). What he tries to do in this essay is to prove this thesis.

In order to understand our present situation, Davies maintains, it is necessary to study the past, especially the immediate past, which for us is the nineteenth century, when the problems and crises of the present day took shape and the first steps towards their solution were made (pp.123-124). Thus he concentrates his attention on this particular century and "its chief movement, Romanticism," considering the Surrealism to be "not a limp offshoot, but a vigorous continuation, a tail, but a most prehensile tail."[35]

He sees especially in Coleridge, Wordsworth and Blake the nascent spirit of Surrealism. Thus after analysing Coleridge's views on fancy and imagination he concludes that "Coleridge abolishes Baconian distinction between reality and phantasy," and as a result poetry becomes an embodiment of "the only complete approach to reality," instead of "being regarded as a rejection or distortion of reality" (p.147). Then he identifies this with the basic stance of Surrealism:

> Surrealism might employ almost the same words to describe its conclusions. It has found itself faced by a violent divorce between the world of action and dream, reality and phantasy, and has protested against this divorce ... (p.147)

What Surrealism has been trying to do is to bridge the gap, to restore the unity, between the two, as evidenced by Davies' quotation of Breton's words: *Je souhaite qu' il ne passe pour avoir tenté rien mieux que de jéter un* fil conducteur *entre les deux mondes par trop dissociés de la veille et du sommeil, de la realité exterieur et interieur, de la raison et de la folie*

... (I hope that it will be known for having tried nothing better than throwing a *conductor wire* between the two far too dissociated worlds of waking and sleeping, of external and internal reality, of reason and folly...) (p.147)

In Wordsworth, he finds a poet creating a new mythology through personification of Nature, not as a means, as the ancients did, to understand and solve the external problems and difficulties caused by natural forces, but as an aid to solve his own internal, psychological problems:

> The mythological moralization of nature established for him an imaginative moral certainty, an emotional conviction of moral being, which filled the place left by the breakdown of his rational moral life. (p.156)

The moving mountain in the episode of the stealing of a boat in his childhood in *The Prelude* is given as an example of Nature turned into "moral being" in the poet's imagination, the "moral certainty" of which helped him, Davies considers, to "bear more easily" his disappointment in the French revolution, his sense of guilt over his own personal failures in the event, in short, "a crisis of conscience". Davies concludes:

> Here, then, is one case at least in which the myth formation has been dominated throughout by an interior problem, by unsolved emotional conflicts, and in which the necessity to conquer external nature plays no part. It would appear that poetry, no longer finding the outer world imminent, had been forced to turn its attention more powerfully than ever before to the solution of interior problems by mythological methods. (p.156)

Although he can present only a single case of this kind of mythology, he argues that, on the basis of the central place Wordsworth occupied in the English Romantic movement and the immense influence his mythology had on "later thought and feeling", the poet could not have been "an eccentric", nor his problems and solutions merely "idiosyncratic" ones. These should, Davies implies, rather be related to "a wide crisis in man's nature at that time," for which he expects "to find further evidence" (p.157).

This he does find in another kind of mythology, the "myths of fatal men and women," which in his view arose, as in the case of Wordsworth, in "a crisis of feeling of human emotion," at the beginning of the nineteenth century (p.163). Considering the view presented by Mario Praz in his *Romantic Agony* that one of the most characteristic aspects of the English Romantic literature "is a peculiar 'erotic sensibility'," a sensibility which is "profoundly algolagnic" and "is obsessed with the idea of pleasure obtained through cruelty, inflicted or received, sadistic or masochistic" (p.160), he recognizes its prototype or breeding ground in the Gothic novels which, though "now unread and almost forgotten, suppressed by a gentleman's agreement", had a great influence, Davies maintains, on the writers of the time, the sensibility expressed in them penetrating into "official literature", as evidenced by Byron with "his monstrous statue of himself as the new Don Juan, the Fatal Man who seduces women by cruelty and evil fascination, etc."; Keats with "his own myth of the Fatal Woman, the woman who tramples men underfoot and ruins them by her deadly charmes," and Shelley who "lived in a family atmosphere of the horror novel" and whose *The Cenci* inescapably shows "the fierceness of algolagnic sensibility" (pp.160-161). He finds the same sensibility running through Beddoes, Tennyson, Browning, the Pre-Raphaelites and Swinburne. However, the most important case, according to Davies, is Blake who "gives to the algolagnic sensibility its purest, and perhaps its most beautiful expression" (p.162), the expression of "melancholia and preoccupation with the strange pleasures of pain – everything that was called *'le mal du siècle'* " (p.163). He believes that the "crisis of human feeling" that gave rise to "these myths of fatal men and women" has come down through the centuries and "unhappily" is still with us in the modern world. Here, too, Davies claims, Surrealism proves to be "the lineal heir to the nineteenth century," for "In its painting, and in its poetry, it has developed a magnificent iconography of melancholia and algolagnia, a mythology designed and apt to assist man in dominating a crisis in his own nature through the imagination ... " (p.163).

The last link he sees between Surrealism and Romanticism is their attitude towards revolution. Most nineteenth century Romantic poets are found to have been more or less involved in the revolutionary movement – Wordsworth, perhaps, being the most famous example – since "they understood ... that bourgeois culture, the culture of pure money, was inhuman and dehumanizing" and they fought it "both by their poesy and by more direct political action" (p.166). As this is exactly what Surrealism tries to do, "In this too, Surrealism follows the nineteenth century."

The logical conclusion to all these parallel comparisons is that "In all the essentials of romanticism, Surrealism continues the earlier movement." The difference between the two lies in it that "Surrealism is organized, orderly and conscious," whereas "romanticism was notoriously inchoate, disorderly, intuitive" (p.168). And in this he recognizes "the greatest debt to dialectical materialism, and something more to psychoanalysts," (p.168), in other words, to Marx and Freud, the two guardian angels of Surrealism.

The emphasis laid on English tradition, especially that of Romanticism in the cases of Read and Davies and that of Gothicism in Breton's case, must in part be due, apart from its legitimate claim, to the particular circumstance in which these essays were written. The book in which they appeared was intended to be the first official introduction in print to Surrealism after the tumultuous reception of the International Surrealist Exhibition, aimed at the English public who seemed to have remained largely hostile or unconvinced or uncomprehending.[36] Obviously, it was important and opportune to show how relevant Surrealism was to English art and literature. David Gascoyne, in his *Short Survey of Surrealism*, which was published a year earlier (1935), already anticipating the English reception, tried to defend Surrealism on the basis of its kinship with English tradition. Considering the future possibility of the "organised international co-operation" of Surrealists – he had also in mind the planned visit by Breton and Éluard to England to hold "a large Surrealist exhibition there," which as we know, materialised the following year – Gascoyne foresees the growth in importance of Surrealism in this century, but at the same time senses a necessity to defend it from the possible objections and negative reactions:

> There will be, of course, objections to such a co-operation. In England, for instance, there will be many to protest that surrealism is foreign to the national temperament, that it cannot grow here as it has no roots in English tradition. Such an objection could only result from a lack of understanding of what surrealism *is*. As a matter of fact, there is a very strong surrealist element in English literature; one need quote only Shakespeare, Marlowe, Swift, Young, Coleridge, Blake, Beddoes, Lear and Carroll to prove this contention. For a writer, or anyone else, to object to an attempt to establish surrealist activity in England, on the grounds that this would mean an "importation from Paris", is just as stupidly provincial as a doctor would be if he objected to the practice of psychoanalysis in England because it originated in Vienna.[37]

It seems as if Gascoyne here was laying out a theme for the later essays of Read and Davies. He then points out the internationaal character of Surrealism, emphasizing its debt not only to the native French tradition but to German and Spanish thoughts – Hegel, Feuerbach, Engels, Marx and "the distinctly southern 'lyricism'" of Dali, Miró, Picasso – and concludes that "Surrealism transcends all nationalism and springs from a plane on which all men are equal" (p.133), which obviously should be interpreted as the unconscious.

The first English language magazine to give support to the Surrealist movement and also virtually the first to introduce it to English and American readers was the Paris-based *Transition*,[38] which was started in April 1927 and despite a temporary suspension of about two years continued publication until 1938. The artistic beliefs of its founder and editor, Eugene Jolas (whom Stuart Gilbert called "a sort of Diaghilev of *avant-garde* literature"[39]), which strongly characterized the whole magazine, were very close to those of the Surrealists, if not altogether identical. They shared the same appreciation of the legacies of Romanticism; supremacy of imagination, significance of the dream and the unconscious, as well as the modern psychological theories, for literature and art.

Like the Surrealists, Jolas recognizes in the concern with the dream and the irrational the common basis or link between the Romantics and the modern writers. Conceding that the dream has been a subject of man's preoccupation since antiquity, he nevertheless stresses the role played by the Romantics in recognizing its true significance:

> Modern interest in the dream began with the romantics ... it was the great, the unique experience of the romantic movement that brought the dream-problem to the attention of the recent era ... The powers of the unconscious, a-logical, daemonic, instinctive were suddenly recognized as having a preponderant influence in life.
>
> The Dionysian principle was discovered... The dream with the romantic poets became the real basis for all creative action. It is for this reason that I have always insisted in *Transition* and other places that this was the modern creator's link with romanticism. Much in that movement seems to us today obsolete, dusty, ready to be thrown overboard. But the great irrationalist researches of the romantic poets continue to fructify our conceptions.[40]

With this belief in mind he reprinted in his magazine many texts of the Romantic writers, especially Novalis, or underlined the declaration of his literary creeds with quotations from Blake's *Marriage of Heaven and Hell*.[41]

Later, in an essay simply entitled, "The Dream", he writes on the signifance of the subject in question and the night-side of life for the modern age, which inadvertently becomes a profession of his literary principle:

> The study of the dream, which was canonized by Coleridge and Novalis more than a hundred years ago, seemed of particular interest in an age that is striving to make poetry didactic and descriptive. I wanted to encourage an examination of the night-mind. Somehow I felt that the nocturnal realities should be studied and incorporated in the poetic scheme in order to wrench apart such

logical facts as seemed to be stumbling blocks for a visionary feeling for life. I was not interested in Freudian symbols, but in symbolism *tout court*. I regarded the dream and everything pre-logical as an integral function in the struggle for a comprehensive attitude towards life. Without having known the nether-worlds of the chthonian any discipline of the intellect is likely to be proble-matical. The creative mind fuses the irrational and the rational.[42]

The study of the dream, for him, "is a poetic-esthetic liberation" which gives "the poetic creation a universal significance that leads to the metaphysical and the mythological in all its fabulous possibilities."

The dream can be the force of "poetic-esthetic liberation" because of its imaginative faculty. In fact, the dream for Jolas is identical with imagination. In the already quoted "Notes on Reality", which begins with a statement: "The creative effort of this age goes towards totality [another name for the "comprehensive attitude towards life"],"[43] he writes on this aspect of the theme to which he repeatedly and tirelessly returns:

> The dream is pure imagination. Here we are verily beyond good and evil. In that world happen the most wonderful, pathological, criminal, beautiful things. The imagination takes revenge on re-ality. All objects in their pragmatic virtue fade. They carry only the poetic emotion. (p.18)

This kinship between poetry and the dream is naturally carried further to their origins, ie, to that between the creative artist and the dreamer, which in part reminds us of Freud's theory of art and literature, although Jolas' view of the function of dreams differs basically from that of Freud, as we shall see later. Thus he continues:

> The creator and the dreamer have identical roots. They both try to return to the primitive condition of humanity and create a condition where the frontiers of the real and the unreal vanish. (pp.18-19)

Indeed, the dream occupies such a central place in his artistic beliefs that he even declares in the same essay that "the absolute importance of the dream for the creative artist must now be assumed" (p.18)

Appreciation of the Romantic heritage, the importance attached to the dream, the idea of the "condition where the frontiers of the real and the unreal vanish" – the Surrealists called it "surreality" – these are all very similar to the Surrealist stances, but Jolas differs from Breton and his followers on several points. For example, he does not, like the Surrealist, exclude the role of consciousness altogether from creative activity. For him, "the subconscious is not enough," and while the "flight from the excessively rational must go on," he believes that "It is blind fanaticism to deny the conscious will as a creative agent" (p.19) – a view quite different from that of the Surrealists, especially of that period for whom automatic writing was virtually the only valid method of creation. This, however, does not mean rejection of the Surrealists, only a recognition of their limitation. Thus, Jolas goes on to write, first acknowledging their achievement or significance:

> I am not one of those who now turns suddenly against surrealism...
> I persist in regarding the surrealist effort as having crystallized a viewpoint in the modern spirit. The importance of the surrealists, which I tried to emphasize when I first introduced them to this review, lay in their recognition of the primal being as a basic element in creative activity. Theirs was a revolt against the hegemony of reason which historically goes back to romanticism and more recently to Freud. (p.19)

The last part of this passage shows that, like the Surrealists, Jolas was also clearly aware of the double heritage of Romanticism and the modern psychological theories, especially of Freud, for modern artists. This appreciation, however, is immediately followed by the description of the shortcomings which he finds in the Surrealists:

> Their mistake lay in the fact that, after applying Freudian and Dadaist discoveries, they did not transcend them. For the transition from life as a biological existence into the formed existence of creation brings with it a concentrated change. The spontaneous emergence of the disinterested symbols is the *a priori* condition of the creative activity. And it is here where synthesist reality begins.

And not, Jolas implies, where it ends, as the Surrealists' aim clearly indicates.

Another point of disagreement between them lay in methodology, in the use of language, in which, in Jolas' opinion, the Surrealists, though revolutionary in spirit, remained tradition-bound. In this again, he pays a conditional tribute to the Surrealists:

> Although my own definition of reality differs from theirs in the implication of methodology, I have no hesitancy in saying that the Surrealists, following in the wake of Dada, were the only ones to recognize the importance of the explorations into the subconscious world. But the movement remained incomplete, in my opinion, because it refused to consider the problem of the word in the struggle for a new reality. Its revolutionary activity did not transcend the traditional style.[44]

For Jolas, it is essential to find a new style, a new language, to express the "new reality", as he formerly wrote:

> The discoveries of the subconscious by medical pioneers as a new field for magical explorations and comprehensions should have made it apparent that the instrument of language in its archaic condition could no longer be used. Modern life with its changed mythos and transmuted concepts of beauty makes it imperative that words be given a new composition and relationship.[45]

Jolas believes that the "new poet", if he really is a new poet, seeks, as he "is aware of the inadequacy of the traditional means of expression," "a form of expression that will attack principally the problem of language," "seeks a new syntax and vocabulary in order to give voice to the enormously complicated world of psychic changes that are the result of the biological and politico-economic metamorphoses today."[46]

The writer who comes nearest to his ideal as the title of the essay quoted above, "The Revolution of Language and James Joyce," indicates, is James Joyce, especially as the author of *Finnegans Wake*. Jolas thinks that in this work, which was still unnamed at that time, the "revolutionary tendency is developed to its ultimate degree ... "[47] There James Joyce, Jolas maintains:

> gives his words odors and sounds that the conventional standard does not know. In his supertemporal and multispatial composition, language is born anew before our eyes. Each chapter has an internal rhythm differentiated in proportion to the contents ... Nothing that the world of appearance shows to interest him, except in relation to the huge philosophic and linguistic pattern he has undertaken to create. A modern mythology is being evolved against the curtain of the past, and a plane of infinity emerges ... Mr. Joyce has created a language of a new richness and power to express the new sense of time and space he wishes to give.[48]

In fact, *Transition* can claim the honour of first publishing *Finnegans Wake*, then entitled simply *Work in Progress*, in serial form before it was published as a book. The 1933 "Advertisement" did not forget to mention this fact: "*Transition* in its 22 issues published seriatim James Joyce's *Work in Progress*." It was also in *Transition* that some of the first critical views and studies of this controversial work appeared during the course of its publication which covered the period of almost 11 years – the essays by such writers as Samuel Beckett, Stuart Gilbert, Frank Budgen and others. Looking back on those early days, Stuart Gilbert reflects in "Transition Days":

One sometimes hears it said that *Work in Progress* 'made' *Transition* – but in some respects, the converse is equally true. The fact that James Joyce's work appeared by instalments with a month's (later on, several months') breathing space ... between them, gave the reader time to study, digest and assimilate it to some extent; whereas, confronted, out of the blue, by that portentous volume, *Finnegans Wake*, he might well have felt discouraged" (p.20).

In his "Homage to the Mythmaker", an article announcing the completion of *Work in Progress* and its imminent appearance in book form,[49] Jolas calls this monumental work of Joyce, "his protean book of the night", in which "the author deals with the dream-phantasies, with the hypnogogic hallucinations, the inner scissions of an entire household, of mankind in general" (p.171). "We know," he says, "that Mr. Joyce's ambition has been to write a book dealing with the night-mind of man."[50] Obviously, Joyce's work won, as regards the subject matter as well as the "revolutionary" use of language, approval and praise of the editor, who had been championing for literature that explored "the night-mind", the irrational side of man, in order to achieve a total comprehensive view of life, as the title of the essay itself amply indicates. Jolas may well have regarded Joyce's work as the fruit or the culmination of his effort to encourage and produce a new kind of literature, both in style and subject matter, which expresses the "new reality" of modern man.[51]

As may have already been clear from some of the quotations, Jolas acknowledges the contribution of such modern psychologists as Freud and Jung, and to a lesser degree of Janet, in establishing this "new sense of life," "new reality," as emphatically as the Surrealists, although the latter's acknowledgement was mainly limited to Freud. Jolas, on the other hand, had reservations with Freud on several points. For example, on Freud's view of artistic creation he writes:

> Although we stand in reverence before the genius of the scientist who in *The I and the It* [*The Ego and the Id*] and more recently in *The Malaise in Civilization* [*Civilization and its Discontents*]has gone beyond his initial point of departure, we feel nevertheless that he does not entirely meet our conceptions of the creative spirit. By reducing everything to the dogma of a neurosis, he eliminates layers of the poetic genesis that are essential for esthetic understanding.[52]

A familiar complaint, especially among literary men, about what Jung called the "reductive method of Freud". Jolas also finds Freud's dream-symbolism less than satisfactory – "I am not interested in Freudian symbolism but symbolism *tout court*" – and does not totally accept his definition of the dream itself:

> The dream is the reflex of the eternal struggle between our instinc-
> tive, unhampered life and our civilized being. For this reason ...
> Freud's definition of the dream as pure wish-fulfilment is not
> entirely correct, since there enter also other elements, such as fear,
> warning, etc.[53]

although he is fully aware of Freud's significance in opening "the door to
the recognition of a world which was dim and obscure before", as many
of his references to Freud in his writings show. At the same time Jolas
rejects direct or blind application of Freud's theories to literature. In a
footnote attached to the emphatic statement that declared "the absolute
importance of the dream for the creative artist," he warns: "It is understood
that I do not consider the childish applications of Freudian theories which
certain English and American writers have indulged in as of the slightest
importance ... With typical pragmatic insensitiveness they have psycho-
logized, celebrating a narrow pan-sexualism as a new 'philosophy of life,'
and using the text-book information they had gained to engage in their
literary game." He gives Eugene O'Neill's *Strange Interlude* as an
extreme example, and criticizes it for working "from the exterior ...
artificially constructing his protagonists around the more familiar 'complexes'."

It seems that Jolas welcomed Jung's theories as a corrective to Freud's
what he called "narrow pan-sexualism". *Transition* prided itself in being,
in the words of the "Advertisement", "The first literary review to introduce the idea of Dr. C. G. Jung ... " It was actually in *Transition* that the
first translation of Jung's article, "Psychology and Poetry," was published.[54] In the enthusiastic description of this article in "Literature and the
New Man", which appeared in the same issue, Jolas' sympathy for Jung
is apparent. In this essay by Jung, according to him, "an epochal step
forward has been made,"in the study of "the enigmatic in the human
soul."[55] For Jolas who believed that "the Freudian symbol of the personal
did not suffice to explain the complexity of the human spirit," it was a
necessary "step forward". The unconscious obtained, through Jung, a
greater significance. Introducing the ideas expressed in Jung's article, he
writes:

> Not only does the unconscious contain the repressed elements of
> the personal life of the creator, says Dr. Jung, but it is also the vessel
> containing ingredients that relate to the collective life of humanity.
> The latter force may be menacing in the supra-personal dementia,
> or else beneficient in the poet's vision, or religious sentiment. But
> the poet gathers these forces in him and presents them through his
> conscious act as a revivified condition of the personal-collective
> unconscious. Past generations emerge and manifest themselves. In

dream and phantasies there are symbols that are identical with those of the sagas and the fairy tales of humanity.

It is in the recognition that in the human being there is a good deal of nocturnal chaos dating back from his primitive ancestors that the discoveries of the new psychology interest us. The night-mind of man crops out in a thousand ways, and although the intellect is the final arbiter and corrective poetry draws its strength from the sources of the hidden forces of nature.

A little earlier in the same essay, Jolas summarizes "the ideas that *Transition* has stood for" as: "the mythos and the dream, ie, the evocation of the instinctive personal and collective universe: the attempt to define the new man in relation to his primal consciousness; the revolution of the word," concluding, "All of these are interdependent functions of the modern spirit." When we compare the above two summaries, we are struck by the similarities that exist between them and by the extent to which Jolas depended upon Jung's theories in forming his literary and artistic principles. Although "Psychology and Poetry" was being publish-ed in 1930, Jung's ideas had been around for well over ten years. Jung's break with Freud happened in 1913, and the first book to mark this break, *Psychology of the Unconscious*, published a year earlier, was translated and published in English as early as 1916. In any case, Jolas, who was the translator of the article, and of many of the German as well as French contributions to the magazine, could have easily read Jung's writings in the original.[56] It seems that Jung played the same role for Jolas as Freud did for Breton and his followers: the psychologist inspired the writer with his literary and artistic creeds, or at least played a crucial role in forming them, and later provided theoretical support for them.

Jolas seems to have been attracted especially by the idea of myth or mythology, of which Jung made much use in his psychological studies, particularly in relation to his theory of dreams, and thus it occupies the central place in his concept of literature. A year before the publication of Jung's article in *Transition*, Jolas wrote:

The new composition must ... become mythological action. The primitive mythos and the modern mythos are fused, and the union of the collective and individual at the point of the immediate conscience produces the universal condition.

. . . .

The new creator is out to make the alliance between the Diony-sian-dynamic and the nocturnal realities. He is out to discover the unity of life. Conquering the dualism between the "it" [id] and the

"I" [Ego], he produces new myths, myths of himself in a dynamic
environment, myths of new machines and inventions, fairy tales and
fables, legends and sagas...[57]

Seven years later, he is found to be making a very similar assertion:

In creative literature, it [*Transition*] is opposed to the photographic,
descriptive or reportorial conception of the narrative and wants to
substitute for the short story and the novel such forms as the modern
magic tale, the myth, the legend, the dream, the saga, the folktale.
In poetry it hopes for an expression of the emotions deriving from
night and dream, from a racial, mythological heritage. It wants to
seek its dialectics in the interplay of polarities.[58]

One of his essays bears the title "Paramyths", which is the name given
to his ideal "literature of the future," an alternative to the traditional novel
and short story, the literature of conventional realism and naturalism. The
"paramyth", according to his prescription, is "a kind of epic wonder tale
giving an organic synthesis of the individual and universal unconscious -
the dream, the day-dream, the mystic vision. In its final form it might be
a phantasmagoric mixture of the poem in prose, the popular tale of
folklore, the psychograph, the essay, the myth, the saga, the hu-
moresque."[59] Seen in this context, we may realize the depth of Jolas'
admiration for Joyce when, paying him a "homage", he described the
writer as the "mythmaker". We also realize, looking at all those quotations, to what extent Jung's theories affected Jolas' literary concepts or his
literary ideals. Together with the Surrealists, Jolas and his *Transition* may
be regarded as one of those cases which show clear signs of influence of
the modern psychologists, their literary principles being directly based on
the psychological theories of the latter.

Transition represented, as did Surrealism, a reaction "against the
pragmatism of the age",[60] against the "evolutionary materialism [that]
dominated the world,"[61] as the nineteenth century Romanticism was a
reaction against the predominance of rationalism of the preceding age.
Both were the effort, at least in intention, to remedy what Jung called
"one-sidedness" of the age, to restore the equilibrium, or totality, of life
which was lost in the prevailing mores of the day, as Jolas puts it: "There
is a certain state of mind which has too long been neglected in literature:
it is the instinctive or automatic condition of our being ... It seems to us
important not to neglect this condition ..."[62] The recognition of this
neglect in modern society is what links the Surrealists and *Transition*
group with Freud and Jung: the psychologists provided theoretical support
to what the writers and the artists perceived intuitively.

After three years of publication of *Transition*, Jolas proudly stated:

The influence of the experiments of *Transition* is making itself felt in the work of the young writers in both England and America. Instead of the purely reportorial – objective realism of the "middle-Westerners", who have been cluttering up the pages of the magazine with their sordid boredom, we re-established the reign of the imagination.[63]

Has the age of "new romanticism" arrived, thanks to the missionary zeal of Eugene Jolas and his *Transition*? It is difficult to verify his claim, but what is undeniable is the considerable contribution which he made to the modern literary world through the introductory role which he assumed for Surrealism as well as the psychological theories of Freud and Jung, and through his association with Joyce and his *Finnegans Wake*. *Transition*, like Surrealism and in fact all the other Modernist movements, was international in its character – indeed, some issues carried a subtitle, such as "An International Quarterly for creative experiment" (Nos.19-20) or "An International Workshop for Orphic Creation" (No.21) – and in its exploration of the possibility of a new kind of literature, it tapped all possible sources of various nationalities. It was, in fact, in *Transition* that the first English translation of Kafka's *Metamorphosis* was published. Besides introducing the new American, British and Irish writers, *Transition*, claims the "Advertisement", "presented new techniques by writers, painters and photographers from Bulgaria, Czechoslovakia, France, Germany, Hungary, Italy, Russia, Spain and many Latin-American countries."

In almost every respect, Jolas and his *Transition,* as well as Surrealism, may be said to have been typically Modernist in character.

CHAPTER EIGHT

VIRGINIA WOOLF THE CRITIC

IT is significant that when Mark Schorer edited a collection of essays on modern British novelists,[1] he used, in place of the usual editor's introduction, Virginia Woolf's essay, "Modern Fiction", under the heading "In General" as an introductory essay for the whole volume. It indicates the editor's recognition of Woolf's awareness of "modernness" of modern fiction and of her supreme articulateness in expressing this awareness, which she undertook in many of her critical writings, "Modern fiction" being perhaps one of the best-known of all. In fact, her effort to promote the cause of the new kind of fiction, in reaction to the conventional novel, amounts almost to a life-long crusade, and her actual works of fiction bear a close relation to this effort, though needless to say they are by no means the illustrations for her theories. In this outspokenness of her aim in the art of fiction and the abundance of critical essays devoted or related to the subject, Virginia Woolf was exceptional among the "modern novelists"[2] and presents a clear contrast particularly to James Joyce, who rarely theorized about his art in the form of criticism preferring, it seems, to remain, in the words of one of his characters, "like the God of creation ... within or behind or beyond or above his handiwork, invisible, refined out of existence, indifferent, paring his fingernails."[3] Whatever artistic beliefs he held we perceive through his works as a whole, or occasional comments of his fictional characters like the above, or fragments of his letters and conversations. The case of D. H. Lawrence, whose essay is used as an epilogue in the same book which is again significant, is rather peculiar in nature in the sense that unlike Joyce and Woolf, Lawrence always had an ambivalent relationship with Modernism, and if we include him among Modernists he was a Modernist in spite of himself. Though equally critical as Virginia Woolf of the author of *The Forsyte Saga*, as his essay "John Galsworthy" (1927) shows, he was at the same time quite antagonistic to Modernism, and the above-mentioned essay, entitled "Surgery for the Novel – or a Bomb" (1936), is a fierce counter-attack on the new tendency in fiction, represented by Proust, Joyce, Dorothy Richardson and, by implication, Virginia Woolf. There was a good reason for F. R. Leavis to include Lawrence in his anti-Modernist pantheon of "Great Tradition." Thus, if we are to choose the most unambiguous and conspicuous representatives of the Modernist phase in the history of the English novel, the choice inevitably falls on James Joyce and Virginia Woolf who, throughout their literary careers, relentlessly pursued the new objectives in the art of fiction through the constant exploration both in form and subject matter.

The particular significance of Virginia Woolf in this context is that she took to herself, as it were, the task of spokesman for the new generation of writers who felt in one way or another the necessity for a change, and searched for a new direction, in their art during the first quarter of this century. Indeed, she may be regarded as the foremost theoretician of this new phase in English fiction and even literature at large, in the sense that she clarifies for us the aspirations and aims of those writers who occupied, to a lesser or a greater degree, the central place in what we now call the Modernist movement or Modernism. In this respect, we may compare her, in spite of the obvious differences, to André Breton, the theoretician of another branch of Modernism, and consider "Modern Fiction" (1919) her First Manifesto and "Mr. Bennett and Mrs. Brown" (1924) the Second Manifesto in the manner of Breton.[4] As the whole period comes to be seen more and more in the historical perspective, as an entity, in spite of the enormous differences among the individual writers, this role of Virginia Woolf as the theoretician of the period, or of Modernism, will no doubt be appreciated more highly, although unlike Breton, whose importance lies more in his theoretical and critical writings than in his fictional works, her primary importance will remain in the field of fiction, nor was she by any means the initiator or the leader of a movement like him.

It was, in fact, Virginia Woolf who first brought to our attention the opposition between what Stephen Spender later called "the contemporary" and "the modern" when, in "Modern Fiction", she made the now famous condemnation of Arnold Bennett, H. G. Wells and John Galsworthy for preoccupying themselves mainly with either the external details or the material aspect of life, classifying them as "materialists" in contrast to the "spiritual" young writers, of whom she names only Joyce as "the most notable". In "Mr. Bennett and Mrs .Brown", published five years later, the same opposition is maintained, though this time with different name tags, ie, "the Edwardians" for the former and "the Georgians" for the latter.

Moreover, the young "Georgians" are now clearly identified as E. M. Forster, D. H. Lawrence, Lytton Strachey, James Joyce and T. S. Eliot. Although the first distinction, that between "materialist" and "spiritual" writers, is based on the substance or the content of their works, and the second on the chronological or the generational difference of the two groups, what Woolf is concerned with in both cases is essentially the same. It is basically an attack on those established writers of her time, Bennett, Wells, Galworthy, whose concept of the art of fiction and the methods they used accordingly were, as she believed, no longer valid, or never were, in the world in which they lived. It is also an equally impassioned plea to the reading public to support the effort and trials made by the younger writers who rejected the conventions of the traditional novel handed down by the literary establishment. Since in her view,

the form of fiction most in vogue more often misses than secures the thing we seek. Whether we call it life or spirit, truth or reality, this, the essential thing has moved off, or on, and refuses to be contained any longer in such ill-fitting vestments as we provide.[5]

For her, this "life or spirit, truth or reality, this, the essential thing" is the most important, vital core of all the novels, and she even maintains that "perhaps without life nothing else is worth while." In "Mr. Bennett and Mrs. Brown", she presents an old lady, Mrs. Brown, a symbol or an incarnation of this "life" or the "eternal human nature", sitting in a railway carriage, which is travelling "not from Richmond to Waterloo, but from one age of English literature to the next",[6] and imagines how Bennett, Wells and Galsworthy would describe her. "Mrs. Brown" does not exist in Wells' Utopia since, in Woolf's view, Wells, "in his passion to make her what she ought to be", would not "waste a thought upon her as she is" (p.327), whereas Galsworthy, preoccupied with the social conditions that produce such women, "would only see in Mrs. Brown a pot broken on the wheel and thrown into the corner" (pp.327-328). Bennett, on the other hand, may not be disturbed by those abstract ideas, and "would observe every detail with immense care", describing in the minutest detail "the advertisement ... the way in which the cushion bulged between the buttons; how Mrs. Brown wore a brooch which had cost three-and-ten-three at Whitworth's bazaar; and had mended both gloves", etc. (p.328), to such an extent that Mrs. Brown herself would finally be completely overlooked: "With all his powers of observation, which are marvellous, with all his sympathy and humanity, which are great, Mr. Bennett has never once looked at Mrs. Brown in her corner" (p.330). This indeed was the main charge that Woolf levelled at all "the Edwardians":

there she sits and not one of the Edwardian writers has so much as looked at her. (p.330)

They are only "interested in something outside" (p.327), in what she described in the earlier essay as "the trivial and the transitory". As a result, "life escapes"[7], "the essential thing" slips from the hands of the Edwardians, and thus their examples are no models for the younger writers. The tools and conventions employed by them, Woolf declares, "those tools are

not our tools, and that business is not our business. For us those conventions are ruin, those tools are death."[8] Hence:

> the men and women who began writing novels in 1910 or therea-
> bouts had this great difficulty to face – that there was no English
> novelist living from whom they could learn their business. (p.326)

Herein was the "awkward predicament" of the "young Georgians". They
had a new vision of "Mrs. Brown", but what they had in front of them
were obsolete tools totally inadequate to handle it. Many of them,
especially Forster and Lawrence, Woolf believes, spoilt their early work
by compromising and using the old tools for the new vision. These, then,
had to be destroyed first:

> And so the smashing and the crashing began. Thus it is that we hear
> all around us, in poems and novels and biographies, even in news-
> paper articles and essays, the sound of breaking and falling, crashing
> and destruction. (pp.333-334)

The age of agreed manners and consensus of values was gone.

She is fully aware of the inevitable experimental nature of the new kind
of literature when, in conclusion, she warns and pleads to the public: "But
do not expect just at present a complete and satisfactory presentment of
her [Mrs. Brown]. Tolerate the spasmodic, the obscure, the fragmentary,
the failure" (p.337). She seems to have been equally aware, however, of
its tremendous potentiality, of the fact that they were witnessing an
emergence of a new era, of an important phase in the history of English
literature, as she declares:

> ... I will make one final and surprisingly rash prediction – we are
> trembling on the verge of one of the great ages of English literature.
> (p.337)

and continues: "But it can only be reached if we are determined never,
never to desert Mrs. Brown." Indeed she belonged, as we now realize, to
the great Age of Modernism, one of the most active and productive periods
in the history of English culture and played, in retrospect, an important
role as its spokesman. In fact, she was one of the first to use the term
"modern" in the sense used by recent scholars of the Modernist movement. In "Modern Fiction", for example, the "young writers", including
herself, who are contrasted with the "materialists" (later renamed "the
contemporary" by Spender) and on whose behalf she so often spoke, are
also called "the moderns"[9]. And for her to be "a modern" above all meant
to be concerned with the life of the spirit, the inner realities of our being.
In this understanding of the most basic issue of Modernism too, she proves
herself to be the forerunner of modern critics (see above, p.7). Towards

the end of "Mr. Bennett and Mrs. Brown", Woolf redefines the perennial quality of Mrs. Brown as

> an old lady of unlimited capacity and infinite variety; capable of appearing in any place; wearing any dress; saying anything and doing heaven knows what. But the things she says and the things she does and her eyes and her nose and her speech and her silence have an overwhelming fascination, for she is, of course, the spirit we live by, life itself.[10]

She argues, in short, that all the actions, words as well as the appearance of a character are of "overwhelming fascination" to us, as they are the very reflection of the human spirit, which she equates with "life itself." That is also the reason why she mentions here not only Mrs. Brown's "speech" but "her silence" as well, for in the life of the spirit, silence is not just the absence of speech but can be as meaningful as, or even richer in meaning than, the speech. Thus silence comes to bear considerable significance to Woolf, which she tried to prove throughout her career, both in her fictional as well as her critical writings. This attitude was already clear in her first manifesto, "Modern Fiction." After rejecting the novels written after the current fashions, saying "Is life like this? Must novels be like this?" she begins one of the most famous, and perhaps overquoted, passages of all the modern critical essays in these words:

> Look within and life, it seems, is very far from being 'like this.' Examine for a moment an ordinary mind on an ordinary day.[11]

Even this short initial passage makes it abundantly clear that "life" for Woolf essentially means life of the spirit, of the mind – "Look within ..." Then she continues to ask, rhetorically, "is it not the task of the novelist to convey *this varying, this unknown and uncircumscribed spirit,* whatever aberration or complexity it may display, *with as little mixture of the alien and external as possible?*" [my italics]. It was precisely for doing, or trying to do this that the "young writers", who are described as "spiritual", are said "to attempt to come closer to life" (p.107). As a result, she comes to the conclusion that if writers are free to write what they choose, and not to be bound by convention, "the point of interest" for "the moderns"

> lies very likely in the dark places of psychology. At once, therefore, the accent falls a little differently; the emphasis is upon something hitherto ignored; at once a different outline of form becomes necessary, difficult for us to grasp, incomprhensible to our predecessors. (p.108)

Here, while speaking of the aspirations of the British "modern" novelists, Woolf perceived the two essential characteristics common to all the Modernist movements: exploration of inner reality and the consequent need for change in form and methods, which inevitably led to the formal experimentations so characteristic of Modernism. She was aware too, like Breton and others, that the new subject matter was "something hitherto ignored", especially in the conventional English novel.

Since her notion of the modern was thus inseparably related to the search for inner truth, to which many of her later essays also bear witness, it followed that for Woolf the essential qualification to be "a modern" was the awareness of or concern for this inner truth or reality. It was exactly for this reason, for example, that she called Sterne "the forerunner of the moderns." By ignoring that famed cathedral, Notre Dame, in preference for "a girl with a green satin purse," Sterne, Woolf maintains, "transfers our interest from the outer to the inner. It is no use going to the guide book; we must consult our own minds ... ," for it is our mind, not the guide-book, which determines what is, and is not, really important for us. "It is all a question of one's point of view. Sterne's eyes were so adjusted that small things often bulked larger in them than big."[12] These lines, written about 1932, echo and reaffirm one of her own assertions in the 1919 manifesto: "Let us not take it for granted that life exists more fully in what is commonly thought big than in what is commonly thought small,"[13] and in this recognition of the significance in the seemingly trivial and insignificant Woolf proves herself to be a true Modernist in line with Joyce as well as Surrealist poets and painters, particularly Marcel Duchamps. It is an attitude which refuses to follow the commonly accepted norms and standards of values but seeks to explore afresh the meanings of whatever confronts us in life according to the true dictates of the mind. Seen in this way Woolf finds in Sterne a strong trait of modernity which anticipates the characteristics of her contemporary Modernists:

> In this preference for the windings of his own mind to the guide book and its hammered high road, Sterne is singularly of our age. In this interest in silence rather than in speech Sterne is the forerunner of the moderns.[14]

She thus feels greater intimacy towards him than towards the pioneers of the conventional novel form: "And for these reasons he is on far more intimate terms with us today than his great contemporaries the Richardsons and the Fieldings."

Conversely, Hemingway, now generally considered as one of the representatives of American Modernism, fails, seen in this way, to qualify as truly "modern". In "An Essay in Criticism" (1927), Woolf, in an attempt to demonstrate how a critic's mind works, assumes the persona of an imaginary critic who, it in time becomes fairly transparent, is herself. The critic Woolf takes Hemingway of *The Sun Also Rises* and *Men Without Women* for illustration, and declares at the outset that the American novelist, "an 'advanced' writer" though he may be in the general opinion, he is so "not in the way that is to us most interesting."[15] She then immediately proceeds to reveal for the reader to take into account the particular stance, or in her words, "prejudice", that is behind this judgement: "the critic is a modernist." When we remember Woolf's earlier statement: "For the moderns 'that', the point of interest, lies very likely in the dark places of psychology," it is not difficult to guess what it is that makes Hemingway not quite interesting for the "modernist" critic, which indeed the ensuing explanation, or definition, confirms:

> Yes, the excuse would be because the moderns make us aware of what we feel subconsciously; they are truer to our own experience; they even anticipate it, and this gives us a particular excitement.

Hemingway, it is conceded, may be "advanced" or "modern" – these terms seem to be synonymous for Woolf here – in that he describes the "immoralities and moralities" of Paris in 1927 or 1928 with candour, "openly, frankly, without prudery" (p.254), which is indeed a great advance from Victorianism, yet "Mr. Hemingway is not modern in the sense given" (p.253) that is, in the sense of the above definition. For, as the characters "are seen from the old angle; the old reticences, the old relations between author and character are observed", "nothing new is revealed about any of the characters" (p.253) in the novel. In other words, what Hemingway's work lacks is the revelation of "what we feel subconsciously," which are "truer to our own experience," and for this reason he is not interesting, not exciting, for the critic who is "a modernist". Thus when the same point is made again: "Mr. Hemingway is not an advanced writer in the sense that he is looking at life from a new angle. What he sees is a tolerably familiar sight" (p.255), it is fairly obvious what is meant by "a new angle". His reputation for being "modern", or "this rumour of modernity", is considered to come "from his subject matter and from his treatment of it rather than any fundamental novelty in his conception of the art of fiction".[16] The critic's final verdict on Hemingway accordingly is that "he is modern in manner and not in vision" (p.258). It is clear for her reader what significance Woolf attached to the respective terms, "manner" and "vision". While the latter meant throughout her career the essential core, the heart, of all artistic creation, the former belonged, in her mind, to the world of the outside, the ephemeral and the transitory.

Despite his novel subject matter and the new and bold "manner" of presenting it, Hemingway, in these two early works at least, was for Woolf essentially a conventional writer, using "the old tools", treading merely the familiar ground, without venturing into, in Bernard Bergonzi's words, "the new territory," opened up for the novelist in the early part of this century. Hemingway is not "modern", Woolf claims, in the sense that he did not explore, and throw new light on, the deeper physchological, or inner, realities which lie beneath the surface of the visible world.

Woolf's predilection for the inner world of the mind, which is reflected in these essays and is at the basis of her artistic beliefs, may have originated, as is often the case, partly in her own temperament, as well as being the natural reaction against the excessive emphasis laid on the material and external aspects of life by her immediate predecessors, but there is substantial evidence in her writings to believe that it was further buttressed by Freud's psychological theories, introduction of which to England almost coincided with Woolf's own launching into a literary career. The above definition, or description, of "the moderns" in the Hemingway essay itself reads almost like a part of the Freudian theory of dreams. The use of the very terms "subconscious" or "unconscious" that crop up frequently in her essays was the result of the spread and popularization of his psychological theories. Although it may be true that, in Woolf's fiction at least, Freud's "specific influence, save in the general area of symbolism" is, as Harvena Richter points out, "difficult to trace,"[17] it is far less difficult a task to spot in her critical essays, which could be by nature more explicit, the marks left by the psychologist. They range from a light hearted and even playful application of his theories to that of a more serious nature which concerns her artistic principles themselves. The best example of the former appears in *A Room of One's Own* (1929), in which she explains how she came to draw "unconsciously" an unattractive picture of the author of *The Mental, Moral and Physical Inferiority of the Female Sex.* Trying to trace the origin of the author Dr. von X's anger, which she believes inspired him to write the book that denigrates women, which in turn caused her to draw that picture, Woolf ponders: "Had he, to adopt the Freudian theory, been laughed at in his cradle by a pretty girl? For even in his cradle the professor, I thought, could not have been an attractive child,"[18] and thus shows her intimate knowledge of Freud's theory of childhood trauma affecting the spiritual life of the adult. Further, while admitting that drawing pictures is an idle act, she maintains: "Yet it is in our idleness, in our dreams, that the submerged truth sometimes comes to the top." Again, it is almost superfluous to recall, in relation to this statement, Freud's theory of dreams or his method of free association. Woolf finally reaches the conclusion that her unconscious anger at the anti-feminist book and its author revealed itself in the picture of the ugly professor: "Anger had snatched my pencil while I dreamt." Although she calls this self-analysis "A very elementary exercise in psychology, not to be dignified by the name of psycho-analysis," it is obvious that her point of reference throughout is the Freudian psychoanalysis. Although the whole tone is mockingly playful, even this example clearly bears relation to her more serious interest in the subject in the other essays.

It becomes clear from what she writes that she held quite a firm conviction that Freud's theories had caused an almost revolutionary change in people's attitude towards themselves and each other, contributing immensely to their appreciation of the deeper layers of their minds. In "Women and Fiction" (1929), while explaining the difficulties and obstacles women, without incomes and their own rooms, generally encounter when they try to create works of art, she states:

> The immense effect of environment and suggestion upon the mind, *we, in our psychoanalytical age*, are beginning to realize.[19] [my italics]

Even in this short passage it is apparent that Woolf had a notion that Freud had introduced a new era into the history of mankind and that her generation belonged to this new "psychoanalytical age". Such expressions as "to be dignified by the name of psychoanalysis," quoted earlier, also indicates the degree of authority and importance she attached to Freudian psychology. It is often believed that when, in "Mr. Bennett and Mrs. Brown", Woolf made that deliberately sensational assertion: "on or about December 1910 human character changed,"[20] she was referring to, or implying, the epoch-making role of the Post-Impressionist Exhibition at the Grafton Galleries,[21] which was indeed the actual initiation of the English public into such Modernist painters as Cezanne, Picasso and Matisse.

While it is true that among her close friends and relations were painters and art critics, including her own sister Vanessa, her husband Clive Bell, and Roger Fry, whose biography she was to write later, that her mode of writing fiction was sometimes compared to painting,[22] and that Woolf herself used a painter as a key figure in *To the Lighthouse*, she seems to have held the art of painting in relatively low esteem, regarding it frankly as "an inferior art",[23] and had rather unfavourable opinions about the painters and the Post-Impressionist Exhibitions themselves. In her letter of November 27th, 1910 to her friend, Violet Dickinson, she writes, referring to the First Exhibition: "Now that Clive [ie, her brother-in-law who was involved in promoting the Exhibition which was organised by Roger Fry] is in the van of aesthetic opinion, I hear a great deal about pictures. I don't think them so good as books." As to the post-impressionists exhibited, she describes them as "a modest sample set of painters, innocent even of indecency", thus finding the public furore they caused incomprehensible. Though her own assessment seems to have been that theirs were no different from "other pictures", she would not call them, she states, anything but "better" just not to make "everyone angry",[24] obviously meaning by "everyone" her friends such as the Bells and Roger Fry. When the Second Exhibition, for which her husband Leonard worked as Secretary, was over, she wrote again to the same recipient (December 24th, 1912): "The Grafton ... thank God, is over; artists are an abominable race. The furious excitement of these people all the winter over their pieces of canvas green and blue, is odious."[25]   In the light of such an attitude on Woolf's part, it seems rather difficult to assume that she attached particular significance to that event, and that her bold statement was directly inspired by the 1910 Exhibition and its effect upon the public, as is often considered.[26] How can "a modest sample set of painters" – indeed a bold statement in retrospect to describe such giants as Cezanne and Picasso – who are "innocent even of indecency" transform the whole human character, all human relations? However important in the Modernist movement the Post-Impressionists may be, as far as Virginia Woolf, especially of this period, is concerned, there is no evidence whatever which enables us to relate her famous pronouncement to them or interpret it as the result recognized by Woolf of the far-reaching influence of those painters on the wide-eyed public. It seems more reasonable to consider, as Anthony Fothergill does, that she attributed the change "not so much to the artistic influence of a Cezanne ... as to more general tendencies,"[27] although the passage he quotes to support his argument: "All human relations have shifted – those between masters and servants, husbands and wives, parents and children, etc." discusses the results rather than the causes for these changes, as he apparently assumes. For in this essay, Woolf does not present the reasons or causes for the change, but only calls attention to the actual situation that demands the corresponding change in the writers' attitudes and methods, as well as in the attitude of the reading public.

The causes themselves must be found in the interaction of various elements in society in the early part of this century, as we discussed in the introductory chapter, which could have affected people's whole outlook on the world, society and human nature. In this respect, Fothergill makes a more significant point later when he calls our attention to the early draft of "Mr. Bennett and Mrs. Brown", where she, in his words, "is far more explicit in attributing this shift in relation to the ideas of Freud, the reading of whose revolutionary accounts of human psychology was absorbing the intelligentsia of the day." It may be worth its while to examine the original typewritten script, which is among the Monks House Papers. In fact, this earlier version of the essay, which was given under the title, "Characters in Fiction", as a lecture to a Cambridge Society, the Heretics, in May 1924, differs substantially from the published version in detail, although the main contentions in both are essentially the same. For example, that statement which proclaims the change in human character "on or about December 1910" itself does not make its appearance there, nor the ensuing passages on the shift in "All human relations", illustrated by the examples from literature – Samuel Butler and Shaw – as well as from real life, such as "the character of one's cook." Instead we have what Woolf describes as "the first of my sweeping statements," which is: "No generation since the world began has known quite so much about character as our generation."[28] This obviously is less sensational, and perhaps less effective, as it does not catch our attention or imagination so dramatically as the one we have now. Nevertheless, the basic claim, at least by implication, that there was in her day a fundamental change in men's attitudes towards each other is common to both statements. Elaborating on her "sweeping [statement]" she writes:

> The average man or woman today thinks more about character than his or her grandparents; character interests them more; *they get closer, they dive deeper into the real amotions* [sic] *and motives of their fellow creatures.*[29] [my italics]

It is after this assertion that she brings in Freud in her wish to prove or support her argument:

> There are scientific reasons why this should be so. If you read Freud you know in ten minutes some facts – or at least some possibilities – which our parents could not possibly have guessed for themselves.[30]

Woolf in effect maintains that it was Freud and his writings that opened the eyes of her contemporaries to the deep-seated secrets of "the real [e]motions and motives" of their fellow human beings, which the older generations, without "help from Dr. Freud" – Woolf's own words[31] – could not have conceived for themselves. She seems to have had second thoughts, however, about this reference to science and Freud, and in the margin, as Faulkner points out, added the handwritten comment: "That is a very debatable point. But [sic] how much can we learn from science [sic] ... & make our case [?] from science."[32] In the final printed version this part, as we know, was completely revised, and the whole passage, including the initial statement itself, was replaced by a new statement and a new argument, thus omitting the direct reference to Freud as well. Yet the gist of the argument, though different in expression, is essentially the same in the two versions and the view expressed in it forms the basis of both texts throughout.

Though Woolf, evidently growing diffident about directly attributing to Freud what she considered an important social change withdrew, perhaps wisely (for how can we attribute a great social change to just a single theory?), his name and the relevant passages from her essay, it is significant all the same that when she first reflected on the dramatic change in men's understanding of and attitude towards each other and called for a corresponding revolution – for it was nothing less than a revolution that she wanted – in the art of fiction, she had at the back of her mind Freud and his theories, which had thrown new light upon human nature and behaviour and which were beginning to exert what has often been termed as "revolutionary" influence on the minds of the educated people at about the same time, although the date given in the final version of the statement, admitted as "arbitrary" by the writer herself, should perhaps be taken as an approximate indication rather than a definite date, as some critics seem to think – she later repeats twice, "about the year 1910".

Describing the feeling of excitement and "exhilaration" of living in London in 1911, which may be regarded as almost the same date as [Dec.] 1910, Leonard Woolf writes, by way of explanation, "Profound changes were taking place in every direction, not merely politically and socially", and mentions Freud, together with Rutherford and Einstein, as "beginning to revolutionize our knowledge of our own minds and of the universe."[33] In fact, there are some significant facts around the dates given by the Woolfs in relation to Freud, which indicates Freud's growing influence in the Anglo-Saxon world, and for that matter the world outside Vienna and Zurich. In 1909, Freud and Jung gave lectures on psychoanalysis in America, which marked their first direct contact with the English speaking public. The following year, 1910, saw the publication of those lectures in English translation in *The American Journal of Psychology*, along with "a comprehensive account" of Freud's theory of dreams by Ernest Jones, thus making his theories accessible to a wider, though still limited, public.[34] Jones, referring to the years 1910-1914, observes: "In these years was launched what was called the 'Psycho-analytical Movement'."

It was in 1910 that the International Psycho-analytical Association was founded under Freud's initiative with Jung as its first President, which was followed by re-organization or formation of Branch Societies in many countries all over the world, including the one in America in 1910 which was later to become the most influential, and the London one in 1913 with Ernest Jones as President. At the beginning of 1911, Freud was made an Honorary Member of the Society for Psychical Research of England, which he called "the first sign of interest from dear old England" (p.99). He also wrote to Jones that he "had to refuse no less than three offers for translating the *Traumdeutung* from Englishmen," as he expected A.A. Brill would soon do it. As it was, the English translation by Brill, the most loyal Freudian in America, of *The Interpretation of Dreams* was published in 1913 on both sides of the Atlantic. It was followed by the publication in English of *The Psychopathology of Everyday Life* in 1914. Jones' comment on Freud of 1909, the year of the American tour, was still more appropriate for Freud of this later date, especially in the English-speaking world: "By this time Freud was in a position where he could look forward to a career of recognition and fame ... From now on he might meet with misunderstanding, criticism, opposition and even abuse, but he could no longer be ignored" (p.73).

Although Britain as a whole was not as enthusiastic about Freud's ideas as was America, even here they began to attract attention and the interest of the intellectuals during the decade of 1910, especially among the literary men, for the reasons discussed in the earlier chapters, and above all, it seems, among the "Bloomsbury Group" of which the Woolfs, together with their close friends, were the central figures. There is a little sketch with the title "According to Freud", written by Lytton Strachey, another prominent member of the group, which may give us some idea about how the "Georgians" became acquainted with Freud's theories and how they reacted to them. The piece consists entirely of a dialogue between two young people, who are in a situation not altogether unlike that of Beatrice and Benedick and whose characters also bear some resemblance to the Shakespearian archetypes. To judge from the heroine's remark, Freud seems to have been received in much the same way as Ibsen, Chekhov or Strindberg had been earlier, and was considered to be part of "modern knowledge." Thus not to know his name or his theories meant to be "out of date"; when Arthur, the young man, confesses that he does not know Freud, the sharp-tongued Rosamund taunts:

Of course not. You are wonderfully out of date. Who *have* you heard of? Schnitzler? Tchekhoff [sic]? I should like to put you through an examination in modern knowledge. Probably you've reached Ibsen, and are beginning to think that you really must take a look at this queer fellow Strindberg everyone's talking about – or was, the year before last. Well, well, I suppose in the end – ten years hence – you'll come and tell me that you've discovered a new writer, called Freud, who's very interesting, and you'll refuse to believe me when I answer ... that I was reading him ten years ago ...[35]

The fact that Freud is here described as "a new writer" indicates that he was regarded by some as a sort of thinker or philosopher, rather than a scientist in the strictest sense as Freud himself seems to have wished throughout his life, and as such was more accessible to the general public than the latter. His name, due to his frank revelation of some of the facts and secrets of the mind which had formerly either been unrealized or suppressed, was synonymous for these people with the truth about the human mind and human nature. The heroine, when she tries to show herself to be up to date and truthful, thus declares: "I am going to prove that I belong to the present day – that I am a contemporary of Dr. Freud because I'm simply going to tell the truth" (p.117). After misunderstanding one another's words and intentions, the two, both highly incensed, part, Arthur returning to his letter writing and Rosamund to the book she had been reading before the act began, namely Freud's *Psychopathology of Everyday Life*. The young man, however, returns presently to collect the fountain pen he has forgotten and left behind. Conversation thus resumed, misunderstandings duly resolved and the couple reconciled, the piece reaches its dénouement not in a conventional happy-ending of a comedy, marriage, but in a way befitting the "modern" young people of the day:

Arthur: Thank goodness, we needn't talk much more. We both thoroughly disgraced ourselves; but luckily there's still time for repentance. Let us repent! – It was a narrow shave, though; we were only saved from utter ruin by –

Rosamund: By your fountain-pen.

Arthur: My ... my *symbolic* fountain-pen?

Rosamund: According to Freud.

Arthur: I'm beginning to think there may be rather more in Dr. Freud than I'd supposed. I must read him. You said you had this book somewhere – ? You must explain him to me.

Rosamund: Yes – in the summer-house. Come along. I'll explain as much as you like.

[They go into the summer-house.][36]

Although the predominant mood of the dialogue is witty, comical and light, in the style of comedy of manners not unlike that of Oscar Wilde, it is not completely frivolous as may be seen from the last speech of Arthur quoted above. The whole piece is based on Freud's thesis expounded in *The Psychopathology* that when we forget something, there is more often than not an unconscious intention or wish behind it: "According to Freud, one never does forget," as the heroine puts it (p.114). Although the editor comments that "This dialogue is another of Strachey's commentaries on the bourgeois war between the sexes" (p.111), it might as well have been an attempt to illustrate in an entertaining way the above contention of Freud, or to show how Freud revealed, as Woolf wrote in her script, "some facts ... or at least some possibilities ... which our parents could not possibly have guessed for themselves."

We may see in this little sketch a reflection of similar scenes among the young people of the time, and especially of Strachey's circle (the editor detects, in the "informality" of its style, "a hint of Strachey's own voice in some of the odd inflections and curious turns of phrase" – p.111), and in this sense it may illustrate one of the possible ways how Freud's theories spread in those early days. The date of composition is considered to be "1914 – the year of the first appearance in English translation of Freud's *Psychopathology of Everyday Life* – or later," (p.111), but it cannot be much later than that, if we judge from the speeches made by the heroine, who declares that "There's fifty years between" herself and Arthur (p.118) who is "thoroughly out of date" and "belongs to the sixties," ie, 1860s, which places the piece definitely within the decade of 1910. The piece is interesting as it conveys to us the impression Freud's ideas made on the educated young of the period, as well as their awareness of the break between themselves and the old tradition and attitudes, epitomized by the term "Victorianism", which was also a favourite subject of Virginia Woolf in her diary, letters and essays.

In his autobiography, Leonard Woolf describes succinctly the nature and extent of Freud's influence among the Bloomsbury group at about the same time:

> In the decade before 1924 in the so-called Bloomsbury circle there was great interest in Freud and psycho-analysis, and the interest was extremely serious. Adrian Stephen, Virginia's brother, who worked ... on mediaeval law, suddenly threw the Middle Ages and law out of the window, and with his wife Karin, became a qualified doctor and professional psycho-analyst. James Strachey, Lytton's youngest brother, and his wife also became professional psychoanalysts. James went to Vienna and was analysed by Freud, and he played an

active part at the Institute of Psycho-Analysis which, largely through Ernest Jones, had been founded in London and was in intimate relations with Freud and the Mecca of psycho-analysis in Vienna, being itself a branch of the International Association of Psycho-Analysis. (p.308)

The statement about James Strachey being psychoanalyzed by Freud must refer to the former's trip to Vienna in 1920 when he, together with his wife Alix, studied psychoanalysis under Freud. In her letter (September 2nd, 1921) to Janet Case, Virginia Woolf writes: "The last people I saw were James and Alix, fresh from Freud – Alix grown gaunt and vigorous – James puny and languid – such is the effect of 10 months' psycho-analysis."[37] It may be naturally assumed that there was conversation, then or later, about their work and experience under Freud. It is clear that Virginia Woolf was surrounded by friends and relatives who had in one way or another close and sometimes direct connection with Freud and Freudian psychology, and had ample opportunities to observe how this affected these people's way of apprehending human behaviour and motives and instigated their acute interest in those subjects. Lytton Strachey, for example, apart from that sketch which directly deals with one of Freud's works, shows subtler traces of his influence elsewhere as well. In the Preface to his best known work, *Eminent Victorians*, he expounds on the method to be used in his history of the Victorian Age:

It is not by the direct method of a scrupulous narration that the explorer of the past can hope to depict that singular epoch. If he is wise, he will adopt a subtler strategy. He will attack his subject in unexpected places; he will fall upon the flank, or the rear; he will shoot *a sudden revealing searchlight into obscure recesses, hitherto undivined.* He will row out over that great ocean of material, and *lower down into it,* here and there, *a little bucket, which will bring up to the light of day some characteristic specimen, from those far depths,* to be examined with a careful curiosity.[38] [my italics]

Though expressed in more abstract terms, this is not very far from Virginia Woolf's attitude in her approach towards literature, with her main interest in the reality beneath the surface "hitherto undivined" or ignored, and explains why she included Strachey and his biographies in the list of "the moderns" or "the Georgians" and their revolutionary works. A line from his life of Florence Nightingale in the book may illustrate his basic attitude towards his subjects stated above: "Beneath her cool and calm demeanour lurked fierce and passionate fire" (p.133). Behind the façade of the gentle "lady with a lamp", he detected "the sign of dominating power," "the traces of a harsh and dangerous temper." In his *Elizabeth and Essex* too, we recognize the influence of the Freudian theory of psychosomatic diseases when, explaining Queen Elizabeth's illness, he rejects the physical causes and attributes it to hysteria, the origin of which is traced back to her experience in childhood when her feelings towards her father must have been profoundly affected by the traumatic event of her mother's execution by that same father.[39]

Leonard Woolf himself, whom Virginia married in 1912, and who thus became the closest person to the novelist, shows, besides his involvement with the publication of Freud's works, which we shall examine later, every sign of the psychologist's influence on his attitudes towards his friends and acquaintances as well as himself. While referring to Freud as revolutionizing "our knowledge of our minds" in the year 1911, he seems to have come to a closer, or direct, contact with his work in 1914, when he read both *The Interpretation of Dreams*, published a year before, and *The Psychopathology of Everyday Life* published that same year, which he read for the purpose of reviewing for a magazine. He seems to have been a constant reader of Freud ever since. Reminiscent of the young couple in Lytton Strachey's sketch, he often resorts to Freud's theories when he tries to understand the deeper causes for the behaviour of, or some personal inclinations in, himself and people around him. Commenting on "the bitterest letter," which he has ever received, from one of his brothers, for whom he was "pure Mr. Hyde" but who did not reveal this long-harboured hatred "until he was over 60 and I over 70", Leonard remarks:

Having read Genesis and its story of Cain and Abel, and later Freud and his elaboration of it, the terrible story of the murderous hatred (suppressed of course) of son for father, father for son, and brother for brother, I ought not to have been astonished by this letter.[40]

and reflects on the savage feelings concealed behind the normal human relations:

When in Ceylon I for the first time saw in the jungle what nature was really like in the crude relation of beast to beast, I was shocked and at first even disgusted at the cold savagery, the pitiless cruelty. But when I contemplate the jungle of human relations, I feel that here are savageries and hatreds – illuminated by Zeus, Jupiter, Christ or Dr. Freud – which make the tiger and the viper seem gentle, charitable, tender-hearted. (p.50)

On Madge Vaughn, daughter of J. A. Symonds and friend of Virginia, he writes:

Madge has worshipped her father as so many daughters have since the time of Electra, in a way which was not fully understood until

the second eating of the apple on the tree of knowledge by Sigmund
Freud. (II, p.49)

Besides showing his knowledge of the theory of the Electra Complex,
the passage reveals the degree of signifance he attached to Freud's ideas
by comparing them to "the second eating of the apple," which indicates
that he regarded them as the initiator of an entirely new era in human
knowledge. He also considered, while commenting on *To the Lighthouse*,
that the attitude of Virginia Woolf and her sister towards their father, Leslie
Stephen, was affected by "a complicated variety of the Oedipus Complex"
(p.117). At another point in the *Autobiography*, recalling a malicious joke
aimed at him during his Ceylon days, he observes:

> It is curious – and then again, if one remembers Freud, it is of course
> not so curious – that I should remember so vividly, after 50 years,
> the incident and the hurt and humiliation ... (II, p.139).

and continues to explain it in Freudian terms:

> It was a joke, but then, of course, it was, deep down, particularly for
> the victims, 'no joke.' Freud with his usual lucidity unravels the
> nature of this kind of joke in Chapter III, 'The Purpose of Jokes',
> of his remarkable book *Jokes and their Relation to the Unconscious*.
> (pp.139-140)

Then he quotes a whole passage from the book mentioned to support
his argument. His character analysis of H. W. Massingham, the editor of
the political journal, *Nation*, for which he worked for some years, is also
essentially Freudian. Holding a conviction, based on the view of several
psychoanalysts, that

> If one looks deep into the minds of those who are on the left in
> politics (including myself), Liberals, revolutionaries, socialists,
> communists and humanitarians, one could find that their political
> beliefs and desires were connected with some very strange goings-
> on down among their ids in their unconscious. (p.256)

He considers that "the conflict in his [Massingham's] character, his gentle
high-mindedness and absurd verbal violence" is the result of existence
"Down below" of strong rival feelings of "the milk of human kindness
and hatred and bitterness", as well as "the grudge against the universe."
Finding an explanation for his "grudge" in Freud's *Civilization and its
Discontents*, Leonard Woolf comments:

> to be even a moderately civilized man is not only difficult but also
> extremely painful. If you have to be as high-minded all the time as
> a Liberal ... editing or writing for *Nation* in 1922, you had to be
> suppressing all the time some very violent and curious instincts

which might, I think, have surprised and shocked even the editor of
the *Nation* had he found them in his unconscious mind.[41]

It is obvious from these examples that for him Freud supplied major
clues for understanding human character and behaviour, and his propensity towards delving beneath the surface into the deeper motives itself must
have developed under Freud's influence. Though for post-Freudians such
total acceptance of Freud's theories, the assumption that all his theories
are scientific facts – the novelist was a little more cautious: she first called
them "some facts" but added presently: "or at least some possibilities" –
may appear rather naïve, it cannot be denied that the knowledge of Freud's
ideas gave him and others like him added dimensions to their understanding of their fellow human beings, which the older generation "could
not possibly have guessed for themselves". At any rate, it is almost
impossible to avoid the impression that observation of the impact these
ideas had upon people around her as well as of the extent of their
penetration into these people's way of thinking must have affected the
novelist a great deal in forming her view of the Freudian influence on
human relations and characters.

Furthermore, Virginia Woolf herself came to have quite close connection, and on one occasion even a personal contact, with Freud. In 1924,
the Hogarth Press, which the Woolfs had established in 1917, took over
the publication of all Freud's papers through a request made by James
Strachey on behalf of the Institute of Psycho-Analysis [the London
Branch of the International Association of Psycho-Analysis] , which had
started in 1921 the publication of the International Psycho-Analytical
Library, in which Freud's papers were included. This was an event given
a special significance by Leonard in his *Autobiography* as "a bold under-
taking" that turned out to be a great success and had a considerable effect
on their Press, which means that there was constant interest in and
demands for Freud's works in the English speaking world. This publishing
venture later developed into the publication of what we now have as the
Standard Edition of all Freud's works under the general editorship of
James Strachey. In Leonard's own words:

> Between 1924 when we took over the library and his death in 1939
> we published an English translation of every book which he wrote,
> and after his death we published his complete works, 24 volumes,
> in the *Standard Edition*. (II, p.310)

This in fact means that Virginia, throughout her literary career, had an
almost constant contact with Freud's works as they underwent publication
in her capacity as his publisher, which seems to have involved every aspect

of the process of producing printed books, as Leonard at one point remarks that both himself and Virginia, as well as the staff on the Press, "were expected to be able to take a hand at any and everything, including packing."[42] It is quite probable that she read many of his works at the stage of proof-reading or as finished products. At any rate, there is little doubt that among modern English writers, Virginia Woolf was in an unusually privileged, or advantageous, position as far as access to Freud's works and witnessing of their impact on the minds of the intelligentsia of her time were concerned.

Through her diaries and letters, Woolf reveals that she read quite a few of Freud's writings, especially towards the end of her life. As late as December 17th 1939, the year of Freud's death and two years before her own, we find an entry in her diary that she "read Freud on Groups,"[43] meaning no doubt his book *Group Psychology*. Earlier in that year, in her letter dated July 15th, she wrote to John Lehmann, who had worked for some time for the Hogarth Press as an assistant: "*Moses* had a very good show – I'm reading it."[44] The English translation of Freud's *Moses and Monotheism* was published in the same year by the Hogarth Press and, judging from her remark above, achieved a considerable success as did the other works by Freud. Apparently she read it just after its publication. Apart from these few instances in which the specific names of the books are given, Woolf often refers to Freud's works without mentioning their titles. It seems she read Freud quite avidly during her last years, and some days before she read *Group Psychology*, ie, on December 8th, 1939, she quotes Freud while commenting on her own mixed feelings about the subject of "shopping": "Ambivalence as Freud calls it (I'm gulping up Freud)" (p.249). Furthermore, in the entry of the following day, she adds:

> Freud is upsetting: reducing one to whirlpool; & I daresay truly. If we're all instinct, the unconscious, what's all this about civilisation, the whole man, freedom &c? His savagery against God good. The falseness of loving one's neighbours. The conscience as censor. Hate ... But I'm too mixed.[45]

Such words as "civilisation" and "God" suggest that she has been reading, as the editor of *The Diary* conjectures (p.250n), *The Future of an Illusion* and *Civilization and its Discontents*. Although we may detect here Woolf's, and many other artists' reservations about the determinist side of Freud, to which point we shall return later, the statements above leave us in little doubt as to the impact of his writings upon her mind. In another entry (Feb. 9th, 1940), she just writes, "Now I'm going to read Freud" (p.266), without giving us any clue as to the title of the book. It is also possible, given her circumstances, that she read more works by the psychologist without mentioning it anywhere.

At all events, it seems fairly certain that Woolf was quite well acquainted, not only through hearsay but through reading directly herself, with the works of Freud, who must have had special significance for her in more than one sense.[46]

The Woolfs' connection with Freud was not limited to business alone, but seems to have extended to the one of more personal nature, which is again revealed by Leonard:

> The greatest pleasure that I got from publishing the Pyscho-Analytical Library was the relationship which it established between us and Freud ... He was not only a genius, but also, unlike many geniuses, an extraordinarily nice man.[47]

He further talks of Freud's "extraordinarily civilized temperament ... which made every kind of relationship with him so pleasant" (*Ibid*, II, p.310). Apparently, the personal frictions which seem to have marred quite a few of Freud's relationships with his followers in the Psycho-Analytical Movement, most notably Jung and Adler, did not exist between the author and the publisher, perhaps largely because the spheres of their activities were completely different. There is also an extremely cordial account by Leonard of the Woolfs' meeting with Freud at his London home which is of considerable interest to us, not only as it gives Leonard's own impressions of the man that might well have been shared by his companion, but mainly because it conveys to us the general atmosphere in which the novelist's direct personal contact with the psychologist took place, which was, as we shall see, full of reverence and warmth. For this reason, we shall quote Leonard's account in full:

> I only once met Freud in person. The Nazis invaded Austria on 11 March 1938, and it took three months to get Freud out of their clutches. He arrived in London in the first week in June and three months later moved into a house in Maresfield Gardens which was to be his permanent home. When he and his family had had time to settle down there, I made discreet enquiries to see whether he would like Virginia and me to come down and see him. The answer was yes, and in the afternoon of Saturday 28 January 1939, we went and had tea with him. I feel no call to praise the famous men whom I have known. Nearly all famous men are disappointing or bores, or both. Freud was neither; he had an aura, not of fame, but of greatness. The terrible cancer of the mouth which killed him only eight months later had already attacked him. It was not an easy interview. He was extraordinarily courteous in a formal, old-fa-

shioned way – for instance, almost ceremoniously he presented Virginia with a flower. There was something about him as of a half-extinct volcano, something sombre, suppressed, reserved. He gave me the feeling which only a very few people whom I have met gave me, a feeling of great gentleness, but behind the gentleness, great strength. The room in which he sat seemed very light, shining, clean, with a pleasant, open view through the windows into a garden .... He spoke about the Nazis. When Virginia said that we felt some guilt, that perhaps if we had not won the 1914 war there would have been no Nazis and no Hitler, he said, no, that was wrong; Hitler and Nazis would have come and would have been much worse if Germany had won the war. (II, pp.311-312)

This must be one of Virginia Woolf's very few direct comments on the subject of politics, which she considered a largely male preoccupation and regarded it with antipathy and near contempt.[48] Also in the light of the latent, and sometimes overt, anti-Semitic sentiments that we often find in her letters and fictional works throughout her life,[49] in spite of the fact that her husband was a Jew (or because of it? – a subject for a biographical study into which we shall not delve here), she seems to have gone out of her usual way to be apologetic and in showing her sympathy for Freud's plight as a Jew at the time, to such an extent as to admit to her share of the collective guilt for it. Woolf herself left only a brief record of this meeting in her diary which, however, extends over two days, January 29th and 30th, 1939. Most of her accounts, which may better be described as jottings, concur with Leonard's, including this exchange with Freud over Hitler. The serious tone with which she states it gives the impression that there was genuine feeling behind those remarks.

Leonard also records an episode which reveals the public's still divided reaction towards Freud, and Freud's own response to it. When he recounted to the psychologist that a man charged with stealing books, including one of his own, was told by the magistrate that "he wished he could sentence him to read all Freud's works", Freud received this, Leonard reports, with amusement as well as deprecation and commented that "His books ... had made him infamous, not famous." Leonard concludes the account of the interview, as if to sum him up, with the laconic remark: "A formidable man."[50]

In Virginia's version, this episode of the thief is abridged into almost shorthand expression: "About his books. Fame? I was infamous rather than famous," followed by the price of his first book and the statement on the following day about Freud's being "Very alert at L's mention of the case ... " (*The Diary*, V, p.202). What she adds to Leonard's record is an almost ruthless description of the terminal cancer patient Freud, to whose condition Leonard referred only indirectly: "A screwed up shrunk very old man: with a monkey's light eyes, paralysed spasmodic movements, inarticulate." To this, however, she immediately adds, "but alert." As we can see, she uses the word "alert" twice in this short space in her diary. In fact, she recognizes in the "screwed up shrunk very old man" "Immense potential ... an old fire", which is "now flickering." This may echo Leonard's recognition in Freud of "something ... as of half extinct volcano", as well as "great strength" behind "[his] great gentleness." Just a few days before this meeting she wrote in a letter: "We are going to see the great Freud on Saturday."[51] In spite of her reservations about a certain aspect of his theories, the epithet Woolf uses here for Freud may indicate her overall attitude towards the pyschologist, in whom, as many of her essays bear witness, she clearly saw one of the spiritual leaders of the age.

In his essay on Modernism, Harry Levin wrote on the influence of the new psychological theories on the art of fiction:

> Fiction was spurred to such feats of self-consciousness by the revelations of psychoanalysis: the Freudian probing for unconscious motives, the Jungian search for universal patterns. It may be an exaggeration to argue that human nature changed in 1910, but Virginia Woolf was bold enough to do so, though probably unaware that the International Psychoanalytical Association had been founded in that year.[52]

When we consider all the circumstances we have examined in which Virginia Woolf was placed in relation to Freud and his ideas at the time of her writing "Mr. Bennett and Mrs. Brown", and especially that the year 1924 when she wrote it was exactly when the Woolfs took over the publication of all Freud's works from the London Branch of the International Psychoanalytical Association through one of their closest friends, James Strachey, who was an active, if not a founding member of the Association and had actually studied under Freud three years before, it seems possible but not very "probable" that the novelist was "unaware" of the fact mentioned by Levin. On the contrary, she must have possessed much greater knowledge about psychoanalysis and its movement than most laymen, and it is highly likely that she knew, or heard, of the formation of its International Association in 1910 – the year she arbitrarily chose in her essay – at least by 1924, if not in that year itself. Levin, however, was essentially right in sensing the link between Freud and Woolf's "bold" declaration on the shift in human character and relations, the link which the original version of the essay, "Characters in Fiction", clearly demonstrates.

When we go through Virginia Woolf's critical writings, her debt to
Freud as well as her recognition of his significance for her age, which she
sometimes plainly acknowledges, becomes increasingly apparent. Above
all her artistic belief, her basic stance as artist, was closely related to
Freud's basic stance as psychologist. It is not that, like those writers
condemned by Eugene Jolas, she applied his theories directly to her works
and constructed them around these theories, but that she shared the
fundamental conviction with the psychologist that the unconscious, or the
inner life of man, which had been neglected so far – in her words
"something hitherto ignored" – is, if not the whole truth itself, of crucial
importance, and holds a vital key to the true understanding of his whole
being. Though she may have had an almost intuitive belief in this and her
interest in and wonder at the mysteries of the human mind must have been
constantly roused by her own recurrent mental disorders, she seems to
have turned, for confirmation of this personal, intuitive conviction, to
Freud, who presented the same idea to the world as a systematic theory
with the endorsement of his clinical studies.

Thus in Virginia Woolf's theory of art, the unconscious, as in Freud's
case, comes to play the most important role, and several of her essays
reveal that the incidental comment made during the light-hearted application of Freudian theory in *A Room of One's Own*: "Yet it is in our
idleness, in our dreams, that the submerged truth sometimes comes to top"
does in fact express Woolf's fundamental belief about the part the unconscious plays in the creative process. In an essay entitled "The Leaning
Tower" (1940), where she analyses and evaluates the achievement of the
younger generation of writers of the 1930s, she discusses the function of
the unconscious at some length, first in general terms:

> Unconsciousness, which means presumably that the under-mind
> works at top speed while the upper-mind drowses, is a state we all
> know. We all have experience of the work done by unconsciousness
> in our daily lives. You have had a crowded day, let us suppose,
> sightseeing in London. Could you say what you had seen and done
> when you come back? Was it not all a blur, a confusion? But after
> what seemed a rest, a chance to turn aside and look at something
> different, the sights and sounds and sayings that had been of most
> interest to you swam to the surface, apparently of their own accord;
> and remained in memory; what was unimportant sank into forget-
> fulness.[53]

then specifically in relation to the writer, maintaining that the creative
process follows the same general rule:

> So it is with the writer. After a hard day's work, trudging around,

seeing all he can, feeling all he can, taking in the book of his mind innumerable notes, the writer becomes – if he can – unconscious. In fact, his under-mind works at top speed while his upper-mind drowses. Then, after a pause, the veil lifts; and there is the thing – the thing he wants to write about – simplified, composed. (p.166)

It is for this reason no doubt that she declares in another essay: "a novelist's chief desire is to be as unconscious as possible."[54] Elaborating on this statement she continues: "He has to induce in himself a state of perpetual lethargy ... so that nothing may disturb or disquiet the mysterious nosings about, feelings around, darts, and dashes, and sudden discoveries of that very shy and illusive spirit, the imagination." We find Woolf here, precisely as the Romantics, closely relating the unconscious to imagination or imaginative faculty. It therefore comes as no surprise when, in concluding the above discussion of the unconscious, she quotes Wordsworth to support her view:

Do we strain Wordsworth's famous saying about emotion recollected in tranquility when we infer that by tranquility he meant that the writer needs to become unconscious before he can create? (p.166)

Obviously, Woolf must have sensed that, whatever the apparent differences, there exists between the kind of literature she believed in and Romanticism essential kinship, that they shared the same creative principle. That she was correct in this may be attested by our earlier surveys of Romanticism and its heritage in Modernism.[55] It seems that in Woolf too, as in Surrealists and others, there was a marriage between Romanticism and modern psychology, especially of Freud, the double tradition or influence we have detected to lie behind the Modernist movement, and in this sense too we may regard her as a writer who typically embodies the spirit of Modernism.

As we have already observed with her contrasting evaluations of Sterne and the early Hemingway (though she might have had a different view of his later phase, eg, of *The Old Man and the Sea*), or of "the Edwardians" and "the Georgians" for that matter, capturing the inner life, or the unconscious, becomes for her one of the primary criteria for appreciating any kind of literature.

Thus, the writers of the 1930s, such as Auden, Spender, Isherwood, C.Day Lewis and Louis MacNeice, whom she called "the leaning-tower writers" for reasons which will later become clear, are valued, in spite of what Woolf regards as their shortcomings, for their "gift of unconsciousness" they are to bequeath to the next generation of writers. Those were the writers who were most affected by what she describes as "a chasm in a smooth road",[56] "the crash" (p.169), ie, the traumatic event of the First World War. For them, as the consequences of the war and ensuing social upheavals, the towers "built of gold [ie, expensive education] and stucco [suburban house]," "the tower[s] of middle-class birth and education," which Woolf claims to have been the main breeding ground of English writers and English literature, are "no longer steady" but "leaning towers".[57] Though the tower dwellers themselves, the writers of the 'thirties tormented by the sense of guilt about their own privileges, felt obliged to subscribe to the political doctrines that tried to topple those very towers by undermining their foundations, the established social orders, and this often made their work didactic and propagandistic.

On the other hand, in a situation of "Everywhere change, everywhere revolution" (p.170), they were forced to become, Woolf maintains, "great egoists, for "When everything is rocking one, the only person who remains comparatively stable," she reasons, "is oneself. When all faces are changing and obscured, the only face one can see clearly is one's own." The result was that their plays, their poems, their novels, all bore marks of autobiography: "they wrote about themselves" (p.177). And it is in this, not in their political propagandas and preachings, that Woolf recognizes their contribution to English literature. Their value lies in that they "wrote about themselves honestly, therefore creatively. They told the unpleasant truths, not only the flattering truths" (p.177). She compares with them the nineteenth century writers unfavourably, because the latter "never told that kind of truth." That "is why", she continues, "so much of the nineteenth century writing is worthless; why for all their genius, Dickens and Thackeray seem so often to write about dolls and puppets, not about full grown men and women; why they are forced to evade the main themes and make do with diversions instead". She quotes Stevenson's complaint that society forced the writers "to avoid half the life that passes us by" and play only with "a little box of toys", in which demand, Woolf accuses, Stevenson – along with Dickens and Thackeray – meekly acquiesced. Woolf admires "the leaning-tower writers" for having "the courage ... to throw that little box of toys out of the window" and "tell the truth", she repeats, "the unpleasant truth, about himself". Because that, she maintains, "is the first step towards telling the truth about other people":

> By analysing themselves honestly, with help from Dr. Freud, these writers have done a great deal to free us from nineteenth-century suppressions. The writers of the next generation may inherit from them a whole state of mind, a mind no longer crippled, evasive,

divided. They may inherit that unconsciousness which, as we guessed – it is only a guess ... is necessary if writers are to get beneath the surface and to write something that people remember when they are alone. For that great gift of unconsciousness the next generation will have to thank the creative and honest egotism of the leaning-tower group. (p.178)

Woolf praises them for their part in removing "nineteenth century suppressions" and establishing "a whole state of mind" – "with help from Dr. Freud"; she is here quite explicit in acknowledging Freud's role as a guide or aide, this time for the writer specifically, in his search for "the truth about himself" and others. The passage suggests that in her mind, as in that of the heroine of Lytton Strachey's sketch, who declared: "I am going to prove ... that I am contemporary of Dr. Freud, because I'm simply going to tell you the truth," the name of Freud was strongly associated with the truths about human nature and telling them honestly.

Furthermore, in extolling the achievement of the writers of the 'thirties, Woolf inadvertently reaffirms her own artistic stance, remarkably consistent throughout her career, which again reveals the essential link that relates Modernism to Romanticism as well as Freudianism, if not altogether identical in their respective entirety. We remember that the "whole state of mind", defined here as "a mind no longer crippled, evasive, divided," was one of the primary ideals of the Romantic writers. It was also the ultimate aim of Freudian psychoanalysis. Woolf then equates it with "unconsciousness," that "under-mind which works at top speed while the upper-mind drowses," and suggests that this "whole state of mind" or "unconsciousness" is a *sine qua non* for writing literary works that "get beneath the surface," "that people remember when they are alone," the two attributes that Woolf often emphasizes when advocating the kind of literature she believed in. We are already familiar with the first, which occupies the central place in her artistic concerns, and was first described in "Modern Fiction" as "the dark places of psychology," the likely "point of interest" of "the moderns." In fact it is at the basis of her argument in virtually all the essays we have so far dealt with. The second refers back to the earlier part of the essay where she discusses the less desirable aspect of the "leaning-tower writers". Comparing them with Wordsworth, Woolf observes that, while we listen to Wordsworth's poetry "when we are alone," and "We remember that in solitude (p.176), the former's didactic propaganda poems with their "loud-speaker strain," which she calls "oratory, not poetry," we listen "in a group, in a classroom" (p.175), and wonders if "the difference between politican's poetry and poet's poetry" lies in the fact that we "listen to the one in company; to the other when we are alone. (p.176)

It is obvious where her sympathy lies – certainly not with "loud-speaker" oratory. Thus, if a particular work is, or is not, to be appreciated "when we are alone," ie, in solitude, it becomes, as in the above passage, another touchstone for Woolf to judge its literary quality, along with its capacity to "get beneath the surface," ie, to reveal the inner and deeper reality, although the two are closely interrelated. It is significant that in Woolf's mind, this what we may call literature of solitude was above all associated with a Romantic poet, Wordsworth. We have already seen in an earlier chapter what individual vision, hence the solitary state of the mind as its prerequisite condition, meant to the Romantics. For Wordsworth particularly, the mind in solitude was of primary interest and importance as the theme for his poetry – eg, "I had learnt betimes to stand unpropped,/And independent musings pleased me so/That spells seemed on me when I was alone" *(The Prelude)* – and "Musing in solitude" *(The Excursion)* was for him an essential mode of creation. Naturally, poems or any kind of work dealing with the mind in solitude, created and composed by a poet or a writer in solitude, may best be appreciated by the reader in solitude, rather than "in company," in a big auditorium, for example. In preferring literature of solitude to that of public affairs or concerns, Woolf proves herself again to be a true descendant of Romanticism. It was no coincidence, therefore, that for Woolf, as well as for most Modernist writers, individual visions or visionary experiences were as vital as for the Romantic poets, though, coming after the "death of God" in modern Europe,[58] the content and the nature of their visions may be quite different from those of the early nineteenth century poets. In fact, individual visions were the focal points of the Modernist writing, and as the Romantics believed in imagination as the creator of those visions, the Modernists valued highly the creative and revelatory faculty of imagination, which is now, as a result of direct or indirect influence of modern psychology, often identified with the unconscious, as in the case of Woolf or André Breton. Their visions leap from "the depths of their unconscious being" which "lie beneath the surface", and their works that deal thus with the most private and inner world may best be appreciated and be remembered by people "when they are alone." In effect, these two qualities that Woolf aims at in literature are inseparably related to one another, and may be considered the two sides of the same coin, ie, Modernism, which has its roots in Romanticism and Freudianism simultaneously.

"The Leaning Tower" is a paper which was read to the Worker's Educational Association in 1940 just a year before Woolf's death, and reflects much of the social change that took place between the two Great Wars, especially in her attitude towards class. As far as her artistic creeds are concerned, however, she reveals herself as loyal to her Modernist principle as at the beginning of her career, and in this respect there is in the paper an echo of much of her earlier writings and especially of "The Narrow Bridge of Art". This is an essay first published in the *New York Herald Tribune* in 1927, and may be considered a sequel to the two earlier essays, "Modern Fiction" and "Mr. Bennett and Mrs. Brown," though far less polemical in tone than its predecessors. If those were the declarations of war on the old orders, or the conventional English novel, this is an exposition in more concrete and dispassionate terms of what is to replace it, of what she envisiges for the literature of the future. If the chief target of her attack in the preceding essays was the prose fiction, the critical focus of this essay is more on traditional poetry and its limitations. The essay is strongly marked by the author's sense of an age in transition – another characteristic of Modernism – and the consequent complexity of the modern mind or sensibility. General "dissatisfaction" with "much modern literature", she explains, results in part from "the failure of poetry to serve us as it has served so many generations of our fathers."[59] The reason for this lies both in poetry itself and the nature of modern consciousness. Having been purified into "the lyric cry of ecstasy or despair," staying aloof from "the common purpose of life," poetry falls short, "is not enough," as a means of expression for her generation, whose "mind is full of monstrous, hybrid, unmanageable emotions":

> That the age of the earth is 3,000,000 years; that human life lasts but a second; that the capacity of the human mind is nevertheless boundless; that life is infinitely beautiful yet repulsive; that one's fellow creatures are adorable but disgusting; that science and religion have between them destroyed belief; that all bonds of union seem broken, yet some control must exist ... (II, p.219)

When writers have to create "in this atmosphere of doubt and conflict", "the fine fabric of a lyric," she argues, "is no more fitted to contain this point of view than a rose leaf to envelop the rugged immensity of a rock" (p.219). It is in short too limited to embrace the whole range and complexity of modern experience. Thus poetry too, though in a different respect from that of the "materialist" fiction, is found wanting in its capacity to express the spirit of the age, for which "Beauty is part ugliness; amusement part disgust; pleasure part pain", when "Emotions which used to enter the mind whole are ... broken up on the threshold" (p.222). Poetic drama, which provided such a supreme vehicle of expression for the

Elizabethans, having, apparently, been irrevocably dead for centuries, Woolf finds only possibility in prose, since "this discord, this incongruity, this sneer, this contrast, this curiosity, the quick, queer emotions which are bred" (p.223) in modern mind, she believes, "submit more readily to prose than to poetry" (p.224), or anything else, for that matter. She even suspects that prose is not only going to take over but has already taken over some of the tasks of poetry.[60]

So the future of literature, she ventures to prophesy, lies in prose, in the exploitation of its so far untapped capacities. As to its form, she thinks that the omnivorous novel – "That cannibal, the novel" – will devour still more art forms and in time produce something completely unrecognizable by that name. For by its absorbtion of the characteristics of other forms of art, the rigid distinction of the conventional genres will cease to exist. The new kind of work "will be written in prose, but in prose which has many of the characteristics of poetry. It will have something of the exaltation of poetry but much of the ordinariness of prose. It will be dramatic and yet not a play. It will be read, not acted."[61] Whatever the name, this will be the form, Woolf considers, flexible enough to capture all those shades of "feelings" that elude traditional poetry and drama. She then proceeds to analyse the content to be contained in the new form in greater detail. Without naming names this time, she rejects again such subject matter as "the houses, incomes, occupations of its characters" of the conventional novel, of what she called "the sociological novel" – "It will make little use of the marvellous fact-recording power, which is one of the attributes of fiction" – and emphasizes its kinship with poetry. "It will resemble poetry," she explains,

> In this that it will give not only or mainly people's relations to each other and their activities together, as the novels have hitherto done, but it will give the relation of the mind to general ideas and its soliloquy in solitude. For under the dominion of the novel we have scrutinized one part of the mind closely and left another unexplored. We have come to forget that a large and important part of life consists in our emotions towards such things as roses and nightingales; the dawn, the sunset, life, death and fate; we forget that we spend much time sleeping, dreaming, thinking, reading alone; we are not entirely occupied in personal relations: all our energies are not absorbed in making our livings. (p.225)

This passage shows us clearly that those standards for which to aim in literature which she mentions in "The Leaning Tower" do indeed derive from her early beliefs, and confirms our view that she wavered little from her original stance throughout her career. It also reveals how strikingly close to Romanticism this original stance was; this manifests itself in such phrases as "the mind's soliloquy in solitude," or "our emotions towards such things as roses and nightingales, the dawn, the sunset, life, death and fate," which, she claims, occupy "a large and important part of life" but have been forgotten "under the dominion of the novel." It is almost impossible to fail to recognize a strong association with Romantic poetry in all those factors of life, to which Woolf calls our attention. They indeed formed the main part of the themes of Romantic poetry and sometimes even served as its titles.

Another point that she reminds us of as having been ignored, though not unrelated to those already discussed, is that much of our time is spent not in company, not in relation with other people, but in "sleeping, dreaming, thinking, reading alone." These, we recall, were also the major concerns of the Romantic poets. The line at the same time inevitably suggests, though not overtly expressed, the underlying link that exists between her artistic stance and the new psychology that took such subjects as sleep and dreams seriously for the first time in the history of modern science and was, as we have seen, exerting a considerable influence on the minds of the educated public at the time. We may even wonder if, without such a background, she would have dared mention them, favourite themes as they had been for Romantic poetry, as the subjects for prose fiction. Her subsequent complaint about the "psychological novelist" echoes Jung's similar view on the subject (see p.87) in that his concern or interest is limited to the "psychology of personal intercourse," to "the remorseless analysis ... of what Tom feels for Judith and Judith does or does not altogether feel for Tom". In other words, he is preoccupied with the characters' psychological reactions only on the conscious and inter-personal levels. This will not do for Woolf, who wants "some more impersonal relationship", who "long[s] for ideas, for dreams, for imagination, for poetry" (p.225), in short, for something of more universal significance which goes beyond or "beneath the surface" of reality. Her earlier statement that "under the dominion of the novel we have scrutinised one part of the mind closely and left another unexplored" (p.225) makes us realize that all this stems from her desire, or quest, for what she later calls "a whole state of the mind".

Thus, according to her prescription, the novel of the future "will give the relations of man to nature, to fate; his imagination; his dreams" (p.226). This so far is little different from the old Romantic stance, but it has an added imprint of the modern age that distinguishes it from Romanticism, in that "it will also give the sneer, the contrast, the question, the closeness and complexity of life." It will, in short, have the characteristics of "that queer conglomeration of incongruous things – the modern mind" (p.226). For this purpose, the most suitable vehicle, she maintains again, is "the democratic art of prose", with "its freedom, its fearlessness, its flexibility", and observes: "With all the suppleness of a tool which is in constant use it can follow the windings and record the changes which are typical of the modern mind" (p.226). She finds proofs for the validity of her assertion in the examples of both "Proust and Dostoevsky". If one of the characteristics of Woolf's fiction is, as is often pointed out, its resemblance to lyrical poetry, it was a natural outcome of her personal beliefs, most manifestly expressed in this essay, which were closely related to the lyrical poems of Romanticism.[62]

We should remind ourselves, however, that these "personal beliefs", deep-rooted though they were, were not merely her personal idiosyncracies but shared by most writers of the Modernist inclination. In fact, as we have already observed, the closing up of genres, especially of prose and poetry, was one of the most distinctive characteristics of Modernism (see pp.23-24). That is also why Joyce's *Ulysses* is sometimes described as a long prose poem. While prose fiction approached poetry, Modernist poets used idioms which were closer to prose, as is indicated by Pound's assertion, based on Stendhal's condemnation of the traditional poetic diction: "As for Stendhal's stricture, if we can have a poetry that comes as close as prose, *pour donner une idée claire et précise*, let us have it ...And if we cannot attain to such a poetry ... for God's sake let us shut up ..."[63] Besides Pound's own works, those of T. S. Eliot, especially of his earlier period, such as "Prufrock" and *The Waste Land*, supremely illustrate this artistic stance. In the field of fiction, Virginia Woolf, together with James Joyce, was its representative advocate and practitioner.

"The Narrow Bridge of Art" is indeed prophetic (Woolf often uses the word "prophecy" in the essay), if not of the future course of all the English novels, which certainly is not the case, of the form and substance of much of her own fictional works to come. They indeed concern greatly with "life, death and fate", with "the relations of man to nature ... his imagination, his dreams", which may also be described as a series of attempts to express "the complexity of life", of "the modern mind".

CHAPTER NINE

THE MODERNIST ACHIEVEMENT

There can be no doubt that she would have written more, had she lived, and it is tempting to consider whether she would not have written differently. The boundaries were marked: moons, mountains and castles lay on the other side. But was she not beginning, in her own gay and brilliant manner, to contemplate a little voyage of discovery? – "Jane Austen".[1]

WHILE admiring, as well as delighting in, the perfection of Jane Austen's art – the art "perfect" within its well-marked "boundaries", which excluded from its confines any hint of the darker side of life such as the tyrannies of instinctual desires, dangers of all sorts, above all of death, man's subliminal fears of which were expressed through the moonlit mountains and ruined castles of the Gothic novels, Virginia Woolf wonders whether, had the novelist lived longer, she might not have produced works quite different in character from those we now possess. She bases her conjecture on the signs of change, the "new element", she recognizes in Austen's last completed novel, *Persuasion*, where she senses that the author "is beginning to discover that the world is larger, more mysterious and more romantic than she had supposed"; "a new sensibility to nature", ie, a sensibility to its beauty as well as its "melancholy"; an altered attitude towards life itself, which makes the heroine's observation of life around her – upon which "until the very end, she is forced to comment ... in silence" – "less of facts and more of feelings than is usual" (p.152).

Developing along these lines and with more experience of life, her later novels, Woolf speculates, would have been very different from the characteristic Austen novel, both in their method and spirit. In the first place, "Her sense of security", which Woolf almost envied elsewhere,[2] "would have been shaken", disturbing the formerly perfect cosmic order. The knowledge of her characters would have been conveyed to the reader, as presaged in *Persuasion*, more by means of reflection than dialogue, since "Those marvellous little speeches ... that shorthand, hit-or-miss method ... would have become too crude to hold all that she now perceived of the complexity of human nature" (p.153). As a result, her speculation continues,

she would have devised a method, clear and composed as ever, but deeper and more suggestive, for conveying not only what people say, but what they leave unsaid; not only what they are, but what life is. (p.153)

And thus, Jane Austen would have become "the forerunner of Henry James and Proust".

By tracing the imaginary development of Austen's later novels, Woolf in fact is expounding her own creeds or ideals in fiction writing. Her description of the would-have-been later phase of the novelist as the "voyage of discovery" could most aptly be applied to the whole literary career of her own, which may indeed be regarded as a "voyage of discovery", of exploration of "not only what people say, but what they leave unsaid". Seen in this way, the title of her first novel, *The Voyage Out* (1915), becomes symbolic not only in relation to the theme of the novel and its young heroine, as is often interpreted, but also in relation to Woolf's entire career as novelist. For, contrary to many earlier criticisms which tended to see a clearer division between her two earliest works, *The Voyage Out* and *Night and Day* (1919), and later, more mature and characteristic novels,[3] there does exist an essential unity and continuity in all her novels and short stories, if not in style, in the author's primary concerns. Jean Guiguet was certainly right when, considering the nine novels of Woolf, he criticized the "dividing-up" method of other critics (David Daiches, R. L. Chambers, etc.) and argued: "the real distinction and value of Virginia Woolf's work lies in the unity of its inspiration, the continuity of her unfailing effort in pursuit of a goal which she envisaged from the very beginning of her literary career."[4] What was this "goal", then? In the very first novel, Terence Hewet, a budding novelist who along with the heroine, Rachel, clearly represents a part of his creator, expresses an ambition for his future work:

> "I want to write a novel about Silence", he said: "the things people don't say. But the difficulty is immense."[5]

That these words are the reflection of the author's own aspiration can be seen from the novel itself which is full of silence, or silent moments. The author confesses as much when she narrates, as silence falls between the heroine and Helen, her aunt and spiritual guide: "Hewet, indeed, might have found excellent material at this time up at the villa for some chapters in the novel which was to be called "Silence, or the Things People Don't Say" (p.269), since in this novel, Woolf herself exploits these silent moments for exploring what "people don't say" – their musings and reflections on the complexities of the inner self and human relationship as well as on the mysteries of life – that constant preoccupation of and the ultimate enigma for Woolf – the dreams and the delusions of the heroine or silent communications between the characters, which in Woolf often meant the truer understanding between people than that achieved through speech (we may remember for example many silent dialogues between Mr. and Mrs. Ramsey in *To the Lighthouse*).

These themes occupy the central place in her later novels, but here this world of the villa centring on Rachel and Helen, in which silence and reflection predominate, exists side by side, making a sharp contrast with the world of the hotel which is presented in the form of the novel of manners, the world full of conversation and movements and thus is dominated by speech and action. Hewet, who comes from the hotel to the villa and achieves spiritual union with Rachel, may be considered a mediator between the two worlds, the world of speech ("what people say") and that of silence ("what they leave unsaid"). Seen from this angle, we may regard *The Voyage Out* as the author's first diffident step towards her ideal novel which, as was stated in her Jane Austen essay, can convey "not only what people say, but what they left unsaid". Thus even this cursory examination of her first novel reveals how closely, and sometimes insep- arably, related Woolf's critical essays are to her fictional works, for, while criticizing or sympathizing with other writers' works, she very often expressed her own artistic ideals and creative principles, which indeed served as the criteria for her critical judgement. This view differs essen- tially from that of Anthony Fothergill who thinks that one of the hazards in reading Woolf's critical essays

> lies in the possible but misleading assumption that Virginia Woolf's critical views can be identified with her intentions and actual achievements in her novels, in terms of which they are often read. The essays may show us what she thought about modern fiction; they will not necessarily reveal the principles by which her own fiction can best be defined.[6]

It is not in such technical details as the "stream of consciousness" method, etc, as Fothergill illustrates, that we can perceive this essential link between her novels and critical writings, but in the basic creative "principles" and artistic creeds which echo and re-echo between both kinds of writings, sometimes using as in the above case exactly the same words, same expressions, and which manifest themselves in the "actual achievements in her novels." The preceding chapter which concentrates on Woolf as critic is indeed based on the same view, for her essays show us not only "what she *thought*" but what she ardently *believed* about modern fiction.

In fact, her artistic creed, her central concerns and beliefs about the art of fiction were remarkably consistent throughout her life, pervading all her writings including, besides her essays, novels and short stories, her diary entries as well as her letters, of which she was a prolific writer. This means that the same continuity, or unity, governs not only among the novels and between those novels and essays but the other kinds of writings as well. This was the reason why Guiguet made such a thorough use of her diary to prove his point.[7] In this respect we might, as T. S. Eliot exhorted about Shakespeare's work, regard all Woolf's writings as an organic whole in which each part illuminates the other. To give another example which shows this continuity among different kinds of writings: in 1919, after the publication of her second novel, *Night and Day,* Woolf wrote in a letter to a friend, while commenting on several aspects of the novel:

> then there's the whole question, which interested me ... of the things one doesn't say; what effect does that have? and how far do our feelings take their colour from the dive underground? I mean what is the reality of any feeling? ... And then there's the question of things happening, normally, all the time.[8]

It is significant that Woolf, explaining what "interested" her while she was writing *Night and Day,* should repeat at one point almost verbatim what Terence Hewit in the previous novel stated : "the things people don't say" – "the things one doesn't say". At the same time she shows her awareness of "the question of things happening, normally, all the time". Indeed, in a manner not completely dissimilar to *The Voyage Out,* this novel too contains the two contrasting worlds: on the one hand, the world of the private visions and dreams of the two protagonists, Katharine and Ralph, and on the other that of their families and friends in which things are "happening, normally, all the time". In this sense the title, *Night and Day,* itself is meaningful and suggestive. We may describe it, using the expression in her essay on Jane Austen, as another attempt of Woolf's to convey "not only what people say but what they leave unsaid". Though this opposition may equally be described as that of speech and silence or as Woolf herself put it in her diary, as that of "facts" and "vision",[9] it is essentially the opposition of the external world and the internal world, the outer, material reality and the inner, emotional or psychological reality. Virginia Woolf's ultimate aim, or wish, as a writer was to capture both simultaneously, to present life in its totality as an amalgamation of the outer and the inner, which after all "life" means to an individual, but objectification of which is possible only in art. Thus the term "whole" appears in her writings with almost obsessional frequency in relation to "life" as well as to "the mind", which were in her case virtually synony-mous. For example, in her diary entries of 1933 she expressed a longing, while she was writing what later became *The Years*, for her creative spirit to career "over the whole of human life",[10] and stated the desired goal for the book: "to give the whole of the present society – nothing less: facts as well as the vision."[11]

As we observed earlier, in her 1940 essay, "The Leaning Tower", she praised Auden and the other writers of the 'thirties for bequeathing "a whole state of mind" to the next generation. Indeed, her chief complaint about the Edwardian novelists, and the traditional English novel for that matter, was that they only caught "half the life", that they "scrutinized one part of the mind [or life] closely and left another unexplored". If we quote a passage from one of her earlier letters and compare what she says there with those statements she made later in life in her diary and in her essays as well as what she achieved or tried to achieve in her novels, it becomes incontestably clear that this quest for wholeness was her lifelong concern which ran through all her writings, regardless of the genre. On August 19th, 1908, some time after she began writing *The Voyage Out*, Woolf wrote to her brother-in-law, Clive Bell, who at that time was a sort of literary confidant for the young author:

> I think a great deal of my future, and settle what book I am to write – how I shall re-form the novel and capture multitudes of things at present fugitive, enclose the whole and shape infinite strange shapes.[12]

Here in this early letter we can see the germ of all her ideals and objectives which she pursued throughout her life: reformation of the novel, which meant to "enclose the whole" of life by capturing what had slipped from the hands of the traditional novel, "something hitherto ignored", as well as the search for the new form, to "shape infinite strange shapes", required by the new artistic vision.

In fact Virginia Woolf's development as a novelist may be considered to have been a process in which she tried to achieve the fusion of the two rival elements of life, facts and vision, speech and silence, company (human relationship) and solitude, night and day, in short the outer and the inner realities, into an integral whole. In the first two novels, these two elements, or the worlds representing them, *are* present, but side by side, as separate entities, forming a sharp contrast. They do not merge into one world, and moving from one to the other is not always smooth. For example, the descriptions of the reveries and dreams of the main characters in *Night and Day* sometimes appear rather artificial and unreal in the realistic settings of the novel which uses basically the conventional method.[13] It was only after the experiment of *Jacob's Room* that she acquired a method suitable for her particular purpose, a method which could describe the inner in relation to the outer. After completing and reading through the novel, Woolf herself wrote in her diary (July 26th, 1922), "There's no doubt in my mind that I have found out how to begin (at 40) to say something in my own voice."[14] It might be said that in her third work Woolf succeeded in writing "a novel about Silence" which Terence Hewet aspired to write but found it immensely difficult, for the novel's emphasis is, in spite of the presence of intermittent and fragmentary dialogues, on the silent thoughts of various characters who surround the titular hero, Jacob. Significantly, Jacob himself is described by one of them as "The silent young man".[15]

One of the reasons for the weakness of the novel as a whole, however, seems to lie precisely in this over-emphasis on silence, on the inner at the cost of the outer, which is not given solid existence outside the minds of the characters.[16] For it is equally difficult to present the whole of life through "silence" alone as through only speech, through "what people say". This novel may be best understood as the necessary adventure for the author to explore her own way during her voyage of discovery, the course of which was inevitably not fully charted, an experiment, in other words, to discover a method to convey the unspoken, inner voices for which the traditional technique, the trodden path, proved insufficient. Although a detailed analysis is beyond the scope of this study, an overall impression gained through the perusal of her novels is that her best works, which to my mind are *Mrs. Dalloway* (1924), *To the Lighthouse* (1927) and, to a lesser degree, *Between the Acts* (1941), are those in which Woolf succeeded in achieving the equilibrium and integral merging of the inner and the outer, that is to say, in which the external and internal worlds exist with equal strength and equal sense of reality, not as a contrast as in her earlier novels but as a synthetic whole.

It might be said that in these works Woolf succeeded in her attempt "to enclose the whole" of life. It is also notable that in them the author provides strong, central characters, who through their experience of the inner and outer worlds function as unifying agents (Clarissa, Mrs. Ramsay and Lily, Isa), and the single, solid outer worlds, with their respective accompaniments of people and objects, which are powerful enough to counterbalance the rich and complex inner life of these characters (London, the sea with the Lighthouse, the village). The minds of the main characters working as catalysts, these factual worlds, despite their material solidity, transform themselves and become invested with multiple meanings and symbolic depths and thus reveal to the reader the complexity and the deeper dimensions of this world and human life, ie, what James in *To the Lighthouse* is made to realize on reaching the lighthouse: "nothing is simply one thing."[17] This, in fact, is one of the central messages of Virginia Woolf's works. A lighthouse is a lighthouse; at the same time it can be as many things as the number of viewers who are looking at it, from near or from afar, and at different stages of their lives. This may be described, using Woolf's own expression in her essay on E. M. Forster, as the "combination of realism and mysticism", which she maintains links Forster with Ibsen. The passage in which Woolf discusses the "realistic power" of Ibsen and shows deeper understanding of his realism than was customary in the older theatrical and literary traditions, may equally be applied to her own three novels discussed above, despite the difference of the medium and style each used:

> A room to him is a room, a writing table a writing table, and a waste-paper basket a waste-paper basket. At the same time, the paraphernalia of reality have at certain moments to become the veil through which we see infinity. When Ibsen achieves this, as he certainly does, it is not by performing some miraculous conjuring trick at the critical moment ... He gives us the effect of ordinary life, as Mr. Forster does, but he gives it us by choosing a very few facts and those of a highly relevant kind. Thus when the moment of illumination comes we accept it implicitly ... We feel simply that the thing we are looking at is lit up, and its depth revealed. It has not ceased to be itself by becoming something else.[18]

It goes without saying that this "combination of realism and mysticism" may be replaced by "facts as well as the vision", fusion of the outer and the inner or any set of the rival elements already mentioned. When she succeeded in realizing in her novels this "combination" or equilibrium or synthesis, and could show the interaction of those contrasting elements in life, Woolf seems to have achieved the goal of her art.[19] That this again was not limited to her novels may be seen from a comment on the third volume of *The Diary*, published in 1980:

> It is the balance between the outer and the inner life which is unique; the implicit understanding of the way they replenish one another[20] ...

The fact that the uniqueness of Woolf's diary can be discussed in practically identical terms with those used above for the discussion of the achievement of her novels may be considered another proof that indicates the aforementioned underlying continuity and kinship which exist among Woolf's different kinds of writings.

After examining the "new" elements in Joyce's *Ulysses* and in the poems of Eliot and the later Yeats, Anthony Cronin describes what he considers is common to them all:

> It is simply that a new dimension of irony, self-knowledge, analysis and complexity had been added which any honest examination of experience must take into account ... And perhaps more important still, a whole range of emotions and feelings, apparently, by the old standards, trivial and unworthy, has been discovered to have dramatic and indeed lyrical possibilities and intensities which were never previously explored.[21]

Calling this "the modern achievement", which in today's terminology may be called "the Modernist achievement", he sums it up as "a return of psychological precision and a gain in honesty, complexity, wholeness" (p.21). He uses the word "return," since he believes that the pioneeer of this "psychological precision" as well as other main characteristics of Modernist poetry, was Baudelaire, who has also figured in this study as one of the major precursors of Modernism: "It is to Baudelaire that we owe the first poetic exploration of those meannesses and diffidences of spirit which the modern movement has finally made accountable to the poet." Although Cronin here is concerned mainly with poetry, regarding *Ulysses* virtually as its extension, his arguments may be applied to the Modernist novel in general, not only to Joyce but also to Woolf and even to Lawrence.

In fact, it is interesting to note in Cronin's statements echoes of Woolf's own artistic beliefs and concerns expressed in her writings which, while preceding examinations of her essays and fictional works may make it sufficiently clear, may be further confirmed by a passage in her essay, "How it Strikes a Contemporary" (1925). In this essay she presents as the particular quality of "the moderns," in contrast to Scott and Austen (and even Wordsworth) who were secure in their shared beliefs and convictions: "the sense of the human being, his depth and the variety of his perceptions, his complexity, his confusion, his self, in short."[22] Then if we remind ourselves of her assertion in "Modern Fiction": "Let us not take it for granted that life exists more fully in what is commonly thought big than in what is commonly thought small," we cover in Woolf's own words the whole ground of what Cronin describes as "the modern achievement."

Such comparison makes us realize once again that, although without doubt Woolf's quest for wholeness did derive from her genuine personal need, as the examination in this study of all kinds of her writings, ranging from the very beginning to the final period of her literary career, abundantly shows, it reflects nevertheless the spirit of an important sector of her age, of the generation of writers we now identify as Modernists, and that she shared many characteristics with them, although manifested by each in his or her characteristically individual way.

If we focus our attention on the novelists, the same reaction against the one-sidedness of the preceding generations and desire to capture the whole of life may clearly be seen in the other representative writers of Modernist fiction, Joyce and Lawrence, in spite of the latter's harsh criticism of the others' methods. As is often pointed out, the whole of *Ulysses* may be considered a massive monument to it over which stands, bearing witness, the modern Trinity, created by Joyce, of Stephen, the intellect, Molly, the flesh and Leopold Bloom the "allroundman",[23] the mediator who embraces both in himself. Lawrence "absolutely" and "flatly" denied that he was "a soul, or a body, or a mind, or an intelligence, or a brain, or a nervous system, or a bunch of glands, or any of the rest of these bits of [him]," maintaining: "The whole is greater than the part" and "I am a man, and alive." For him "a man alive" meant a whole being. With characteristic feverish ardour, he claimed that the superiority of Lawrence, the novelist, to "the saint, the scientist, the philosopher, and the poet" lay in his capacity to "get the whole hog" instead of, as they did, "different bits of man alive." For, in his own words,

> The novel is the one bright book of life. Books are not life. They are tremulations on the ether. But the novel as a tremulation can make the whole man alive tremble. Which is more than poetry, philosophy, science or any other book tremulation can do.[24]

What he tried in his novels was to recover, especially through a new relationship between men and women, this wholeness of "man alive", which he believed to have been destroyed by excessive intellectualism and materialism of modern civilization.

This quest for wholeness, which was at the centre of Modernist literature, was thus the legacy of the whole Romantic movement, handed down via such mediators as Baudelaire, Nietzsche and Dostoevsky. The examination of the Romantic ancestry in this study, we believe, will provide sufficient ground for justifying the view that one root of Modernism was indeed in this earlier movement, a view also shared by such critics as Randall Jarrell and Peter Faulkner. It was not just a coincidence that Woolf found a close affinity between her own creative principle and that of Wordsworth; nor was it an accident that a study could be carried out at all about the correlation between Romantic poetry and Lawrence's novels as is made clear by the subtitle, "D. H. Lawrence and English Romanticism."[25]

Sharing essentially the same concern and wish for the totality and integrity of life, Modernists reacted in much the same way to what they regarded as the one-sidedness of society, the result largely of the nineteenth century positivism, as the Romantics did to the eighteenth century rationalist domination: to turn their eyes inwards with particular intensity, as if to compensate for and counterbalance the lost equilibrium. This was indeed the main tenet of Woolf's "Modern Fiction": "For the moderns 'that', the point of interest, lies very likely in the dark places of psychology ... the emphasis is upon something hitherto ignored ..." For the reasons examined earlier, this tendency was particularly strong and conspicuous in the field of the English novel, and the desire to get beyond or beneath the phenomenal world was common to most Modernist writers. Although in this study only the case of Virginia Woolf has been examined in detail for being the most representative in various other aspects as well, on this particular point D. H. Lawrence also left quite a few testimonies, as a passage from one of his letters illustrates:

> It is not your brain that you must trust to, nor your will – but to that fundamental pathetic faculty for receiving the hidden waves that come from the depths of life, and for transferring them to the unreceptive world. It is something which happens below the consciousness, and below the range of the will – it is something which is unrecognizable and frustrated and destroyed.[26]

As the examinations and analyses of the foregoing chapters have made clear, this shift of the focus, or deepening of perspective, about man and the world demanded a corresponding radical change in the writer's attitude to his craft. In order to convey this new awareness, the altered visions of reality, each writer had to discover new style, new form, since the traditional realism was no longer useful or appropriate. The exploration of what Eugene Jolas called "the new reality" inevitably meant the exploration of and experimentation with new form and new style. This was indeed a part, and an important part at that, of *The Struggle of the Modern*. In a letter to Edward Garnett (April 17th, 1913), Lawrence reveals the kind of problem these novelists had:

> All the time, underneath, there is something deep evolving itself out in me. And it is *hard* to express a new thing, in sincerity. And you should understand, and help me to the new thing ... (p.190)

Lawrence, Joyce, who was determined "to encounter for the millionth time the reality of experience and to forge in the smithy of my soul the uncreated conscience of my race"[27], and Woolf, who considered the revelation of the "unknown and uncircumscribed spirit" of man "the task of the novelist", were all aware that they were expressing a "new thing", and that for the "new thing" the conventional technique, the old "tools" would not do. More recently, the case of Doris Lessing, though on an individual scale, recapitulates the situation in which those writers were placed about three-quarters of a century earlier. In an interview given some years ago, Lessing commented on the change of her style, her moving "away from realism" with *The Golden Notebook*: to the interviewer who reminded her of her former admiration for "the nineteenth century realist novel as a high point of literature", she answered: "The reason why I don't write realistically any more is because I simply cannot put what I see inside realism, and that's true I think with nearly all writers."[28] She had to abandon realism when her progressive, optimistic views based on her earlier sympathy wth Communism no longer fitted experience and realities of life. For Lessing, as well as for Joyce, Woolf and Lawrence, to be content with conventional realism must have seemed, in Walter Allen's words, "to be content with unreality." In a significantly titled chapter, "The Modern as Vision of the Whole", Stephen Spender observed:

> I consider that early in this century, and perhaps up to the 1930's, the best work of the modern expressed ... tension between past and present, which could only be expressed in a revolutionary kind of art. What Joyce, Eliot, Lawrence, Pound, Yeats, Virginia Woolf were doing could only be done in ways which are today sometimes dismissed as 'experimental'.[29]

If, as he defines later, what constitutes "the whole" for Spender is "this tension between past and present" or "The confrontation of the past with present"[30] and different from what has been examined here in Woolf, as well as Joyce and Lawrence, his argument about the "revolutionary" and "experimental" nature of the works of the writers mentioned, among whom he includes the above three, is nevertheless an appropriate comment on our case as well. Being exploratory, the new form, the new style for expressing, to use Lawrence's words, "the new thing" which had evolved from "underneath" the writer's conscious world, could not but be "experimental", and as there had been no precedent, no model, at least in the mainstream of the English novel, was destined to be "revolutionary". Virginia Woolf was perfectly aware of this, as is clearly shown in her plea at the end of "Mr. Bennett and Mrs. Brown": "do not expect just at present a complete and satisfactory presentment of [Mrs. Brown – life]. Tolerate the spasmodic, the obscure, the fragmentary, the failure."

Lacking the native model, as Woolf again explicitly complained, "from whom they could learn their business," the novelists with the Modernist inclination sought either direct models or sources of inspiration in writers of other countries. It is a well-known fact that Joyce acknowledged his debt to a French writer, Éduard Dujardin and his novel, *Les Lauriers sont coupés* (1888), in developing his "revolutionary" method of stream of consciousness or internal monologue which became a most useful tool for describing the state of mind of the fictional characters, ie, for presenting "the new thing", the revelation of the inner reality. Ellmann reports that Joyce addressed Dujardin "in letters as *'Maître'*," though he also indicates that Joyce believed he was giving his master more credit than he truly deserved ('cake for bread'),[31] for it was Joyce himself who exploited and drew out the full potentialities of *le monologue intérieur* from an obscure work all but forgotten during its author's lifetime. His debt to Dujardin was, as Leon Edel points out,[32] also his debt to French symbolism, since Dujardin was a member and his novel a product of the the Symbolist movement. Thus, together with the close affinity of his concept of "epiphany" with that of "correspondances" of Baudelaire, the initiator of the movement, Joyce proves himself to be aligned with French Symbolism in more than one sense, in his basic creative principle as well as technique, rather than with the "great tradition" of the English novel.

Virginia Woolf who, as her complaint above clearly shows, was particularly conscious of this "awkward predicament" of the "young Georgians", ie, the Modernist writers in England, wrote in another essay that as the result of the dearth of "living heroes to worship and destroy" during the reign of Edward VII, "the Georgians read Russian novels in translation; how they benefited and suffered ... "[33] That there was a cult of Dostoevsky as well as Nietzsche during the initial years of the Modernist era was already mentioned.[34]

Woolf's admiration for Russian novelists such as Chekhov, Dostoevsky and Tolstoy, is apparent in many of her critical essays. In "Modern Fiction", after rejecting "the materialists" she went so far as to say : "The most elementary remarks upon modern English fiction can hardly avoid some mention of the Russian influence, and if the Russians are mentioned one runs the risk of feeling that to write of any fiction save theirs is a waste of time."[35] She herself was involved in translating and publishing some of Tolstoy's and Dostoevsky's writings. Particularly strong, however, seems to have been the influence or the impact of Dostoevsky on Woolf, about whom she remarked, "It is directly obvious that he is the greatest writer ever born,"[36] and "Out of Shakespeare there is no more exciting reading."[37] A passage from her "The Russian Point of View" may help us to perceive the kinship which she must have felt with the world of Dostoevsky's novels:

> a new panorama of the human mind is revealed. The old divisions melt into each other. Men are at the same time villains and saints; their acts are at once beautiful and despicable. We love and we hate at the same time. There is none of that precise division between good and bad to which we are used. (p.243)

This is indeed very close to Woolf's own descriptions of "the modern mind" in her essays, such as "The Narrow Bridge of Art." There are signs that, especially in the earlier part of her career, she used Dostoevsky as a sort of standard against which her own works were to be judged. While she was writing *Mrs. Dalloway*, which was still called *The Hours*, she questioned herself:

> what do I feel about *my* writing? – this book, that is, *The Hours* ... One must write from deep feeling, said Dostoevsky. And do I? Or do I fabricate with words, loving them as I do? No, I think not ...[38]

After some digression, she asks again as if to confirm: "Am I writing *The Hours* from deep emotion?" It is significant that it was precisely in this novel that she conceived the use of the Dostoevskian doubles, Clarissa and Septimus Warren Smith, to present the inclusive vision of "life and death, sanity and insanity". Although this again needs more detailed analysis, Woolf's two earliest novels may also be best understood in relation to Dostoevsky. It seems to me that in those novels Woolf was not, as often criticized,[39] simply using the conventional method; she was in my view rather trying to create a world similar to Dostoevsky's in which the visionary and everyday worlds intermingle without clear-cut divisions, and in which traditional realism co-exists in perfect harmony with the more abstract, even mystical and fantastic writings.[40] If "the abstract and the metaphorical" in them strike us as being "at odds with their traditional mould,"[41] it may be due not so much to the fact that she used the traditional technique at all as to the lack of her skill in integrating the two worlds, which was done superbly by the master.[42] After all, they were her first two novels. To view them in this way seems to enable us to see better the essential continuity between these early works and her later novels. The feverish intensity of Dostoevsky, however, may have been less in agreement with her own temperament than another foreign author whom she read later than Dostoevsky but often mentioned or discussed alongside the Russian writer, especially when she wanted to give examples of those who had achieved what the native writers had failed to do, a sort of antithesis to English novelists, as in "Phases of Fiction" (1929), where she expounds on both as the writers who shared "the same power of illuminating the consciousness from its roots to the surface."[43]

Although there is neither intention nor space in this study to step further into the slippery terrain of the question of influence, there is no doubt that she found another kindred spirit, ideal writer, in another foreigner whom she described in a way reminiscent of her earlier description of the ideal modern fiction: "Proust ... is so porous, so pliable, so perfectly perceptive that we realize him only as an envelope, thin but elastic, which stretches wider and wider and serves not to enforce a view but to enclose a world" (p.83). At times she even appears to be apprehensive of the effect which Proust has on her. Trying to describe the impression of the party with the members of the upper classes which she attended the night before, Woolf writes in her diary (November 18th, 1924), "No doubt Proust could say what I mean – that great writer whom I cannot read when I'm correcting, so persuasive he is. He makes it seem easy to write well; which only means that one is slipping along on borrowed skates."[44] This entry reveals Woolf's profound admiration for the French novelist as well as the degree of his power over her, due most probably to the proximity of their sensibilities, or temperaments, and artistic concerns, from which she even felt she had to defend herself in order to maintain her independence as an artist. Several months later, after completing *Mrs. Dalloway*, she compared her achievement with that of Proust (April 8th, 1925):

> I wonder if this time I have achieved something? Well, nothing anyhow compared with Proust, in whom I am embedded now. The thing about Proust is his combination of the utmost sensibility with the utmost tenacity. He searches out these butterfly shades to the last grain. He is as tough as catgut and as evanescent as a butterfly's bloom. And he will, I suppose, both influence me and make me out of temper with every sentence of my own.[45]

It is revealing that Woolf resorted to the Russian and French novelists for the criteria against which to judge, both in the course of writing and after completion, her own novel. The general impression is, however, that technically her two earliest works have greater affinities with Dostoevsky, while the later novels, in which she established her own style, have more in common with Proust. This latter impression seems to have been shared by Woolf's contemporaries, to judge from the rather comical episode concerning her being called the "English Proust", reported by Richard Kennedy who worked as office boy for the Hogarth Press between 1928 and 1929.[46]

All this shows Woolf's break with the native tradition, at least in the sphere of fiction, and her receptivity to the foreign influence, in which again she may be seen to embody the spirit of Modernism, its international nature. As to Lawrence, being an untypical Modernist and against almost everybody, except perhaps Homer and Shakespeare, it is not immediately clear as the other two whom he really admired or regarded worthy to be his mentor. Yet there appears to be a growing tendency among critics to focus attention on Nietzsche's influence on Lawrence.[47] It is also possible that Lawrence sought his ideals more in other places and cultures than other artists, as may be seen in his reaction to New Mexico and the Red Indian ritual and religion, which he encountered after the peregrinations through Southern Europe (Sicily), Ceylon, Tahiti, California and Australia. On the impact of this old and alien culture, he wrote:

> I think New Mexico was the greatest experience from the outside world that I have ever had. It certainly changed me for ever. Curious as it may sound, it was New Mexico that liberated me from the present era of civilization, the great era of material and mechanical developments.[48]

and on the aboriginal people:

> The Red Indian, as a civilized and truly religious man, civilized beyond taboo and totem, as he is in the south, is religious in perhaps the oldest sense, and deepest of the word ... go to Taos Pueblo on some brilliant snowy morning and see the white figure on the roof; or come riding through at dusk on some windy evening ... and you will feel the old, old root of human consciousness still reaching down to depths we know nothing of; and of which, only too often, we are jealous. (pp.127-128)

Whatever their form, this brief survey reveals to us that the experimentalism, for which particularly Joyce and Woolf were censured, and cosmopolitanism, or internationalism – for it cannot be an accident that both Joyce and Lawrence died in self-imposed exile – which these novelists shared with other Modernists were not the result of mere whims of fashion but stemmed from the genuine need of each writer to express his or her new vision of life, new awareness of the "hitherto ignored" side of human reality, "the new thing" in Lawrence's words, in the most satisfactory way. In short, such features as experimentalism and cosmopolitanism of Modernist fiction were part and parcel of its concern with and emphasis on the inner realities, which in its turn derived from these novelists' desire to capture life in its totality, their quest for the wholeness of life.

Indeed, the Modernist achievement in the field of the English novel lies, to my mind, in its exploration of the inner world of man, and the resulting integration between the inner and the outer elements of life, which had rarely been dealt with in traditional English literature, except in poetry and in the "sub-literary" form of fiction, and of course, Shakespeare. These writers, Joyce, Woolf and even Lawrence, were accordingly acutely aware that they were attempting something new in the genre which they were using. Although what they considered to constitute the inner realities, and "the whole" for that matter, may have had points of difference due to the temperament as well as life experience of each, they shared the same desire to go beyond or beneath the surface realities and to illuminate the dark chaos, be it beneficial or threatening, of the depths of the human mind. And in their best works, they achieved the delicate equilibrium between the inner and the outer worlds, and observed the interaction between the two, which was in fact the basis of Woolf's "moment of illumination" discussed earlier, or Joyce's "epiphany", defined in his *Stephen Hero* as "a sudden spiritual manifestation, whether in the vulgarity of speech or of gesture or in a memorable phase of the mind itself," as well as, we may add, commonplace objects.[49]

In Lawrence, what comes closest to these ideas may be his concept of "symbols" which, according to him, "stand for units of *human* feeling, human experience."[50] Thus it follows that another factor to link them together is the use of symbolism, since it was an integral part of, and the essential means of presenting, those moments of revelation, examples of which are abundant in most of their works. No doubt it was partly this that brought their novels closer to poetry, which is another oustanding feature of Modernist fiction. In all this, they may be said to have opened up a new vista, new perspective, or new dimension for the English novel, and despite the natural reactions which succeeded them, what they achieved, each in his or her highly individual manner, has become a lasting legacy that shines for its distinction, and for some critics such as John Holloway, quoted at the outset of this study, outshines all that have followed since. In this sense, it is remarkable that Virginia Woolf seems to have felt this almost intuitively when in 1924 she made the "rash prediction": "we are trembling on the verge of one of the great ages of English literature", though with the wisdom of hindsight we can correct her and say, as Bernard Bergonzi pointed out,[51] that they were in fact in the midst, or rather towards the close, and not on the verge of, one of the great ages of English literature, the age of Modernism.

Now when we consider the Modernist movement, it is, as the earlier examinations in this study have made it clear, almost imperative to remember the contribution made by the spread of Freudian psychology, to its formation as well as to its reception by the public. We may even doubt, if not whether the great age came into existence at all, whether

Modernist art and literature acquired those particular characteristics with which we now identify them, without the timely advent of the new psychological theories. Ronald W. Clark, while listing the unfavourable reactions to Freud in "intellectual circles", including Virginia Woolf,[52] concedes: "Yet it was in literature and biography that the ramifications already opened up by psychoanalysts were most far-reaching", (p.419) and comments that despite the critical views of some writers, "Katherine Mansfield, Elizabeth Bowen and certainly Virginia Woolf ... all wrote in a manner which would have been barely comprehensible before the coming of Freud."[53] And we may add, "certainly" Joyce and to a certain extent Lawrence too, especially in his basic ideas about the human mind.

The foregoing study of Woolf's critical essays leaves us in little doubt that the novelist was clearly aware of the role played by Freud in modern, and particularly Modernist literature. Her letters to the then Harvard student Harman H. Goldstone (March 19th, 1932) are sometimes used as proof that Woolf never read Freud's works or was indifferent to them, as she writes in answer to one of his enquiries, "I have not studied Dr. Freud or any psychoanalyst – indeed I think I have never read any of their books [which is clearly not true]; my knowledge is merely from superficial talk."[54] Yet in the light of what has been revealed through her essays and diaries, it is difficult to take what she says here at its face value. These remarks seem to have been made as a kind of smoke-screen or self-defence by a creative writer who feared to be identified with any particular theoretical system, which she knew would only restrict and impoverish the meaning of her works. Besides, as was already mentioned, Woolf never made a mechanical application of Freud's theories to her fictional works nor approved of those written on that principle. There is even an unsigned review by her, entitled "Freudian Fiction", of such a book, in which she makes critical comments on the method; "It simplifies rather than complicates, detracts rather than enriches," and on the chartacters: "In becoming cases they ceased to be individuals."[55] Apart from the obviously Oedipal implication of the Father-Son relationship borne out by many expressions and images of James' death-wish against Mr. Ramsey, the only instance in her fictional works that has direct connection with Freudian psychology may be found in *Between the Acts* in the form of another fragment of conversation among the spectators of the pageant, in which we overhear someone saying:

> Take the idiot. Did she mean, so to speak, something hidden, the unconscious, as they call it? But why always drag in sex ...? It's true, there's sense in which we all, I admit, are savages still. Those

women with red nails. And dressing up – what's that? The old
savage, I suppose ...[56]

Woolf here may well be recording the prevailing attitude of the general
public to Freud's theories, but it is also possible to assume that the author
is expressing her own view through the mouth of an unrecognizable
character in the crowd. Whichever the case, the passage conveys to the
reader an idea that the true significance of Freud (though not mentioned
by name) did not lie in the details of his theories but in his central thesis
which drew attention to the continuing existence in the unconscious of
the primitive instinctual forces, the "old savage" – the thesis particularly
persuasive after the carnage of World War One, and in retrospect on the
eve of another, still greater holocaust – and which, together with the War,
put an effective end to the comfortable nineteenth century optimism of
eternal human progress. A similar point may be made with Lawrence who
was a relentless critic of Freud's determinist attitude, for the same reason
as the above spectator's, maintaining, "All is not *sex*"[57] and "when Freud
makes sex accountable for everything he as good as makes it accounting
for nothing" (p.19), but who nevertheless recognized the psychologist's
contribution in bringing out into the open the subject treated so far as
taboo. In the Introduction to *Fantasia of the Unconscious*, he paid tribute
to Freud:

> We are thankful that Freud pulled us somewhat to earth, out of all
> our clouds of superfineness. What Freud says is partly true. And
> half a loaf is better than no bread. (p.17)

Yet the true significance of Freud for Lawrence may be found in his
role as instigator or the motive force which set off the development of
Lawrence's own notions and beliefs about the unconscious, which came
to mean for him the deepest source of life, and formed the core of his
major fictional works. His two essays on the unconscious were, after all,
written as a reaction to Freud's theory of the subject, as its corrective, as
it were. If Joyce reacted against the scientific, which in this case was
synonymous with the determinist, side of Freudian psychology, as most
writers including Woolf and Lawrence did, he too was far from unsym-
pathetic to its basic tenet which held dreams and the unconscious activities
of the mind as significant. His brother, Stanislaus Joyce, wrote: "The
revelation and importance of the subconscious had caught his interest.
The epiphanies became more frequently subjective and included dreams
which he considered in some way revelatory."[58] Despite his ostensible
indifference, Joyce shows, as we have already observed, his familiarity
with psychoanalytical theories in various references in his works.

No less, if not more, important than the direct or indirect contact with Freud's ideas themselves was the general atmosphere or climate which resulted from the spread of those ideas. The signifcance of the fact that Joyce was surrounded by Surrealists and other *avant-garde* artists who were strongly influenced by Freud at the time of his writing *Ulysses* and especially *Finnegans Wake* has often been pointed out.[59] This point has also been examined in this study in relation to the contribution made by Eugene Jolas, the sympathizer of Surrealism, and his magazine *Transition*, which advocates the new artistic principles based largely on the legacy of Romantic literature and the theoretical framework derived from Freud and Jung.

Attention must be paid at the same time to the receiving side of the created works, the reading public on whom also, as was discussed in the initial chapter, the effect of Freudian psychology, especially after World War One, was considerable. The height of Modernist literature indeed coincided with the penetration, in whatever form, of the new psychological ideas among the general public. The "introversion of the novel" was achieved partly through the introversion of public consciousness as well. When Thomas Mann, who admitted that his *Death in Venice,* in which the protagonist's dream plays an important role, "was created under the immediate influence of Freud,"[60] said in his speech on Freud's eightieth birthday, "psychoanalysis is the greatest contribution to the art of the novel" (p.295), he may well have represented the feelings of many writers of the period. We may consider the already quoted Address, signed by 197 writers and artists, including Mann himself and Virginia Woolf, and presented to the psychologist on the same occasion, its testimony. As far as Modernist art and literature are concerned, Graham Hough's comparison of Freud's status to that of "Plato in the Renaissance" does not seem to be far-fetched.

The reason for this close relationship between the two fields, which would normally be considered mutually exclusive, must surely lie in the particular nature of the kind of psychology pioneered by Freud. In her perceptive study of the psychologist, Marie Jahoda, when reassessing his achievements from the viewpoint of a psychologist, finds significance in the very fact that Freud continues to be a subject of controversy among psychologists, that they have not yet come to an agreement as to where to place him: whether he was "the founder of a new psychology or a poet; a philosopher or a philosoper manqué; a positivist or a metaphysician" etc.[61] which she ultimately relates to "the problems of psychology as a science (p.3). Johoda traces the cause for this "unfinished debate" about Freud partly to the contradictions and inconsistencies in his own writings, which she considers derive from the dilemma within Freud himself. As was touched on earlier, and as Jahoda emphasizes in her study, idealogically Freud hung on to his "faith in psychology as a natural science" (p.142) in the nineteenth century positivist or determinist sense and thus "held fast to [his] self-image as a natural scientist" (p.14).

Yet in practice, as Jahoda points out, finding such "physiological reductionism" inadequate to deal with the actual complexities of human behaviour and psychology observed in his clinical work, he had to create "a psychological language which [had] room for all psychological phenomena" (p.145), based on a comprehensive understanding of man, ie, man as a whole being, instead of studying him under neatly divided categories such as memory or perception or learning or attitude change, each in isolation (here again we may sense his kinship with the romantics and the Modernist writers). In short, "Freud's reductionist belief is in contrast to what he actually did",[62] and out of this dilemma or conflict, Jahoda argues, was born paradoxically another great legacy of his, a new outlook or possibility for future psychology, "a comprehensive psychology" which is not just a natural science but also includes humanities (and even art and literature) (pp.147-148). Jahoda, who regards psychoanalysis as a combination of natural, social and humanistic sciences, maintains that "so far his is the only system of psychological thought which embodies so broad a view of the subject" (p.148). Freud's such "interdisciplinary" approach, she thinks, "promises ... to advance psychology" (p.159).

Jahoda's reappraisal of Freud is based on her view that his dilemma is finally the "dilemmas of all psychology", as well as her realization that "psychology is reflexive and its practitioners are driven by their own work to ask questions which no science can answer" (p.161). As Jahoda herself gives some examples, such realization and the kind of approach of which Freud set an example seem to be gaining ground among psychologists. More recently, Anthony Storr, one of the best-known psychologists in Britain today, who was trained both in medicine and psychology, made a similar point. Stating that psychiatrists "often find themselves confronted with human problems about which science has nothing to say,"[63] and reminding us of Freud's abandonment of his work based on the physiological approach, *Project for a Scientific Psychology*, which is also discussed by Jahoda, Storr wrote on the nature of psychotherapy:

> Psychotherapy is not, and cannot be, a scientifically-based procedure in the sense in which a medical treatment can be; for understanding another person is in principle different from understanding a disease.

and emphasized the importance of the interdisciplinary training for the profession:

> The training which a psychotherapist needs is much more in the area of the humanities than in that of science. A knowledge of philosophy, of comparative religion, of the history of ideas, and of the great novels of the world is far more help in understanding the motives of human beings and what makes their lives worth living than any amount of physiology, anatomy or biochemistry.[64]

For he believes that

> Those emotional problems which remain in the province of the psychotherapist (and they will not be few) will increasingly be recognized as part of the human condition, inseparable from our peculiarities as a species; the inevitable concomitants of our tendency towards alienation from our own bodies and relation with other human beings which cannot be divorced from our capacity for metaphor, symbol, abstraction and innovation.

Although, curiously, Storr consistently emphasizes Freud's determinist side (is it because of his Jungian background?), this sort of recognition and practice, however tentative, originated, as Jahoda points out, in Freud, who regarded creative writers as "valuable allies" and used to the full materials from literature (Shakespeare, Sophocles, Ibsen, etc.), philosophy (Nietzsche in particular), anthropology and so on in his psychological studies. These ideas and reflections of the more recent psychologists help us recognize the common ground which Freud shared with literary men and understand the attraction felt, willingly or unwillingly, by so many writers and artists towards his ideas which to a certain degree still exists today. Jahoda's analysis of Freud's dilemma also helps to explain why so often the same writers or artists showed simultanously sympathy and aversion towards him: they sympathized with the creative thinker in Freud but rejected the positivist or determinist scientist in him. David Lodge demonstrated an awareness of this intrinsic affinity between literature and Freud's theories, as well as those of Jung which essentially derived from the former, when he included Freud's "The Relation of the Poet to Day-Dreaming" and Jung's "Psychology and Literature" in his *Twentieth Century Literary Criticism* (1972), alongside the essays by W. B. Yeats, Henry James, T. S. Eliot, Virginia Woolf, D. H. Lawrence, etc. To treat Freud and Jung on exactly the same footing as great writers and critics is another way of recognizing their importance for twentieth century literature, which transcends the normal boundary separating two different fields. Their psychological theories, particularly those of Freud, were important for writers and artists both as the source of inspiration, the root, and as the backdrop for the whole cultural scene of the period roughly between 1910 and 1930 and a few years more. It may not be an exaggeration to say that Modernism is defined by the presence of Freud, or at least by the attitude towards man represented by Freudianism.

As is common in most human undertakings, Modernism too had its excesses, in which artistic experiments, or rather explorations, went beyond the point of comprehension or endurance of the reading public, and there was an inevitable reaction – it could also be considered a natural process in the chain of actions and reactions – against Modernism, especially during the post-war years of the 1950s. Robin Rabinovitz, who made a special study of this phenomenon, quotes the view of the novelists of the 'fifties, who regarded Joyce's *Finnegans Wake* and Woolf's *The Waves* as the main culprits which brought about the alienation of "ordinary readers" from the novel.[65] What those later novelists reacted against, however, was not simply experiment, as Rabinovitz seems to assume throughout and as the title of his book itself suggests,[66] but more basically the introversion of the novel in Modernism, of which experimentalism was only one of its consequences. Thus the eyes of those novelists were turned back to the external world, their main concerns becoming social problems or phenomena or both, and they took for their models precisely those writers rejected by Modernists, the Victorian and the Edwardian novelists of the realist tradition. For Kingsley Amis, who is considered by Rabinovitz one of the "leaders in a return to traditional forms in the novel" (p.4), reaction against Modernism meant also reaction against Freud, when in his successful first novel *Lucky Jim* (1954) he caricatured Freud's theory by giving to a litter of three kittens belonging to the Welch household, the main target of his criticism and satire, the names Super-Ego, Ego and Id, of which Id was said to be the only survivor.[67] As the cats were "christened" by Mrs. Welch, it is possible that in the mind of the author the kind of people who should be chastised by his satire were identified as Freud enthusiasts. This point is made still clearer, especially in relation to Modernist fiction, in the film version of the novel, in which Bertrand, Professor Welch's son and the villain of the piece who is clearly disliked by the author, is changed from the painter in the novel to a novelist who is particularly interested in the subconscious, or the psychological probings of his characters' minds. Yet Rabinovitz in conclusion observes that those who reacted against Modernism produced works which neither approached the quality of their models nor those which matched those of the novelists they rejected, and quotes a remark made in 1958 by Anthony Quinton:

There is no one among the leading novelists of the last thirteen years who has managed to evoke any sustained and passionate partisanship one way or another; they are tractable and commodious figures who can be fitted into our lives without disrupting them. No one has made the sort of claims for the importance of his work made by, or on behalf of, Joyce, Lawrence or even Virginia Woolf.[68]

This comment is curiously reminiscent of Marie Jahoda's observation on those who came after Freud, including his critics:

the best of them are aware that much of the contemporary research literature in the technical psychological journals consists of 'elegant trivialities', ... that is, of sophisticated quantitative methods applied to insignificant questions. But they also sense that Freud was never trivial; his questions remain significant.[69]

The same may perhaps be said of the writers of Modernist fiction. They were never concerned with trivial questions and even trivial matters gained permanent significance by passing through the sensibilities and perceptions of those novelists. Paradoxically, the novels of Joyce, Woolf or Lawrence still remain fresh today, while those of the later novelists who reacted against them look rather dated. [We may compare this with the similar contrast between Osborne's *Look Back in Anger* (1956) and that belated manifestation of Modernism in the theatre, Beckett's *Waiting for Godot* (1955).] This must be due to the fact that the questions with which they grappled in their works were of a permanent and universal nature, such as the mysteries of life and death, those of the closest but most intractable being, the self, the related problem of bringing to light the inarticulate, hidden part of the human mind – weren't these what Shakespeare too was most concerned about? – the meaning of human relationships, especially those between men and women, and the relation between art and life; in short, the fundamental questions which arise out of human existence itself, which do not disappear or alter with the changes in the political or social systems. Joined to these concerns was their single-minded dedication to their art, based on their sense of mission and faith in art which almost bordered on religious beliefs. Joyce gave a superb expression to this when through Stephen's thought he described himself as "a priest of eternal imagination, transmuting the daily bread of experience into the radiant body of everlasting life."[70]

It may be said that such attitudes and such subject matter as discussed above, which in the tradition of English literature had usually belonged to the realm of poetry, was for the first time incorporated into the field of fiction – which indeed was Virginia Woolf's aspiration – and that the English novel has become that much richer. And in this we can recognize

a great contribution made to English literature by such Modernist writers
as Joyce, Woolf and Lawrence. In relation to Virginia Woolf's "best
novels", David Daiches observed:

> Perhaps the greatest fictional art weaves together the world of action
> and the world of introspection, the sense of the dailiness of daily
> living and the moods of private illumination which illumine and
> even transfigure routine ... [71]

The statement may equally be applied to the best novels of James Joyce
or D. H. Lawrence. For what they achieved in those works was, as was
discussed already, the fusion of the inner and the outer, "the world of
introspection" and "the world of action". It is noteworthy that Daiches'
remark is almost a paraphrase of Joyce's description, or definition, of an
artist quoted earlier. As to Virginia Woolf, however, Daiches almost
contradicts himself later when he classifies her as "a minor novelist" for
the reason that "one's response to her novels will depend in the last
analysis on one's temperament. [72]

This is a curious argument, and makes one wonder how it is possible
to acknowledge the greatness of an artist's works and in the next breath
rate her as "minor", ie, "unimportant" (OED) or even second-rate, simply
because there are readers who cannot appreciate or understand them. We
may again extend the same argument to Joyce and ask: is *Ulysses*, not to
say *Finnegans Wake*, understood and appreciated without any resistance
by all readers? There are even those who vehemently react against
Lawrence's whole approach towards life and art. This too seems to be a
question of temperament. I take up this point particularly, as this sort of
patronizing attitude towards Virginia Woolf had been, in my view, too
common among critics, as is also manifest in Anthony Quinton's expression, "or *even* Virginia Woolf [my italics]", until recently, when the tide
seems to have taken a turn in the direction in which her status as a major,
not "minor", novelist of the modern period is clearly recognized. This
impression is strengthened by the increasing flow of publications on
Woolf, either as the sole subject, or as one of the Modernist triumvirate
of the English novel. [73]

This change seems to have coincided with, or resulted from, the
establishment of the term and the concept of Modernism in recent years,
which has revealed much of what had been considered Woolf's personal
idiosyncrasy was in fact a manifestation, individualistic, to be sure, of the
larger spirit of the age. As the understanding of the phenomenon of
Modernism increased, the recognition of Woolf's representative status
seems to have grown, so that now it even happens, as far as the discussion

of Modernist fiction is concerned, that critics only mention Joyce and
Woolf, as in the case of Jeremy Hawthorn's article on "The Modernist
Novel" (see p.18), or include Lawrence with qualifications, as in this
study, or place him in an auxiliary or secondary role.[74]

If Virginia Woolf has by now gained fully-deserved recognition as a
major novelist, there still remains one aspect of her work which is often
neglected, or has not received due appreciation: her criticial writings. In
concluding his article on Virginia Woolf as critic, René Wellek summed
up his view of this side of Woolf as follows:

> Though she may not have contributed importantly to a theory of
> literature or even of the novel, Virginia Woolf has accomplished the
> task of the critic: she has characterized many of the main novelists
> and judged them acutely blending characterization and judgement
> ... (p.437)

While Wellek's assessment certainly applies to some portion of
Woolf's large critical output, it by no means covers the whole and ignores
the most important contribution she made in her capacity as critic. In
order to understand and appreciate this aspect of Woolf's achievement
fully, we have to pay special attention to her major critical essays in which
she expounded and advocated her ideas of the new novel forcefully and
consistently, although these same ideas are also scattered among her minor
essays, serving as the basis of her judgement or evaluation of certain
writers or works.

A significant fact was that, in expressing her own ideals and aspirations
for the novel, Woolf was aware that she was speaking for a whole
generation of writers, which means that her essays must be seen in a wider
context and not just as personal outpourings. In the midst of the cultural
turmoil, and fully participating in it herself, she had a clearsighted
understanding of what was happening around her. Arnold Bennett, one
of the main targets of her criticism, knew this when he described Woolf
as the "real champion of the younger school," and remarked: "she alone,
so far as I know, came forward and attacked the old." As a result, her
essays, while being impassioned manifestos, became a series of lucid
accounts of "the situation of the novel" and literature of her time.

As was stated at the outset and examined in detail in the section on
Woolf, she was the first, at least in the field of the English novel, to
distinguish clearly between the old and the new modes of writing and gave
perceptive exposition of the latter, calling it "modern" or "modernist",
which foreshadowed, we may even say prepared the way for, the analyses
of the later scholars and critics of Modernism, as to its characteristics as

well as its affiliations. That Spender's *The Struggle of the Modern*, one of the milestones in the development of the concept of Modernism in English literature, was inspired by and partly based on Woolf's ideas has already been touched upon.

In the light of these considerations, it becomes difficult to maintain the view that Woolf as critic did not "[contribute] importantly to a theory of literature or even of the novel", since out of her essays emerges the earliest, even if embryonic, theory of Modernist literature and fiction, and as such is, in my view, invaluable material for scholars and critics who study the subject. As it is, this side of Woolf's contribution still awaits greater appreciation and the attention that it deserves.

NOTES

(Further details of works mentioned may be found in the Bibliography)

INTRODUCTION

1. "The Literary Scene", in *The Modern Age, The Pelican Guide to English Literature, VII*, ed. Boris Ford (Harmondsworth: Penguin Books, 1961), p.99.
2. *The Evening Standard* (2nd December, 1926), p.5, quoted in Samuel Hynes, *Edwardian Occasions: Essays on English Writing in the Early Twentieth Century* (London: Routledge & Kegan Paul, 1972), p.33.
3. Anthony Fothergill's section dealing exclusively with "Virginia Woolf's Critical Essays" [its title] in Peter Faulkner's *Modernism* (London: Methuen, 1977), pp.29-38 and René Wellek's short article, "Virginia Woolf as Critic", *The Southern Review* (Louisiana, 1977), pp.419-437, may be considered as examples of the few early attempts.

CHAPTER ONE – What was Modernism? The Question of Terminology

1. Preface, *The Modern Tradition*, ed. Richard Ellmann and Charles Feidelson (NY: Oxford University Press, 1965), p.v.
2. Reprinted in *Modern Essays* (London: Collins, 1971), p.39
3. See esp.Introduction, *A Reader's Guide to Great Twentieth-Century English Novels* (London: Thames and Hudson, 1959).
4. *The Tradition of the New* (1959; rpt. London: Thames and Hudson, 1962). p.214.
5. *Image and Experience: Studies in a Literary Revolution* (1960: rpt. Lincoln: University of Nebraska Press, 1960), p.8.
6. *Modernism*, p.ix. He also discusses Hough's adoption of the term "Imagism".
7. *The Struggle of the Modern* (London: Hamish Hamilton, 1963), p.256.
8. "What Was Modernism" in *Refractions: Essays in Comparative Literature* (NY: Oxford University Press, 1966), p.281.
9. Ellmann and Feidelson, p.vi.
10. Spender's adoption of these terms may possibly have been inspired by a short passage in Levin's "What was Modernism?" that preceded his book, where Levin too makes a similar, though not exactly the same, distinction, without further elaborating on it: "Now, we are all contemporaries; about that we have no option, so long as we stay alive. But we may choose whether or not we wish to be modern..." (p.276). The term "modern" at any rate was apparently very much in the air at the time.
11. *The Idea of the Modern in Literature and the Arts*, ed. Irving Howe (1967; rpt. NY: Horizon Press, 1968). The Introduction subtitled "The Idea of the Modern", was reprinted in Howe's later book, *The Decline of the New* (1971) as the initial chapter, "The Culture of Modernism". See Chapter One, p.15.
12. "The Advent of Modernism 1900-1920", *The Sphere History of Literature in the English Language, VII: The Twentieth Century*, ed. B. Bergonzi (London: Sphere Books, 1970), p.18.
13. Bergonzi, while showing a certain reservation about some of Woolf's views, recognizes the accuracy of her perception and judgement and comments: "Virginia Woolf's [critical] instinct was remarkably sure" (p.18).
14. These commentaries invited a severe rebuke from Kermode, who criticized them for their "dogmatic" approach and "slapdash, unexamined history" and commented: "the list within its limits is not unreasonable; only comments are deplorable". – *Modern Essays*, p.44.
15. For example, on Graham Greene, whom Spender excluded from his discussions, and his

The Power and the Glory (1940), Connolly writes: "Graham Greene is one of the few Catholic writers who is also a modernist" (p.81). Thus, Kermode, after complaining about "his abuse" of such key words as "modernism" and "sensibility", gives his verdict rather impatiently: by such practice, "Mr. Connolly simply obscures this interesting issue; his book will add confusion where there is enough already." – *Modern Essays*, p.43.

16. "The Fate of the Avant-Garde", in Howe, p.144.

17. *On Modernism: The Prospects for Literature and Freedom* (Cambridge, Massachussetts: MIT Press, 1967), p.3.

18. *A Question of Modernity* (London: Secker & Warburg, 1966), p.13.

19. *French Literature and its Background, The Twentieth Century* (London: Oxford University Press, 1970), p.6, pp.1-20.

20. *Age of the Modern and Other Literary Essays* (Carbondale & Edwardville: Southern Illinois University Press, 1971), p.118.

21. *The Decline of the New* (London: Gollancz, 1971), p.vii.

22. *The Social Context of Modern English Literature* (Oxford: Blackwell, 1971), pp.69-70.

23. *The Twentieth Century Mind*, ed. C. B. Cox and A. E. Dyson (London: Oxford University Press, 1972), III, p.324.

24. *Modernism: 1890-1930*, ed. M. Bradbury and J. McFarlane (Harmondsworth: Penguin Books, 1976), p.13. The Preface, from which these quotations are taken, is dated 1974.

25. *Working with Structuralism* (Boston/London: Routledge & Kegan Paul, 1981), p.72.

26. It is interesting to compare David Lodge's use of these terms in the two books discussed in the text with the critical language of the same author's earlier books, for it seems to recapitulate quite neatly in a single critic the general pattern of the changing fortunes of the critical terms we have observed so far, and thus sums it up equally neatly. In his first book of criticism, *Language of Fiction* (London, Routledge & Kegan Paul, 1966), published in the middle of our second period, "modernism" or "modernist" hardly makes its appearance; instead, we have characteristically, "The Modern Movement in Fiction", "The 'modern' novel", and indeed, an essay on "The Modern, the Contemporary and the Importance of Being Amis", where he names at the outset James, Conrad, Joyce, Lawrence, Forster and Virginia Woolf as "the important modern novelists" and adds: " 'Modern' has, in fact, become a qualitative rather than a chronological term; and to anyone with an elementary knowledge of recent literary history it is obvious that, in Britain, 'the contemporary novel is no longer "modern" ' (p.243. The quotation at the end comes from Frederick Karl, *A Reader's Guide to the Contemporary English Novel* (1963), p.4). Inevitably, the passage is almost immediately followed by the discussion of *The Struggle of the Modern*, in which, the author comments, Spender "emancipates 'contemporary' as well as 'modern' from a chronological significance", thus showing clearly the characteristic signs of the peak of the second period. In the next book, *The Novelist at the Crossroads*" (London: Routledge & Kegan Paul, 1971), which comes at the very end of this period, Spender's terminology that seems to have gained such ground in the 'sixties is nowhere to be seen; in its place we have references, albeit in passing, to "modernist experimentalism" (as opposed to the "realistic novel"), "the Modernist movement" and "modernism". Although the book covers the subjects very similar to those of the later books, these terms, unlike in the latter, are not discussed in their own right here. The only exception may be Kermode's idea of "neo-modernism" in Part IV: "Fiction and Modernism", which gets more detailed attention (p.168). However, both "neo-modernism" and "Modernism" in this section will later be called "postmodernism". All in all, the book seems to reflect the transitional stage of the early 'seventies, when the idea of "Modernism" was not yet altogether crystallized, but the term was increasingly being preferred to "the modern". While his essay, "The Language of Modernist Fiction: Metaphor and Metonymy", included in Penguin *Modernism* may be said to retain some of this transitional character, the title – "modern", according to the author, "in its qualitative as well as merely chronological significance" (p.481)- the last two books, which were written after *Modernism,* drop the "qualitative" sense of the word "modern" completely, reducing it to a term of "merely chronological signifance", thus enabling "modern fiction" in these later books to contain "two [opposing] kinds" or three kinds of fiction, or for that matter any number of different types of fiction", that belong to "the modern period". The word's "qualitative" function was taken over by

"modernism", which by now seems to have established itself, together with its derivatives, as a "key" critical term. As was mentioned already, the vicissitude of these critical idioms in Lodge's writings would seem to confirm our impression of the general critical trend.

27. This poet will be discussed in a later chapter. See p.91.

28. *Fontana Dictionary of Modern Thought*, ed. Alan Bullock and Oliver Stallybrass (London: Collins, 1977), p.395.

29. *The Uses of Fiction: Essays on the Modern Novel in Honour of Arnold Kettle*, ed. Douglas Jefferson and Graham Martin (Milton Keynes: The Open University Press, 1982), p.42.

30. Peter Faulkner writes in his *Modernism* that it was in the 1920s that the term Modernism began to be used in the present sense, and names as an example *A Survey of Modernist Poetry* (1927) by Laura Riding and Robert Graves. He comments, however, that "the authors tend to use the adjective 'modern' rather than 'modernist' in most of the text ..." (p.x). This predilection for the adjective "modern" in the sense of "modernist" apparently went on for quite some time, several decades in fact, until it finally almost overshadowed the latter towards our second period, although in its noun form, "modernism", seems to have fared slightly better. Thus, Donald Davie, discussing what is "modern" poetry in *Articulate Energy* (London: Routledge & Kegan Paul, 1955) observed: " 'modern', in fact, has taken over the functions of the now outmoded adjective 'modernist' ..." (p.147). Clearly, the critical world was preparing its way for the phase when the word "modern" dominated the scene, and Spender's choice of this word for his book may be considered a result or a reflection of this general critical climate. In any case, we can see interesting reversals of the critical fashion, or trend, here.

CHAPTER TWO – The Nature and Roots of Modernism

1. Bullock and Stallybrass, p.396

2. Bradbury and McFarlane, p.92

3. *The Social Context*, p.92

4. "The Birth of the Modern", p.1

5. Faulkner, p.33

6. *The English Novel* (1954; rpt. Harmondsworth: Penguin Books, 1970), pp.341-342.

7. Bradbury and McFarlane, p.82

8. *The Idea of the Modern*, p.14

9. *Consciousness and Society: the Reorientation of European Social Thought: 1890-1930* (1958; rpt. London: MacGibbon & Kee, 1959), p.34.

10. *The Sense of an Ending: Studies in the Theory of Fiction* (1967; rpt. Oxford: University Press, 1968), p.97.

11. Bradbury and McFarlane, p.84.

12. *Between the Acts* (1941; rpt. Harmondsworth, Penguin Books, 1953), p.138.

13. *Refractions*, p.294

14. "The Double Image", in Bradbury and McFarlane, p.67. McFarlane himself singles out Freud's theory of dreams as the most significant for modern literature (p.85).

15. *The Age of the Modern* (p.100).

16. *Image and Experience*, p.108. He also compares Freud with Plato in that they both, as he thinks, gave a low status to the artist, Plato banishing him from his ideal *Republic* and Freud identifying him with the neurotic. This view, however, seems rather problematical, since Freud in a sense holds the artist in high esteem as one who possesses to an exceptional degree the power of sublimation, an important faculty in Freud's psychological system that, he believes, forms the basis of civilization. See p.71, Chapter 4, *"The Role of the Psychologists-(1) – Sigmund Freud."*

17. Nigel Walker, "A New Copernicus?" , *Freud and the 20th Century*, ed. B. Nelson (London: Allen & Unwin, 1958), p.23.

18. "The History of a Dream", *Transition*, No. 18 (1929), p.37.

19. *Sigmund Freud: Life and Work, III* (London: The Hogarth Press, 1957), p.471.

20. "Note", *Transition*, No. 14 (Fall, 1928), pp.180-181.
21. *The Struggle of the Modern*, p.51.
22. "The Freudian Revolution Analyzed, " in Nelson, p.13.
23. "The End of the Line" , *The Idea of the Modern*, p.158.
24. *Consciousness and Society*, p.34.
25. *"Delusions and Dreams in Jensen's Gradiva"* (1907), *The Standard Edition of the Complete Psychological Works of Sigmund Freud*, ed. James Strachey (London: The Hogarth Press and the Institute of Psycho-Analysis, 1953-1974), IX, pp.43-44. The Standard Edition will henceforth be cited as *S.E.* This paper, along with Freud's views on art and literature, is discussed in a later chapter.
26. *The Liberal Imagination* (London: Secker & Warburg, 1951), p.35.
27. *Puzzles and Epiphanies* (London: Routledge & Kegan Paul, 1962), p.61.

CHAPTER THREE – Modernism and the English Novel

1. *The Romantic Novel in England* (Cambridge, Massachussetts: Harvard University Press, 1972), p.21.
2. C. J. Rawson, "Fielding and Smollett", *Sphere History of Literature in the English Language*, IV, ed. Roger Lonsdale (London: Sphere Books, 1971), p.294. For earlier examples, see also *The Pelican Guide to English Literature*, IV (Harmondsworth, 1957) and David Daiches' *A Critical History of English Literature* (London, 1960), Vol. II.
3. Samuel Chew, *The Nineteenth Century and After, A Literary History of England*, IV (NY, 1967), p.1196, quoted by Robert D. Hume, "Gothic versus Romantic: A Revaluation of the Gothic Novel", *PMLA* 84 (March 1969), p.282.
4. Horace Walpole, *Shorter Novels*, III (London: Dent & Sons, 1930), p.102.
5. *The Romance* (London: Methuen, 1970), p.57.
6. *The Literature of Terror* (London & NY: Longman, 1980), p.425
7. *The Romantic Novel*, p.1.
8. See especially Chapter 4, "Gothic and Romanticism" (pp.99-129).
9. *The Situation of the Novel* (1970; rpt. Harmondsworth, Penguin Books, 1972), p.25.
10. *The Turn of the Novel: the Transition to Modern Fiction* (1966; rpt. London, Oxford & NY: Oxford University Press 1970), p.xv.
11. *Possibilities: Essays on the State of the Novel* (London, Oxford & NY: Oxford University Press, 1973), p.81.
12. *Collected Essays* (London: Hogarth Press, 1966), II, pp.69-70, hereafter cited as *C.E.*
13. *C.E.* I, pp.131-133.
14. Karl and Magalaner, p.34.
15. "Psychology and Art Today" (1935), reprinted in *The English Auden: Poems, Essays and Dramatic Writings, 1927-1939*, ed. E. Mendelson (London: Faber & Faber, 1977), p.341. Auden was an ardent admirer of Freud and often found support in his theories for his own poetic beliefs. See, eg, Richard Hoggart, *Auden: An Introductory Essay* (London, 1951), pp.117-129 and John Blair, *The Poetic Art of W. H. Auden* (New Jersey, 1965), pp.39 and 75.
16. Walter Allen , *Tradition and Dream* (1964; rpt. Harmondsworth, Penguin Books, 1965), p.26. Karl and Magalaner comment specifically on this point: "It is striking that the novelists with whom we are concerned did not on the whole absorb Freud's ideas so much as take to an atmosphere in which the development of character and personality had been transformed into something new."– p.34.
17. Bradbury, *The Social Context*, p.86. Virginia Woolf, who had recognised radical change in "all human relations" around the year 1910, saw still greater significance in 1914 when "suddenly, like a chasm in a smooth road, the war came", "the crash came", putting an end to the old order completely. – "The Leaning Tower", *C.E.* II, pp.167-169. For D. H. Lawrence, "It was in 1915 the old world ended".– *Kangaroo* (1923; rpt. Harmondsworth: Penguin Books, 1968), p.240.
18. *Tradition and Dream*, p.27.

19. *The Rise and Fall of the Man of Letters* (London: Weidenfeld & Nicholson, 1969), p.252.
20. *Freudianism and the Literary Mind* (1945; rpt. Baton Rouge, Louisiana: Louisiana University Press, 1967), p.48.
21. *Ibid*, p.66. Hoffman examines in detail the process of the spreading of Freud's theories in America in Chapter II of the book (pp.44-58).
22. For his attitude towards Freud and Jung, see eg, Richard Ellmann, *James Joyce* (1959; rpt. London: Oxford University Press, 1966), pp.450, 480, 525, 672, etc. Ellmann mentions the fact that Joyce "disparaged" his friend's knowledge of psychoanalysis "but found [it] useful" (p.405), and notes further that despite his constant disavowal of any interest in psychoanalysis, "he partly belied himself by the keen interest he took in the notebook Frank Budgen kept to record his dreams; Joyce's interpretations showed the influence of Freud" (p.450).
23. The best known of such references is to the psychologists themselves: "when they were jung and easily freudened ..." – *Finnegans Wake* (1939; rpt. Faber & Faber, 1968), p.115. On Joyce's intimacy with and references to Freud's theories, see, eg, Hoffman, pp.119-125, or W. Y. Tyndall, *A Reader's Guide to James Joyce* (London, 1959), p.260.
26. For example, Harry Levin in *James Joyce: A Critical Introduction* (London, 1960), Clive Hart in *Structure and Motif in Finnegans Wake* (London, 1962), or W. Y. Tindall in *A Reader's Guide to 'Finnegans Wake'* (London, 1969).

CHAPTER FOUR – The Role of the Psychologists (1)– Sigmund Freud

1. W. H. Auden, *Collected Shorter Poems: 1927-1957* (London: Faber & Faber, 1966), p.168.
2. *The Republic*, The Loeb Classical Library, translated by Paul Shorey (London: Heinemann, 1963), p.335.
3. *The Interpretation of Dreams*, translated and edited by James Strachey (1953; rpt. London: Allen & Unwin, 1954), pp.134, 582n.
4. *Freud and the 20th Century*, p.15. Freud himself observes: "We psycho-analysts were not the first and not the only ones to utter this call to introspection; but it seems to be our fate to give it its most forcible expression and to support it with empirical material which affects every individual." – *Introductory Lectures on Psycho-Analysis*, S.E. XVI, p.285.
5. *Ibid*, pp.284-285.
6. "Sigmund Freud in his Historical Setting" in *The Spirit of Man, Art and Literature, The Complete Works of C. G. Jung*, XV, translated by R. F. C. Hull (London: Routledge & Kegan Paul, 1966), p.34. (Hereafter the *Complete Works* will be cited as *C.W.*) The essay was first published in 1932.
7. F. J. Hoffman, while conceding that there was "no lack of discussion of Freudianism before and during the war", observes that it was the postwar 'twenties "which were to witness the real penetration of Freudianism into the thought of England and America." – *Freudianism and the Literary Mind*, p.58.
8. *S.E.* XX, p.54.
9. *The Interpretation of Dreams*, p.xxxii.
10. *New Introductory Lectures on Psycho-Analysis*, S.E. XXII, p.7.
11. *Five Lectures on Psycho-Analysis*, S.E. XI, p.33.
12. Though we find in Shakespeare's plays many speeches to the same effect which express the contemporary popular ideas of the dream, Shakespeare shows in his great tragedies deeper insight and an attitude quite original for his time. The subject is discussed in my dissertation, *Shakespeare and the Early Literature of Dreams*. (Shakespeare Institute, The University of Birmingham, 1969).
13. Jung, *C.W.* XV, p.44.
14. An historical survey of man's ambivalent attitude towards dreams may also be found in my dissertation mentioned above.
15. *The Interpretation of Dreams*, p.121. This theory is repeatedly found in the book as well as in the other works of Freud.
16. *Ibid*, p.279.

17. Quoted by David Stafford-Clark, *What Freud Really Said* (Harmondsworth: Penguin Books, 1969), pp.58 and 65.

18. *Introductory Lectures*, S.E. XV, p.175.

19. *Ibid*, pp.175-176. In *The Interpretation of Dreams*, Chapter VI, Section C, 4, pp.310 ff.

20. *The Interpretation of Dreams*, p.352.

21. *Introductory Lectures*, S.E. XV, p.158.

22. *The Interpretation of Dreams*, p.399.

23. *Ibid*, p.360.

24. Although it may not surely be the final answer to these points raised by Freud, we may quote the conclusion reached by the later researchers of dreams: " ... viewing our growing library of dreams, we may begin to see in what percentage of our dreams these points of theory hold. Not all dreams protect sleep, or fulfil wishes, or exhibit a covert form of repressed behaviour. Sometimes dreams seem to follow a sequence and develop a theme. Sometimes memory fails. Dream researchers are not seeking a single formula to describe all dreams, and indeed in the laboratory they must analyze far more than merely dreams." –Gay G. Luce and Julius Segal, *Sleep and Dreams* (London: Panther Books, 1969), p.249.

25. *Introductory Lectures*, S.E. XV, p.210.

26. Quoted in *The Interpretation of Dreams*, p.549.

27. To give some examples of the works referred to by Freud: Charles Darwin, *The Descent of Man* (London, 1875), etc.

J. G. Frazer, *Totemism and Exogamy* (London, 1910); *The Golden Bough* (London, 1911-1914.)

W. Wundt, *Mythus und Religion* (Leipzig, 1906); *Elemente der Völkerpsychologie* (Leipzig, 1912).

E. Durkheim, *"La prohibition de l'inceste et ses origines" - Année sociolog, I, 1 (1898); Les formes élémentaires de la vie religieuse: Le système totemique en Australie* (Paris, 1912), etc.

A. Lang, *The Secret of the Totem* (London, 1905).

J. J. Atkinson, *Primal Law* (London, 1903).

28. *Totem and Taboo*, S.E. XIII, p.141.

29. This is not surprising when we think of the central position Freud attributed to the Oedipus complex. For the discussion of these later works, see p.57.

30. Here it must be remembered that we are talking mainly about a male child. As for little girls, Freud at first thought that the exact opposite takes place, ie, "a girl's affection is for her father", and regarding her mother as her rival, she conceives a death-wish against her which is revealed in the dreams of the mother's death. (*The Interpretation of Dreams*, pp.256-260). He modified this view later, postulating that both boys and girls at an early stage share the same incestuous wish for their mothers but later, when girls realize their difference from boys, out of disappointment in the apparent inferiority of their sexual organs, they turn their attachment and love towards their fathers, and reject their mothers who share the same destiny. Freud called this the "Electra complex", finding the prototype of the situation in the story of Electra in the Greek myth who plots to kill her mother, Clytemnestra, in revenge for Agamemnon, her father, who had already been murdered by Clyemnestra and her lover (Cf. "Some Psychological Consequences of the Anatomical Distinction between the Sexes", *Collected Papers*, 5 (1925), *Female Sexuality* (1931), *New Introductory Lectures* (1933)). However, Freud does not seem to have been so clear or sure of the sexuality in little girls, and of women, for that matter, as of boys or men. He often mentioned the "impenetrable obscurity" of female sexuality and once wrote: "We know less about the sexual life of little girls than of boys. But we need not feel ashamed of this distinction; after all, the sexual life of adult women is 'a dark continent' for psychology." - *The Question of Lay Analysis*, S.E. XX, p.212.

31. *The Interpretation of Dreams*, p.262.

32. *Ibid*, pp.264. The Editor's footnote identifies these lines as "Lewis Cambelle's translation [1883] 1. p.982 ff."

33. In a footnote added to *The Interpretation of Dreams* in 1919, Freud states that this psycho-analytic interpretation was later taken over by Ernest Jones, who published it in a more amplified form in his "The Oedipus Complex as an Explanation of Hamlet's

Mystery." This in turn was expanded into a book published in 1949 under the title *Hamlet and Oedipus.*

34. *The Interpretation of Dreams,* p.266.

35. In a footnote added in 1914, Freud writes: "None of the findings of psycho-analytic research has provoked such embittered denials, such fierce opposition - or such amusing contortions – on the part of the critics as this indication of the childhood impulses towards incest which persist in the unconscious. An attempt has even been made recently to make out, in the face of all experience, that the incest should only be taken as 'symbolic'... " (p.263).

36. For example, Erich Fromm criticized Freud's theory on the grounds that "the Oedipus complex is symptomatic of the patriarchal society; it is not universal, and the rivalry between father and son does not occur in societies where patriarchal authority does not exist." – Quoted by J. A. C. Brown: *Freud and the Post-Freudians* (Harmondsworth: Penguin Books, 1969), p.163.

   More recently, in his conversation on "dynamic psychology", psychologist and psychoanalyst Anthony Storr observes that "There's an enormous area of research about cultural differences which will have to be undertaken, " and take the Oedipus complex as an example. He believes that "the Oedipus complex ... is a product of the small family", and supports his view with the report by a Nigerian psychiatrist who gave "a completely different picture of what went on in the Nigerian family which is much more extended and where the children are looked after by many more adults, and so you don't get these intense rivalries. Indeed, they have a quite different concept of individuality. They don't think of a person as being a separate individual in his own right, but only as part of the family. You don't have a psychiatric patient there: you have the family as a patient and not just one person." -"Nature and Human Nature - Anthony Storr discusses 'dynamic psychology' with Renford Bambrough," *The Listener,* Vol. 85 (1971), p.814.

37. *The Interpretation of Dreams,* p.536

38. *An Outline of Psycho-Analysis, S.E.* XXIII, p.145

39. A detailed discussion on the relation between the "super-ego" and "conscience" may be found in Chapters VII and VIII of his *Civilization and its Discontents.*

40. *S.E.* XXIII, p.146.

41. *The Future of an Illusion, S.E.* XXI, p.43.

42. *Totem and Taboo, S.E.* XIII, pp.142-143; pp.156-157. Also see pp.83-85.

43. *Civilization and its Discontents, S.E.,* XXI, p.132.

44. *Ibid,* p.145. Though unpopular among psychologists, this work has often been highly regarded by literary men as cultural criticism or a serious reflection on the essential nature of civilization. For example, Lionel Trilling, in his *Beyond Culture* (1965), includes it among the ten books which he prescribed for his students as the "prolegomenon" for the study of modern literature.

45. *Freudianism and the Literary Mind,* p.66.

46. *The London Times,* 4th December, 1929, 10e, quoted by Hoffman, p.66.

47. *Five Lectures, S.E.* XI, p.53.

48. "Two Encyclopedia Articles, " (1923), *S.E.* XVIII, p.256.

49. *Five Lectures, S.E.* XI, p.54.

50. *Civilization and its Discontents, S.E.* XXI, p.97.

51. "Leonardo da Vinci and a Memory of his Childhood", *S.E.* XI, p.136.

52. *S.E.* XXI, pp.82-83. On beauty, he further states: "Beauty has no obvious use; nor is there any clear cultural necessity for it. Yet civilization could not be without it."

53. "Delusions and Dreams in Jensen's *Gradiva*" (1907), *S.E.* IX, 8. In this passage alone, we may detect the influence of Shakespeare *(Hamlet).*

54. *S.E.* II, pp.160-161.

55. "Jensen's *Gradiva*", *S.E.* IX, p.44.

56. "Freud and Literature", *The Liberal Imagination* (1950; rpt. London: Secker & Warburg, 1951), p.34.

57. "Jensen's *Gradiva*", *S.E.* IX, p.7.

58. *S.E.* XIV, p.318.

Notes – to pages 55 to 62

59. In "Jensen's *Gradiva*", we find his own profession of his intention to adhere to the actual text: "It is so easy to draw analogies and to read meanings into things. Is it not rather we who have slipped into this charming poetic story a secret meaning very far from its author's intentions? ... For the moment ... we have tried to save ourselves from making any such tendentious interpretation by giving the story entirely in the author's own words" - *S.E.* IX, p.43.

60. "Leonardo", *S.E.* XI, p.136, and "Dostoevsky", S.E. XXI, p.177.

61. *Ibid,* p.112. For Jung's criticism of this interpretation and his argument of the archetype of "two mothers" as its alternative, see pp.77-78. The criticisms of Freud's essay on Leonardo by other writers (some of them art critics) and himself are discussed by Ronald W. Clark in his *Freud: The Man and the Cause* (London: Jonathan Cape and Weidenfeld & Nicolson, 1980), pp.347-348.

62. Cf. Freud's discussion of "Those Wrecked by Success" in "Some Character Types". See pp.104-105.

63. "Freud's case history of Dostoevsky", *The Times Literary Supplement*, 18 July, 1975, pp.807-808.

64. A question has been raised by a practising psychoanalyst on the applicability of psychoanalytical theories to biographical and critical studies of creative artists. Charles Rycroft casts doubt on the view, which he considers widely held among general public and psychoanalysts, that "the conceptual system used by psychoanalysts to explain neuroses can be applied without significant modification to creative activity, and that, as a result, it is possible to write 'pathobiographies' of creative people, in which their products can be interpreted as having been caused by their prior, and mostly childhood, experiences, " on the ground that the relationship between a critic and his subject is essentially different from that between an analyst and his patient. Unlike the doctor for whom confirmations and repudiations from his patient are available, it is impossible for the "psychoanalytical critic-biographer" to confirm his interpretations on his subject – "The interpretations the analyst-critic makes are in no sense the result of mutual endeavour and exploration, as are those that emerge at the end of a successful therapeutic analysis." Psychoanalytical studies of creative people, he points out, consequently "tend to have a curious 'up in the air' quality". "They may, and indeed often do, sound plausible and even convincing, " he continues, "but their logical status remains uncertain, since it is unclear in what sense the interpretations arrived at can be asserted to be true." - "The Artist as Patient, " *The Times Literary Supplement*, 22 September, 1972, pp.1089-1090.

65. *S.E.* VII, p.305.

66. In the present essay, however, his interest is centred on drama, which he continues to analyse in detail, dividing it into five categories, namely, religious drama, social drama, drama of character, psychological drama and psycho-pathological drama. The dramatic conflict in the first three, Freud observes, takes place between the hero and the outside forces, be they human or divine, whereas in psychological and psycho-pathological drama the struggle occurs in the hero's own mind. Furthermore, the conflict in psychological drama arises between the two conscious impulses, while that in the psycho-pathological drama (which incidentally seems first to have induced him to write the piece) takes place between a conscious impulse and a repressed one. As the first and one of the most successful of the latter kind of drama, Freud quotes *Hamlet*, and by analyzing its success in comparison with modern failures, he prescribes the conditions required for writing a successful psycho-pathological drama.

67. "The Relation of the Poet to Day-Dreaming" (1908), *Collected Papers*, IV, The International Psycho-Analytical Library, No. 10, edited by J. D. Sutherland (London: The Hogarth Press and the Institute of Psycho-Analysis, 1957), p.174. The same essay, with minor alterations, is included in the *Standard Edition*, IX, under the title, "Creative Writers and Day Dreaming."

68. *Ibid,* p.176. Unlike children's play, however, adults' fantasies which, according to Freud, are in nature either erotic or ambitious or both together, are usually jealously concealed. It is, says Freud, mainly through the confessions of neurotic patients for whom these fantasies have become overpowering, that we gain knowledge of the secret contents of adults' fantasies.

69. Arnold Kettle, *An Introduction to the English Novel* (London: Hutchinson University Library, 1959), I, p.29.
70. For example:
    Five Lectures on Psycho-Analysis (1910), *S.E.* XI, pp.49-50.
    Introductory Lectures on Pyscho-Analysis (1916-1917), *S.E.* XVI, pp.375-377.
    An Autobiographical Study (1925-1926), *S.E.* XX, pp.64-65.
    Civilization and its Discontents (1930), *S.E.* XXI, pp.12 and 17-18.
71. Perhaps we had better be acquainted here with Freud's idea of neurosis:
    The neuroses have no psychical content that is peculiar to them and that might not equally be found in healthy people. Or, as Jung has expressed it, neurotics fall ill of the same complexes against which we healthy people struggle as well. Whether that struggle ends in health, in neurosis or in a countervailing superiority of achievement, depends on quantitative considerations, on the relative strength of the conflicting forces. – *Five Lectures*, *S.E.* XI, p.50. A similar view is found in "Leonardo da Vinci", *S.E.* XI, p.131.
72. *Introductory Lectures*, *S.E.* XVI, p.376.
73. *S.E.* XI, p.50
74. *S.E.* XVI, p.376.
75. *S.E.* XX, pp.64-65.
76. Lionel Trilling, *Freud and the Crisis of our Culture* (Boston: The Beacon Press, 1955), pp.15-16. A slightly shortened version of this essay is included in his *Beyond Culture*, under a new title, "Freud: Within and Beyond Culture."
77. Ernest Jones, *Sigmund Freud*, III, pp.219-220. Jones considers the style of the Address to be "unmistakably Thomas Mann's" (p.219).
78. *Age of the Modern*, (p.104).

CHAPTER FIVE – The Role of the Psychologists (2) – C. G. Jung

1." Sigmund Freud in his Historical setting", *C.W.* XV, p.34.
2. *Ibid*, p.35. Perhaps here Jung is exaggerating Freud's "negative" attitude towards "accepted cultural values", for, though his method of argument may be said to be reductive, his attitude towards culture or civilization was, as we have seen, far from negative.
3. *Ibid*, pp.35-36. In "In Memory of Sigmund Freud", his obituary published just after the death of Freud in 1939, he repeats: "Freud has to be seen against [his] cultural background". *C.W.* XV, p.46.
4. *C.W.* XV, pp.37-40.
5. We have already encountered some examples when we discussed the applicability of the theory of the Oedipus complex (see p.91). A compact general survey of these criticisms by later psychologists is made in J. A. C. Brown's *Freud and the Post-Freudians*.
6. C. G. Jung, "The Archetypes of the Collective Unconscious" (1934), *C.W.* IX, Part I, p.3.
7. C. G. Jung, *Modern Man in Search of a Soul.* (1930; rpt. London: Routledge & Kegan Paul, 1966), pp.36-37.
8. "The Archetypes", *C.W.* IX, pp.3-4.
9. "The Concept of the Collective Unconscious" (1936), *C.W.* IX, Part I, p.42.
10. Also "The Archetypes", *C.W.* IX, p.3.
11. *Ibid* "The Archetypes", *C.W.* IX, p.5.
12. C. G. Jung, *Pyschology of the Unconscious, A Study of the Transformations and Symbolisms of the Libido*, trans. Beatrice M. Hinkle (London: Kegan Paul, Trench, Trubner, 1918), p.35. – This was first published in German in 1912, was later revised by the author and included in the *Complete Works* V under a different title, *Symbols of Transformation* (1956). The first English translation by B. M. Hinkle was published in New York in 1916, followed by the British version, reprint of the same, in 1917.

13. See Sigmund Freud, "Leonardo da Vinci and a Memory of his Childhood", *S.E.* XI, pp.63-137. See also above, p.63.

14. "The Concept of the Collective Unconscious", *C.W.* IX, pp.44-45. Also in "The Psychology of the Unsconscious", *Two Essays on Analytical Psychology, C.W.* VII, p.64. Freud, as we have seen, makes a similar point: see pp.63-64.

15. *Two Essays, C.W.* VII, pp.64-65.

16. Jung's theory of archetypes, together with his idea that man's psyche retains the marks of the evolutionary past, has been subject to strong attacks from other psychologists who charge him with being unscientific. For example, J. A. C. Brown, of the Freudian school, writes: "Evolution takes place slowly over millions, not thousands, of years; it takes place by natural selection based on chance variations and mutations, and the effect of civilization, if any, is to reduce the influence of selection by reducing competition; so far as we have been unable to discover the brain contains no innate ideas of any sort, much less archetypes of the elaborate kind described by Jung; the 'mind', however one defines the term, 'evolved' in the period of which we have knowledge by accumulating past experiences. In the matter of the racial unconscious, Jung is supported by no scientist anywhere, since there is no evidence that the biological equipment of any race is basically different from that of any other" – *Freud and the Post-Freudians*, p.110.

17. *Modern Man*, p.30.

18. "The Archetypes", *C.W.* IX, p.5. - Jung, who criticized Freud for ignoring cultural differences, in his turn is criticized for overlooking the same factor in his comparison of myths and symbols. Avis M. Dry, in her critical study, asks, " ... is there not an echo of the early nineteenth century anthropology in Jung's method of comparing myths and symbols in isolation from the cultures of which they are components, ie, without consideration of the interrelationships and modifying factors within the cultures themselves...?" and gives an example, reported incidentally by a Jungian psychologist, where Jung's method proved invalid. This "omission of differences relevant for precison of understanding", she continues, is the very thing "of which some critics are likely to accuse Jung and his school." – *The Psychology of Jung* (London: Methuen, 1961), p.110.

19. *Modern Man*, p.161.

20. "The Archetypes", *C.W.* IX, p.6.

21. *Ibid*, p.7. This view of Jung may be called "naturalization of the human psyche" in contrast to Freud's idea of "humanization of natural phenomena", through which, he considers, primitive man tried to achieve psychological control over them. - See *The Future of an Illusion, S.E.* XXI, pp.16-22.

22. "The Archetypes", *C.W.* IX, p.7.

23. According to Jung, this means "a sequence of fantasies produced by deliberate concentration". The sources of dreams, says Jung, are often repressed instincts which strive to become conscious and consequently tend to influence the conscious life of the dreamer. If a patient is in this state of mind, he is to contemplate any one fragment of fantasy that seems significant to him, until its context becomes clear. In the process, while elaborating the fantasy by adding further fantasies, he produces, observes Jung, material rich in archetypal images and associations. – "The Concept of the Collective Unconscious", *C.W.* IX, p.49.

24. "The Relations between the Ego and the Unconscious"– *Two Essays, C.W.* VII, p.128.

25. *Modern Man*, p.18.

26. "General Aspects of Dream Psychology" (1916), *The Structure and the Dynamics of the Psyche, C.W.* VIII, p.252.

27. "On the Nature of Dreams" (1945), *Ibid*, p.285.

28. *Modern Man*, p.20.

29. *The Structure and Dynamics, C.W.* VIII, pp.289-290.

30. *Modern Man*, pp.24-26.

31. Jung discusses similarity between the "mother" symbol and the "horse" symbol in *Psychology and the Unconscious* (later *Symbols of Transformation*), pp.282-283 and 308.

32. *Modern Man*, pp.27-30.

33. *Two Essays, C.W.* VII p.171.

34. *The Structure and Dynamics, C.W.* VIII, p.292.

35. *Two Essays*, *C.W.* VII, p.155.
36. *Two Essays*, *C.W.* VII, p.192. – The notion of persona, or mask, the terms being of dramatic origin, are naturally often found among poets and writers, especially among Jung's contemporaries. T. S. Eliot, for example, makes an extensive use of personae or masks in his poetry, not to mention his plays, the best example of which may be "The Love Song of J. Alfred Prufrock". The poet who made it the core of his beliefs not only in art but in life as well was W. B. Yeats. In *"Per Amica Silentia Lunae"*, *Mythologies* (London: Macmillan, 1959), he writes, quoting his old diary:

"I think all happiness depends on the energy to assume the mask of some other life, on a rebirth as something not one's self ... If we cannot imagine ourselves as different from what we are, and try to assume that second self, we cannot impose a discipline upon ourselves though we may accept one from others. Active virtue, as distinguished from the passive acceptance of a code, is therefore theatrical, consciously dramatic, the wearing of a mask ... " (p.334).

As can be seen from the quotation, however, the signifance artists attach to the mask is not entirely the same as that of Jung. It is not just a façade or social role as in Jung's case, but is endowed with the more positive function of overcoming and transcending the limitation of the self, an enlargement and enrichment in imagination of the possibilities of one's existence, either in art or in life. (We may also call to mind Fernando Pessoa, a Portuguese poet who assumed, when writing poetry, four different names or personae, to explore the different aspects of his inner self). All the same, this notion of the mask is one of the indications to show how closely Jung's mind was working to that of the literary man.

37. *Aion*, *C.W.* II, p.8.
38. "The Archetypes", *C.W.* IX, p.28.
39. *Two Essays*, *C.W.* VII, p.187.
40. In his footnote, Jung quotes Erwin Rousselle who calls the "spinning woman" the "animal soul".
41. *Aion*, *C.W.* II, p.13.
42. "The Archetypes", *C.W.* IX, p.28.
43. *Two Essays*, *C.W.* VII, pp.205-206.
44. *Aion*, *C.W.* II, p.16.
45. *C.W.* XV, pp.65-83.
46. This is one of the instances which show a curiously close kinship between Jungian theories and the prevalent literary theories of the time. The passage quoted above reminds us, for example, of the famous dictum of T. S. Eliot: "the poet has, not a 'personality' to express, but a particular medium which is only a medium and not a personality, in which impressions and experiences combine in peculiar and unexpected ways." – "Tradition and the Individual Talent", *Selected Essays* (London: Faber & Faber, 1951), pp.19-20.
47. *C.W.* XV, p.72.
48. *C.W.* XV, p.79.
49. With characteristic caution, Jung italicises the word "seems" and adds, "I use the word 'seems' because our own bias may prevent a deeper appreciation of it."
50. This was followed in 1930 by an English translation by Eugene Jolas for his own monthly magazine *Transition* under the title "Psychology and Poetry". It provided the magazine with the theoretical ground for the new lirerarary principles it was advocating. The essay was translated again later by W. S. Dell and C. F. Baynes and published, together with other essays, in *Modern Man in Search of a Soul* (1933). It is also included in Vol. XV of the Collected Works.
51 *Modern Man*, p.179.
52. Fernando Pessoa, *Obra Poética*, ed. Maria Aliete Galhoz (1960; 5th edition, Rio de Janeiro: José Aguilar Editora, 1974), p.394. Incidentally, Gabriel Josipovici, who has a section on Fernando Pessoa (1888-1935) in his *The Lessons of Modernism*, considers this poet, little known outside the Portuguese-speaking world, one of the "five grey-suited gentlemen", along with Cavafy, Kafka, Eliot and Borges, who for him represent "what is most radical in the literature of the past hundred years ... what embodies most clearly the essential spirit of modernism" (p.26).

Notes – to pages 83 to91

53. *Writers at Work*, selected by Kay Dick (Harmondsworth: Penguin Books, 1972), pp.17-18.

54. *Modern Man*, pp.198-199.

55. *C.W.* VII, p.225. Even his discussion of Longfellow's narrative poem, *Hiawatha,* though lengthy, has to be regarded essentially as supporting material for his theory rather than its application to the field of literary criticism. Describing it as a "poetical compilation of Indian myths", he treats it as folk material, with very little reference to the author, or the compiler, Longfellow himself, so that it is rather difficult to consider it a discussion of "a work of art" or "an artist". Jung uses the epic to provide the "mythological foundations" to the fantasies of one of his patients, to trace the "archetypal" material of those fantasies. The only time Longfellow is mentioned in his own right as the creator is when Jung regrets the introduction by the poet of "the white man's Saviour in the guise of the Supreme representative of Christianity and Christian morals" (p.395) at the end of the hero's life. - *C.W.* V, pp.312-357, 395 and 461.

56. " 'Ulysses': A Monologue", *The Spirit in Man, Art and Literature, C.W.* XV, p.109.

57. Here Jung repeats the thesis of his earlier papers and writes: "The artist does not follow an individual impulse, but rather a current of collective life which arises not directly from consciousness but from the collective unconscious of the modern psyche." - *Ibid*, p.117.

58. *Ibid,* p.122. "Like every true prophet, " Jung continues, "the artist is the unwitting mouthpiece of the psychic secrets of his time, and is often as unconscious as a sleep-walker. He supposes that it is he who speaks, but the spirit of the age is his prompter, and whatever his spirit says is proved true by its effect."

59. "Picasso" , *The Spirit in Man, Art and Literature, C.W.* XV, p.135.

60. In a footnote, added later (1934) in response to a controversy provoked by this comment, Jung explains at length that by this he does not mean that Picasso was a schizophrenic and that he is merely referring to the "disposition" or the psychological "habitus" of the painter. – *C.W.* XV, p.137.

61. For example, R. S. Peters described his psychological theories as "so mysterious as to be almost undiscussable" – Brett's *History of Psychology* (London, Allen & Unwin, 1952), p.695, cited by Dry (p.xi).

62. Richard Burgin, *Conversations with Jorge Luis Borges* (NY: Holt, Reinhart & Winston, 1969), p.109. It must be added, however, that there were on the other hand writers and artists, like Surrealists and Virginia Woolf, who showed their interest only in Freud, ignoring Jung, at least officially, completely. D. H. Lawrence also preferred the clear stance of Freud to what he thought a rather vague attitude of Jung – see *Fantasia of the Unconscious and Psychoanalysis and the Unconscious* (1923; rpt. Harmondsworth: Penguin Books, 1971), p.19.

63. *Freud and the Post-Freudians*, p.43.

CHAPTER SIX - The Romantic Ancestry

1. William Blake, *Complete Writings,* ed. Geoffrey Keynes (Oxford: Oxford University Preass, 1966), p.794.

2. William Wordsworth, *Poetical Works* (Oxford: Oxford University Press, 1973), p.62. Wordsworth's poems are all quoted from this edition.

3. Samuel Taylor Coleridge, *Biographia Literaria,* edited by George Watson (London: Dent, 1967), p.49.

4. Samuel Taylor Coleridge, *Poetical Works,* edited by E. H. Coleridge (Oxford: Oxford University Press, 1969), p.240. All quotations of Coleridge's poems are from this edition.

5. *The Common Pursuit* (1952; rpt. Harmondsworth: Penguin Books, 1962), p.186.

6. Quoted by Fred Inglis, *Keats* (London: Evans Brothers, 1971), p.33. Inglis himself describes Keats in similar terms to those of F. R. Leavis on Blake quoted above: " ... we come upon Keats as one of the first Romantics and a poet ... who looked upon himself with some triumph as solitary artist (in the widest sense of the word), in some sense at odds with society. This wasn't so with men like Pope and Johnson or even Swift. They

felt themselves of a society even when they were lambasting its wickedness. They shared its best moral insights and standards."

7. "Annotations to Reynolds" in *Ibid*, p.477.
8. "The Life of William Blake", in *The Letters of W. Blake*, ed. A. G. B. Russell (London, Methuen, 1906), p.18.
9. *Energy and Imagination* (Oxford: Clarendon Press, 1970), p.202.
10. *Biographia Literaria*, Vol. II, Ch. XXII, p.268.
11. See Norman Fruman, *Coleridge, the Damaged Archangel* (London: George Allen & Unwin, 1972), pp.365-412. The author makes analyses, both literary and psychoanalytical, of these dreams, and relates them to Coleridge's poems, especially *Kubla Kahn*, *The Ancient Mariner* and *Christabel*.
12. *The Notebooks of Samuel Taylor Coleridge, I, 1794-1804*, edited by Katherine Coburn (London: Routledge and Kegan Paul, 1957), p.1727.
13. *Collected Letters of Samuel Taylor Coleridge, II: 1801-1806*, edited by E. L. Griggs (Oxford: Clarendon Press, 1956), p.1009.
14. Fruman, pp.334-350.
15. *Nineteenth Century Studies*, edited by H. Davis et al. (Ithaca, NY: Cornell University Press, 1940), pp.39-40.
16. *The Notebooks, II:* 1804-1808, edited by K. Coburn (London: Routledge & Kegan Paul, 1962), p.2086, 15. 52, f40v.
17. Keats, *Poetical Works*, edited by H. W. Garrod (Oxford: Oxford University Press, 1970). All quotations of Keats' poems are from this edition.
18. Shelley, *Poetical Works*, edited by Thomas Hutchinson (London: Oxford University Press, 1971), p.637.
19. James Thomson, *The City of Dreadful Night and Other Poems* (London: P.J. and A. E. Dobell, 1919), p.3.
20. Novalis, *Hymns to the Night*, translated by Mabel Cotterell (London, Phoenix Press, 1948), p.27.
21. "Fragments", *Transition*, No. 18 (Nov. 1929), p.78.
22. Quoted by René Wellek, *Confrontations: Studies in the Intellectual and Literary Relations between Germany, England and the United States during the Nineteenth Century* (Princeton: Princeton University Press, 1965), p.16.
23. Quoted by Ralph Tymms, *German Romantic Literature* (London: Methuen, 1955), pp.154-155.
24. "Fragments", p.75.
25. Paul van Tieghem, in his survey of the Romantic movement in Europe, observes that Romanticism in England was above all an affair in the field of poetry, and while it produced "the modern historical novel" of Scott, the "typically romantic" novels found in Germany and France never came into existence in England:

    Le profond renouvellement que marque le romantisme anglais intéresse surtout la poésie. Au théâtre, toute liberté était acquise depuis longtemps dans la patrie de Shakespeare; quand au roman ... il s'annexe une domaine nouveau, éminemment romantique, lorsque Scott inaugure le roman historique moderne: mais pour des raisons morales ou autres, nous ne voyons pas naître outre-Manche le roman passionel, si typiquement romantique, des Allemandes et surtout des Français. – Le romantisme dans la littérature européene (Paris: Editions Albin Michel, 1948 et 1969), p.135.
26. Foreword in E. T. A. Hoffmann, *Selected Writings of E. T. A. Hoffmann*, edited and translated by L. J. Kent and E. C. Knight (Chicago: University of Chicago Press, 1969), I p.2.
27. E. T. A. Hoffmann , *The Best Tales of Hoffmann*, edited by E. F. Bleiler (NY: Dover Publications, 1967), p.22.
28. Tymms, p.160.
29. *The Best Tales of Hoffmann*, p.104.
30. Tymms, p.366.
31. "Introduction", *Selected Writings of E. T. A. Hoffmann*, pp.44-45.

32. For the discussion of his influence, see the above Introduction, by Kent and Knight.

33. Gérard de Nerval, *Selected Writings of Gérard de Nerval*, translated, with Introduction and Notes, by Geoffrey Wagner (London: Peter Owen, 1958), p.115.

34. eg, L.-H. Sebillotte, *La Vie Secréte de Gérard de Nerval* (Paris: Corti, 1948), discussed in the Introduction by Geoffrey Wagner, p.28.

35. "Foreword" to *Selected Writings of E. T. A. Hoffmann*, p.2.

36. *Literary Origin of Surrealism: A New Mysticism in French Poetry* (London: University of London Press, 1969), p.32. During her discussion of Nerval's influence on the Surrealists, she also points out what she considers to be the basic misunderstanding of Nerval by the Surrealists.

37. *Hyperion, or the Hermit in Greece*, trans. W. R. Trask (1797-1799; rpt. London: The New English Library, 1965), p.93.

38. "The Night-Side of Life", *Transition*, No. 27 (April-May 1938), p.209.

39. The editors of *The Modern Tradition* define the symbolists in these words: "Though not all romantics are symbolists, the symbolist is a kind of romantic, one who singles out and develops the romantic doctrine of creative imagination" (p.6).

40. *Modern French Poets on Poetry* : An Anthology, arranged and annotated by Robert Gibson (Cambridge: University Press, 1961), p.59. As it was imagination, Baudelaire maintains, that taught man the moral significance of colour, shape, sound and fragrance creating a new spiritual world, it is right for imagination to rule over the world: *"C'est l'imagination qui a enseigne a l'homme le sens moral de la couleur, du contour, du son et du parfum. Elle a crée, au commencement du monde, l'analogie et la métaphore. Elle décompose toute la création et, avec les matériaux amassés et disposés suivant des règles dont on ne peut trouver l'origine que dans le plus profond de l'âme, elle crée un monde nouveau, elle produit la sensation du neuf. Comme elle a crée le monde (on peut bien dire cela, je crois, même dans un sens religieux), il est juste qu'elle le gouverne."*

41. *La Nature est un temple où des vivants piliers*
Laissent parfois sortir de confuses paroles;
L'homme y passe à travers des forêts de symboles
Qui l'observent avec des regards familiers.
– from *"Correspondances"* in Charles Baudelaire, *Les Fleurs du Mal* (1857; rpt. Paris: Editions Garnier Frères, 1954), p.14.

42. George Steiner discusses the pervasive influence of the Gothic romance on European literature and analyses Dostoevsky's case in detail in his *Tolstoy and Dostoevsky* (1959; rpt. Harmondsworth: Penguin Books, 1967), pp.177-195.

43. *Dostoevski the Adapter: A Study in Dostoevsky's Use of the Tales of Hoffmann* (Chappell Hill: University of North Carolina Press, 1954), p.5. Passage also gives a brief survey of the "veritable Hoffmann craze" in Russia during 1835, when Hoffmann's *Tales* were greatly admired and imitated by major Russian writers, who regarded him rather as a philosophical thinker. It seems to have declined rapidly after 1841, along with Russian Romanticism itself (pp.2-6).

44. The letter of 9th August, 1838 to his brother, Michael Dostoevsky, in *Letters of Fyodor Michailovitch Dostoevsky to his Family and Friends*, translated by E. C. Mayne (London: Peter Owen, 1962), p.4.

45. *Notes from the Underground; The Double*, trans. Jessie Coulson (1864; 1846; rpt. Harmondsworth: Penguin Books, 1972), p.177.

46. The influence of Russian novelists, above all, Dostoevsky, on Woolf seems to me quite considerable, especially in her early novels, and deserve greater attention. This point will be raised in another chapter.

47. Steiner considers this novella to be of great significance: "Had Dostoevsky written nothing else, he would have been remembered as one of the master builders of modern thought", *Tolstoy and Dostoevsky*, (p.201).

48. The translator of the Penguin edition of the story informs us that the direct motive for writing it "was the publication in 1863 of Chernyshevsky's novel *What is to be Done?* which postulates the attainment by mankind of perfect virtue and happiness by the pursuit of enlightened self-interest." – p.10.

49. *Notes from the Underground*, p.33.

50. *The Brothers Karamazov*, translated by Constance Garnett (1912; rpt. London: Heinemann, 1974), pp.677-678.

51. The letter of 26th February, 1869 to N. N. Strachov, literary critic, in *Letters*, pp.166-167.

52. *Fyodor Dostoevsky, The Notebooks for "The Possessed"*, edited by E. Wasiolek and translated by Victor Terras (Chicago and London: University of Chicago Press, 1968), pp.200 and 375.

53. Indeed Steiner, while stressing the difference of the media each used, does compare Dostoevsky's achievements to Shakespeare's, and further implies that the novelist himself was aware of their resemblance. Discussing the above passage in the *Notebooks*, which presents Shakespeare as a prophet, Steiner concludes: "Doubtless this judgement hints at Dostoevsky's image of himself" (p.157). Though seen from a different angle, this comparison also seems to have suggested itself to Virginia Woolf, who apparently regarded them as the two greatest writers. There is an entry on the subject of satire in her diary (6th May, 1935) which reads: "Ideas that struck me: That the more complex a vision the less it lends itself to satire: the more it understands the less it is able to sum up and make linear. For example: Shre [Shakespeare] and Dostoevsky, neither of them satirise ..." – *The Diary of Virginia Woolf*, IV, *1931-1935*, edited by Anne Olivier Bell (London: The Hogarth Press, 1982), p.309.

54. Quoted by Ronald Hayman, *Nietzsche: A Critical Life* (London: Weidenfeld & Nicolson, 1980), p.304.

55. *Sigmund Freud*, III, pp.292-293.

56. *New Introductory Lectures, S.E.* XXII, p.104.

57. See Hayman, pp.290-291.

58. *Beyond Good and Evil*, S. 191. *The Complete Works of Friedrich Nietzsche*, XII, translated by Helen Zimmern, edited by Oscar Levi (Edinburgh, T. N. Foulis, 1911). Hereafter cited as *CWFN*. It is significant that this comment on reason is almost an exact replica of Dostoevsky's remark in his letter to his brother, dated 31st October, 1838. After distinguishing between reason and the soul: "Reason is a material capacity, etc, " he writes " *Reason is a tool*, a machine, which is driven by the spiritual fire [my italics]." - *Letters*, p.7. Perhaps we may understand his idea better if we think of reason as a highly sophisticated computer which yet cannot have the final value judgement or emotion.

59. *Beyond Good and Evil*, S. 17. The German quotation is from *Jenseits von Gut und Böse*, S. 17, *Nietzsche: Werke*, VI, 2, edited by G. Colli & M. Montinari (Berlin: Walter de Gruyter, 1968).

60. *Ibid*, S. 54. He expresses a similar view on the same subject in *The Will to Power* (pp.483-484), this time setting Descartes clearly as a target.

61. *Ibid*, S. 17. The translator of *The Complete Works* renders *"Es denkt"* as "One thinks", instead of "It thinks", and translates *"ich"* sometimes as "I" and at other times as "ego". Thus the passage: *"dass dies 'es' gerade jenes alte beruhmte 'Ich' sei, ist, milde geredet, etc."* becomes: "that this 'one' is precisely the famous old 'ego', is to put it mildly, etc." However, "one" in English is usually an indirect way of saying "I", and, put in this way, the distinction Nietzsche is so repeatedly trying to make between "es" or the thinking process and *"ich"*, ie, his emphasis on the unconscious aspect of our mental activity, will be completely lost, which explains some alterations made in the translation quoted above. (Hayman, in his discussion which partly covers the same subject gives, to my mind, more appropriate translation (pp.290-291.)

62. *Beyond Good and Evil*, S. 108.

63. *The Interpretation of Dreams*, pp.548-549. See also Chapter 4.

64. In his autobiography, Jung himself reflects that he "alone logically pursued the two problems which most interested Freud", ie, "the problem of 'archaic vestiges'" and that of sexuality. – *Memories, Dreams and Reflections*, translated by Richard & Clara Winston (1961: rpt. London: Collins, 1972), p.192.

65. Quoted in *Psychology of the Unconscious* (*Wandelungen und Symbole der Libido*), p.28.

66. *Human, All-Too-Human*, Part I, S. 380. *CWFN*, VI, translated H. Zimmern, edited by Oscar Levy (Edinburgh: T. N. Foulis, 1910). See p.82.

67. After the quotation from Nietzsche, which again shows a remarkable affinity with Freud's theory of the "archaic or regressive" character of dreams, Jung tells us that Freud, through

dream analysis, and "independent of Nietzsche", reached a similar standpoint to that of the philosopher's. Ernest Jones in his turn informs us that on several occasions Freud related that "Nietzsche had in no way influenced his ideas" (*Sigmund Freud,* II, p.385). H. Stuart Hughes, on the ground of this report, concludes that "it is only when we come to Jung that we find a specific Nietzschean inheritance" *(Consciousness and Society,* p.106). In view of what we have already examined on this subject, it seems rather difficult to deny Nietzsche's influence on Freud so categorically.

68. *Human, All-Too-Human,* Part II, I, S. 76.
69. *Beyond Good and Evil,* S. 193.
70. *The Birth of Tragedy, CWFN,* I, translated by W. A. Haussmann, edited by Oscar Levy (Edinburgh: T. N. Foulis, 1910), pp.22-23.
71. *The Will to Power,* p.1051, *CWFN,* XV, translated by A. M. Ludovici, and edited O. Levi (Edinburgh: T. N. Foulis, 1913).
72. *The Birth of Tragedy,* I, p.22.
73. Hayman, p.2.

CHAPTER SEVEN – Surrealism and its Sympathisers

1. André Breton, *Manifestes du surréalisme* (1924).
2. "Literature and the New Man". *Transition,* No. 19-20.
3. Bradbury and McFarlane, p.293.
4. The opposition and struggle between the conservative forces and the rebels in Paris at this period is concisely described by Eric Cahm in his "Revolt, Conservation and Reaction in Paris", *Ibid,* pp.162-171.
5. David Gascoyne, one of the initiators of the Surrealist movement in England, said of Breton: " ...one thing is certain: that except for André Breton the surrealist movement could never have existed, for it is as difficult to imagine it without him as it is to imagine psycho-analysis without Freud." – *A Short Survey of Surrealism* (London: Cobden-Sanderson, 1935), p.58.
6. André Breton, *Manifestes du surréalisme* (1924 and 1930; rpt. Paris: Gallimard, 1979) p.11.
7. Patrick Waldberg, *Surrealism* (London, Thames & Hudson, 1968), p.16.
8. Breton, p.12.
9. Immediately after the above statement, Breton continues: *"Si les profondeurs de notre espirit recèlent d'etranges forces capables d'augmenter celles de la surface, ou de lutter victorieusement contre elles, il y a tout intérêt à les capter, à les capter d'abord, pour les soumettre ensuite, s'il y a lieu, au contrôle de notre raison. "* (If the depth of our mind conceals strange forces capable of augmenting or overpowering those on the surface, it is most desirable to capture them, first to capture them and then, if it is necessary, to place them under the control of reason). This in fact is an extremely concise summary of the Freudian theory of the unconscious C. W. Bigsby, writing on the kinship between the Surrealists and the Romantics, observes: "Like the romantics (Hoffmann, Novalis, Coleridge, Nerval, Baudelaire), who had concerned themselves with dreams, hypnosis, somnambulism, madness and hallucinations, they were fascinated by the unconscious ... But, above all, the surrealists join with the romantics in their justification of the imagination in the face of rationalism and materialism." – Dada and Surrealism (London: Methuen, 1972), pp.58-59. In fact, as discussed in the previous chapter, imagination and the unconscious were two almost inseparably linked concepts for the Romantics.
10. *"Il y a un homme coupé en deux par la fenêtre* (There is a man cut in two by the window)." – Breton, p.32.
11. Anna Balakian finds, "in spite of Breton's admiration for Freud and his efforts to bring Freud's attention to the application he had found for the interpretation of dreams on a poetic basis"; a certain discrepancy between Freud's attitude towards the arts and Breton's basic tenets. She believes that another psychologist exercised more direct influence on Breton:

... there was another source nearer to André Breton, and written in the only language he read with ease: the works of Pierre Janet, professor of Pyschiatric medicine ... Professor Janet had been the teacher of Jung, and his works were on the required reading list of medical students of Breton's vintage. The resemblance between Jung's notion of the collective self and the surrealists' concept of what Paul Éluard was to call "*Les Dessous d'une vie*" is due to the fact that they both derive from Pierre Janet, whose character as psychologist was quite different from Freud's. If we examine the monumental works of Janet, we come upon the very vocabulary that André Breton was to transform into a lexicon for surrealism, thereby attributing to words like "reality", "nature", "anguish", "*amour fou*", "automatism" and "human liberty" meanings they never had in literary writings. – *André Breton: Magus of Surrealism* (NY: Oxford University Press, 1971), p.28.

Balakian confirms this view with an account of a confidential talk given to her by a fellow Surrealist, which gives much credibility to it. However, if Janet's influence was overshadowed by that of Freud in the mind of Breton, it may have been partly due to the fact that Freud's figure then was beginning to loom large on the cultural scene of post-war Europe, his theories finally gaining popularity and even prestige, but even more to the fact that Breton, for whose Surrealist credo the dream formed an essential part, felt stronger allegiance to Freud for whom too dreams had crucial importance. Janet, while contributing to the study of the Unconscious, apparently did not elaborate, or throw new light, on this aspect of psychic activity. As to the implied linguistic problem, Breton could have read Freud's works in French, since by that time they had been translated into many languages. Even at the time Breton was forming the Surrealist movement, André Gide was seeking permission to publish Freud's writings in his *Nouvelle Revue Française*. (See Ernest Jones, II, p.23.). Obviously, he did not have to know German to become acquainted with Freud's theories.

12. Balakian gives another version of the genesis of *Les Champs magnetiques* and automatic writing recounted to her by Philippe Soupault:

> It was Philippe Soupault, Breton's earliest literary collaborator, who mentioned Pierre Janet when, a few months after the death of André Breton, he related to me the circumstances under which they undertook *Les Champs magnetiques*, their first joint venture in automatic writing. The term came from Pierre Janet at the same time that the vision of magnetic fields was inspired by graphic displays of electric patterns of magnetism, and the work derived thus in its double connotation from the scientific rather than the literary frame of reference.

Among the works of Pierre Janet there is a thick volume called *L'Automatisme psychologique* (1st edition 1889, 9th edition 1921, indicating how available the work was to students of psychology). Several things are striking in Janet's notion of automatic writing, which of course he uses as a channel for therapy, but in so doing, unlike Freud, he is constantly aware of its implication for the exploration of the normal mind. – *Ibid*, pp.28-29.

It may be argued on Freud's behalf that he too was "constantly aware" of his theories' "implication for the exploration of the normal mind." The dividing line between the normal and the abnormal, to begin with, was not very distinct for him, and the study of dreams was important precisely because not only the mentally sick but also normal people dream. That is why he claimed that the interpretation of dreams was "the royal road to a knowledge of the unconscious." (See p.47.)

Very likely, Breton introduced automatic writing by combining Janet's technique of automatism with Freud's method of free association, but must have found greater significance, in relation to his artistic creeds, in Freud's theories than in those of Janet. After all, Janet remains to this day in the specific field of psychology, while Freud has been considered to be a part of the whole cultural phenomenon.

13. In a footnote to the *Second Manifesto* (1930), Breton, explaining why he emphasizes the use of automatic writing and recounting of dreams, maintains that once you experience the "inner dream-world", the world governed by premediated actions will appear, in comparison to the former, "only a poor show": "*Ceux qui s'y sont livré sans réserves, si bas qu'ensuite certains d'entre eux soient redescendus, n'auront pas un jour été projeté*

si vainement en pleine féerie interieur. *Aupré de cette féerie, le retour à toute activité préméditée de l'esprit ... n'offrira à leurs yeux qu'on pauvre spectacle."* – Breton, p.121.

14. Robert Short in Bradbury and McFarlane, p.301. Patrick Waldberg elaborates a similar view: "Judging from the contents of Breton's *Manifesto* alone, one might see in surrealism only a shoot of the Romantic tree, on which would be grafted amazing branches of symbolism and which would be made stranger still by a cutting from Freudian theory. We can in fact find in Novalis, Arnim and Nerval, in Lautreamont, Rimbaud and Mallarmé, most of the assertions which comprise the text of the Manifesto. The difference is that the intuitions and accounts of individual experience that we find in these poets have been brought together by Breton into a body of doctrine which is a kind of Declaration of the Rights (and Duties) of the Poets." – *Surrealism*, pp.17-18.

15. " ... *ce romantisme dont nous voulons bien, historiquement, passer aujourd'hui pour la queue, mais alors la queue tellement prehensile ...* " – Breton, p.110.

16. For Breton too childhood is an ideal state which "approaches closest the true life." Surrealism is a means to resurrect it: *"L'esprit qui plonge dans le surréalisme revit avec exaltation la meilleure part de son enfance ... C'est peut-être l'enfance qui approche le plus de la 'vraie vie'; l'enfance au-delà de laquelle l'homme ne dispose, en plus de son laissez-passer, que de quelques billets de faveur; l'enfance où tout concourait cependant à la possession efficace, sans aléas, de soi-même. Grâce au surréalisme, il semble que ces chances revienne.* – *Ibid*, pp.54-55. Miró may be said to represent this aspect of Surrealism best in visual form, as Guy Weelen comments: "Miró with his penetrating eye recaptures the graces of childhood ... " – *Introduction to Miró: 1924-1940* (London: Methuen, 1960).

17. " ... *nous disons ... qu'avoir cent ans d'existence pour lui [le romantisme] c'est la jeunesse ...* " – Breton, p.34.

18. André Breton , *What is Surrealism?* (1934), reprinted in Ellman and Feidelson's *The Modern Tradition*, p.607.

19. *Freudianism and the Literary Mind*, p.60.

20. *Manifestes*, pp.98-99.

21. See Maurice Nadeau, *The History of Surrealism*, translated by Richard Howard (Penguin Books, 1973), p.208. Patrick Waldberg, who was a member of the Surrealist movement for ten years, assesses the political side of the movement: "One can say with complete objectivity that surrealists were quite ineffectual in their various political stands. It was paradoxical, in fact, to attempt to make Marxism, founded on reason, compatible with the surrealist priority given to dreams and to irrational modes of knowledge. And, anyway, the workers' movements mistrusted the poets, who were all of bourgeois origin, and whose zeal and verbal excesses exasperated them" (p.18). On the hostility of English Socialists and Communists towards Surrealism, Julian Symons writes in his *The Thirties: A Dream Revolved* (1960: rpt. London: Faber & Faber, 1975), p.88.

Tom Stoppard, in his *Travesties*, makes an hilarious parody of this opposition or contradiction between the Communists, radicals in politics, and the avant-garde artists, radicals in art, represented respectively by Lenin and Tristan Tzara, the Dadaist, which may be perfectly applicable to the case of the Surrealists.

22. "Legitime Défense", reprinted as "Legitimate Defence" (September 1926) in Nadeau (p.275). In this pamphlet, Breton tried to defend the Surrealist stand in relation to Marxism, ie, the above-mentioned synthesis of Surrealism and Marxism, arguing that it is perfectly possible simultaneously to seek Proletarian revolution in the external world on the one hand and continue with complete freedom the exploration of the inner world on the other.

23. "Limits not Frontiers of Surrealism" in *Surrealism*, edited by Herbert Read (1936, rpt. London: Faber & Faber, 1971) p.106. In this essay, Breton expounds for the benefit of the British public the basic principles and characteristics of Surrealism, including its allegiance to the ideas of Marx and Freud, as well as its debt to foregoing poets and writers. Throughout the essay, the influence of Freud is prevalent and conspicuous, manifest in the terminology and the basic artistic conception, as may be recognisable in the passages quoted here.

24. *Ibid*, pp.107-108.

25. *Dada and Surrealism*, p.59.

26. *Manifestes*, p.24. On the contrary, he quotes Lewis's *Ambrosio, or the Monk* as one of the works that best expresses "the marvellous (le merveilleux)", one of the ideals he cherishes: " *le merveilleux est toujours beau, n'importe quel merveilleux est beau, il n'y a même que le merveilleux qui soit beau.*"

27. *Dada and Surrealism*, p.29. Robert D. Hume reached a similar conclusion earlier in his article, "Gothic versus Romantic" (pp.282-290). While considering the appearance of the Gothic novel as "one symptom of a widespread shift away from neo-Classical ideals of order and reason, toward romantic belief in emotion and imagination" (p.282) and thus conceding that Gothic and Romantic writings are "closely related chronologically" and "share many characteristics", he thinks in the final analysis "they remain quite distinct". Though Gothic and Romantic writers share the same "concern with ultimate questions and lack of faith in the adequacy of reason or religious faith to make comprehensible the paradoxes of human existence", they diverge in their way of solving these problems. Whereas the Romantics find in imagination a means of escape from the limitations of the human condition, "The Gothic writers, though possessed by the same discontent with the everyday world, have no faith in the ability of man to transcend or transform it imaginatively. Their explorations lie strictly within the realm of this world and they are confined to the limits of reason. Thus they cannot present the sensed order found by the romantics in their highest flights. The Gothic literary endeavour is not that of the transcendent romantic imagination; rather, in Coleridge's terms, Gothic writers are working with fancy, which is bound to the 'fixities and definities' of the rational world" (p.289).
By making the above distinction, however, Hume, as he expressly states, does "not mean to denigrate the Gothic novel."

28. *Surrealism*, p.109. Here we seem to hear an echo of Jung rather than Freud.

29. Julian Symons gives a vivid and amusing description of the event in his *The Thirties*, pp.85-87. For a more detailed account, see Paul C. Ray, *The Surrealist Movement in England* (Ithaca and London: Cornell University Press, 1971), pp.134-166.

30. *Surrealism*, p.20.

31. In his exhaustive study of the English Surrealist movement, Paul C. Ray calls our attention to the fact that Read allowed this introductory essay to be reprinted several times under the title, "Surrealism and Romanticism", which clearly indicates the importance attached to it by the author (*The Surrealist Movement in England*, p.121). Ray also traces some of the changes which took place in the course of time in Read's stance as regards his artistic beliefs (pp.108-133).

32. *Surrealism*, p.21. Read originally preferred to use the term "supernaturalist" to "surrealism", restricting the use of the latter to the particular movement initiated by Breton. In *Art and Society* (London: Faber & Faber, 1945) too, as Ray points out, he makes a similar claim, saying that it would be possible to show "how closely the romantic theory of poetry as elaborated by a great critic like Coleridge, or even by an honest Victorian like A. C. Bradley, corresponds to the theory of Surrealism" (p.124).

33. *Surrealism*, pp.20-21.

34. Paul C. Ray points out that "Read was among the first to make use of psychoanalysis", and that "Psychoanalysis provided Read with a vocabulary particularly well suited to describing the creative process, ". He discusses some of Read's writings in which he makes direct use of Freud's terminology such as "the id", "the ego" and "super-ego" in order to analyze a creative process (Ray, pp.109-116). However, this does not mean that Read accepted Freud's theories all in all. For example, while conceding that "art is closely linked" with the repressed instincts, he rejects the theory of sublimation, considering that "sublimation usually involves a conformity to collective ideals which completely submerges the individuality of the artist." – *Surrealism*, p.55.

35. *Ibid*, p.124. The last phrase is, of course, a quotation from Breton's *Second Manifesto: "la queue tellement préhensile"* (see above, p.47).

36. Paul C. Ray describes the reactions to the Exhibition as "a mixed bag", ranging "from the stupid and the violent to the ironic and supercilious to the intelligent but unsmypathetic; there is, however, nowhere to be found a fully appreciative review of the exhibition or fully sympathetic reaction to the Surrealist endeavour", though he admits that "The exhibition did, without any doubt, have a considerable impact upon London;

references to it continued to crop up with regularity during the next year or two", and that it stimulated interest in individual Surrealists, both English and Continental, such as Picasso, Ernst, Magritte, Miró, Klee, etc, who continued to have exhibitions until the early years of the war. - (p.166)

37. *A Short Survey of Surrealism*, p.132

38. In its No. 22 issue (February, 1933), the magazine prints its own "Advertisement", one of the claims of which reads: " *Transition* was the first to introduce Surrealism to the English-speaking world: it published in English versions the work of surrealist painters at a time when surrealism was unknown." Actually, some of the Dadaist and Surrealist writings had already been published before in *The Little Review*, but it was not a systematic or consistent effort, as in the case of *Transition*, to introduce or advocate the new movement to the public, as may be seen from Ray's remark: "Interestingly enough, no explanation or theoretical justification of Dada-Surrealism ever appeared in *The Little Review*" (Ray, p.68).

39. "Transition Days", in *Transition Workshop*, edited by Eugene Jolas (NY: The Vanguard Press, 1949), p.20.

40. "Vertigral Workshop", *Transition*, No. 24 (June 1936), pp.109-111.

41. Eugene Jolas *et al*, "Revolution of the Word – Proclamation", *Transition*, Nos. 16-17 (June 1929), p.13. For example, the second article of this "Proclamation" reads: "The imagination in search of a fabulous world is autonomous and unconfined. (Prudence is a rich, ugly old maid courted by Incapacity ... Blake)." It is signed by 15 other signatories besides Jolas, including Stuart Guilbert.

42. *Transition*, Nos. 19-20 (June, 1930), p.47.

43. *Transition*, No. 18 (Nov. 1929), p.15.

44." Literature and the New Man", Transition, Nos. 19-20 (June 1930), p.14.

45. "The Revolution of Language and James Joyce", *Transition*, No. 11 (February 1928), p.110.

46. "Vertigral Workshop", *Transition*, Nr. 24 (June 1936), pp.111-112.

47. "The Revolution of Language and James Joyce", p.110. Along with Joyce, Jolas lists the names of other experimenters in language such as Leon-Paul Fargue, Gertrude Stein and the German poets, August Stramm and Hans Arp.It is interesting to note that in this earlier article Jolas still regarded the Surrealists as the innovators of language: "The revolution of the surrealists who destroyed completely the old relationship between words and thought remains of immense significance. A different association of words on planes of the spirit makes it possible for these poets to create a universe of beauty the existence of which was never suspected before ... André Breton, demoralizing the old psychic processes by the destruction of logic, discovered a world of magic in the study of the dream via the Freudian explorations into the subconscious strata and the automatic expression of interior currents." (p.111).

48. "The Revolution of Language and James Joyce", pp.113-114.

49. *Transition* No. 27 (April-May, 1938), p.169.

50. *Ibid*, p.169. Defending *Finnegans Wake* from its censure for being "obscure", Joyce himself told one of his friends: "They compare it, of course, with *Ulysses*. But the action of *Ulysses* was chiefly in the daytime, and the action of my new work takes place at night. It's natural things should not be so clear at night, isn't it now?" – Ellmann, p.603.

51. Richard Ellmann writes: "Jolas found in *Finnegans Wake* the principal text for his revolution of the word." – *Ibid*, p.601.

52. "Literature and the New Man", p.15

53. "Notes on Reality", p.18.

54. *Transition*, Nos. 19-20 (June 1930).

55. "Literature and the New Man", p.15.

56. Ellmann tells us that "Jolas was fluent in English, French and German, and like Joyce, was fascinated by words." – Ellmann, p.600.

57. "Notes on Reality", p.19.

58. "Vertigral Workshop", p.109. Elsewhere, this "dialectics in the interplay of polarities" is described as "a new romanticism ... which achieves magic by combining the interior and the exterior, the subjective and the objective, the imaginary and the apparently real",

which is very similar to the Surrealist synthesis. - Jolas, Elliot Paul and Robert Saga, "First Aid to the Enemy", *Transition,* No. 9 (December 1927), p.175.

59. *Transition,* No. 23 (July 1935), p.7. Later it was included, under the same title, in *Transition Workshop* (1949).

60. "Literature and the New Man", p.13.

61. "Notes on Reality", p.15.

62. "Notes", *Transition,* No. 14 (Autumn 1928), p.181.

63. "Literature and the New Man", p.14.

CHAPTER EIGHT – Virginia Woolf the Critic

1. *Modern British Fiction* (NY, Oxford University Press, 1961). The book includes essays on Hardy, Conrad, F. Madox Ford, E. M. Forster, Lawrence, Joyce and Woolf, each being considered to represent, in some sense or other, to a greater or lesser degree, the characteristics of "the modern" in modern British fiction.

2. Consequently, she is in general highly regarded as a critic as well, as Hermione Lee's following comment illustrates: "If she had written no novels, she would have a place in twentieth-century letters as a considerable essayist". *The Novels of Virginia Woolf* (London: Methuen, 1977), p.11.

3. *A Portrait of the Artist as a Young Man* (1916, rpt. London: Jonathan Cape, 1968), p.219.

4. Quentin Bell, Woolf's nephew and biographer, regards the latter virtually as her manifesto: "It was as near as she came to an aesthetic manifesto", and "Mr. Bennett and Mrs. Brown" is, in fact, Virginia's own private manifesto" – *Virginia Woolf: A Biography,* II (St. Albans: Triad/Paladin, 1976), pp.104-105.

5. "Modern Fiction", *Collected Essays,* II (London: The Hogarth Press, 1966), p.105.

6. *C.E.* I, p.330.

7. *C.E.* II, p.105.

8. *C.E.* I, p.330.

9. *C.E.* II, p.108.

10. *C.E.* I, p.337.

11. *C.E.* II, p.106.

12. "The Sentimental Journey", *C.E.* I, p.97.

13. "Modern Fiction", *C.E.* II, p.107.

14. *C.E.* I, p.97.

15. *C.E.* II, p.253.

16. *C.E.* II, pp.253-254.

17. Virginia Woolf: *The Inward Voyage* (Princeton, NJ: Princeton University Press, 1970), p.64.

18. *A Room of One's Own* (London: The Hogarth Press, 1929), p.47.

19. *C.E.* II, p.142.

20. *C.E.* I, p.320.

21. See, for example, Kettle, *An Introduction to the English Novel,* II, p.92; Bradbury, *The Social Context,* p.85; Lee, *The Novels of Virginia Woolf,* p.17.

22. Eg, Clive Bell's article on her "painterly vision" in *Dial,* December 1924) included in *Virginia Woolf: The Critical Heritage,* edited by R. Majumdar and A. McLaurin (London: Routledge & Kegan Paul, 1975), pp.138-147. Her method is often compared with that of the Impressionists or the Post-Impressionists. See, eg, Kettle, pp.19-21; Lee, pp.15-17.

23. Quoted by Quentin Bell, II, p.7.

24. *The Flight of the Mind: The Letters of Virginia Woolf, I: 1888-1912,* edited by N. Nicolson (London: The Hogarth Press, 1975), p.440.

25. *The Question of Things Happening: The Letters of Virginia Woolf, II: 1912-1922,* edited by N. Nicolson (London: The Hogarth Press, 1976), p.15.

26. To give a typical example, Arnold Kettle writes on what he calls the "explicit" date, December 1910, restating, according to him, what was first suggested by J. Isaacs: "this

curious and apparently arbitrary date refers to the opening at the Grafton Galleries of the most famous of the post-Impressionist exhibitions." (We may also remember that "the opening" took place in November, and not in December – a small point, but if we take the date as "explicit", it will matter.) Commenting further that "Virginia Woolf was, of course, a member of a circle deeply, one might say passionately, involved in this event, with an implication that Woolf herself was "passionately involved", which, as we have seen, seems to be far from the case, though perfectly appropriate for Clive Bell and Roger Fry, to whom he also refers. Kettle maintains that "there can be little doubt that Virginia Woolf herself responded deeply both to the works of art involved and to the aims behind post-Impressionist painting." – Kettle, II, p.92. However, Woolf's own expressions, such as "a modest sample set of painters" or "furious excitement ... over their pieces of canvas coloured green and blue, is odious", do not seem at all to endorse such a view. However, this does not exclude the possibility that she shared some characteristics and the same artistic ideals with the Post-Impressionist painters.

27. "Virginia Woolf's critical essays", in Peter Faulkner's *Modernism*, p.35.
28. "Characters in Fiction", p.3. Monks House Papers, Manuscripts Section, University of Sussex Library.
29. The word spelt "amotions" must be a typing error for "emotions".
30. When quoting the passage beginning with "If you read Freud, etc" in his essay in *Modernism*, Fothergill added a phrase at the end in brackets, which reads: " ... which our parents could not possibly have guessed for themselves [about the ambitions and motives of their fellow creatures]" (p.35), using the earlier line typed by Woolf as "amotions and motives, etc." as explanation and interpreting "amotions" as ambitions". The script is in fact full of uncorrected typing errors as it was not originally intended to be read by the public. Most of the time the errors involve one letter, missing, superfluous, misplaced or wrong, eg, "fesl" for "feel", "hey" for "they", "lothes" for "clothes", "seetle" for "settle" (all on p.6) and "mena" for "mean" (p.8). If we examine the case of "amotions", in order to turn it to "ambitions", we must replace one letter with two, while "emotions", which is our reading, requires, as in most cases, changing only one letter. Moreover, when we consider Woolf's main concerns, "ambitions" hardly seems to be one of them, whereas "emotions" is one of the words which we encounter most often in her essays, along with "unconscious", etc. For that matter, Freudian psychology, to which the line was related, was mainly concerned with men's hidden "emotions and motives" rather than "ambitions", the latter being the domain more of the Adlerian psychology.
31. "The Leaning Tower", *C.E.* II, p.178.
32. "Characters in Fiction", p.3. Woolf's handwriting is not always easy to decipher, and this could also cause different readings. Fothergill transcribes this as: " 'that is a very debatable point' she says: 'how much can we make our own from science[?]' " (p.35).
33. *An Autobiography, II: 1911-1969* (1964, 1967, 1969; rpt. Oxford: Oxford Univ. Press, 1980), p.21.
34. *Sigmund Freud*, II, p.83. Jones' essay on *Hamlet* had already appeared in the preceding and in fact the first issue of the journal in the same year.
35. *The Really Interesting Question and Other Papers*, edited by Paul Levy (London: Weidenfeld & Nicolson, 1972), p.113.
36. *Ibid*, p.120. In an earlier scene Rosamund, trying to explain Freud to Arthur, says, "What is he? He's a doctor. But you'd better find out the rest for yourself, for no doubt you'll be shocked if I were to explain him to you. You'll find the book in there ... *The Psychopathology of Everyday Life*. I'll leave you with it; and before dinner you will have learnt all about the impossibility of accidents, and the unconscious self, and the sexual symbolism of fountain pens [she takes up his], and – but I see you're blushing already" (pp.113-114), which helps us to imagine the kind of shock those who were just emerging from their Victorian mores received from Freud's books and theories.
37. *The Letters*, II, p.482.
38. *Eminent Victorians* (1918; rpt. London: Chatto & Windus, 1938), p.vii.
39. *Elizabeth and Essex: A Tragic History* (London: Chatto & Windus, 1928), pp.19-22.
40. *An Autobiography*, I: 1880-1911 (1960, 1961; rpt. Oxford: Oxford Univ. Press, 1980), p.50.

41. *Ibid*, p.256. There are more examples of this kind in the same book, *An Autobiography*, II, pp.22-23, 136 and 220.

42. *Ibid*, p.315. Richard Kennedy, in his memoir, also describes the novelist often working as a compositor, setting type for printing (see Chapter 9, p.246, note 46). An episode from the same book in which the office boy Kennedy takes Freud's *Collected Papers* to lunch with him (p.71) illustrates the easy access people at the Hogarth Press had to the psychologist's works.

43. *The Diary of Virginia Woolf, V. 1936-1941, edited by Anne Olivier Bell (London: The Hogarth Press, 1984), p.252*

44. *Leave the Letters Till We're Dead: The Letters of Virginia Woolf, VI: 1936-1941*, edited by Nigel Nicolson (London: The Hogarth Press, 1980), p.346.

45. *The Diary*, V, p.250

46. Quentin Bell, in relation to the novelist's mental illness, which he believes would not have responded to psychoanalytical treatment, observes: "In her later years she showed little interest in and less enthusiasm for the discoveries of Freud and could not have been persuaded to consult a psychiatrist" (*Virginia Woolf*, II, 19n). The speculation about the clinical applicability of psychoanalysis to Woolf's case apart, the comment does not seem to agree with the evidence which we find in her letters or diary entries. Moreover, in 1940, a year before her death, she was to give credit to Freud for his "help" to the writers in her essay "The Leaning Tower". In view of these facts, it does not seem very likely that her interest in Freud's ideas or her appreciation of his contribution to literature and society diminished greatly towards the end of her life. In fact, the contrary seems to be the case.

47. *An Autobiography*, II, p.310.

48. Cf. *The Letters*, II, pp.xvii-xviii.

49. For example, *The Letters*, I, p.184; *The Years* (1937; rpt. London: Granada, 1977), pp.259-260.

50. *An Autobiography*, II, p.312.

51. To Ethel Smith (Tuesday, January 24th, 1939). *The Letters*, VI, p.311.

52. *Refractions*, p.289.

53. *C.E.* II, p.166.

54. "Professions for Women", *Ibid*, p.287.

55. Although Hermione Lee, as regards this passage on Wordsworth, observes, and rightly: "Clearly Virginia Woolf inherits something of the Romantic idea of the potency of the imagination, working at a depth below the conscious mind" (p.28), this was not, as she seems to suggest, Woolf's personal idiosyncrasy but was one of the hallmarks of Modernism or Modernist writers, Woolf being unmistakably one.

56. *C.E.* II, p.167.

57. *C.E.* II, pp.170-171.

58. Leonard Woolf, in relation to his own "loss of religious faith" around his 14th birthday, makes an interesting comment on this subject: "As regards God himself, it is interesting to observe that by 1894 his position had already become precarious. No one, not even the believers, believed that he would take any steps against me for becoming an athiest. He had become as aloof, intermittent and tenuous as a comet, and just as ineffective to impinge upon matter or to punish a sinner ... In less than a century his position had suffered a change almost exactly like that of the British monarchy. He had become a constitutional instead of an absolute God ... All that remained to the deity was in fact *caput mortuum*." – *An Autobiography*, I, pp.24-25.

59. *C.E.* II, "The Narrow Bridge of Art", p.218.

60. The acuteness of her perception here may be testified by John Bayley's comment in his essay, "Prose or Poetry", which essentially echoes her view 30 years later: "Those who deplore the plight of contemporary poetry often ignore the fact that many of the former functions of the poet have been taken over by the novelist: the change is simply one of form." – *The Romantic Survival: A Study in Poetic Evolution* (London: Chatto & Windus, 1957), p.15.

61. *C.E.* II, "*Narrow Bridge of Art* ", p.224.

62. For example, David Lodge, comparing Woolf with James Joyce, writes: "It might be said

that whereas his writing aspired to the condition of myth, hers aspired to the condition of lyrical poetry." – *The Modes of Modern Writing* (London: Edward Arnold, 1977), p.177. It seems, however, rather difficult to make a clear division between the two novelists, since Joyce's novels have their lyrical moments and Woolf's often uncertain mythical dimension.

63. Quoted by Cronin, p.14.

CHAPTER NINE – The Modernist Achievement

1. "Jane Austen" (1925?), *C.E.* I, p.152.
2. See, eg, Woolf's essay "How it Strikes a Contemporary", *C.E.* II, p.159.
3. One of the extreme examples may be Karl and Magalaner's comment on *The Voyage Out*: "Her first novel ... is a wholly conventional book in content and traditional expository style" (p.129). Joan Bennett, aware of some of the unusual qualities in them elsewhere, ignored these two early novels completely when she discussed "The Form of the Novels". – *Virginia Woolf: Her Art as a Novelist* (1945; rpt. London: Cambridge University Press, 1964), pp.91-111.
4. *Virginia Woolf and her Works*, translated by Jean Stewart (London: The Hogarth Press, 1965), p.194. Guiguet went so far as to state: "One may say that Virginia Woolf ... spent her life re-writing the same book, of which she has given us nine different versions." (p.196)
5. *The Voyage Out* (London: The Hogarth Press, 1915; 10th imp.1975), p.262.
6. Faulkner, p.30.
7. As Anne Olivier Bell's complete version of *The Diary* was not published at this time, what Guiguet used was Leonard Woolf's edited version.
8. To Janet Case (19th November, 1919), *The Letters*, II, p.400.
9. *The Diary*, IV, pp.129 and 151.
10. *Ibid*, IV, p.134.
11. *Ibid*, IV, p.151.
12. *The Letters*, I, p.356.
13. The reason for this occasional awkwardness, however, seems to lie not so much in the method itself as in the nature of some of the "dreams" which have very little to do with the actual world or existence of the characters, for such moments of awkwardness occur in my view when the main characters withdraw into rather infantile escapist day-dreams rather than serious reflections on life and human relationship as in *The Voyage Out* or at less awkward moments of the same novel.
14. *The Diary*, II, p.186.
15. *Jacob's Room* (1922; rpt. Harmondsworth: Penguin Books, 1965), p.56.
16. It may also be argued that what causes the weakness is the absence of a central and unifying element, be it a character, a place or an object, as in the case of her later novels like *Mrs. Dalloway* and *To the Lighthouse*. Even Jacob is presented mainly through fragmentary impressions of other characters which never amount to an integral whole, and as his inner self is rarely-described he remains curiously vacuous.
17. *To the Lighthouse* (1927; rpt. Harmondsworth: Penguin Books, 1964), p.211.
18. "The Novels of E. M. Forster", *C.E.* I, p.346.
19. From this point of view, it may be said that in *The Waves* (1931), and *The Years* (1937) the author failed in creating this wholeness, precisely because she did not achieve the equilibrium, the equal strength of the outer and the inner. *The Waves*, which might be called another "novel of silence", inclines too heavily towards the inner world, to such an extent as to make the outer world – the sea, the birds, the trees, etc, – appear merely reflections of the minds of the characters or of those inaudible voices, without having the independent existence of its own, while *The Years*, which seems to have been written as a reaction to *The Waves* and is crowded with too many facts and events, leans too heavily on the outer elements.
20. Rosemary Dinnage's review of *The Diary of Virginia Woolf, III: 1925-1930*, edited by

Anne Olivier Bell (London, The Hogarth Press, 1980), in *The Times Literary Supplement*, 18th April, 1930, p.435.

21. *A Question of Modernity*, p.20.

22. *C.E.* II, p.159.

23. *Ulysses* (1922; rpt. Harmondsworth: Penguin Books, 1969), p.234. Frank Budgen, reporting his conversation with Joyce, reveals how the author came to conceive of Ulysses-Bloom out of his wish to create a "complete all-round character" (Joyce's own words), which Joyce believed no writer had ever presented in literature. – Budgen, *James Joyce and the Making of 'Ulysses'* (1960; rpt. London, Oxford University Press, 1972), pp.15-18.

24. "Why the Novel Matters", *A Selection from Phoenix*, edited by. A. A. H. Inglis (1936, 1968; rpt. Harmondsworth, Penguin Books, 1971), p.185.

25. Colin Clark, *River of Dissolution: D. H. Lawrence and English Romanticism* (London: Routledge & Kegan Paul, 1969). It is of particular interest in relation to this book to learn through the Introduction that the study was inspired by Middleton Murry's earliest criticism of Lawrence and especially by his oversight, his lack of awareness of a protagonist's "quest for wholeness" (p.ix) in one of Lawrence's novels.

26. *The Letters of D. H. Lawrence*, edited with an Introduction by Aldous Huxley (London: Heinemann, 1932), p.232.

27. *A Portrait of the Artist*, p.257.

28. "The Book Programme", BBC World Service, April 4th, 1980.

29. *The Struggle of the Modern*, p.79.

30. *Ibid*, p.80. It is certainly true that this sense of the "confrontation of the past with the present" occupies an important place in the Modernist awareness, as already observed in relation to Woolf's statement on the shift in human character, Strachey's sketch on Freud and Lawrence, who saw the dividing line "in 1915 [when] the old world ended", or as may be seen in Joyce's juxtaposition of the old, genial Headmaster, Mr. Deasy, who holds the optimistic and progressive view of history of the nineteenth century, believing: "All history moves towards one great goal, the manifestation of God", with young Stephen, for whom "History ... is a nightmare from which I am trying to awake" in the "Nestor" episode (*Ulysses*, p.40). It is doubtful, however, whether we could take this "confrontation", as Spender thinks, for "the fundamental aim of modernism."

31. *James Joyce*, p.534.

32. Leon Edel, *The Modern Psychological Novel* (1961; rpt. New York: Grosset & Dunlap, 1964), p.31.

33. "On Re-reading Novels", *C.E.* II, p.122.

34. René Wellek too, while discussing the reactions of the English-speaking world to Dostoevsky in his *Introduction to Dostoevsky: A Collection of Critical Essays* (Englewood Cliffs, NJ: Prentice Hall, 1962), refers to "the tremendous emotional reactions to Dostoevsky in England during and shortly after the First World War", and comments: "A Dostoevsky cult existed for a few years and certainly many English novelists show that they have read him and have tried to evoke his mood or draw Dostoevskean characters" (p.12), giving, as examples, the works of Hugh Walpole and Aldous Huxley.

35. *C.E.* II, p.109.

36. In her letter to Lytton Strachey (1st September, 1912), while she was reading *"Crime et Châtiment"*, *The Letters*, II, p.5.

37. "The Russian Point of View" [1925?], *C.E.* I, p.242. In this essay, Woolf describes Dostoevsky's novels as "seething whirlpools, gyrating sandstorms, waterspouts which hiss and boil and suck us in. They are composed purely and wholly of the stuff of the soul. Against our wills we are drawn in, whirled around, blinded, suffocated and at the same time filled with giddy rapture". The reference to Shakespeare comes just after this passage.

38. *A Writer's Diary*, p.57.

39. For example, Jean Guiguet writes: "Forster and Lawrence – and Virginia Woolf herself – spoilt their earliest writings by trying to use the conventions and technique of the Edwardians instead of discarding these obsolete tools." – p.39.

Notes – to pages 202 to 207

40. For that matter, Woolf's concept of the ideal novel which presents "not only what people say, but what they leave unsaid" echoes, whether she read it directly or not, Dostoevsky's view of reality stated in the already quoted passage from *The Notebooks for 'The Possessed'*: "The whole of reality is not exhausted by everyday life, for a huge part of it is present in it in the form of a still latent unexpressed, future Word" (p.375). Incidentally, in 1922, Woolf undertook the translation of "Stavrogin's confession" in *The Possessed* in collaboration with S. S. Koteliansky (*The Letters*, II, p.516n).

41. Hermione Lee, p.53.

42. We must remember that in those early years, Woolf was avidly reading or translating Dostoevsky's works, as her letters and essays show, and especially in *Night and Day* there is a direct quotation of Dostoevsky's words, which works like a *leitmotif* throughout the novel: "It's life that matters, nothing but – life – the process of discovery – the everlasting and perpetual process, not the discovery itself at all." – *Night and Day* (London: The Hogarth Press, 1919; 9th Imp. 1971), p.132. There is also a scene in which a character shows amazement at hearing that the other has not read *The Idiot* and becomes derisive when he admits to having read *War and Peace* (p.368).

43. *C.E.* II, p.85.

44. *The Diary*, II, p.322.

45. *The Diary*, III, p.7.

46. In *A Boy at the Hogarth Press* (London: Heinemann, 1972), a memoir made largely of his letters and diary entries written during his days at the Woolfs' publishing house, Kennedy gives us glimpses of the novelist from an unusual angle. His conversation with her while working together at the Press one day in 1928, when he was 16, is an example:

    In the printing room when Mrs. W. is setting type and I am machining we work in silence, unless of course, she is in one of her happy moods – if she's going to a party or been walking around London, which she often does. [This, together with the other statements to similar effect, reveals that Woolf's favourite themes such as London or the significance of parties for human relationship had solid bases in her real life experiences.]

    Today I interrupted her to ask her what Proust was like, as a reviewer had called her the 'English Proust'. At first she did not understand because I had pronounced Proust to rhyme with Faust and not boost. But she laughed and said she couldn't do French cooking, but it was delicious. (p.66).

    He then compares Leonard with Proust's character ("LW is rather like Swann", p.67) and discusses the difference and similarity between Virginia and another personage: "Of course, Mrs. W. is not at all like Odette, but they are both rather wayward creatures, worshipped by their husbands" (p.68). Earlier, in his letter to a school friend, he describes Virginia Woolf in these terms: "Mrs. Woolf, wife of the manager, is a very celebrated author and, in her own way, more important than Galsworthy" (p.25), which may indicate that at this time, with her two major works, *Mrs. Dalloway* and *To the Lighthouse*, behind her, Woolf was already a well-established figure in the mainstream of the literary world, replacing the old guard, such as Galsworthy.

47. For example, John Burt Foster's *Heirs to Dionysus: A Nietzschean Current in Literary Modernism* (Guildford: Princeton University Press, 1982), has a chapter on Lawrence and his *Women in Love* to trace the German philosopher's influence on Lawrence. The other writers chosen by Foster for this particular study are Gide, Mann and Malraux.

48. "New Mexico" (1928), *A Selection from Phoenix*, p.126.

49. *Stephen Hero* (1944; rpt. London: Jonathan Cape, 1969), p.216. Later, "the clock of the Ballast Office" is added by Stephen as being "capable of an epiphany". After the sentence quoted in the text, Joyce continued: "He [Stephen = Joyce] believed that it was for the man of letters to record these epiphanies with extreme care, seeing that they themselves are the most delicate and evanescent of moments."

50. *A Selection from Phoenix*, p.544.

51. *Sphere History*, VII, p.19.

52. *Freud, the Man and the Cause*, pp.417-418. As to Woolf, Clark quotes from her letter (2nd October, 1924) in which she makes a rather derisive comment on Freud's attachment

of sexual significance to a mundane incident in life (*The Letters*, III, pp.134-135). As this is the only instance I know of her negative reaction to Freud, while the evidence to the contrary abound, it does not seem justifiable to make it represent Woolf's whole attitude. This may be understood as an expression of her rejection of the determinist side of Freud, his "pan-sexualism" which, though never openly expressed in her essays, is echoed by an anonymous spectator in *Between the Acts* : "But why always drag in sex ..." (see p.207).

53. *Freud, the Man and the Cause*, p.420.

54. *The Sickle Side of the Moon: The Letters of Virginia Woolf, V, 1932-1935*, edited by Nigel Nicolson (London: The Hogarth Press, 1979), p.36. Perhaps a similar statement in her next letter to Goldstone (August 16th, 1932), is closer to the truth: "I ... have only a very amateurish knowledge of Freud and the psychoanalysts; I have made no study of them" (*Ibid*, p.91), since this was the case with most educated laymen. We must also remember that Woolf was surrounded by first-class specialists of the Freudian school, which may have made her belittle her knowledge and emphasize her amateur status.

55. "Freudian Fiction", *The Times Literary Supplement*, 25th March, 1920, p.199. This was a review of *An Imperfect Mother*, a novel by J. D. Beresford.

56. *Between the Acts*, pp.138-139. The passage also reflects one of the main motifs of the novel, the continuity of the world and human existence from prehistoric times to the present, which is presented by, eg, the "favourite reading – *An Outline of History* " of Mrs. Swithin whose thoughts also often wander back to the time when Piccadilly was still covered with "rhododendron forests", when England was not yet severed from the Continent and was inhabited by primaeval monsters and beasts, or by the history of the village which goes back beyond Roman times, or the pageant itself which begins with the birth of England as an island and traces its history to the present day, and above all, the apocalyptic "vision of Europe, bristling with guns, poised with planes", ie. the coming to life of the "old savage" in modern guise, which will put an end to all this continuity: "At any moment guns would rake that land into furrows; planes splinter Bolney Minster into smithereens and blast the Folly" (p.42).

57. *Fantasia of the Unconscious*, p.17.

58. *My Brother's Keeper* (1958; rpt. London/Boston: Faber & Faber, for 1982), p.135.

59. See, for example, R. M. Adams, *Surface and Symbol: The Consistency of James Joyce's 'Ulysses'* (NY: Oxford University Press, 1962), pp.247-248 and Erwin Steinberg, *The Stream of Consciousness and Beyond in 'Ulysses'* (Pittsburgh: University of Pittsburgh Press, 1958), pp.286-296. Steinberg in particular makes detailed analyses of the affinities between the experimental works, both literary and plastic, of Marcel Duchamp, as well as Breton and others, and Joyce's techniques. He also refers to Jolas and Joyce's association with him.

60. Quoted in Clark, p.418.

61. *Freud and the Dilemmas of Psychology* (London: The Hogarth Press, 1977), p.1.

62. *Ibid*, p.147. R. W. Clark also quotes a comment addressed to Freud by one of the earliest defectors, the swiss psychologist Bleuler: "no matter how great your scientific accomplishments are, psychologically you impress me as an artist", and contrasts it to Freud's own persistent claim that "psychoanalysis [is] a science" (Clark, p.294).

63. "The Therapist at School", a review of Donald Light's "Becoming Psychiatrists", *The Times Literary Supplement*, 29th May, 1981, p.599.

64. Storr on the other hand hopes that maladies of biochemical origins will be more clearly defined as psychiatry advances, and be given psychiatric treatment.

65. *The Reaction Against Experiment in the English Novel, 1950-1960* (NY/London: Columbia University Press, 1967), p.5. Indeed, we may regard these two works, as was already mentioned in relation to *The Waves*, as examples in which the authors, either giving in to the fascination of, or paying exclusive attention to, the inner world, failed to achieve the equilibrium of the inner and the outer. In such cases their visions tend to become either too private or idiosyncratic – moreover, in the case of Joyce there is evidence that he tried to make communication more difficult than was necessary – and ultimately the "ideal reader" must therefore be the author himself rather than the insomniac.

66. Writing in 1967, when the term "Modernism" was not yet established, Rabinovitz

Notes – to pages 211 to 216

constantly refers to the Modernist writers, mainly Joyce and Woolf, as "experimental novelists" or "experimentalists", though occasionally he resorts to the habit of the critics during the second period of my analysis, ie, the use of the terms, "the modern" and "the contemporary", made prevalent by Stephen Spender, whose *The Struggle of the Modern* is also discussed here. His consistent use of the term "experimentalists" and other variants of "experiment", without any consideration and examination of the motives and needs of those novelists, makes them appear to be experimenting for the sake of experiment, just for "faddishness ... [and] new gimmicks", to use John Wain's phrase quoted by the author (p.8). For Rabinowitz. unlike for the novelists of the 'fifties, and in the general critical climate of the period, the word "experimental" does not necessarily have denigrating connotations. The concluding chapter, "Drawbacks of Traditionalism", makes it clear that the contrary is the case, although again the author offers little explanation for the merit of the "experimentalists".

67. Amis describes the attitude of the hero, or rather the anti-hero, to the cat: "He [Dixon] admired it for never allowing either of the senior Welches to pick it up.'Scratch 'em', he whispered to it; 'pee on the carpets.' It began to purr loudly." – *Lucky Jim* (London: Gollancz, 1954), p.184.

68. Rabinovitz, p.168.

69. Jahoda, p.160.

70. *A Portrait of the Artist*, p.225. Joyce himelf was acutely conscious of the religious implication of the "radiant image of the eucharist" in this line. (As is often pointed out, even after his rejection of the career of priest, Joyce's spiritual tie with the Catholic religion was never completely severed.) The central concept of "epiphany", for that matter, was also borrowed from religion.

71. *The Novel and the Modern World* (Chicago/London: University of Chicago Press, 1960), p.189.

72. Daiches, p.191.

73. Some of the former category have been discussed in this study; an example of the latter is Robert Kiely's *Beyond Egotism: The Fiction of James Joyce, Virginia Woolf and D.H. Lawrence* (Cambridge/Mass. /London: Harvard University Press, 1980).

74. This seems to be, for example, the case of the "Harvester Annotated Critical Bibliographies" series. The reviewer of its first volume, Alistair Davies' *An Annotated Critical Bibliography of Modernism* (Brighton, 1983), informs us that, while one section is allocated to D. H. Lawrence in this volume, alongside those on general studies of Modernism, Yeats, Wyndham Lewis and T. S. Eliot, independent volumes are going to be devoted to both Joyce and Woolf – Edward Mendelson, "Picking through the wreckage", *The Times Literary Supplement*, 26th August, 1983, p.901. Although the book came out too late for the author of this study either to benefit from it or to analyse it, the publication of a bibliography of Modernism, the first such venture in the history of criticism, is a clear indication of the recent critical climate, and seems to confirm the basic stance of this book.

BIBLIOGRAPHY

Adams, R. M. *Surface and Symbol: The Consistency of James Joyce's 'Ulysses'*. NY: Oxford University Press, 1962.
Allen, Walter. *Tradition and Dream*. 1964; rpt. Harmondsworth: Penguin Books, 1965.
Amis, Kingsley, *Lucky Jim*. London: Gollancz, 1954.
Auden, W. H. *Collected Shorter Poems, 1927-1957*. London: Faber & Faber, 1966.
   – The English Auden: *Poems, Essays and Dramatic Writings, 1927-1939*. Edited by Edward Mendelson. London: Faber & Faber, 1977.

Balakian, Anna: *André Breton: Magus of Surrealism*. NY: Oxford University Press, 1971.
   – *Literary Origin of Surrealism: A New Mysticism in French Poetry*. London: University of London Press, 1969.
Baudelaire, Charles. *Les Fleurs du Mal*. 1857; rpt. Paris: Editions Garnier Frères, 1954.
Bayley, John. *The Romantic Survival: A Study in Poetic Evolution*. London: Chatto & Windus, 1957.
Beer, Gillian. *The Romance*. The Critical Idiom. London: Methuen, 1970.
Begin, Albert. "The Night-Side of Life", *Transition*, No.27 (April-May 1938), pp.197-218.
Bell, Quentin. *Virginia Woolf: A Biography*. 2 Vols. 1972; rpt. St. Albans; Triad/Paladin, 1976.
Bennett, Joan. *Virginia Woolf: Her Art as a Novelist*. 1945; rpt. London: Cambridge University Press, 1964.
Bergonzi, Bernard. *The Situation of the Novel*. 1970; rpt. Harmondsworth: Penguin Books, 1972.
   – editor *The Twentieth Century. The Sphere History of Literature in the English Language, V.* London: Sphere Books, 1970.
Bigsby, C. W. *Dada and Surrealism*. The Critical Idiom. London, Methuen, 1972.
Blair, John B. *The Poetic Art of W. H. Auden*. New Jersey: Princeton University Press, 1965.
Blake, William. *Complete Writings*. Edited by Geoffrey Keynes. Oxford: Oxford University Press, 1966.
   – *The Letters of William Blake*. Edited by A. G. B. Russell. London: Methuen, 1966.
Bradbury, Malcolm and McFarlane, James, editors. *Modernism: 1890-1930. Pelican Guides to European Literature*. Harmondsworth: Penguin Books, 1976.
Bradbury, Malcolm. *Possibilities: Essays on the State of the Novel*. London/Oxford/NY: Oxford University Press, 1973.
   – *The Social Context of Modern English Literature*. Oxford: Blackwell, 1971.
Breton, André. *Manifestes du surréalisme*. 1924 and 1930; rpt. Paris: Gallimard, 1979.
Brown, J. A. C. *Freud and the Post-Freudians*. 1961; rpt. Harmondsworth: Penguin Books, 1964.
Budgen, Frank: *James Joyce and the Making of 'Ulysses'*. 1960; rpt. London: Oxford University Press, 1962.
Bullock, Alan and Stallybrass, Oliver, editors. *Fontana Dictionary of Modern Thought*. London: Collins, 1977.
Burgin, Richard, editor, *Conversations with Jorge Luis Borges*. NY: Holt, Reinhart & Winston, 1969.

Cannell, Kathleen. "The History of a Dream", *Transition*, No.18 (1929), p.37.
Clark, Colin. *River of Dissolution: D. H. Lawrence and English Romanticism*. London: Routledge & Kegan Paul, 1969.
Clark, Ronald W. *Freud: The Man and the Cause*. London: Jonathan Cape and Weidenfeld & Nicolson, 1980.

Coleridge, S. T. *Biographia Literaria.* editor, George Watson. London: Dent, 1967.
– *Collected Letters of Samuel Taylor Coleridge*, II: 1801-1806. Edited by E. L. Griggs. Oxford: Clarendon Press, 1956.
– *Poetical Works.* edited by E. H. Coleridge. Oxford: Oxford University Press, 1969.
– *The Notebooks of Samuel Taylor Coleridge, I: 1794-1804*, Edited by Katherine Coburn. London: Routledge & Kegan Paul, 1957.
– *The Notebooks of Samuel Taylor Coleridge, II: 1804-1808.* Edited by Katherine Coburn. London: Routledge & Kegan Paul, 1962.
Connolly, Cyril. *The Modern Movement: One Hundred Key Books from England, France and America: 1800-1950.* London: Andre Deutsch/Hamish Hamilton, 1965.
Cox, C..B. and Dyson, A.E. editors. *The Twentieth Century Mind.* 3 vols. London: Oxford University Press, 1972.
Cronin, Antony. *A Question of Modernity.* London: Secker & Warburg, 1966.

Daiches, David. *A Critical History of English Literature.* 2 vols. London: Secker & Warburg, 1960.
– *The Novel and the Modern World.* Chicago and London: University of Chicago Press, 1960.
Davie, Donald: *Articulate Energy: An Enquiry into the Syntax of English Poetry.* London: Routledge & Kegan Paul, 1955.
Davis, H. et al. editors. *Nineteenth Century Studies.* Ithaca, NY: Cornell University Press, 1940.
Dick, Kay, editor. *Writers at Work.* Harmondsworth: Penguin Books, 1972.
Dinnage, Rosemary. Review of *The Diary of Virginia Woolf,III: 1925-1930*, edited by Anne Olivier Bell. *The Times Literary Supplement*, 18th April, 1980, p.435.
Dostoevsky, Fyodor. *The Brothers Karamazov.* Translated by Constance Garnett. 1912; rpt. London: Heinemann, 1974.
– *Letters of Fyodor Michailovitch Dostoevsky to his Family and Friends.* Translated by E.C. Mayne. London: Peter Owen, 1962.
– *The Notebooks for 'The Possessed'.* Edited by E. Wasiolek and translated by Victor Terras. Chicago and London: University of Chicago Press, 1968.
– *Notes from the Underground; The Double.* Translated by Jessie Coulson. 1864 & 1846; rpt. Harmondsworth: Penguin Books, 1972.
Dry, Avis M. *The Psychology of Jung.* London: Methuen, 1961.

Edel, Leon. *The Modern Psychological Novel.* 1961: rpt. NY: Grosset & Dunlap, 1964.
Eliot, T.S. *Selected Essays.* London: Faber & Faber, 1951.
Ellmann, Richard. *James Joyce.* 1959; rpt. London: Oxford University Press, 1966.
Ellmann, Richard and Feidelson, Charles, editors. *The Modern Tradition.* NY: Oxford University Press, 1965.
Eysenck, H. J. *Sense and Nonsense in Psychology.* Harmondsworth: Penguin Books, 1968.

Faulkner, Peter. *Modernism.* The Critical Idiom. London: Methuen, 1977.
Ford, Boris, editor. *From Dryden to Johnson. The Pelican Guide to English Literature, IV.* 1961: rpt. Harmondsworth, Penguin Books, 1968.
– Editor. *The Modern Age. The Pelican Guide to English Literature, VII.* 1961; rpt. Harmondsworth: Penguin Books, 1964.
Foster, John Burt. *Heirs to Dionysus: A Nietzschean Current in Literary Modernism.* Guildford: Princeton University Press, 1982.
Frank, Joseph. "Freud's Case-History of Dostoevsky", *The Times Literary Supplement*, 18 July, 1975, pp.807-808.
Freud, Sigmund. *The Interpretation of Dreams.* Translated and edited by James Strachey, 1953; rpt. London: Allen & Unwin, 1954.
– "The Relation of the Poet to Day-Dreaming", *Collected Papers*, IV. The International

Psycho-Analytical Library, 19. Edited by J. D. Sutherland. London: The Hogarth Press and the Institute of Psycho-Analysis, 1957.
- *The Standard Edition of the Complete Works of Sigmund Freud*. 24 vols. edited by James Strachey. London: The Hogarth Press, 1953-74.
Friedman, Alan. *The Turn of the Novel: The Transition to Modern Fiction*. 1966; rpt. London/Oxford/NY: Oxford University Press, 1970.
Fruman, Norman. *Coleridge, The Damaged Archangel*. London: George Allen & Unwin, 1972.

Gascoyne, David. *A Short Survey of Surrealism*. London: Cobden-Sanderson, 1935.
Gibson, Robert, editor, *Modern French Poets on Poetry: An Anthology*. Cambridge: Cambridge University Press, 1961.
Gilbert, Stuart. "Transition Days", *Transition Workshop*. Edited by Eugene Jolas. NY: The Vanguard Press, 1949.
Gross, John. *The Rise and Fall of the Man of Letters*. London: Weidenfeld & Nicolson, 1969.
Guiget, Jean. *Virginia Woolf and her Works*. Translated by Jean Stewart. London: The Hogarth Press, 1965.

Hart, Clive. *Structure and Motif in Finnegans Wake*. London: Faber & Faber, 1962.
Hawthorn, Jeremy. "Individuality and Characterization in the Modernist Novel", *The Uses of Fiction: Essays on the Modern Novel in Honour of Arnold Kettle*. Edited by Douglas Jefferson and Graham Martin. Milton Keynes: The Open University Press, 1982.
Hayman, Ronald. *Nietzsche: A Critical Life*. London: Weidenfeld & Nicolson, 1980.
Hoffmann, E. T. A. *The Best Tales of Hoffmann*. Edited by E. F. Bleiler, NY: Dover Publications, 1967.
- *Selected Writings of E. T. A. Hoffmann*. Edited and translated by L. J. Kent and E. C. Knight. Chicago: University of Chicago Press, 1969.
Hoffmann, Frederick J. *Freudianism and the Literary Mind*. 1945; rpt. Baton Rouge, Louisiana: Louisiana University Press, 1967.
Hoggart, Richard. *Auden: An Introductory Essay*. London: Chatto & Windus, 1951.
Hölderlin, Friedrich. *Hyperion, or the Hermit of Greece*. Translated by W. R. Trask. 1797-1799; rpt. London: The New English Library, 1965.
Hough, Graham. *Image and Experience: Studies in a Literary Revolution*. 1960; rpt. Lincoln: University of Nebraska Press, 1960.
Howe, Irving. *The Decline of the New*. London: Gollancz, 1971.
- Editor, *The Idea of the Modern in Literature and the Arts* 1967; rpt. NY, Horizon Press, 1968.
Hughes, H. Stuart. *Consciousness and Society: The Reorientation of European Social Thought: 1890-1930*. 1958; rpt. London: MacGibbon & Kee, 1959.
Hume, Robert D. "Gothic versus Romantic: A Revaluation of the Gothic Novel", *PMLA* 84 (March 1969), pp.282-290.
Hynes, Samuel. *Edwardian Occasions: Essays on English Writing in the Early Twentieth Century*. London: Routledge & Kegan Paul, 1972.

Inglis, Fred. *Keats*. London: Evans Brothers, 1971.

Jahoda, Marie. *Freud and the Dilemmas of Psychology*. London: The Hogarth Press, 1977.
Jolas, Eugene. "Advertisement", *Transition*, No.22 (February 1933)
- "The Dream", *Transition*. Nos.19-20 (June 1930), pp.46-47.
- "Homage to the Mythmaker", *Transition*, No.27 (April-May, 1938), pp.169-175.
- "Literature and the New Man", *Transition*, Nos.19-20 (June 1930), pp.13-19.
- "Notes on Reality", *Transition*, No.18 (November 1929), pp.15-20.
- "Notes", *Transition*, No.23 (Autumn 1928), pp.180-185.
- "Paramyths", *Transition*, No.23 (July 1935), p.7.

– "The Revolution of Language and James Joyce", *Transition* No.11 (February 1928), pp.109-116.
– "Vertigral Workshop", *Transition*, No.24 (June 1936), pp.109-114,
– et al. "Revolution of the Word-Proclamation", *Transition*,Nos.16-17 (June 1929), p.13.
– et al. "First Aid to the Enemy", *Transition*, No.9 (December 1927), p.175.
Jones, Ernest. *Sigmund Freud: Life and Work.* 3 vols. London: The Hogarth Press, 1953-1957.
Josipovici, Gabriel. "The Birth of the Modern: 1885-1914", *French Literature and its Background, VI, The Twentieth Century.* Edited by John Cruikshank. London/Oxford/NY: Oxford University Press, 1970.
– *The Lessons of Modernism and Other Essays.* London: Macmillan, 1977.
– *The World and the Book: A Study of Modern Fiction.* 1971; rpt. St. Albans: Paladin, 1973.
Joyce, James. *Finnegans Wake.* 1934; rpt. London: Faber & Faber, 1964.
– *A Portrait of the Artist as a Young Man.* 1916; rpt. London: Jonathan Cape, 1968.
– *Stephen Hero.* 1944; rpt. London: Jonathan Cape, 1969.
– *Ulysses.* 1922; rpt. Harmondsworth: Penguin Books, 1969.
Joyce, Stanislaus. *My Brother's Keeper.* 1958; rpt. London/Boston: Faber & Faber, 1982.
Jung, C.G. *The Complete Works of C. G. Jung.* 20 Vols. London: Routledge & Kegan Paul, 1953-1971.
– *Memories, Dreams, Reflections.* 1963; rpt. London: Collins/Fontana, 1967.
– *Modern Man in Search of a Soul.* 1930; rpt. London: Routledge & Kegan Paul, 1966.
– *Psychology of the Unconscious: A Study of the Transformations and Symbolisms of the Libido.* Translated by Beatrice M. Hinkle. London: Kegan Paul, Trench, Trubner, 1918.

Kampf, Louis. *On Modernism: The Prospects for Literature and Freedom.* Cambridge, Mass.: MIT Press, 1967.
Karl, Frederick R. and Magalaner, Marvin, editors. *A Reader's Guide to Great Twentieth Century English Novels.* London: Thames & Hudson, 1959.
Keats, John. *Poetical Works.* Edited by H. W. Garrod. Oxford: Oxford University Press, 1970.
Kelley, Alice van Buren. *The Novels of Virginia Woolf: Fact and Vision.* Chicago and London: University of Chicago Press, 1973.
Kennedy, Richard. *A Boy at the Hogarth Press.* London: Heinemann, 1972.
Kermode, Frank. *Modern Essays.* 1958; rpt. London: Collins, 1971.
– *Puzzles and Epiphanies.* London: Routledge & Kegan Paul, 1962.
– *The Sense of an Ending: Studies in the Theory of Fiction.* 1967; rpt. Oxford: Oxford University Press, 1968.
Kettle, Arnold. *An Introduction to the English Novel.* 2 vols. London; Hutchinson University Library, 1951-1953.
Kiely, Robert. *Beyond Egotism: The Fiction of James Joyce, Virginia Woolf and D. H. Lawrence.* Cambridge, Mass./London: Harvard University Press, 1972.
Kirkpatrick, B. J. editor, *A Bibliography of Virginia Woolf.* The Soho Bibliographies, IX. Oxford: Clarendon Press, 1980.

Lawrence, D. H. *Fantasia of the Unconscious and Psychoanalysis and the Unconscious.* 1923; rpt. Harmondsworth: Penguin Books, 1968.
– *Kangaroo.* 1923; rpt. Harmondsworth: Penguin Books, 1968.
– *The Letters of D. H. Lawrence.* Edited and introduced by Aldous Huxley. London: Heinemann, 1932.
– *A Selection from Phoenix.* Edited by A. A. H. Inglis. 1936, 1968; rpt. Harmondsworth: Penguin Books, 1971.
Leavis, F. R. *The Common Pursuit.* 1952; rpt. Harmondsworth, Penguin Books, 1962.
Lee, Hermione. *The Novels of Virginia Woolf.* London: Methuen, 1977.

Lessing, Doris. Interview in *"The Book Programme"*. BBC World Service, 4th April, 1980.
Levin, Harry. *Refractions: Essays in Comparative Literature*. NY: Oxford University Press, 1966.
Lodge, David. *Language of Fiction*. London: Routledge & Kegan Paul, 1966.
  – *The Modes of Modern Writing: Metaphor, Metonymy and the Typology of Modern Literature*. London: Edward Arnold, 1977.
  – *The Novelist at the Crossroads*. London: Routledge & Kegan Paul, 1971.
  – *Working with Structuralism*. Boston/London: Routledge & Kegan Paul, 1971.
  – Editor. *Twentieth Century Literary Criticism*. London/NY: Longman, 1972.
Lonsdale, Roger, editor. *Dryden to Johnson. Sphere History of Literature in the English Language, IV*. London: Sphere Books, 1971.
Luce, Gay Gaer and Segal, Julius. *Sleep and Dreams*. London: Panther Books, 1969.

Majumdar, R. and McLaurin, A. Editors. *Virginia Woolf: The Critical Heritage*. London: Routledge & Kegan Paul, 1975.
Mendelson, Edward. "Picking through the Wreckage", *The Times Literary Supplement*, 26th August, 1983, p.901.
Moore, H. T. *Age of the Modern and Other Literary Essays*. Carbondale & Edwardville: Southern Illinois University Press, 1971.

Nadeau, Maurice. *The History of Surrealism*. Translated by Richard Howard. Harmondsworth: Penguin Books, 1973.
Nelson, Benjamin, editor, *Freud and the 20th Century*. London: Allen & Unwin, 1958.
Nerval, Gérard de. *Selected Writings of Gérard de Nerval*. Translation, introduction and notes by Geoffrey Wagner. London: Peter Owen, 1958.
Nietzsche, Frichrich. *Beyond Good and Evil. The Complete Works of Friedrich Nietzsche*, XII. Edited by Oscar Levi and translated by Helen Zimmern. Edinburgh: T. N. Foulis, 1911.
  – *The Birth of Tragedy. The Complete Works of Friedrich Nietzsche, I*. Edited by Oscar Levi and translated by W. A. Haussmann. Edinburgh, T. N. Foulis, 1910.
  – *Human, All-Too-Human. The Complete Works of Friedrich Nietzsche, VI*. edited by Oscar Levi and translated by Helen Zimmern. Edinburgh: T.N. Foulis, 1910.
  – *Jenseits von Gut und Böse. Nietzsche: Werke*, VI 2. Edited by G. Colli and M. Montinari. Berlin: Walter de Gruyter, 1968.
  – *The Will to Power. Complete Works of Friedrich Nietzsche*, XV. Edited by Oscar Levi and translated by A. M. Ludovici. Edinburgh: T. N. Foulis, 1913.
Novalis. "Fragments", *Transition* No.18 (November 1929), pp.77-78.
  – *Hymns to the Night*. Translated by Mabel Cotterell. London: Phoenix Press, 1948.

Paley, Morton D. *Energy and Imagination*. Oxford: Clarendon Press, 1970.
Passage, Charles E. *Dostoevski the Adapter: A Study in Dostoevski's Use of the Tales of Hoffmann*. Chappell Hill: University of North Carolina Press, 1954.
Pessoa, Fernando. *Obra Poética*. Edited by Maria Aliete Galhoz. 1960; rpt. Rio de Janeiro: José Aguilar Editora, 1974.
Plato. *The Republic*. The Loeb Classical Library. Translated by Paul Shorey. London: Heinemann,. 1963.
Punter, David. *The Literature of Terror*. London/NY: Longman, 1980.

Rabinovitz, Robin. *The Reaction Against Experiment in the English Novel, 1950-1960*. NY/London: Columbia University Press, 1967.
Ray, Paul C. *The Surrealist Movement in England*. Ithaca/London; Cornell University Press, 1971.
Read, Herbert. *Art and Society*. London: Faber & Faber, 1945.
  – Editor. *Surrealism*. 1936; rpt. Faber & Faber, 1971.

Richter, Harvena. *Virginia Woolf: The Inward Voyage*. Princeton, NJ: Princeton University Press, 1970.
Rosenberg, Harold. *The Tradition of the New*. 1959; rpt. London: Thames & Hudson, 1962.
Rycroft, Charles. "The Artist as Patient", *The Times Literary Supplement*, 22nd September, 1972, pp.1089-1090.

Schorer, Mark. *Modern British Fiction*. NY: Oxford University Press, 1961.
Shakespeare, William. *The Complete Works*. Edited by Peter Alexander, London & Glasgow: Collins 1951.
Shelley, P. B. *Poetical Works*, Edited by Thomas Hutchinson. London: Oxford University Press, 1971.
Spender, Stephen. *The Struggle of the Modern*. London: Hamish Hamilton, 1963.
Stafford-Clark, David. *What Freud Really Said*. Harmondsworth: Penguin Books, 1969.
Steinberg, Erwin. *The Stream of Consciousness and Beyond in 'Ulysses'*. Pittsburg: University of Pittsburgh Press, 1958.
Steiner, George. *Tolstoy and Dostoevsky*. 1959; rpt. Harmondsworth: Penguin Books, 1967.
Storr, Anthony. "Nature and Human Nature". *The Listener*, Vol.85, 1971, p.814.
– "The Therapist at School", *The Times Literary Supplement*, 29 May, 1981, p.599.
Strachey, Lytton. "According to Freud", *The Really Interesting Question and Other Papers*. Edited by Paul Levy. London: Weidenfeld & Nicolson, 1972.
– *Elizabeth and Essex: A Tragic History*. London: Chatto & Windus 1928.
– *Eminent Victorians*. 1918; rpt. London: Chatto & Windus, 1938.
Symons, Julian. *The Thirties: A Dream Revolved*. 1960; rpt. London: Faber & Faber, 1975.

Thomson, James. *The City of Dreadful Night and Other Poems*. London: P. J. and A. E. Dobell, 1919.
Tieghem, Paul van. *Le romantisme dans la littérature européene*. Paris: Editions Albin Michel, 1948 & 1949.
Tindall, William Y. *A Reader's Guide to 'Finnegans Wake.'* London: Thames & Hudson, 1959.
– *A Reader's Guide to James Joyce*. London: Thames & Hudson, 1959.
Trilling, Lionel. *Beyond Culture*. 1965; rpt. Harmondsworth: Penguin Books, 1967.
– *Freud and the Crisis of our Culture*. Boston: The Beacon Press, 1955.
– *The Liberal Imagination*. London: Secker & Warburg, 1951.
Tymms, Ralph. *German Romantic Literature*. London: Methuen, 1955.

Waldberg, Patrick. *Surrealism*. London: Thames & Hudson, 1968.
Walpole, Horace. *Shorter Novels*, III. London: Dent & Sons, 1930.
Weelen, Guy. *Miró: 1924-1940*. London: Methuen, 1960.
Wellek, René. *Confrontations: Studies in the Intellectual and Literary Relations between Germany, England and the United States during the Nineteenth Century*. Princeton: Princeton University Press, 1965.
– "Virginia Woolf as Critic", *The Southern Review*, N.S. 13 (Louisiana 1977), pp.419-437.
– Editor. *Dostoevsky: A Collection of Critical Essays*. Twentieth Century Views. Englewood Cliffs, New Jersey: Prentice Hall, 1962.
Woolf, Leonard. *An Autobiography*. 2 Vols. 1960, 1961, 1964, 1967, 1969; rpt. Oxford/NY/Toronto/Melbourne: Oxford University Press, 1960.
Woolf, Virginia. *Between the Acts*. 1941; rpt. Harmondsworth: Penguin Books, 1953.
– *Characters in Fiction*. Monks House Papers, Manuscripts Section, University of Sussex Library.
– *Collected Essays*, 4 vols. Edited by Leonard Woolf. London: The Hogarth Press, 1966-1967.

– *The Diary of Virginia Woolf*, 5 vols. Edited by Anne Olivier Bell. London: The Hogarth Press, 1977-1982.
– "Freudian Fiction", *The Times Literary Supplement*, 25 March, 1920, p.199.
– A Haunted House and Other Stories. London: The Hogarth Press, 1944.
– *Jacob's Room*. 1922; rpt. Harmondsworth; Penguin Books, 1965.
– *The Letters of Virginia Woolf*. 6 vols. Edited by Nigel Nicolson. London: The Hogarth Press, 1975-1980.
– *Mrs. Dalloway*. 1925; rpt. Harmondsworth: Penguin Books, 1964.
– *Night and Day*. London: The Hogarth Press, 1919.
– *Orlando*. London: The Hogarth Press, 1928.
– *A Room of One's Own*. London: The Hogarth Press, 1929.
– *To the Lighthouse*. 1927; rpt. Harmondsworth: Penguin Books, 1964.
– *The Voyage Out*. London: The Hogarth Press, 1915.
– *The Waves*. 1931; rpt. Harmondsworth: Penguin Books, 1964.
– *A Writer's Diary*. Edited by Leonard Woolf. London: The Hogarth Press, 1953.
– *The Years*. 1937; rpt. London, Granada, 1977.
Wordsworth, William. *Poetical Works*. Edited by Thomas Hutchinson and the Rev. Ernest de Selincourt. Oxford: Oxford University Press, 1973.

Yeats, W. B. *Mythologies*. London: Macmillan, 1959.

INDEX OF NAMES

264

GENERAL INDEX

270